TABLE OF CONTENTS

CHAPTER 1: SCOPE OF CRIMINAL LIABILITY 1

    I. PRINCIPALS. UCMJ ART. 77. 1

    II. ACCESSORY AFTER THE FACT. UCMJ ART. 78. 8

    III. LESSER INCLUDED OFFENSES. UCMJ ART. 79. 10

CHAPTER 2: INCHOATE OFFENSES 1

    I. ATTEMPTS. UCMJ ART. 80. 1

    II. CONSPIRACY. UCMJ ART. 81. 8

    III. SOLICITATION. UCMJ ART. 82 and ART. 134. 15

CHAPTER 3: MILITARY OFFENSES 1

    PART I: ABSENCE, DISOBEDIENCE, AND RELATED OFFENSES

    I. UNAUTHORIZED ABSENCE. 1

    II. ABSENCE WITHOUT LEAVE. UCMJ ART. 86. 1

    III. MISSING MOVEMENT. UCMJ ART. 87. 7

    IV. DESERTION. UCMJ ART. 85. 9

    V. DEFENSES TO UNAUTHORIZED ABSENCE. 12

    VI. PROTECTED STATUS. 19

    VII. DISRESPECT. 22

    VIII. DISOBEDIENCE: PERSONAL ORDER. UCMJ ART. 90(2) & 91(2) . 24

    IX. VIOLATION OF A LAWFUL GENERAL REGULATION / ORDER. UCMJ ART. 92(1). 28

    X. FAILURE TO OBEY LOCAL ORDERS. UCMJ ART. 92(2). 31

    XI. THE LAWFULNESS OF ORDERS. 32

    XII. DERELICTION OF DUTY. UCMJ ART. 92(3). 35

    XIII. ENLISTMENT DEFINED. 38

XIV. FRAUDULENT ENLISTMENT, APPOINTMENT, OR SEPARATION. UCMJ ART. 83. 40

XV. EFFECTING UNLAWFUL ENLISTMENT, APPOINTMENT, OR SEPARATION. UCMJ ART. 84. 41

XVI. CRUELTY AND MALTREATMENT. UCMJ ART. 93. 42

XVII. FRATERNIZATION. UCMJ ART. 134. 43

XVIII. IMPERSONATING AN OFFICER, WARRANT OFFICER, OR NONCOMMISSIONED OFFICER. UCMJ ART. 134. 47

XIX. MALINGERING. UCMJ ART. 115. 48

XX. LOSS, DAMAGE, DESTRUCTION, OR WRONGFUL DISPOSITION OF MILITARY PROPERTY. UCMJ ART. 108. 50

PART II: THE GENERAL ARTICLES

I. CONDUCT UNBECOMING AN OFFICER. UCMJ ART. 133. 56

II. THE GENERAL ARTICLE. UCMJ ART. 134. 59

PART III: WARTIME RELATED OFFENSES AND ESPIONAGE

I. WARTIME-RELATED OFFENSES. 75

II. MISBEHAVIOR BEFORE THE ENEMY. UCMJ ART. 99 77

III. WAR TROPHIES 78

IV. STRAGGLING. UCMJ ART. 134. 79

V. ESPIONAGE. UCMJ ART. 106A. 79

CHAPTER 4: CONVENTIONAL OFFENSES 1

I. OFFENSES AGAINST THE PERSON. UCMJ Arts. 128, 120a, 134 1

II. HOMICIDES. UCMJ ARTs. 118, 119, & 134. 7

III. KIDNAPPING. UCMJ ART. 134. 19

IV. MAIMING. UCMJ ART. 124. 20

V. SEXUAL OFFENSES. 22

VI. OFFENSES AGAINST PROPERTY. 53

VII. OFFENSES AGAINST THE ADMINISTRATION OF JUSTICE. 83

VIII. "EVIL WORDS" OFFENSES. 101

IX. DRUG OFFENSES. 105

CHAPTER 5: DEFENSES 1

I. "SPECIAL DEFENSES" vs. "OTHER DEFENSES." 1

II. PROCEDURE. 1

III. ACCIDENT. 2

IV. DEFECTIVE CAUSATION / INTERVENING CAUSE. 5

V. DURESS. 6

VI. INABILITY / IMPOSSIBILITY 9

VII. ENTRAPMENT. 12

VIII. SELF-DEFENSE. 14

IX. DEFENSE OF ANOTHER. 16

X. INTOXICATION. 17

XI. MISTAKEN BELIEF OR IGNORANCE. 18

XII. JUSTIFICATION. 23

XIII. ALIBI. 26

XIV. VOLUNTARY ABANDONMENT 27

XV. MISCELLANEOUS DEFENSES. 27

XVI. STATUTE OF LIMITATIONS 30

XVII. FORMER JEOPARDY (ART. 44, UCMJ) 32

CHAPTER 6: MENTAL RESPONSIBILITY 1

I. INTRODUCTION. 1

II. REFERENCES. 1

III. MENTAL RESPONSIBILITY. 1

IV. PARTIAL MENTAL RESPONSIBILITY. 3

V. INTOXICATION. 4

  VI. COMPETENCY TO STAND TRIAL. 4

  VII. THE SANITY BOARD. 8

  VIII. TRIAL CONSIDERATIONS. 10

CHAPTER 7: PLEADINGS 1

  I. THE CHARGING DECISION. 1

  II. PLEADINGS GENERALLY. 3

  III. MULTIPLICITY. 9

  IV. LESSER INCLUDED OFFENSES. 10

  V. UNREASONABLE MULTIPLICATION OF CHARGES. 12

  APPENDIX A 14

  APPENDIX B 16

CHAPTER 8: IMPROPER SUPERIOR-SUBORDINATE RELATIONSHIPS & FRATERNIZATION 1

  I. REFERENCES. 1

  II. INTRODUCTION. 1

  III. IMPROPER SUPERIOR - SUBORDINATE RELATIONSHIPS. 1

  IV. FRATERNIZATION AND RELATED OFFENSES 5

  V. CASE LAW 7

  APPENDIX: AR 600-20 FRATERNIZATION (EXTRACT) 11

CHAPTER 1: SCOPE OF CRIMINAL LIABILITY

I. **PRINCIPALS. UCMJ ART. 77.**

   A. Principal Liability Defined.

      1. Text. "Any person punishable under this chapter who: (1) commits an offense punishable by this chapter or aids, abets, counsels, commands, or procures its commission; or (2) causes an act to be done which if directly performed by him would be punishable by this chapter; is a principal." Article 77.

      2. Purpose. Article 77 directs that a person need not personally perform the acts necessary to constitute an offense to be guilty of that offense. It eliminates the common law distinctions between principals in the first degree, principals in the second degree, and accessories before the fact. All of these parties to an offense are deemed principals, are equally guilty of the offense, and may be punished to the same extent.

   B. Who are "Principals?" The MCM creates two categories of individuals that can be guilty of an offense as a principal: 1) Perpetrators & 2) Other Parties.

      1. Perpetrators. "A perpetrator is one who actually commits the offense, either by the perpetrator's own hand, or by knowingly or intentionally inducing or setting in motion" acts by an agent or instrument which results in the commission of the offense. MCM, pt. IV, ¶ 1b(2)(a).

         a) *United States v. Perry*, 27 M.J. 796 (A.F.C.M.R. 1988) (holding accused liable as a perpetrator where, although accused never touched the stolen property, he directed another airman to grab a paper bag that had been left temporarily unguarded at a local bar).

         b) Suppose Person A intentionally causes an innocent Person B to commit an offense's act against Person B's will. The offense's *mens rea* requirement may be satisfied by Person A's criminal intent. In such a case, only Person A is guilty of a crime. *United States v. Minor*, 11 M.J. 608 (A.C.M.R. 1981) (holding accused liable as a principal to sodomy, where accused makes himself a party to the co-accused's threat compelling a victim's boyfriend to commit sodomy on victim).

         c) Authority of government "agent" or "decoy," however, may prevent liability as a perpetrator. *United States v. Sneed*, 38 C.M.R. 249 (C.M.A. 1968). Accused proposed theft of military property to two other soldiers. Soldiers informed military authorities and were told to go along with the proposal. Accused subsequently directed one Soldier to load military property on a truck and directed the other Soldier to drive away with the military property. Because the Soldiers were government "agents or decoys," the government never lost control or possession of the military property and their acts did not constitute a wrongful taking. Under the circumstances, the accused never acquired possession, dominion, or control; conviction for larceny reversed, and lesser included offense of attempted larceny affirmed. *See also United States v. Klink*, 14 M.J. 743 (A.F.C.M.R. 1982) (larceny upheld where accused, along with assistance of two government operatives, actually took goods from a government warehouse, carried them to a dock, loaded them into getaway vehicle, and helped drive them away).

      2. Other Parties. "If one is not a perpetrator, to be guilty of an offense committed by the perpetrator, the person must" meet the two requirements listed at MCM, pt. IV, ¶ 1b(2)(b).

         a) Aider and Abettor. Case law still predominantly describes the MCM's "Other Party" liability as "aider and abettor liability." Aiding and abetting requires the following proof: "(1) the specific intent to facilitate the commission of a crime by another; (2) guilty knowledge on the part of the accused; (3) that an offense was being committed by someone; and (4) that the accused assisted or participated in the commission of an offense." *United States v. Pritchett*, 31 M.J. 213 (C.M.A. 1990). See discussion below regarding the basis for principal liability.

b) Co-conspirators.

(1) Article 77 is broad enough to encompass vicarious liability of co-conspirators. *United States v. Browning*, 54 M.J. 1, 7 (C.A.A.F. 2000) (holding that prosecution could prove larceny and fraudulent claim charges on theory that accused was perpetrator, aider and abettor, *or* co-conspirator, even though conspiracy was not on the charge sheet).

(2) A conspirator may be convicted of substantive offenses committed by a co-conspirator, provided such offenses were committed in furtherance of the agreement while the agreement continued to exist and the conspirator remains a party to it. MCM, pt. IV, ¶ 5c(5); *Pinkerton v. United States*, 328 U.S. 640 (1946); *United States v. Browning*, 54 M.J. 1 (C.A.A.F. 2000); *United States v. Gaeta*, 14 M.J. 383 (C.M.A. 1983) (members were properly instructed on liability for co-conspirator's drug distribution; citing *Nye and Nissen v. United States*, 336 U.S. 613 (1949)); *United States v. Figueroa*, 28 M.J. 570 (N.M.C.M.R. 1989) (guilty plea to drug distribution by one co-conspirator to another co-conspirator was provident even though accused did not physically participate in the distribution).

c) Basis for Liability: Actus Reus (Assist, encourage, advise, instigate, counsel, command, procure)

(1) Article 77 requires an affirmative step on the part of the accused to be liable as an aider and abettor. *United States v. Thompson*, 50 M.J. 257 (1999). The evidence was legally sufficient for a conviction of rape as a principal where the accused participated in getting the victim helplessly intoxicated, knew a friend was going to have intercourse with the victim, did nothing to dissuade the friend when he looked to the accused for approval, and provided the friend with a condom.

(2) *United States v. Speer*, 40 M.J. 230 (C.M.A. 1994). An accused aids and abets the offense of drug distribution when he verifies purchase price and accepts the cash payment from the buyer, even though the delivery of the drugs has been completed, because he facilitates the "financial climax of the deal." The court adopts the "criminal venture" approach to aiding and abetting.

(3) *United States v. Bolden*, 28 M.J. 127 (C.M.A. 1989). Accused was guilty of larceny as an aider and abettor where he suggested and assisted a "sham" marriage to obtain quarters allowance and a false rental agreement that overstated the monthly rent.

(4) *United States v. Patterson*, 21 C.M.R. 135 (C.M.A. 1956). An accused who blocked a door with the intent of preventing the escape of the victim from his assailant aided and abetted the assailant.

(5) *United States v. Jacobs*, 2 C.M.R. 115 (C.M.A. 1952). Accused and three others broke into a private home and assaulted the occupant. Although the accused did not personally take property from victim, he

aided and abetted the others in committing a robbery and was liable as a principal. The "assault provides the necessary act of assistance, and accordingly we have before us much more than mere presence at the scene of the crime."

d) Basis for Liability: Mens Rea (Shared Criminal Intent with Perpetrator)

(1) In the case of an accomplice, the intent element may be satisfied with "proof that the accomplice shared in the perpetrator's criminal purpose and intended to facilitate the intent of the perpetrator with respect to the commission of the offense." *United States v. Mitchell*, 66 M.J. 176 (C.A.A.F. 2008) (in a guilty plea for aiding and abetting an indecent assault, the accused admitted to acting with the specific intent to gratify the principal's lust and sexual desires and the court concluded that there was no need to demonstrate that the aider and abettor intended to gratify his own lust and sexual desires).

(2) The requisite *mens rea* for aiding and abetting is sharing the criminal intent or purpose of the active perpetrator of the crime. *United States v. Jacobs*, 2 C.M.R. 115, 117 (C.M.A. 1952) ("[t]he proof must show that the aider or abettor . . . participated in it as in something he wished to bring about, that he sought by his action to make it successful") (prosecution under Articles of War, because offense pre-dated effective date of the UCMJ); *United States v. Bolden*, 28 M.J. 127 (C.M.A. 1989); *United States v. Gosselin*, 62 M.J. 349 (2006) (record did not reflect a shared "criminal purpose" of introducing drugs onto the base).

(3) *United States v. Fullen*, 1 M.J. 853 (A.F.C.M.R. 1976). Accused agreed with two others to lure the victim to a dark area where they would grab and rob the victim. According to the accused, he was unaware that one of his companions was going to strike the victim with a pipe. After the victim fell to the ground, the accused took the victim's wallet, which contained $9. Accused was guilty of robbery, because the intended grabbing would have been an assault sufficient for the compound offense of robbery.

(4) *United States v. Patterson*, 21 C.M.R. 135 (C.M.A. 1956). Accused pulled victim to the floor, and co-accused hit victim with chair. Later the same day, the co-accused struck victim several times in the face with a large belt buckle. Victim tried to flee, but accused blocked access to the door and co-accused bit victim's ear. Notwithstanding accused's claim that he did not intend that an *aggravated* assault be committed, the facts belie his claim and support conviction of aggravated assault. Principals are chargeable with results that flow as natural and probable consequences of the offense subjectively intended.

(5) An aider or abettor may be guilty of an offense of greater or lesser seriousness than the perpetrator, depending on his level of intent. MCM, pt. IV, ¶ 1b(4). *United States v. Jackson*, 19 C.M.R. 319 (C.M.A. 1955). Accused and co-accused assaulted the victim. Co-accused stabbed the victim, who subsequently died. Both accused were convicted of premeditated murder at a joint trial. Court affirmed co-accused's conviction but reversed accused's conviction, because of failure to instruct on lesser included offense of involuntary manslaughter. The

aider and abettor may be guilty in a different degree from the principal, and the law holds each accountable according to the turpitude of his own motive. *Compare United States v. Richards*, 56 M.J. 282 (2002) (intent to kill or inflict great bodily harm by kicking the victim sufficient to establish guilt as an aider and abettor of voluntary manslaughter even though death caused by co-accused stabbing the victim).

e) Presence at the Scene of the Crime. Appellate courts have considered the extent to which presence at the scene of the crime constitutes a sufficient act or evinces sufficient intent to establish Article 77 liability.

(1) Presence is not necessary. Presence at the scene of a crime is not necessary to make one a party to the crime and liable as a principal. *See United States v. Carter*, 23 C.M.R. 872 (A.F.B.R. 1957) Accused who loaned his car to a friend with the knowledge that it was going to be used in the commission of a larceny was guilty of larceny on aiding and abetting theory, even though he did not know all the details of how the crime was to be committed and was not present at the commission of the crime.

(2) Presence is not sufficient. Mere presence at the scene of crime does not make one a principal. MCM, pt. IV, ¶ 1b(3)(b). *See United States v. Shelly*, 19 M.J. 325 (C.M.A. 1985) (holding that mere presence in a misappropriated vehicle did not make the accused liable as a principal); *United States v. Waluski*, 21 C.M.R. 46 (C.M.A. 1956) (holding that mere presence was insufficient to support finding that accused aided and abetted the driver in the culpably negligent operation of a vehicle); *United States v. Johnson*, 19 C.M.R. 146 (C.M.A. 1955) (holding that mere presence with group of pedestrians who robbed a passerby was insufficient to support conviction as aider and abettor); *United States v. Guest*, 11 C.M.R. 147 (C.M.A. 1953) (holding that evidence was insufficient to support conviction as aider and abettor of murder and larceny, even though the accused was present at the scene of the murder, robbery, and subsequent discussion of the sale of the stolen property, because he did nothing to encourage or aid the murder or the larceny); *United States v. Gosselin*, 62 M.J. 349 (2006) (mere presence in the car with drugs not enough to establish guilt, citing *United States v. Burroughs*, 12 M.J. 380 (C.M.A. 1982)).

(3) Presence may be a factor in establishing liability. United States v. Pritchett, 31 M.J. 213 (C.M.A. 1990).

(4) *United States v. Cobb*, 45 M.J. 82 (C.A.A.F. 1996). Evidence was legally sufficient to support accused's conviction as an aider and abettor to robbery when he was present at crime, fully aware of his companion's impending crime, expected and in fact was offered a share of the proceeds, and may have held perpetrator's feet as he leaned out of vehicle to effect robbery.

(5) *United States v. Pritchett*, 31 M.J. 213 (C.M.A. 1990). The fact that the wife shared an apartment with the accused, the fact that 166 grams of marijuana were stored in a coffee can in a dresser in the only bathroom in the apartment, the fact that the accused knowingly permitted his residence to be used as a respository for the drugs, the fact that the accused was found caught after the sale in possession of a purse that contained marked bills from the drug sale, and the fact that the appellant's fingerprints were

found on several foil wrapped pieces in the can were sufficient to show that the accused aided and abetted his wife's possession with intent to distribute marijuana. Additionally, his immediate presence during the drug sale, "his preliminary drug talk, and his maintenance of a drug-sale safe house" were sufficient to constitute active encouragement and assistance to support a conviction for aiding and abetting his wife's drug distrubition. Finally, the accused's facilitation of his wife's drug distribution, the fact that the sale took place in a common area of the home while the accused was at home, and the fact that the money from the controlled buy was found in the accused's possession were sufficient to show that the accused aided and abetted his wife's distribution of marijuana.

(6) *United States v. Dunn*, 27 M.J. 624 (A.F.C.M.R. 1988). Accused's presence at the scene of a shoplifting, perpetrated as part of the accused's criminal training, was sufficient to establish his guilt for larceny as an aider and abettor.

(7) *United States v. Hatchett*, 46 C.M.R. 1239 (N.M.C.M.R. 1973). Hitchhiker sat in back seat of vehicle between accused and active perpetrator. As car moved along, active perpetrator robbed victim. Accused was guilty of robbery. He was aware the victim was given ride in order to be robbed and his presence in the rear seat of the vehicle "ensured the victim could not escape."

f) Failure to Stop Crime. Failure to stop a crime does not constitute aiding and abetting unless there is an affirmative duty to interfere (*e.g.*, a security guard). If a person has a duty to interfere, but fails to do so, that person is a party to the crime *if* such noninterference is intended to and does operate as an aid or encouragement to the perpetrator. MCM, pt. IV, ¶ 1b(2)(b). *See United States v. Thompson*, 22 M.J. 40 (C.M.A. 1986) (holding no general duty of NCOs to prevent crime absent "identifiable regulation, directive, or custom of the service."); *United States v. Simmons*, 63 M.J. 89 (2006) (duty of NCO to prevent crime within unit may arise, but failure to act must be accompanied by shared criminal purpose).

(1) Liability found. *See United States v. Shearer*, 44 M.J. 330 (1996) (affirming conviction after of guilty plea to aiding and abetting flight from the scene of an accident where accused admitted that he had a duty to report the identity of the driver to Japanese authorities at the scene of the accident); *United States v. Crouch*, 11 M.J. 128 (C.M.A. 1981) (motor pool guard allowed friends to steal tools); *United States v. Ford*, 30 C.M.R. 31 (C.M.A. 1960) (evidence showed that security guard told perpetrators about unsecured building and his failure to interfere was intended to encourage fellow guards to steal unsecured property).

(2) No liability found. *See United States v. Epps*, 25 M.J. 319 (C.M.A. 1987) (under the facts, failure to stop barracks larceny did not make accused an aider and abettor); *United States v. Shelly*, 19 M.J. 325 (C.M.A. 1985) (government failed to prove the existence of duty of senior vehicle occupant to ensure the safe operation of the vehicle); *United States v. McCarthy*, 29 C.M.R. 574 (C.M.A. 1960) (after advising subordinates not to steal hubcaps, lieutenant's failure to take active measures to prevent crime committed in his presence did not establish his guilt as a principal); *United States v. Lyons*, 28 C.M.R. 292 (C.M.A.

1959) (holding that a truck guard who accepted money to "see nothing" not liable as an aider or abettor where he was not told why he was offered the money and there was no evidence that he participated in the venture as something he desired to bring about); *United States v. Fuller*, 25 M.J. 514 (A.C.M.R. 1987) (soldier, whose job was fuel handler, had no duty to prevent burning of barracks room).

g) Duty to Report Crime. As a general rule, mere failure to report a crime does not by itself make one an aider and abettor. However, statutory exceptions to this rule may exist in certain circumstances. *See, e.g.,* 18 U.S.C. §793(f) (defining criminal offense to fail to report illegal disposition of national defense information). Also, the services can require that personnel report offenses that they observe. Thus, failure to report a crime may be a dereliction under some circumstances. *See United States v. Heyward*, 22 M.J. 35 (C.M.A. 1985) (Air Force regulation imposing special duty to report drug abuse did not violate the Fifth Amendment, because it did not compel members to report their own illegal acts but only those of other members) *cert. denied,* 479 U.S. 1011 (1986); *United States v. Bland*, 39 M.J. 921 (N.M.C.M.R. 1994) (upholding Navy regulation imposing a general duty to report crime which has been observed).

C. Principals Are Independently Liable.

1. One may be convicted as a principal, even if the perpetrator is not identified or prosecuted, or is acquitted. MCM, pt. IV, ¶ 1b(6).

2. *Standefer v. United States*, 447 U.S. 10 (1980). A defendant can be convicted of aiding and abetting the commission of a federal offense, despite the prior acquittal of the alleged actual perpetrator of the offense.

3. *United States v. Minor*, 11 M.J. 608 (A.C.M.R. 1981). Co-accused forced victim's boyfriend to commit sodomy on victim by threatening him and accused aided and abetted threat by encouraging victim's boyfriend to comply. The accused was properly convicted of sodomy as a principal, because the amenability of the actual perpetrator to prosecution is not a requirement for criminal liability as an aider and abettor. The actor need not be subject to the UCMJ.

4. *United States v. Crocker*, 35 C.M.R. 725, 739-40 (A.F.B.R. 1964). Accused and Holloway engaged in assault with a knife upon the victim. The evidence established that Holloway fatally stabbed the victim. Holloway was acquitted of murder, and but found guilty of aggravated assault. The accused was convicted of unpremeditated murder, and the court affirmed the conviction. The acquittal of the active perpetrator has no effect on the accused's case.

5. *United States v. Duffy*, 47 C.M.R. 658 (A.C.M.R. 1973) (officer who ordered NCO to kill prisoner guilty as principal despite acquittal of NCO based on lack of mental capacity).

D. Liability for Other Offenses. The statutory principal is criminally liable for all offenses embraced by the common venture and for offenses likely to result as a natural and probable consequence of the offense directly intended. MCM, pt. IV, ¶ 1b(5).

1. *United States v. Knudson*, 14 M.J. 13 (C.M.A. 1982). Accused loaned money to Shaw to buy LSD to be resold at a profit, drove Shaw to off-post residence to buy LSD, and informed prospective buyer that Shaw still had LSD. Evidence was sufficient for conviction of wrongful introduction and wrongful distribution of LSD. If there is a concert of purpose to do a criminal act, all probable results that could be expected are chargeable to all parties concerned. "The fact that the accused did not know in advance of

the particular transfers or the parties to whom the transfers would be made does not relieve him of criminal responsibility."

    2. *United States v. Waluski*, 21 C.M.R. 46 (C.M.A. 1956). Accused and Hart stole a jeep. Hart drove away from scene at high rate of speed and ran over a pedestrian, killing him. Because there was no evidence that accused actively aided and abetted the operation of the vehicle, accused could not be convicted of involuntary manslaughter.

    3. *United States v. Wooten*, 3 C.M.R. 92, 97 (C.M.A. 1952). Aider and abettor of larceny of 250 pairs of Army issue trousers also liable for wrongful disposition of military property, because it was a natural and probable consequence of the theft.

    4. *United States v. Self*, 13 C.M.R. 227 (A.B.R. 1953). Accused and two co-accused wrongfully appropriated jeep and drove away. When stopped at a checkpoint, co-accused shot and killed a sentinel. Accused was in the back seat and did nothing during the events at the checkpoint. Where an accused has combined with others in the perpetration of an unlawful act under such circumstances as will, when tested by experience, probably result in the taking of human life, he is equally responsible for a homicide flowing as a natural consequence of such unlawful combination. The court reversed the conviction for murder, because the larceny of the vehicle, however, was not "so desperate a design that its execution might naturally or probably result in the taking of human life."

E. Withdrawal as a Principal. A person may withdraw from a common venture or design and avoid liability for any offenses committed after the withdrawal. To be effective the withdrawal must:

    1. Occur before the offense is committed;

    2. Effectively countermand or negate the assistance, encouragement, advice, instigation, counsel, command, or procurement; *and*

    3. Be clearly communicated to the would-be perpetrators or to appropriate law enforcement authorities in time for the perpetrators to abandon the plan or for law enforcement authorities to prevent the offense. MCM, pt. IV, ¶ 1.b.(7).

F. Pleading.

    1. All principals are charged as if each was the perpetrator. R.C.M. 307(c)(3) discussion, ¶ H(i).

    2. *United States v. Vidal*, 23 M.J. 319 (C.M.A. 1987). Accused and PFC Hunt kidnapped German woman. Accused drove car to secluded area. PFC Hunt and then the accused had sexual intercourse with her in the back seat. Accused charged with a single specification of rape, but the specification did not indicate whether he was the perpetrator or an aider and abettor. The court affirmed the conviction, because the standard rape specification is sufficient to charge accused as perpetrator or aider and abettor, and the prosecution is not required to elect between those two theories. *See also United States v. Westmoreland*, 31 M.J. 160 (C.M.A. 1990) (judge can instruct, and accused can be convicted, under an aiding and abetting theory, even though case has not been presented on that theory); *United States v. Dayton*, 29 M.J. 6 (C.M.A. 1989) (government is entitled to prosecute the accused for distribution of LSD on the alternate theories that he is guilty as a perpetrator or as an aider and abettor).

G. Relationship to Inchoate Crimes.

    1. Attempts. For an accused to be guilty as an aider and abettor to an attempt, the actual perpetrator must have actually attempted the commission of the underlying offense. *United States v. Jones*, 37 M.J. 459 (C.M.A. 1993). Accused aided and abetted perpetrator who took "substantial step" with intent to distribute cocaine to an undercover

officer. Perpetrator's failure to go through with the transaction did nothing to alter her or accused's liability.

2. Solicitation.

a) The crime of solicitation is complete when the solicitation or advice is communicated. Conviction as a principal for aiding and abetting, however, requires that the completion or attempt of a crime.

b) Solicitation pertains to inducing an action in the future; aiding and abetting pertains to involvement in ongoing activity. *United States v. Dean*, 44 M.J. 683 (A. Ct. Crim. App. 1996) (holding that accused's call to her co-conspirator "don't let him get into the door" made during ongoing beating was aiding and abetting rather than solicitation).

Solicitation may exist even when the object is predisposed to the crime. *United States v. Hays*, 62 M.J. 158 (2005) (holding that appellant's request for photographs of a sexual encounter between "JD" and a nine-year old girl immediately after the appellant's inquiry into whether JD had engaged in sexual intercourse with the nine-year-old girl was a serious request to commit carnal knowledge). The court further stated that neither the MCM nor the UCMJ precludes a conviction for solicitation because the object is predisposed towards the crime (rejecting the requirement set forth in *Dean*, 44 M.J. 683 (A. Ct. Crim. App. 1996)).

II. ACCESSORY AFTER THE FACT. UCMJ ART. 78.

A. Introduction.

1. Text. "Any person subject to this chapter who, knowing that an offense punishable by this chapter has been committed, receives, comforts or assists the offender in order to hinder or prevent his apprehension, trial or punishment shall be punished as a court-martial may direct." Article 78.

2. Not a Lesser included Offense of the Underlying Offense--Must Be Independently Charged. *United States v. Price*, 34 C.M.R. 516 (A.B.R. 1963) (holding that neither accessory after the fact nor receiving stolen property were lesser included offenses of larceny); *United States v. Greener*, 1 M.J. 1111 (N-M.C.M.R. 1977). *But see United States v. Michaels*, 3 M.J. 846 (A.C.M.R. 1977) (permitting accused to enter a substitute plea of accessory after the fact to larceny, even though not a lesser included offense of the referred larceny charge).

3. Acquittal of the Principal Actor Is No Defense. *United States v. Marsh*, 32 C.M.R. 252 (C.M.A. 1962) (holding that an accused can be convicted of a violation of Article 78 without regard to the separate conviction or acquittal of the principal actor).

4. Principal Offender Need Not Be Subject to the UCMJ. *United States v. Michaels*, 3 M.J. 846 (A.C.M.R. 1977); *United States v. Blevins*, 34 C.M.R. 967 (A.F.B.R. 1964) (holding that military accused can be convicted of a violation of Article 78 without regard for the amenability of the principal offender to military jurisdiction).

5. Failure to Report Offense. The mere failure to report an offense will not make one an accessory after the fact. However, such failure may violate a lawful order or regulation and thus constitute an offense under Article 92. *See supra* ¶ I.C.5., this chapter. Also, a positive act of concealment *and* failure to report a serious offense can constitute the offense of misprision of a serious offense under Article 134. *See infra* ¶ II.D., this chapter.

B. Acts Sufficient for Accessory After the Fact.

1. *United States v. Davis*, 42 M.J. 453 (C.A.A.F. 1996). Accused who falsely informed investigators that he did not know who committed larceny but hinted that someone other than the actual thief was responsible gave "assistance" to the actual offender, thereby making accused an accessory after the fact to larceny.

2. *United States v. Foushee*, 13 M.J. 833 (A.C.M.R. 1982). Providing Q-tips and alcohol to clean blood off the knife used in an assault and to treat offender's injured ankle constituted receipt, comfort, and assistance for the purposes of hindering or preventing the apprehension or trial of the offender. However, where evidence showed only that the accused knew the principal perpetrator had stabbed the victim with the knife but did not know the perpetrator intended to kill or inflict grievous bodily harm, accused could be convicted of being accessory after the fact to assault with a dangerous weapon but not assault with intent to murder. *See also United States v. Marsh*, 32 C.M.R. 252 (C.M.A. 1962) (advising perpetrator of theft to get rid of stolen goods and thereafter consuming liquor bought with proceeds); *United States v. Tamas*, 20 C.M.R. 218 (C.M.A. 1955) (concealing proceeds of a theft for purpose of assisting thief); *United States v. Blevins*, 34 C.M.R. 967 (A.F.B.R. 1964) (concealing and transporting proceeds of theft).

3. *United States v. Michaels*, 3 M.J. 846 (A.C.M.R. 1977). Where accused has responsibility to protect particular property, accused is an accessory after the fact when he accepts money not to disclose completed larcenies.

C. Liability as a Principal Distinguished.

1. The co-perpetrator of the offense of possession of heroin cannot be an accessory after the fact to the same offense. *United States v. McCrea*, 50 C.M.R. 194 (A.C.M.R. 1975).

2. Act of principal must occur before or during the crime. If the act is after the crime, then it must have been part of an agreement or plan before commission of the offense, for the accused to be guilty as a principal rather than an accessory after the fact. *See United States v. Greener*, 1 M.J. 1111 (N.C.M.R. 1977) (one who is not a party to the original larceny scheme but who after the theft removes purloined goods from a cache is an accessory after the fact).

One is not an accessory after the fact if the offense is still in progress when the assistance is rendered. Even though the perpetrator of a larceny has consummated the larceny as soon as any taking occurs, others may become aiders and abettors by participating in the continuing asportation of the stolen property. *United States v. Bryant*, 9 M.J. 918 (C.M.R. 1980). *But see United States v. Manuel*, 8 M.J. 822 (A.F.C.M.R. 1979). Notwithstanding that larceny is a continuing offense, accused may be convicted of accessory after the fact when, with the intent to assist the active perpetrator avoid detention and prosecution, he advises the active perpetrator to destroy the stolen property. The purpose of the assistance is critical. If it is to secure the fruits of the crime, he is a principal, but if it is to assist the perpetrator in avoiding detection and punishment, he is an accessory after the fact.

D. Liability for Misprision of a Serious Offense Distinguished. *See* ¶ VI.G, ch. 4.

1. One can be an accessory to *any* offense; however, misprision requires an offense punishable by confinement for more than one year. MCM, pt. IV. ¶ 95c(2).

2. An accessory must "receive," "comfort" or "assist" a principal "in order to hinder or prevent his apprehension, trial or punishment." MCM, pt. IV, ¶ 2. Misprision requires a positive act to conceal a felony, but it does not require intent to benefit the principal. MCM, pt. IV, ¶ 95.c.(1).

3. Act Sufficient for Misprision. *United States v. Sanchez*, 51 M.J. 165 (C.A.A.F. 1999). Disposal of knife used in aggravated assault and formulation of plan to avoid detection amounted to affirmative assistance supportive of a misprision conviction.

4. Acts Insufficient for Misprision. *United States v. Maclin*, 27 C.M.R. 590 (A.B.R. 1958) (reversing conviction for misprision, because accused who was burying stolen property did not know the prior theft was a felony); *United States v. Assey*, 9 C.M.R. 732 (A.F.B.R. 1953) (lending money to larceny perpetrator to replace stolen goods was not a "positive act of concealment").

III. LESSER INCLUDED OFFENSES. UCMJ ART. 79.

A. Introduction.

1. Text. "An accused may be found guilty of an offense necessarily included in the offense charged or of an attempt to commit either the offense charged or an offense necessarily included therein." Article 79.

2. Evolution of the Doctrine.

a) The Court of Military Appeals formerly construed Article 79 and its "necessarily included" language to mean offenses that are "fairly embraced" in the pleadings and proof of the greater offense. *United States v. Baker*, 14 M.J. 361 (C.M.A. 1983).

b) In 1989, the Supreme Court held that Fed.R.Crim.P. 31(c) should be construed to include only lesser included offenses as established by the statutory elements. *Schmuck v. United States*, 489 U.S. 705 (1989).

c) In *United States v. Teters*, 37 M.J. 370, 376 (C.M.A. 1993), the Court of Military Appeals stated, "In view of the identity of language of Article 79 and Fed.R.Crim.P. 31(c), we will apply the Supreme Court's more recent holding and abandon the 'fairly embraced' test for determining lesser included offenses as a matter of law."

d) *United States v. Foster*, 40 M.J. 140 (C.M.A. 1994). Citing *Schmuck*, the court held: "One offense is not necessarily included in another unless the elements of the lesser offense are a subset of the elements of the charged offense" (emphasis omitted). This formulation of the test for multiplicity and lesser included offenses created a significant issue for offenses charged under Art. 134, which requires proof of an element not required for proof of offenses under Arts. 80–132: that the conduct was prejudicial to good order and discipline or service-discrediting. The court held that the phrase "necessarily included" in Art. 79 "encompasses derivative offenses under Article 134." An offense under Art. 134 may, "depending on the facts of the case, stand either as a greater or lesser offense of an offense arising under an enumerated article." This is because "the enumerated articles are rooted in the principle that such conduct *per se* is either prejudicial to good order and discipline or brings discredit to the armed forces; these elements are implicit in the enumerated articles."

e) *United States v. Weymouth*, 43 M.J. 329 (C.A.A.F. 1995). The CAAF refined its holdings in *Teters* and *Foster*, adopting the "pleadings-elements" approach: "In the military, the specification, in combination with the statute, provides notice of the essential elements of the offense" (emphasis omitted). The court cautions that it did not retreat to the "fairly embraced" test rejected in *Teters*: "Either the elements alleging the greater offense (by the statute and pleadings) fairly include all of the elements of the lesser offense or they do not. As alleged, proof of the greater offense must invariably prove the lesser offense; otherwise the lesser offense is not included."

f) *United States v. Jones*, 68 M.J. 465 (C.A.A.F. 2010). The CAAF definitely abandoned principles announced in *Foster* and *Weymouth* and returned to the "elements test" announced in *Teters*.

B. Fair Notice: A Fundamental Principle

1. The Constitution requires that an accused be on notice as to the offense that must be defended against. *Jackson v. Virginia*, 443 U.S. 307 (1979); *Schmuck v. United States*, 489 U.S. 705 (1989).

2. This due process principle of fair notice mandates that an the accused know for what offense and under what legal theory he may be convicted. A lesser included offense meets this notice requirement if it is a subset of the greater offense alleged. *See United States v. Medina*, 66 M.J. 21 (C.A.A.F. 2008); *United States v. Miller*, 67 M.J. 385 (C.A.A.F. 2009); *United States v. Jones*, 68 M.J. 465 (C.A.A.F. 2010).

C. The Rule.

1. " Under the elements test, one compares the elements of each offense. If all of the elements of offense X are also elements of offense Y, then X is an LIO of Y. Offense Y is called the greater offense because it contains all of the elements of offense X along with one or more additional elements." *United States v. Jones*, 68 M.J. 465, 470 (C.A.A.F. 2010).

2. There are two expressions of the elements test that appear to be valid, even after *Jones:*

a) A lesser included offense exists when the elements of the greater offense must invariably prove the lesser offense. *United States v. Weymouth*, 43 M.J. 329, 335 (1995).

b) An offense is included in another only if the greater offense "could not possibly be committed without committing the lesser offense." *United States v. Oatney*, 45 M.J. 185, 188 (C.A.A.F. 1996) (holding that communicating a threat was not a lesser included offense of obstruction of justice for purposes of multiplicity). Stated another way, "To be necessarily included in the greater offense, the lesser must be such that it is impossible to commit the greater without first having committed the lesser." *United States v. Weymouth*, 43 M.J. 329, 332 (C.A.A.F. 1995); *United States v. Swemley*, No. 20090359 (N.-M. Ct. Crim. App. Apr. 29, 2010)(unpub.)

3. In *Foster,* the court referenced the language in the MCM describing two types of LIOs: "quanititative LIOs" and "qualitative LIOS." *United States v. Foster*, 40 M.J. 140, 144 (C.M.A. 1994); 2008 MCM, pt. IV, ¶ 3(b)(1).

a) A "quantitative subset" exists when the elements of the lesser offense are contained within the elements of the greater offense. *United States v. Foster*, 40 M.J. 140 (C.M.A. 1994); 2008 MCM, pt. IV, ¶ 3(b)(1)(a). This is the type of LIO that *Jones* most clearly describes.

b) A "qualitative subset" exists in two situations: (1) all of the elements of the lesser offense are included in ther greater but one or more of the elements is legally less serious, and (2) all of the elements of the lesser offense are included in the greater but the mens rea is legally less serious. *United States v. Foster*, 40 M.J. 140, 146 (C.M.A. 1994); 2008 MCM, pt. IV, ¶ 3(b)(1)(b&c). It is unclear whether this type of lesser offense is "necessarily included" in a greater offense after *Jones*.

4. When comparing elements of offenses to determine whether an Article 134 offense stands as a lesser included offense to an offense under Articles 82 through 132, the CAAF has held that Articles 82 through 132 are not *per se* prejudicial to good order and discipline or service discrediting. Clauses 1 and 2 of Article 134 are not *per se* included in every enumerated offense. *United States v. Miller*, 67 M.J. 325 (C.A.A.F. 2009).

5. Clauses 1 and 2 are not per se lesser included offenses of offenses charged under Clause 3 of Article 134. *United States v. Medina*, 66 M.J. 21 (C.A.A.F. 2008). *See infra* ch. 7, ¶ IV.

6. Listings of LIOs in the MCM are not binding on the courts. Until Congress says otherwise, LIOs are determined based on the elements defined by Congress for the greater offense. The President does not have the power to make one offense an LIO of another by simply listing it as such in the MCM. *United States v. Jones*, 68 M.J. 465, 471–72 (C.A.A.F. 2010). Practitioners should not rely on the LIOs listed under each punitive article in Part IV of the MCM, but should use the list as a guide and then apply the elements test to be sure that the lesser offense is necessarily included.

D. Instructions.

1. If there is some evidence admitted at trial that reasonably raises a lesser included offense, then the military judge has a *sua sponte* duty to give an instruction on the lesser included offense. *United States v. Miergrimado*, 66 M.J. 34 (C.A.A.F. 2008); *United States v. Rodwell*, 20 M.J. 264, 265 (C.M.A.1985); *United States v. Davis*, 53 M.J. 202 (C.A.A.F. 2000) (reversing involuntary manslaughter conviction for failing to instruct on lesser included offense of negligent homicide); *United States v. Wells*, 52 M.J. 126 (C.A.A.F. 1999) (reversing premeditated murder conviction for failing to instruct on lesser included offense of voluntary manslaughter).

2. If the military judge fails to give an instruction, defense failure to object constitutes waiver, absent plain error. R.C.M. 920(f); *United States v. Pasha*, 24 M.J. 87, 91 (C.M.A. 1987); *United States v. Mundy*, 9 C.M.R. 130 (C.M.A. 1953). The defense may waive an LIO instruction in order to pursue an "all or nothing" trial strategy and there is no rule that prevents the Government from acquiescing in such a strategy. *See United States v. Upham*, 66 M.J. 83, 87 (C.A.A.F. 2008). The military judge need not oblige, however. As one court observed, "Such a litigation tactic remains viable in military jurisprudence, but it is far from being an absolute right or the unilateral prerogative of the defense." *United States v. Swemley*, No. 200900359 (N.M. Ct. Crim. App. Apr. 29, 2010) (unpub.).

3. An instruction on a lesser included offense is proper when an element of the charged greater offense, which is not required for the lesser included offense, is in dispute. *United States v. Miergrimado*, 66 M.J. 34 (C.A.A.F. 2008); *United States v. Griffin*, 50 M.J. 480 (C.A.A.F.1999) (holding that factual issue as to whether accused *intended* to stab victim with a knife, which he knowingly held in his hand, did not require an instruction on the lesser included offense of simple battery, because proof of intent to use the dangerous weapon is not required for the greater offense).

THIS PAGE INTENTIONALLY LEFT BLANK

CHAPTER 2: INCHOATE OFFENSES

I. **ATTEMPTS. UCMJ ART. 80.**

   A. Introduction.

   1. Text. "An act, done with specific intent to commit an offense under this chapter, amounting to more than mere preparation and tending, even though failing, to effect its commission, is an attempt to commit that offense." Article 80(a).

   2. Elements. MCM, pt. IV, ¶ 4b.

      a) The accused did a certain overt act;

      b) The act was done with the specific intent to commit a certain offense under the code;

      c) The act amounted to more than mere preparation; and

      d) The act apparently tended to effect the commission of the intended offense.

   3. Advisement of Elements During Guilty Plea. Military judge must adequately advise and explain each of the four elements of attempt to an accused. *United States v. Redlinski*, 58 M.J. 117 (C.A.A.F. 2003).

   B. Overt Act.

   1. Generally.

      a) The overt act need not be alleged in the specification. *United States v. Mobley*, 31 M.J. 273 (C.M.A. 1990); *United States v. Marshall*, 40 C.M.R. 138 (C.M.A. 1969).

      b) The overt act need not be illegal. *United States v. Johnson*, 22 C.M.R. 278 (C.M.A. 1957) (accused guilty of attempted desertion where all acts occurred within limits of legitimate pass).

   2. Specific Intent.

      a) The overt act must be done with the specific intent to commit an offense under the UCMJ.

      b) Applications.

         (1) Attempted murder requires specific intent to kill, even though murder may require a lesser intent. *See United States v. Roa*, 12 M.J. 210 (C.M.A. 1982) (explaining that, because an attempt requires a specific intent, there can be no "attempt" to commit involuntary manslaughter "by culpable negligence"); *United States v. Allen*, 21 M.J. 72 (C.M.A. 1985) (finding circumstantial evidence sufficient to prove intent to kill required for attempted murder).

         (2) Attempted rape requires specific intent to have sexual intercourse by force and without consent, even though rape is general intent crime. *United States v. Sampson*, 7 M.J. 513 (A.C.M.R. 1979); *cf. United States v. Adams*, 13 M.J. 818 (A.C.M.R. 1982) (assault with intent to commit rape).

         (3) In a prosecution for attempted violation of a lawful general regulation, under Article 92(1), the accused must have had the specific intent to commit the proscribed act, and it is immaterial whether the

accused knew the act violated any particular provision of any particular regulation. *United States v. Foster*, 14 M.J. 246 (C.M.A. 1982).

(4) No attempted sale of heroin where accused intentionally sold brown sugar. *United States v. Collier*, 3 M.J. 932 (A.C.M.R. 1977).

(5) Transferred or concurrent intent doctrine may be applied to attempted murder. *United States v. Willis*, 43 M.J. 889 (A.F.C.C.A. 1996), *aff'd*, 46 M.J. 258 (C.A.A.F. 1997).

3. More Than Mere Preparation.

a) Preparation consists of devising or arranging the means or measures necessary for the commission of the offense. The required overt act must go beyond preparatory steps and be a direct movement towards the commission of the offense. MCM, pt. IV, ¶ 4c(2); *United States v. Jackson*, 5 M.J. 765 (A.C.M.R. 1978) (holding that approaching and asking other soldiers if they want to buy a "bag" or "reefer" was not an attempt, but affirming it as a solicitation).

b) For the accused to be guilty of an attempt, the overt acts tending toward commission of the consummated offense must amount to more than mere preparation and constitute at least the beginning of its effectuation. However, "[t]here is no requirement under the law of attempts that the trip to the doorstep of the intended crime be completed in order for the attempt to have been committed." *United States v. Anzalone*, 41 M.J. 142 (C.M.A. 1994) (affirming assault by attempt, where accused retrieved his rifle, locked and loaded a round in the chamber, and started toward the victim's tent, even though he was stopped before he reached a point where he could have actually inflicted harm); *United States v. Owen*, 47 M.J. 501 (A.C.C.A. 1997) (holding that giving middle-man a map, automobile license number, and guidance on method for "hit man," where accused believed "hit man" had already arrived in town for the job, was sufficient overt act for attempted murder).

c) The line of demarcation between preparation and a direct movement towards the offense is not always clear. Primarily the difference is one of fact, not law. *United States v. Choat*, 21 C.M.R. 313 (C.M.A. 1956) (attempted unlawful entry).

d) After a guilty plea where the accused admits that her acts went beyond mere preparation and points to a particular action that satisfies herself on this point, appellate courts will not find actions that fall within the "twilight zone" between mere preparation and attempt to be substantially inconsistent with the guilty plea. *United States v. Smith*, 50 M.J. 380 (C.A.A.F. 1999).

e) Words alone may be sufficient to constitute an overt act. *United States v. Brantner*, 28 M.J. 941 (N.M.C.M.R. 1989) (a recruiter's request to conduct a "hernia examination" was an act deemed more than mere preparation for a charge of attempted indecent assault).

4. "Substantial Step."

a) The overt act must be a "substantial step" toward the commission of the crime. Whether the act is only preparatory or a substantial step toward commission of the crime must be determined on a case-by-case basis. *United States v. Jones*, 32 M.J. 430 (C.M.A. 1991) (holding that soliciting another to destroy car, making plans to destroy it, and finally delivering the car and its keys to that person on the agreed day of the auto's destruction constituted substantial step toward larceny from insurance company); *United States v. Williamson*, 42

M.J. 613 (N.M.C.C.A. 1995) (accused's acts of putting knife in his pocket and "going after" intended victim, without some indication of how close he came to completing the crime or why he failed to complete it, were not factually sufficient to constitute a substantial step toward the commission of the intended crime); *United States v. Church*, 29 M.J. 679 (A.F.C.M.R. 1989), *aff'd*, 32 M.J. 70 (C.M.A. 1991) (planning wife's murder, hiring undercover agent to kill wife, making payments for killing, and telling agent how to shoot wife constituted substantial step toward murder).

b) The "Test." *United States v. Byrd*, 24 M.J. 286 (C.M.A. 1987).

(1) The overt act must be a substantial step and direct movement toward commision of the crime.

(2) A substantial step is one strongly corroborative of the accused's criminal intent and is indicative of resolve to commit the offense.

c) The accused must have engaged in conduct that is strongly corroborative of the firmness of the accused's criminal intent. *United States v. Byrd*, 24 M.J. 286 (C.M.A. 1987) (accepting money from undercover agent and riding to an off-post location to purchase marijuana was not strongly corroborative of the firmness of the accused's intent to distribute marijuana); *United States v. Presto*, 24 M.J. 350 (C.M.A. 1987) (after agreeing to try to get marijuana for undercover agent, placing phone calls to drug supplier was not a substantial step toward distribution of marijuana); *United States v. LeProwse*, 26 M.J. 652 (A.C.M.R. 1988) (offering to pay two boys to remove their trousers was strongly corroborative of the firmness of the accused's intent to commit indecent liberties); *see also United States v. Jones,* 32 M.J. 430, 432 (C.M.A. 1991) ("It is not the acts alone which determine the intent of the person committing them. The circumstances in which those acts were done are also indicative of a person's intent.").

5. Tending to Effect the Commission of the Offense.

a) *United States v. McGinty*, 38 M.J. 131 (C.M.A. 1993) (the accused's running his fingers through the victim's hair and hugging him was an affirmative step toward committing indecent acts).

b) The overt act need not be the ultimate step in the consummation of the crime. It is sufficient if it is one that in the ordinary and likely course of events, would, if not interrupted by extraneous causes, result in the commission of the offense itself. *United States v. Johnson*, 22 C.M.R. 278 (C.M.A. 1957) (although within the 50 mile limit of his pass, the accused's walking to within the prohibited distance from the East German border, after unsuccessful attempts to get taxi drivers to cross the border, was sufficient overt act for attempted desertion); *United States v. Gugliotta*, 23 M.J. 905 (N.M.C.M.R. 1987) (overt act sufficient to constitute direct movement to commission of robbery where accused and accomplices made plans, procured implements, and went to the site of the crime with the tools for purpose of robbing exchange).

C. Defenses.

1. Factual Impossibility. Factual impossibility is not a defense to attempt. If the accused's act would constitute a crime if the facts and circumstances were as the accused believed them to be, then he may be found guilty of an attempt to commit the intended crime, even though it was impossible to commit the intended crime under the actual circumstances. MCM, pt. IV, ¶ 4c(3).

a) The defense of factual impossibility does not preclude conviction of attempted conspiracy where the other purported conspirator is an undercover government agent. *United States v. Anzalone*, 43 M.J. 322 (C.A.A.F. 1995) (attempted conspiracy to commit espionage); *see also United States v. Valigura*, 54 M.J. 187 (C.A.A.F. 2000); *United States v. Baker*, 43 M.J. 736 (A.F.C.C.A. 1995) (conspiracy would have been completed, but for the fact that informant did not share accused's criminal intent); *United States v. Roeseler*, 55 M.J. 286 (C.A.A.F. 2001) (factual impossibility not a defense to attempted conspiracy where accused agreed to murder the fictitious in-laws of a fellow member of his platoon; because the impossibility of the fictitious victims being murdered was not a defense to either attempt or conspiracy, it was not a defense to the offense of attempted conspiracy).

b) *United States v. Thomas*, 32 C.M.R. 278 (C.M.A. 1962). The accused and two companions committed sexual intercourse with a female, whom they believed to be unconscious, under circumstances amounting to rape. The female, however, was dead at the time of the sexual intercourse. Conviction for attempted rape affirmed.

c) *United States v. Dominguez*, 22 C.M.R. 275 (C.M.A. 1957). The accused injected himself with a substance he believed to be a narcotic drug. Regardless of the true nature of the white powdery substance, accused was guilty of attempted use of a narcotic drug.

d) *United States v. Riddle*, 44 M.J. 282 (C.A.A.F. 1996). The accused could be convicted of attempted conspiracy to steal military pay entitlements to which he was entitled by law or regulation, where he did not believe he was married at the time, even if he was married at the time.

e) *United States v. Church*, 29 M.J. 679 (A.F.C.M.R. 1989) *aff'd* 32 M.J. 70 (C.M.A. 1991). Evidence supported the accused's conviction for attempted premeditated murder of his wife, although the person he hired to kill his wife was an undercover agent.

f) *United States v. Wilson*, 7 M.J. 997 (A.C.M.R. 1979). The accused came upon another person who was unconscious. Beside the person was a hypodermic needle and syringe used by him to inject heroin. The accused destroyed the needle and syringe to hinder or prevent the person's apprehension for use and possession of narcotics. Because this person was probably dead at the time the items were destroyed, the accused cannot be found guilty of accessory after the fact in violation of Article 78. Because the accused believed the person was alive at the time he destroyed the needle and syringe, however, he may be found guilty of attempted accessory after the fact.

g) *United States v. Longtin*, 7 M.J. 784 (A.C.M.R. 1979). The accused sold a substance, which he believed to be opium, as opium. The laboratory test was inconclusive, and the Government could not prove it was opium. The court affirmed the conviction for attempted sale of opium. Had the facts and circumstances been as he believed them to be, he could have been convicted of sale of opium.

h) *United States v. Powell*, 24 M.J. 603 (A.F.C.M.R. 1987) (attempted larceny even though bank denied loan application).

2. Voluntary Abandonment.

a) A person who, with the specific intent to commit a crime, has performed an act that is beyond mere preparation and a substantial step toward commission of the offense may nevertheless avoid liability for the attempt by voluntarily abandoning the criminal effort. *United States v. Byrd*, 24 M.J. 286 (C.M.A. 1987) (recognizing voluntary abandonment as an affirmative defense in military justice).

b) It is a defense to a completed attempt that the person voluntarily and completely abandoned the intended crime, solely because of the person's own sense that it was wrong, prior to the completion of the crime. MCM, pt. IV, ¶ 4c(4) (added to the MCM in 1995).

c) When the actions of the accused have progressed into their last stages and the victim has already suffered substantial harm, voluntary abandonment is not a defense to attempt. *United States v. Smauley*, 42 M.J. 449 (C.A.A.F. 1995) (upholding guilty plea to attempted carnal knowledge).

d) The defense of voluntary abandonment is "unavailable if the criminal venture is frustrated by any circumstance that was not present or apparent when the actor began his criminal course of conduct that makes the accomplishment of the criminal purpose more difficult." *United States v. Haney*, 39 M.J. 917 (N.M.C.M.R. 1994) (citing *United States v. Rios*, 33 M.J. 436 (C.M.A 1991)).

e) Applications.

    (1) *United States v. Schoof*, 37 M.J. 96 (C.M.A. 1993) (fact that accused, later the same day, solicited someone to assist him in continuing to pursue the same crime of delivering classified microfiche to the Soviet Embassy undermined his claim that he had completely renounced his criminal purpose).

    (2) *United States v. Rios*, 33 M.J. 436 (C.M.A 1991) (accused did not voluntarily abandon attempted robbery where he merely postponed the criminal conduct to a more advantageous time and transferred the criminal effort to a different but similar victim); *see also United States v. Haney*, 39 M.J. 917 (N.M.C.M.R. 1994) (defense of voluntary abandonment not available to an accused where he and another sailor tried to rob a vending machine by drilling a hole in the glass and the glass shattered, "prompt[ing] their conclusion that continuing in the endeavor would be a 'bad idea'").

    (3) *United States v. Collier*, 36 M.J. 501 (A.F.C.M.R. 1992) (holding that when an attempted murder has proceeded so far that injury results, abandonment is not available as a defense).

    (4) *United States v. Wilmouth* 34 M.J. 739 (N.M.C.M.R. 1991) (accused's failure to deliver classified information because of inability to locate agent could not be attributed to a change of heart).

    (5) *United States v. Miller*, 30 M.J. 999 (N.M.C.M.R. 1990) (abandoning a course of action is not voluntary when it is motivated by circumstances that increase the probability of detection and apprehension).

    (6) *United States v. Walthers*, 30 M.J. 829 (N.M.C.M.R. 1990) (where the record indicated that the accused abandoned attempt to steal a car stereo, after breaking into the car, because of his own sense that it was wrong, the guilty plea to attempted larceny was improvident).

D. Pleading.

1. Overt act need not be alleged. *United States v. Marshall*, 40 C.M.R. 138 (C.M.A. 1969).

2. Attempted drug offenses.

a) *United States v. Showers*, 45 C.M.R. 647 (A.C.M.R. 1972). Specification alleging that the accused "did . . . on or about 31 August 1971 attempt to sell some quantity of a habit forming drug, to wit: Heroin" was fatally defective, because it fails to allege that the attempt was wrongful. *Accord United States v. Brice*, 38 C.M.R. 134 (C.M.A. 1967); *but see United States v. Simpson*, 25 M.J. 865 (A.C.M.R. 1988) (omission of the word "wrongful" from one of four drug distribution specifications not a fatal defect where defendant pled guilty), *aff'd*, 27 M.J. 483 (C.M.A. 1988).

b) *United States v. Guevara*, 26 M.J. 779 (A.F.C.M.R. 1988). Conviction for attempted use of a controlled substance, alleged in the generic, affirmed. Accused intended to use some type of controlled substance.

3. Attempted Robbery.

a) All the *essential* elements of robbery must be alleged in an attempted robbery specification. *United States v. Rios*, 15 C.M.R. 203 (C.M.A. 1954) (specification failing to allege the attempted taking was from the person or the presence of the victim was fatally defective).

b) *United States v. Hunt*, 7 M.J. 985 (A.C.M.R. 1979) (specification failing to allege the attempted taking was from the person or the presence of the victims was fatally defective; conviction of attempted larceny affirmed), *aff'd* 10 M.J. 222 (C.M.A. 1981).

c) *United States v. Ferguson*, 2 M.J. 1225 (N.C.M.R. 1976) (specification alleging, in part, that the accused did "attempt to rob a wallet, the property of PFC Hoge," was fatally defective).

d) *United States v. Wright*, 35 C.M.R. 546 (A.B.R. 1964) (specification alleging that accused "attempted to commit the offense of robbery by entering the Wolfgang Roth Insurance and Loan Agency, wearing a mask and armed with a pistol," was fatally defective).

E. Attempt as a Lesser Included Offense.

1. Text. "An accused may be found guilty of an offense necessarily included in the offense charged or of an attempt to commit either the offense charged or an offense necessarily included therein." Article 79.

2. *United States v. Banks*, 7 M.J. 501 (A.F.C.M.R. 1979). Attempted destruction of military property was a lesser included offense of sabotage, prosecuted under Article 134(3) and 18 U.S.C. § 2155.

3. The specification alleging the greater offense and the facts of the case put the defense on notice of the existence of the lesser offense of attempt. *See United States v. LaFontant*, 16 M.J. 236 (C.M.A. 1983) (affirming lesser included offense of attempted possession of LSD, even though members had not been instructed thereon, because the accused was convicted of actual possession and there was evidence that accused consciously and intentionally possessed a substance he believed to be LSD); *United States v. Guillory*, 36 M.J. 952 (A.C.M.R. 1993) (plea of guilty to attempted possession provident where inquiry

establishes guilt to greater offense of possession with intent to distribute, even though military judge did not advise accused of elements of attempt).

4. Specific intent requirement. *United States v. Roa*, 12 M.J. 210 (C.M.A. 1982) (attempt requires specific intent even where greater offense does not).

F. Attempts Expressly Enumerated in Substantive Offenses.

1. While most attempts should be charged under Article 80, the attempts listed below are specifically addressed under the article defining the primary offense and should be charged accordingly. MCM, pt. IV, ¶ 4c(6).

   a) Article 85 (desertion).

   b) Article 94 (mutiny).

   c) Article 100 (subordinate compelling surrender).

   d) Article 104 (aiding the enemy).

   e) Article 106a (espionage).

   f) Article 128 (assault).

2. Attempted Conspiracy. Attempted conspiracy is a viable offense under the UCMJ. *United States v. Riddle*, 44 M.J. 282 (C.A.A.F. 1996) (affirming conviction for attempted conspiracy to steal military pay entitlements). Attempted conspiracy is applicable where an accused agrees with an undercover *United States v. Anzalone*, 43 M.J. 322 (C.A.A.F. 1995) (holding that attempt and conspiracy statutes did not prohibit charge of attempted conspiracy to commit espionage, when other alleged conspirator is an undercover government agent); *United States v. Roeseler*, 55 M.J. 286 (C.A.A.F. 2001) (affirming conviction for attempted conspiracy to murder fictitious in-laws of fellow soldier).

3. Solicitation. "Soliciting another to commit an offense does not constitute an attempt." MCM, pt. IV, ¶ 4c(5).

4. Attempted drug offenses.

   a) If the accused believed the substance was an illegal drug, but the prosecution cannot prove it or the substance was actually not an illegal drug, then the accused can be convicted of attempting to commit the drug offense. *United States v. Dominguez*, 22 C.M.R. 275 (C.M.A. 1957) (attempted use of narcotic drug); *United States v. Longtin*, 7 M.J. 784 (A.C.M.R. 1979) (attempted sale of opium, where laboratory test inconclusive); *United States v. Gray*, 41 C.M.R. 756 (N.C.M.R. 1969) (attempted possession of marijuana and mescaline, where substances were not seized).

   b) If the accused did not believe the substance was an illegal drug, however, the accused did not attempt to commit a drug offense. *United States v. Collier*, 3 M.J. 932 (A.C.M.R. 1977) (where accused was putting one over on the heroin buyer by selling him brown sugar, guilty plea to attempted transfer of heroin was improvident); *United States v. Giles*, 42 C.M.R. 960 (A.F.C.M.R. 1970) (accused who knows he has been deceived by seller, but nevertheless smokes substance hoping to achieve a "high," was not guilty of attempted use).

   c) If the accused sold fake drugs, he can be charged and convicted of larceny by false pretenses, under Article 121. *See United States v. Williams*, 3 M.J. 555 (A.C.M.R. 1977) (sale of fake LSD) *rev'd on other grounds* 4 M.J. 336 (C.M.A. 1978).

5. Attempted Adultery. *United States v. St. Fort*, 26 M.J. 764 (A.C.M.R. 1988) (man returned home unexpectedly and found his wife clad only in bathrobe and the accused naked in a closet).

II. CONSPIRACY. UCMJ ART. 81.

A. Introduction.

1. "Any person subject to this chapter who conspires with any other person to commit an offense under this chapter shall, if one or more of the conspirators does an act to effect the object of the conspiracy, be punished as a court-martial may direct." Article 81.

2. Public Policy Rationale. The concerted activity of a conspiracy is much more dangerous to society than the acts of individuals. The criminal enterprise is more difficult to detect because of its secrecy, is more likely to succeed because of the combination of strengths and resources of its members, and may continue to exist even after the initial object of the conspiracy has been achieved. *See United States v. Feola*, 420 U.S. 671, 693-94 (1975); *United States v. Rabinowich*, 238 U.S. 78, 88 (1915).

3. Elements. MCM, pt. IV, ¶ 5b.

a) The accused entered into an agreement with one or more persons to commit an offense under the code; and

b) While the agreement continued to exist, and while the accused remained a party to the agreement, the accused or at least one of the co-conspirators performed an overt act for the purpose of bringing about the object of the conspiracy.

B. Parties to a Conspiracy.

1. Two or more persons are required in order to have a conspiracy. MCM, pt. IV, ¶ 5c(1).

a) Co-conspirators need not be subject to the UCMJ. *United States v. Rhodes*, 29 C.M.R. 551 (C.M.A. 1960) (co-conspirator was a foreign national).

b) At least two parties must be culpably involved. There must be a "meeting of minds" regarding the criminal object of the conspiracy. *United States v. Valigura*, 54 M.J. 187 (C.A.A.F. 2000) (adhering to the traditional "bilateral theory" and rejecting the modern "unilateral theory"; no conspiracy where only co-conspirator was an undercover agent; affirming conviction for attempted conspiracy); *United States v. LaBossiere*, 32 C.M.R. 337 (C.M.A. 1962). ("it is well settled that there can be no conspiracy when a supposed participant merely feigns acquiescence with another's criminal proposal in order to secure his detection and apprehension by proper authorities.").

2. Acquittal of accused's co-conspirators in a separate trial does not preclude conspiracy conviction of the accused. *United States v. Garcia*, 16 M.J. 52 (C.M.A. 1983) (overruling the former "rule of consistency").

C. "Bilateral Theory" of liability.

1. Conspiracy, under Article 81, requires a "meeting of the minds" to achieve the purported criminal goal. *United States v. Valigura*, 54 M.J. 187 (C.A.A.F. 2000); *United States v. LaBossiere*, 32 C.M.R. 337 (C.M.A. 1962) (if only two persons involved, one cannot be a government agent); *United States v. Duffy*, 47 C.M.R. 658 (A.C.M.R. 1973) (mentally incapacitated co-accused not culpably involved).

2. The law does not require 'consistency of verdicts.' If one of two co-conspirators is acquitted of conspiracy in a previous trial, the other co-conspirator may still be tried and convicted of conspiracy. *United States v. Garcia*, 16 M.J. 52, 57 (C.M.A. 1983).

3. An accused may be convicted of attempted conspiracy with an undercover law enforcement agent. *United States v. Anzalone*, 43 M.J. 322 (C.A.A.F. 1995); *United States v. Valigura*, 54 M.J. 187 (C.A.A.F. 2000).

4. Attempted conspiracy does not require an agreement or shared intent among the expected conspirators with respect to the object of the conspiracy. *United States v. Roeseler*, 55 M.J. 286 (C.A.A.F. 2001) (accused agreed to murder fictitious parents-in-law of fellow member of platoon).

D. The Agreement.

1. No particular words or form of agreement are required, only a common understanding to accomplish the object of the conspiracy. This may be shown by the conduct of the parties. The agreement need not state the means by which the conspiracy is to be accomplished or what part each conspirator is to play. *United States v. Whitten*, 56 M.J. 234 (C.A.A.F. 2002) (agreement formed by circling back to take a duffel bag after spotting it outside a vehicle while driving through housing area); MCM, pt. IV, ¶ 5c(2).

   a) "Object of the conspiracy."

      (1) *United States v. Shelton*, 62 M.J. 1 (C.A.A.F. 2005). The MJ instructed on lesser included offenses of unpremeditated murder and conspiracy to commit unpremeditated murder. MJ told the members that they would have to find "that at the time of the killing, the accused had the intent to kill or inflict great bodily harm on PFC Chafin." MJ erred. If the intent of the parties to the agreement was limited to the infliction of great bodily harm, their agreement was to commit aggravated assault, not unpremeditated murder.

      (2) *United States v. Denaro*, 62 M.J. 663 (C.G. Ct. Crim. App. 2006). Object must be a UCMJ offense. Interfering with a urinalysis constitutes the Article 134 offense of wrongfully interfering with an adverse administrative proceeding, thereby establishing the unlawful object of the conspiracy.

   b) *United States v. Billings*, 58 M.J. 861 (A. Ct. Crim. App. 2003) (evidence established an agreement by the accused to commit robbery where accused was leader of the gang and she silently concurred when a subordinate outlined the robbery plan as a way to make money for the gang and evidence suggested that the accused shared in the proceeds) *aff'd*, 61 M.J. 163 (C.A.A.F. 2005).

   c) *United States v. Cobb*, 45 M.J. 82 (C.A.A.F. 1996) (evidence established agreement to commit robbery, where accused brought co-conspirators together, knew of their criminal venture, and expected to share in the proceeds).

   d) *United States v. Garner*, 43 M.J. 435 (C.A.A.F. 1996) (affirming conviction for conspiracy to steal insurance funds where accused hired a fellow soldier to kill accused's wife with promise to share her life insurance proceeds).

   e) *United States v. Barnes*, 38 M.J. 72 (C.M.A. 1993) ("existence of a conspiracy is generally established by circumstantial evidence and is usually manifested by the conduct of the parties themselves").

f) *United States v. Matias*, 25 M.J. 356 (C.M.A. 1987) (conduct of accused and roommate was sufficient evidence of an agreement between them to sell marijuana), *cert. denied*, 485 U.S. 968 (1988).

g) *United States v. Jackson*, 20 M.J. 68 (C.M.A. 1985) (without saying a word, the co-conspirator joined the accused in a conspiracy to commit larceny).

h) *United States v. Brown*, 41 M.J. 504 (A. Ct. Crim. App. 1994) (conspiracy to organize a strike manifested by circumstantial evidence) *aff'd*, 45 M.J. 389 (C.A.A.F. 1996).

i) *United States v. Dickey*, 41 M.J. 637 (N-M. Ct. Crim. App. 1994), *vacated and remanded*, 43 M.J. 170 (C.A.A.F. 1995), *aff'd*, 46 M.J. 123 (C.A.A.F. 1996) (agreement to commit rape need not be expressed but only need be implied).

j) *United States v. Pete*, 39 M.J. 521 (A.C.M.R. 1994) (mere involvement in "gripe sessions" at which soldiers discussed leaving post without authority to protest conditions did not amount to a conspiracy).

k) *United States v. Walker*, 39 M.J. 731 (N-M.C.M.R. 1994) (affirming conviction for conspiracy to distribute marijuana where accused acted as a lookout and knew his associates were selling marijuana), *aff'd*, 41 M.J. 79 (C.M.A. 1994).

l) *United States v. Graalum*, 19 C.M.R. 667, 697-98 (A.F.B.R. 1955) ("conduct of the alleged co-conspirators, their declarations to or in the presence of each other, and other circumstantial evidence" clearly manifested agreement to commit bribery).

m) *United States v. Triplett*, 56 M.J. 875 (A. Ct. Crim. App. 2002) (accused's acts of straddling victim's chest and placing hands on her throat to facilitate rape by co-conspirator established that accused and co-conspirator formed an agreement to rape victim).

n) *United States v. Brown*, 9 M.J. 599 (A.F.C.M.R. 1980) (accused's involvement in first two of four thefts was insufficient to establish that the scope and object of the conspiracy, of which the accused was a member, included the last two thefts).

2. Mere presence is insufficient basis for inference of agreement. *United States v. Wright*, 42 M.J. 163 (C.A.A.F. 1995) (evidence that accused agreed to be present to assist if necessary and to assist in disposal of the victim's body was sufficient proof of agreement to commit premeditated murder); *United States v. Mukes*, 18 M.J. 358 (C.M.A. 1984) (conspiracy requires "deliberate, knowing, and specific intent to join the conspiracy, not . . . that [the accused] was merely present when the crime was committed").

3. A conditional agreement is sufficient for conspiracy if the accused believes that the condition is likely to be fulfilled. *United States v. Wright*, 42 M.J. 163, 166-67 (C.A.A.F. 1995) (citing federal case law).

4. Single Agreement to Commit Multiple Crimes. A single agreement to commit multiple offenses is a single conspiracy.

a) *United States v. Mack*, 58 M.J. 413 (C.A.A.F. 2003). Accused was convicted separately of conspiracy to commit check forgery and conspiracy to commit larceny of the check proceeds. On appeal, the government acknowledged there was only one agreement and thus, only one conspiracy. The court consolidated the two conspiracy specifications. "[O]ne agreement cannot be taken to be several agreements and hence several conspiracies because it envisages the violation of several statutes rather than one."

    b) *United States v. Pereira*, 53 M.J. 183 (C.A.A.F. 2000). Accused pled guilty to and was convicted of separate specifications of conspiracy to commit murder, conspiracy to commit robbery, and conspiracy to commit kidnapping. The record established that the accused and his co-conspirators formed only one agreement to commit all the underlying offenses. As a matter of law, there was only one conspiracy, and the court consolidated the three specifications into one specification.

5. Complex Conspiracies. The scope and structure of conspiracies will vary considerably. The simplest form is a single bilateral agreement to commit a single crime. From that simple model, conspiracies may evolve into highly complex networks involving agreements between multiple parties to commit multiple crimes. In some cases, separate conspiracies are linked together by one or more common members. The scope and structure of the conspiracy has critical implications for determining liability of co-conspirators for crimes committed in furtherance of the conspiracy, resolving of evidentiary issues, and presenting a coherent theory to the panel. Two common metaphors used to describe complex conspiracies are the "wheel with spokes" conspiracy and the "chain" conspiracy.

    a) A "totality of the circumstances" analysis is the correct approach when determining the number of conspiracies in a given case. Federal court decisions have identified a variety of factors that may be relevant to determining whether a single or multiple conspiracies exist. Among such factors are the following: (1) the objectives of each alleged conspiracy; (2) the nature of the scheme in each alleged conspiracy; (3) the nature of the charge; (4) the overt acts alleged in each; (5) the time each of the alleged conspiracies took place; (6) the location of each of the alleged conspiracies; (7) the conspiratorial participants in each; and (8) the degree of interdependence between the alleged conspiracies. *United States v. Finlayson*, 58 M.J. 824 (A. Ct. Crim. App. 2003) (applying the eight factors to find one conspiracy where the accused used two suppliers, one of whom also supplied the other, and later had his wife join him in his drug distributing venture).

    b) Under the "wheel" metaphor, establishing a single conspiracy requires that the prosecution prove that the spokes are bound by a "rim," which is the concerted action of all the parties working together with a single design for the accomplishment of a common purpose. The circumstances must lead to an inference that some form of overall agreement existed. This agreement may be inferred from the parties' acts or other circumstantial evidence. *United States v. Kenny*, 645 F.2d 1323, 1334-35 (9th Cir. 1981) (finding a single conspiracy in the form of a "wheel" with the defendant as a central "hub" dealing in individual transactions with the other defendants as "spokes"), *cert. denied*, 452 U.S. 920 (1981).

    c) The government need not show direct contact or explicit agreement between the defendants. It is sufficient to show that each defendant knew or had reason to know of the scope of the conspiracy and that each defendant had reason to believe that their own benefits were dependent upon the success of the entire venture. *United States v. Kostoff*, 585 F.2d 378, 380 (9th Cir. 1978).

d) Once the existence of a conspiracy has been established, evidence of only a slight connection is necessary to convict a defendant of knowing participation in it. *United States v. Dunn*, 564 F.2d 348, 357 (9th Cir. 1977).

E. Overt Act.

1. The overt act must be independent of the agreement, and it must take place during or after the agreement. MCM, pt. IV, ¶ 5c(4)(a). *United States v. Kauffman*, 34 C.M.R. 63 (C.M.A. 1963) (the act of receiving the name and address of his contact, which was not separate from the agreement, was not a sufficient overt act for conspiracy to wrongfully communicate with agents of East Germany); *United States v. Schwab*, 27 M.J. 559 (A.C.M.R. 1988) (accused's conversations with his alleged co-conspirator, his statement that he put money aside, and co-conspirator's notes and sketches did not satisfy the overt act requirement for conspiracy to commit larceny and wrongful sale of firearms); *United States v. Farkas*, 21 M.J. 458 (C.M.A. 1986), *cert. denied*, 479 U.S. 857 (1986) (act done prior to agreement is not a sufficient overt act).

2. The overt act must be done by one or more of the co-conspirators, but not necessarily the accused. MCM, pt. IV, ¶ 5c(4)(a); *see United States v. Yarborough*, 5 C.M.R. 106 (C.M.A. 1962) (in conspiracy to intentionally inflict self-injury, the government could have alleged overt acts proven to be committed by the co-conspirator, but the government alleged overt acts by the accused that it did not prove).

3. An overt act by one conspirator is the act of all; the overt act may be performed by any member of the conspiracy. Each conspirator is equally guilty even though each does not participate in, or have knowledge of, all of the details. MCM, pt. IV, ¶ 5c(4)(c); *see United States v. Figueroa*, 28 M.J. 570 (N.M.C.M.R. 1989).

4. The overt act need not be criminal. Although committing the intended offense may constitute the overt act, it is not essential. Mere preparation may be enough, as long as it manifests that the agreement is being executed. MCM, pt. IV, ¶ 5c(4)(b); *United States v. Choat*, 21 C.M.R. 313 (C.M.A. 1956) (obtaining crowbar with which to break and enter a store was sufficient overt act for conspiracy to commit larceny); see *United States v. Brown*, 41 M.J. 504 (A.C.C.A. 1994) (agreement may be contemporaneous with the offense itself in a conspiracy to organize a strike), *aff'd,* 45 M.J. 389 (C.A.A.F. 1996).

5. At least one overt act must be alleged and proved; *United States v. McGlothlin*, 44 C.M.R. 533 (A.C.M.R. 1971) (holding that specification alleging conspiracy to commit pandering but not alleging any overt act in furtherance of the conspiracy was fatally defective). Government may allege several overt acts, but need prove only one; *United States v. Reid*, 31 C.M.R. 83 (C.M.A. 1961).

6. Substitution of proof of an unalleged overt act does not necessarily constitute a fatal variance, as long as there is "substantial similarity" between the alleged overt act and the overt act proven at trial. *United States v. Collier*, 14 M.J. 377 (C.M.A. 1983); see *United States v. Moreno*, 46 M.J. 216 (C.A.A.F. 1997) (where basic facts remain unchanged, amendment of alleged overt act the day before trial was permissible minor change).

F. Wharton's Rule.

1. Some offenses require two or more culpable actors acting in concert. There can be no conspiracy where the agreement exists only between the persons necessary to commit such an offense. Examples include dueling, bigamy, incest, adultery, and bribery. MCM, pt. IV, ¶ 5c(3).

2. *Iannelli v. United States*, 420 U.S. 770, 782-86 (1975). Defendant and seven others were convicted of conspiracy to violate and violating 18 U.S.C. § 1955, a federal statute

making it a crime for five or more persons to operate a prohibited gambling business. Convictions for both offenses were affirmed. Wharton's Rule "has current vitality only as a judicial presumption, to be applied in the absence of legislative intent to the contrary. The classic Wharton's Rule offenses—adultery, incest, bigamy, dueling—are crimes that are characterized by the general congruence of the agreement and the completed substantive offense. The parties to the agreement are the only persons who participate in commission of the substantive offense, and the immediate consequences of the crime rest on the parties themselves rather than society at large."

3. Rule does not apply where the substantive offense does not demand concerted criminal activity, such as drug use or distribution. *United States v. Crocker*, 18 M.J. 33, 38-39 (C.M.A. 1984) (drug distribution); *United States v. Johnson*, 58 M.J. 509 (N-M. Ct. Crim. App. 2003) (drug use); *United States v. Osthoff*, 8 M.J. 629 (A.C.M.R. 1979).

4. Rule does not apply when the conspiracy involves the cooperation of a greater number of persons than is required for commission of the substantive offense. *See United States v. Crocker*, 18 M.J. 33, 38 (C.M.A. 1984) (affirming conspiracy conviction where accused accepted money and agreed to buy drugs for another airman on a trip to Amsterdam; Wharton's Rule did not apply because only one party to a drug distribution need have a criminal intent); *United States v. Jiles*, 51 M.J. 583 (N.M. Ct. Crim. App. 1999) (holding Wharton's Rule did not apply to conspiracy to distribute marijuana).

5. *But see United States v. Parada*, 54 M.J. 730 (C.G. Ct. Crim. App. 2001) (Application of Wharton's Rule to drug offenses is a highly fact-dependent determination in which the extent of the enterprise in time and reach are prime considerations. Conspiracy to distribute marijuana where the only parties involved were the accused, who mailed the drugs, and his friend, who received them, was unnecessary "piling-on" of charges); *United States v. Viser*, 27 M.J. 562 (A.C.M.R. 1988) (holding Wharton's Rule does not apply to drug offenses).

6. Wharton's Rule does not apply to conspiracy to violate an anti-black marketing regulation. *United States v. Wood*, 7 M.J. 885 (A.F.C.M.R. 1979) (reasoning that the regulation could be violated by one person).

G. Duration.

1. Termination. A conspiracy terminates when the object of the conspiracy is accomplished, the members withdraw, or the members abandon the conspiracy. *United States v. Beverly*, 14 U.S.C.M.A. 468, 471 (C.M.A. 1964).

a) *United States v. Jimenez Recio*, 537 U.S. 270 (2003) Conspiracy does not automatically terminate simply because the Government has defeated its object. Thus, defendants may be convicted of conspiracy, even absent proof they joined the conspiracy before its defeat.

b) *United States v. Ratliff*, 42 M.J. 797 (N-M.C.C.A. 1995). Accused and four other Marines conspired to rob enough other Marines to finance a trip to Raleigh, North Carolina. After successfully getting money from one robbery victim but then failing to get money from two other victims that ran away, it was obvious that the co-conspirators did not think that they had attained the object of their conspiracy. Therefore, a statement made by a co-conspirator, at that time, was not hearsay, under MRE 801(d)(2)(E).

c) *United States v. Hooper*, 4 M.J. 830 (A.F.C.M.R. 1978). Accused charged with conspiring to violate and violating an Air Force regulation proscribing demonstrations in foreign countries by burning a cross. Later, an alleged co-

conspirator stated that the accused lit the fire. The statement was admissible only if it was made during and in furtherance of the conspiracy. "It is well settled that a conspiracy ends when the objectives thereof are accomplished, if not earlier by abandonment of the aims or when any of the members of the joint enterprise withdraw therefrom." The object of the conspiracy was the erection and burning of the cross. When that was accomplished, the conspiracy terminated.

2. Withdrawal.

a) An individual is not guilty of conspiracy if he effectively withdraws before the alleged overt act is committed. An effective withdrawal must consist of affirmative conduct that is wholly inconsistent with adherence to the unlawful agreement and that shows that the party has severed all connection with the conspiracy. A conspirator who effectively withdraws from the conspiracy after the performance of the alleged overt act remains guilty of conspiracy and of any offenses committed pursuant to the conspiracy up to the time of the withdrawal, but he is not liable for offenses committed by the remaining conspirators after his withdrawal. MCM, pt. IV, ¶ 5c(6).

b) *United States v. Miasel*, 24 C.M.R. 184 (C.M.A. 1957). Accused and six others agreed to commit sodomy upon a fellow soldier in the stockade. The group forced the victim to lie down while the accused climbed on top of the victim. The accused declined to try to commit sodomy. The group took the victim out of the room and committed forcible sodomy upon him, but the accused did not leave the room with the group and had no further participation in the venture. "The failure of the accused to accompany the group when they left the barracks is indicative of an affirmative act on his part to effect a withdrawal and constitutes conduct wholly inconsistent with the theory of continuing adherence."

c) Mere inactivity does not constitute withdrawal. *United States v. Rhodes*, 28 C.M.R. 427 (A.B.R. 1959), aff'd 29 C.M.R. 551 (C.M.A. 1960). From 1951 to 1953, the accused, while stationed at the United States embassy in Moscow, agreed to supply information to Soviet agents. In 1953, he returned to the United States and did not again actively participate in the conspiracy. In 1957, a co-conspirator committed an overt act. Accused was guilty of conspiracy. "[I]t is no defense to the charge of conspiracy that appellant was inactive [in the conspiracy] subsequent to June 1953.

3. A conspiracy is presumed to continue, until the contrary is shown. *United States v. Graalum*, 19 C.M.R. 667 (A.F.B.R. 1955) (affirming conviction for conspiracy to commit bribery, where accused did not effectively withdraw prior to the performance of the overt act by the co-conspirator).

H. Vicarious Liability.

1. A co-conspirator may be convicted for substantive offenses committed by another co-conspirator, provided such offenses were committed while the agreement continued to exist and were in furtherance of the agreement. MCM, pt. IV, ¶ 5c(5); *Pinkerton v. United States*, 328 U.S. 640 (1946); *United States v. Browning*, 54 M.J. 1 (C.A.A.F. 2000); *United States v. Gaeta*, 14 M.J. 383 (C.M.A. 1983) (members were properly instructed on liability for co-conspirator's drug distribution); *United States v. Figueroa*, 28 M.J. 570 (N.M.C.M.R. 1989) (guilty plea to drug distribution by co-conspirator was provident).

2. *United States v. Billings*, 58 M.J. 861 (A.C.C.A. 2003) (accused's silent consent as approval authority for all gang activity supported conviction for robbery even though other gang members carried out the crime) *aff'd*, 61 M.J. 163 (2005).

3. *United States v. Finlayson*, 58 M.J. 824 (A.C.C.A. 2003) (dicta) (accused could be criminally liable for the actions of other conspirators before he joined the conspiracy).

4. Article 77 is broad enough to encompass vicarious liability of co-conspirators. *United States v. Browning*, 54 M.J. 1, 7 (C.A.A.F. 2000) (holding that prosecution could prove larceny and fraudulent claim charges on theory that accused was perpetrator, aider and abettor, or co-conspirator, even though conspiracy was not on the charge sheet).

5. A co-conspirator's statement may be admissible under MRE 801(d)(2)(E) even though conspiracy is not a charged offense. *United States v. Knudson*, 14 M.J. 13 (C.M.A. 1982).

I. Punishment.

1. Conspiracy to commit an offense is distinct and separate from the offense that is the object of the conspiracy. The accused can be convicted and punished separately for both the conspiracy and the underlying offense. Also, commission of the intended offense may constitute the overt act required for conspiracy. MCM, pt. IV, ¶ 5c(8); *Pinkerton v. United States*, 328 U.S. 640 (1946); *United States v. Dunbar*, 12 M.J. 218 (C.M.A. 1982); *United States v. Washington*, 1 M.J. 473 (C.M.A. 1976); *United States v. Nagle*, 30 M.J. 1229 (A.C.M.R. 1990).

2. Conspiracy to commit a crime and solicitation to commit the same crime are separate offenses. *See United States v. Ramsey*, 52 M.J. 322 (C.A.A.F. 2000); *United States v. Carroll*, 43 M.J. 487 (C.A.A.F. 1996).

3. Conspiracy to commit a crime and attempted commission of the same crime are separate offenses, because each offense requires proof of a separate element. *United States v. Stottlemire*, 28 M.J. 477 (C.M.A. 1989).

4. Where the theft of two separate items was contemplated by the conspiracy, the value of the items can be aggregated to calculate the maximum punishment available for the conspiracy. *United States v. Crawford*, 31 M.J. 736 (A.F.C.M.R. 1990).

III. SOLICITATION. UCMJ ART. 82 AND ART. 134.

A. Introduction. Solicitation may be charged under either Article 82 or Article 134, depending on the crime solicited.

1. Article 82 covers solicitation to commit the offenses of desertion (Article 85), mutiny (Article 94), misbehavior before the enemy (Article 99), or sedition (Article 94).

2. Article 134 covers solicitation to commit offenses other than these four named offenses.

B. Discussion.

1. Instantaneous offense. The offense is complete when a solicitation is made or advice given with the specific wrongful intent to influence another or others to commit an offense. It is not necessary that the person or persons solicited or advised agree to or act upon the solicitation or advice. MCM, pt. IV, ¶ 6c(1).

2. Form of solicitation. Solicitation may be by means other than word of mouth or writing. Any act or conduct that reasonably may be construed as a serious request or advice to commit an offense can be considered solicitation. It is not necessary that the accused act alone; the accused may act through other persons in committing this offense. MCM, pt. IV, ¶ 6c(2).

3. The prosecution must prove the accused had the specific intent that the offense actually be committed. *United States v. Taylor*, 23 M.J. 314 (C.M.A. 1987); *United States v. Benton*, 7 M.J. 606 (N.C.M.R. 1979).

4. An express or implicit invitation to join in a criminal plan is a solicitation. The context in which an alleged statement was made can be considered to determine its criminal nature as a solicitation. *United States v. Williams*, 52 M.J. 218 (C.A.A.F. 2000) (where accused and other person had used drugs together and the other person was informed of the accused's international drug smuggling operation, including the employment of a third party for drug buying trips to Turkey, the accused's statement, "Are you ready to go; you got your passport?" to which the other person promptly answered, "I'm not going to go," could reasonably be construed as an invitation to join the criminal enterprise).

5. The person solicited must know that an offense is contemplated. *United States v. Higgins*, 40 M.J. 67 (C.M.A. 1994) (guilty plea to solicitation improvident where accused asked soldier to withdraw money from ATM machine but did not tell him that the ATM card did not belong to accused); *United States v. Conway*, 40 M.J. 859 (A.F.C.M.R. 1994) (person solicited need not know the specific statute but must understand that the invitation is to engage in wrongful conduct and that the conduct has been made criminal by law); *United States v. Davis*, 39 M.J. 1110 (A.F.C.M.R. 1994) (plea to solicitation improvident where accused asked person to cash "girlfriend's check," and solicitee believed the act was properly authorized and thus legal).

6. The person solicited need not be subject to prosecution by court-martial. *United States v. Conway*, 40 M.J. 859 (A.F.C.M.R. 1994) (accused who requested to see his 15-year-old stepdaughter naked, when child was aware of improper purpose, was guilty of solicitation); *See also United States v. Harris*, 2003 C.C.A. Lexis 269 (N-M.C.C.A. 2003).

7. The person solicited may be predisposed toward the crime. *United States v. Hays*, 62 M.J. 158 (2005) (holding neither the MCM nor the UCMJ precludes a conviction for solicitation because the object is predisposed towards the crime (rejecting the requirement set forth in *Dean*, 44 M.J. 683 (Army Ct. Crim. App. 1996)).

C. Miscellaneous Issues.

1. Accomplice liability distinguished. If the solicitee commits the intended offense, the solicitor may be liable for the commission of the crime as a principal under Article 77. MCM, pt. IV, ¶ 1.b.(2)(b).

2. Pleading. Incorrectly charging an Article 134 solicitation under Article 82 may be amended as a minor change. *United States v. Brewster*, 32 M.J. 591 (A.C.M.R. 1991).

THIS PAGE INTENTIONALLY LEFT BLANK

CHAPTER 3: MILITARY OFFENSES
PART I: ABSENCE, DISOBEDIENCE, AND RELATED OFFENSES

I. **UNAUTHORIZED ABSENCE.**

    A. Introduction.

        1. Scope. As used in this chapter, Absence without authority refers to offenses under three articles of the Uniform Code of Military Justice:

            a) Article 85: Desertion and attempted desertion.

            b) Article 86: Failure to go to appointed place of duty, leaving appointed place of duty, and absence without leave.

            c) Article 87: Missing movement.

    B. Charges. Unauthorized absences are punishable under Articles 85, 86 and 87 and not under Article 134. *United States v. Deller*, 12 C.M.R. 165 (C.M.A. 1953) (allegation that accused absented himself without leave "with the wrongful intention of permanently preventing completion of basic training and useful service as a soldier" was not an offense in violation of Article 134; however, the court affirmed a conviction under Article 85).

II. **ABSENCE WITHOUT LEAVE. UCMJ ART. 86.**

    A. Failure to Go to Appointed Place of Duty (Failure to Repair). UCMJ art. 86(1).

        1. Elements. MCM, pt. IV, ¶ 10.b.(1).

            a) A certain authority appointed a certain time and place of duty for the accused;

            b) The accused knew of that time and place; and

            c) The accused, without authority, failed to go to the appointed place of duty at the time prescribed.

        2. Pleadings. The "appointed place of duty" addressed in Article 86(1) refers to a specifically appointed place of duty rather than a general place of duty. A specification listing only the accused's unit does not list a specific place of duty and is fatally defective. *United States v. Sturkey*, 50 C.M.R. 110 (A.C.M.R. 1975). *See also United States v. Coleman*, 34 M.J. 1020 (ACMR 1992). The appointed place need not be alleged with as much specificity in nonjudicial proceedings. *United States v. Atchison*, 13 M.J. 798 (A.C.M.R. 1982).

            a) The offense requires that the accused actually knew the appointed time and place. MCM, pt. IV, ¶ 10.c.(2). *But see United States v. Adams*, 63 M.J. 223 (2006) (holding the Art. 112a theory of "deliberate avoidance" satisfies the knowledge requirement for ALL Art. 86 offenses).

            b) "Appointed place of duty" includes the place(s) where a restricted soldier is required to sign-in. *United States v. High*, 39 M.J. 82 (C.M.A. 1994).

            c) Ordinarily, violation of an order to report to a particular place, though charged under Article 92, constitutes no more than a failure to repair. The maximum punishment is therefore limited to that for failure to repair. *United States v. Hargrove*, 51 M.J. 408 (C.A.A.F. 1999) (accused guilty of failure to go to appointed place of duty, rather than disobeying a lawful order, when order was to sign-in hourly when not working); *United States v. Henderson*, 44 M.J. 232

(C.A.A.F. 1996) (accused's failure to comply with staff sergeant's order to get dressed and be at morning formation 45 minutes later constituted offense of failure to repair rather than willfully disobeying an NCO); *United States v. Baldwin*, 49 C.M.R. 814 (A.C.M.R. 1975); MCM, pt. IV, paragraphs 14.c.(2)(b) and 16.e.(2).

    d) On the other hand, if the order to return to duty was issued in performance of a proper military function and not for the purpose of increasing the punishment, the accused may be convicted and punished for both offenses. *United States v. Pettersen*, 17 M.J. 69 (C.M.A. 1983); *see generally* MCM, pt. IV, paragraph 14c(2)(a)(iii) (stating that an order must have a proper military purpose and not be designed to increase punishment).

3. "Without Proper Authority." *United States v. Duncan*, 60 M.J. 973 (Army Ct. Crim. App. 2005). Appellant told his squad leader that he had to take his son to the hospital, and based on that false information his squad leader gave him permission to miss the formation. Appellant claimed that this evidence was a matter inconsistent with his plea. An absence from a unit, organization, or place of duty is without authority if it is preceded by false statements, false documents, or false information provided by an accused.

B. Leaving Place of Duty. Article 86(2).

    1. Elements. MCM, pt. IV, ¶ 10b(2).

        a) A certain authority appointed a certain time and place of duty for the accused;

        b) The accused knew of that time and place; and

        c) The accused, without authority, went from the appointed place of duty after having reported to that place.

    2. Pleadings. See supra ¶ A.2., this chapter.

C. Absence Without Leave. Article 86(3).

    1. Elements. MCM, pt. IV, ¶ 10.a.(3).

        a) The accused absented himself from his unit, organization or place of duty at which he was required to be;

        b) The absence was without proper authority from anyone competent to give him leave; and

        c) The absence was for a certain period of time.

    2. Several aggravated forms of AWOL permit increased punishment. MCM, pt. IV, ¶ 10.e.(3)-(5). Note that two of these aggravated offenses contain an intent element. For the elements and a discussion of these aggravated forms of AWOL, see MCM, pt. IV, paragraphs 10.b.(3), (4) and 10.c.(4). Unless otherwise indicated, the discussion of AWOL in this section refers to the standard, non-aggravated form of AWOL.

    3. Definition of Terms.

        a) "Unit" refers to a military element such as a company or battery.

        b) "Organization" refers to a larger command consisting of two or more units. One can be AWOL from an armed force as a whole. *United States v. Vidal*, 45 C.M.R. 540 (A.C.M.R. 1972); *see United States v. Brown*, 24 C.M.R. 585

(A.F.B.R. 1957) (holding the United States Air Force was both an organization and a place of duty).

c) "Place of duty at which the accused was required to be" is a generic term designed to broadly cover places such as a command, quarters, station, base, camp or post. *United States v. Brown*, 24 C.M.R. 585 (A.F.B.R. 1957). Note that this definition is different from "a place of duty" under Article 86(1) and 86(2), which refers to a specific "appointed place of duty."

d) An individual may be absent from more than one unit. *United States v. Mitchell*, 22 C.M.R. 28 (C.M.A. 1956); *United States v. Green*, 14 M.J. 766 (A.C.M.R. 1982).

4. A specification alleging the wrong unit requires dismissal. *United States v. Walls*, 1 M.J. 734 (A.F.C.M.R. 1975); *United States v. Riley*, 1 M.J. 639 (C.G.C.M.R. 1975); *United States v. Holmes*, 43 C.M.R. 446 (A.C.M.R. 1970) (holding that dismissal for fatal variance does not preclude retrial for unauthorized absence from correct unit).

5. An Article 86(3) specification must allege the accused was absent from his unit, organization, or other place of duty at which he was required to be. Failure to allege that the accused was required to be there is fatal. *United States v. Kohlman*, 21 C.M.R. 793 (A.F.C.M.R. 1956). Absence from a unit cannot be supported when the member is in fact present in the unit, albeit casually. *United States v. Wargo*, 11 M.J. 501 (N.C.M.R. 1981). *But see United States v. Phillips*, 28 M.J. 599 (N.M.C.M.R 1989) (affirming conviction of accused who remained on the installation but in another unit's barracks). *See also United States v. Cary*, 57 M.J. 655 (N-M. Ct. Crim. App. 2002) (accused was allowed to leave local area and live with cousin, conditioned upon the requirement he call his unit daily to report status; accused's failure was not an unauthorized absence, but rather a failure to perform a particular task).

6. The specification must allege that the absence was "without authority." Failure to do so may be a fatal defect. *United States v. Fout*, 13 C.M.R. 121 (C.M.A. 1953), *overruled in part by United States v. Watkins*, 21 M.J. 208 (C.M.A. 1986) (omission not fatal when first challenged on appeal, accused pled guilty, another AWOL specification to which the accused pled guilty contained the phrase "without authority," and no prejudice evident).

7. Mere failure to follow unit checkout procedure by accused who was granted leave does not constitute AWOL. *United States v. Dukes*, 30 M.J. 793 (N.M.C.M.R. 1990).

8. A definitive inception date is indispensable to a successful prosecution for unauthorized absence. *United States v. Hardeman*, 59 M.J. 389 (C.A.A.F. 2004).

9. Computing the Duration of the Absence. MCM, pt. IV, ¶ 10.c.(9).

a) An unauthorized absence is complete the moment the accused leaves the unit without authority. It is not a continuing offense. *See United States v. Jackson*, 20 M.J. 83 (C.M.A. 1985); *United States v. Lynch*, 47 C.M.R. 498 (C.M.A. 1973); *United States v. Newton*, 11 M.J. 580 (N.C.M.R. 1980) (accused's plea improvident when he admitted his absence actually began before the date alleged in the specification which constituted an admission to an uncharged offense). *But see United States v. Brock*, 13 M.J. 766 (A.F.C.M.R. 1982) (plea to "13 October" absence not improvident as it was embraced by "on or about" 14 October specification). Leave is considered an absence from duty, and one in an AWOL status cannot take leave. *United States v. Kimbrell*, 28 M.J. 542 (A.F.C.M.R. 1989); *United States v. Ringer*, 14 M.J. 979 (N.M.C.M.R. 1982).

b) The duration of an absence must be proved in order to determine the legal punishment for the offense. *United States v. Lynch*, 47 C.M.R. 498 (C.M.A. 1973); *see also United States v. Simmons*, 3 M.J. 398 (C.M.A. 1977).

c) The duration of an absence alleged in a specification may be decreased but not enlarged by the court. *United States v. Turner*, 23 C.M.R. 674 (C.G.B.R. 1957), *rev'd on other grounds*, 25 C.M.R. 386 (C.M.A. 1958); *United States v. Scott*, 59 M.J. 718 (Army Ct. Crim. App. 2004) (holding plea improvident for charged period when accused signed in with CQ and departed the next day; citing MCM pt. IV, ¶ 10c(11), the court divided the period of absence into two shorter absences under the same specification and affirmed the findings and sentence); An accused may be found guilty of two or more separate unauthorized absences under one specification, but the maximum punishment may not increase. MCM, pt. IV, ¶ 10c(11).

d) If a member is released by the civilian authorities without trial, and was on authorized leave at the time of arrest or detention, the member may be found guilty of unauthorized absence only if it is proved that the member actually committed the offense for which detained, thus establishing that the absence was the result of the member's own misconduct. MCM, pt. IV, ¶ 10.c.(5). *But see United States v. Sprague*, 25 M.J. 743 (A.C.M.R. 1987) (holding guilty plea provident where accused admitted his arrest on a warrant for contempt of court was his own fault, despite the fact that he was released without trial).

e) If a service member is given authorization to attend civilian court proceedings, pursuant to UCMJ Article 14, and is put in civilian jail as a result, the ensuing absence is not unauthorized. *United States v. Urban*, 45 M.J. 528 (N-M. Ct. Crim. App. 1996).

10. Termination of the Absence: Return to Military Control.

a) Surrender to military authority. If an accused presents himself to military authorities and notifies them of his AWOL status, the surrender terminates the absence. MCM, pt. IV, ¶ 10.c.(10)(a).

(1) *United States v. Coglin*, 10 M.J. 670, 672 (A.C.M.R. 1981) lists three factors which must be found to constitute an effective voluntary termination:

(a) "[T]he absentee must present himself to competent military authority with the intention of returning to military duty;"

(b) "[T]he absentee must identify himself properly and must disclose his status as an absentee;" and

(c) "[T]he military authority, with full knowledge of the individual's status as an absentee, exercises control over him."

(2) Casual presence. *United States v. Rogers*, 59 M.J. 584 (Army Ct. Crim. App. 2003) (affirming conviction when accused pled guilty and said she was "sometimes" on post during the charged periods, but admitted she had no intent to return and did not turn herself in to her unit; casual presence on post for personal reasons did not voluntarily terminate

her absence). The opinion contains a pattern instruction for voluntary termination issues.

(3) Intent to return to duty. The soldier must voluntarily submit or offer to submit to military authorities with a bona fide intention to return to duty. *United States v. Self*, 35 C.M.R. 557 (A.B.R. 1965).

b) Military Control.

(1) Where an accused thwarted an attempt to exercise control by refusing to submit to lawful orders, military control was not established. *United States v. Pettersen*, 14 M.J. 608 (A.F.C.M.R. 1982), *aff'd* 17 M.J. 69 (C.M.A. 1983).

(2) Telephone contact alone will not effect a return to military control. *United States v. Anderson*, 1 M.J. 688 (N.C.M.R. 1975); *see also United States v. Sandell*, 9 M.J. 798 (N.C.M.R. 1980) (rejecting claim of constructive termination where accused informed recruiter by telephone he wished to surrender, but before surrendering to a captain at the reserve center, accused became frightened and departed the center).

(3) Civilian bail/bond. *United States v. Dubry*, 12 M.J. 36 (C.M.A. 1981) (accused's surrender to military authority was not complete because the terms of his civilian bail made him unavailable to return to unrestricted military control).

(4) Where the record reflects the accused 1) may have submitted himself to military authorities, and 2) military authorities failed to exercise control over the accused, a substantial basis in law and fact exists to question the providence of the accused's plea of guilty to unauthorized absence (relative to the calculation of the termination date of the accused's absence). *United States v. Phillipe*, 63 M.J. 307 (C.A.A.F. 2006); *see also United States v. Pinero*, 60 M.J. 31 (C.A.A.F. 2004) (AWOL soldier who returned to his unit to submit to a urinalysis that lasted five hours, and then went AWOL again, terminated his initial AWOL when he returned to submit to the urinalysis).

c) Knowledge of absentee's status.

(1) "[K]nown presence at a military installation will not constitute termination where the absentee, by design and misrepresentation, conceals his identity or duty status." *United States v. Self*, 35 C.M.R. 557 (A.B.R. 1965).

(2) Casual presence at a military installation, unknown to proper authority and primarily for the absentee's own purposes, does not end the unauthorized absence. *United States v. Williams*, 29 M.J. 504 (A.C.M.R. 1989) (if an absentee temporarily submits himself to military control but does not disclose his status as an absentee, the AWOL is not terminated); *United States v. Self*, 35 C.M.R. 557 (A.B.R. 1965); *United States v. Murat Acemoglu*, 45 C.M.R. 335 (C.M.A. 1972) (going to American embassy to find out information on how to surrender was not enough to terminate AWOL); *United States v. Baughman*, 8 M.J. 545 (C.G.C.M.R. 1979).

(3) Constructive knowledge of absentee's status. An unauthorized absence may be terminated by the exercise of control over the absentee by military authorities having a duty to inquire into the absentee's status, if they could have determined such status by reasonable diligence. *United States v. Gudatis*, 18 M.J. 816 (A.F.C.M.R. 1984). *But see United States v. Jackson*, 2 C.M.R. 96 (C.M.A. 1952) (After the accused went AWOL, he was tried by summary court-martial for other offenses in a different area of Korea. During World War II and the Korean Conflict, summary courts-martial were convened in areas where large troop concentrations existed, and courts often did not know the accused soldiers' status. Thus, the AWOL did not terminate in this case, because the accused did not inform the summary court-martial of his status and went AWOL after the court-martial.)

d) Apprehension of a known absentee by military authorities terminates an unauthorized absence.

(1) The authorities need not be of the same armed force as the accused. *United States v. Coates*, 10 C.M.R. 123 (C.M.A. 1953).

(2) But, record of trial must evince military authority's knowledge of status and intent to exercise control. *United States v. Gaston*, 62 M.J. 404 (2006) (action by "dorm manager" informing the accused that his squadron was looking for him not enough to constitute termination by apprehension; dorm manager did not indicate why unit was looking for accused and once notified, accused voluntarily surrendered by going to the front of the dorm).

e) Apprehension of a known absentee by civil authorities, acting at the request and on behalf of military authorities, terminates an unauthorized absence. *United States v. Garner*, 23 C.M.R. 42 (C.M.A. 1957); *see also United States v. Hart*, 47 C.M.R. 686 (A.C.M.R. 1973).

(1) Where a service member is apprehended by civilian authorities for a civilian offense, and the authorities indicate a willingness to turn the member over to military control, the failure or refusal of military officials to take control of the member constructively terminates the absence. *United States v. Lanphear*, 49 C.M.R. 742 (C.M.A. 1975). *But see United States v. Bowman*, 49 C.M.R. 406 (A.C.M.R. 1974) (holding that the Army has no affirmative duty to seek the release of a service member it knows is in civilian jail pending civilian charges).

(2) Defense counsel must determine all relevant facts concerning an accused's apprehension by civilian authorities and return to military control to competently advise an accused before entering a guilty plea to an unauthorized absence terminated by apprehension. *United States v. Evans*, 35 M.J. 754, 757 n.1 (N.M.C.M.R. 1992).

f) Delivery to military authority. If a known absentee is delivered by anyone to military authority, this terminates the absence. MCM, pt. IV, ¶ 10.c.(10)(c).

11. For a discussion of trial defense counsel's obligations concerning disclosure of documents, see *United States v. Province*, 45 M.J. 359 (C.A.A.F. 1997) (in which defense counsel, during pretrial negotiations, gave prosecutors a written pass given to the accused,

thus allowing the government to sever one long AWOL charge into two AWOL charges; the court held defense counsel was not unethical or ineffective because counsel used the document to secure a favorable deal for his client and because the government could have obtained the document elsewhere).

D. *Mens Rea* Under Article 86, UCMJ.

1. Specific intent is not an element of the Article 86 offenses, but it is necessary to plead and prove specific intent for certain aggravating factors (*e.g.*, intent to avoid field maneuvers or field exercises). MCM, pt. IV, ¶¶ 10c(3) and (4).

2. Unauthorized absence requires is a general intent crime, whereas desertion under Article 85 requires specific intent. *United States v. Holder*, 22 C.M.R. 3 (C.M.A. 1956).

E. Attempts. Attempted AWOL may be a lesser included offense of desertion and attempted desertion. *United States v. Evans*, 28 M.J. 753 (A.F.C.M.R. 1989), *aff'd*, 29 M.J. 331 (C.M.A. 1989).

F. Multiplicity/Unreasonable Multiplication of Charges.

1. Multiplicity: AWOL & breaking restriction covering same time period. *United States v. Hudson,* 58 M.J. 357 (C.A.A.F. 2004).

2. Unreasonable multiplication of charges: multiple failures to repair & dereliction of duty. *United States v. Taylor*, 26 M.J. 7 (C.M.A. 1988).

G. Lesser included Offenses.

1. Article 86(1) is not a lesser included offense of Article 86(3). *United States v. Reese*, 7 C.M.R. 292 (A.B.R. 1953).

2. Article 86(3) is not a lesser included offense of Article 86(1) or (2). *United States v. Sturkey*, 50 C.M.R. 110 (A.C.M.R. 1975).

III. MISSING MOVEMENT. UCMJ ART. 87.

A. Background. The offense of missing movement is a relative newcomer to military criminal law, arising from problems encountered in World War II when members of units or crews failed to show up when their units or ships departed. Article 87 was designed to cover offenses more serious than simple AWOL but less severe than desertion. *United States v. Smith*, 2 M.J. 566 (A.C.M.R. 1976), *aff'd*, 4 M.J. 210 (C.M.A. 1978) (not discussing the missing movement offense).

B. Elements. MCM, pt. IV, ¶ 11.b.

1. That the accused was required in the course of duty to move with a ship, aircraft or unit;

2. That he knew of the prospective movement of the ship, aircraft, or unit;

3. That the accused missed the movement; and

4. That the missed movement was either through design or neglect.

C. Two Forms of Missing Movement.

1. Through design.

a) "Design" refers to doing an act intentionally or on purpose. It requires specific intent to miss the movement. MCM, pt. IV, ¶ 11.c.(3).

b) Missing movement through design, the more serious offense, has a maximum punishment of dishonorable discharge, total forfeitures, and confinement for two years. MCM, pt. IV, ¶ 11.e.(1).

2. Through neglect.

a) "Neglect" means the omission to take such measures as are appropriate under the circumstances to assure presence with a ship, aircraft, or unit at the time of a scheduled movement, or doing some act without giving attention to its probable consequences in connection with the prospective movement, such as a departure from the vicinity of the prospective movement to such a distance as would make it likely that one could not return in time for the movement. MCM, pt. IV, ¶ 11.c.(4).

b) The maximum punishment for missing movement through neglect is a bad conduct discharge, total forfeitures, and confinement for one year. MCM, pt. IV, ¶ 11.e.(2).

D. General Requirements.

1. "Movement" includes neither practice marches of short duration with a return to the point of departure nor minor changes in location of a unit such as from one side of a post to another. MCM, pt. IV, ¶ 11c(1). Movement missed must be substantial in terms of duration, distance and mission. Thus, missing a port call for MAC flight constituted missing movement of an aircraft within meaning of Article 87. *United States v. Graham*, 16 M.J. 460 (C.M.A. 1983); *United States v. Blair*, 24 M.J. 879 (A.C.M.R. 1987) *aff'd*, 27 M.J. 438 (C.M.A. 1988). *But see United States v. Gibson*, 17 M.J. 143 (C.M.A. 1984) (failure to report for an ordinary commercial flight does not constitute missing movement as it is not the type of movement contemplated by Article 87).

2. In a case involving missing movement involving a civilian aircraft, the government must show that the accused was required to travel on that aircraft. *United States v. Kapple*, 40 M.J. 472 (C.M.A. 1994).

3. The accused must have actual knowledge of the prospective movement. Knowledge of the exact hour or even of the exact date of the movement is not required. MCM, pt. IV, ¶ 11c(5).

4. The accused's knowledge may be shown by circumstantial evidence. *United States v. Chandler*, 48 C.M.R. 945 (C.M.A. 1974) (reversing conviction because the evidence was legally insufficient to prove actual knowledge).

5. Some authority supports the proposition that UCMJ Article 87 does not reach every instance in which a service member misses a movement but is applicable only when the accused has an essential mission related to the movement, *e.g.*, is an integral member of the unit or crew whose absence would potentially disrupt the mission. *Compare United States v. Gillchrest*, 50 C.M.R. 832 (A.F.C.M.R. 1975) (finding that service member missing a commercial aircraft to Turkey as part of PCS did not meet Congressional intent behind the missing movement offense) *and United States v. Smith*, 2 M.J. 566 (A.C.M.R. 1976) *aff'd*, 4 M.J. 210 (C.M.A. 1978) (holding that missing movement to site of two-day bivouac 12 miles downrange did not constitute missing movement; "[h]ard and fast rules relating to the duration, distance and mission of the 'movement' are not appropriate, but rather those factors plus other concomitant circumstances must be considered collectively, in order to evaluate the potential disruption of the unit caused by a soldier's absence"), *with United States v. Lemley*, 2 M.J. 1196 (N.C.M.R. 1976) (holding that accused, who

was being escort from brig and missed specific Pan Am flight listed on orders, did miss "movement") *and United States v. St. Ann*, 6 M.J. 563 (N.C.M.R. 1978)(holding that missing a commercial flight while on orders constitutes missing movement even when the accused is not a member of the crew or traveling with his unit).

6. Going AWOL and proceeding to a place more than 1200 miles away was a failure to exercise due care contemplated in missing movement through neglect. *United States v. Mitchell*, 3 M.J. 641 (A.C.M.R. 1977).

7. Missing a two-week winter exercise that took place on the same installation as the unit's location in Alaska supported missing a movement by design. *United States v. Jones*, 37 M.J. 571 (A.C.M.R. 1993).

8. An eight-hour "dependent's cruise" by aircraft carrier is not a "minor" change in the location of the ship. The focus of the statutory prohibition is upon the movement itself, and not its purpose. *United States v. Quezada*, 40 M.J. 109 (C.M.A. 1994).

9. An essential element of missing movement is that the movement actually occurred. This element may be inferred if the accused holds a ticket for a regularly scheduled commercial flight. *United States v. Kapple*, 36 M.J. 1119 (A.F.C.M. R. 1993), *rev'd on other grounds*, 40 M.J. 472 (C.M.A. 1994).

10. Missing the move, rather than a particular mode of travel, is the gravamen of missing movement. *United States v. Smith*, 26 M.J. 276 (C.M.A. 1988).

11. Military judge erred by using the accused's plea of guilty to AWOL as evidence to establish an essential element of a separate charge of missing movement to which a plea of not guilty had been entered. *United States v. Wahnon*, 1 M.J. 144 (C.M.A. 1975).

E. Multiplicity and Lesser included Offenses.

1. An accused cannot be punished for both AWOL of minimal duration and missing movement through neglect or through design when the same absence forms the basis for both charges. *United States v. Baba*, 21 M.J. 76 (C.M.A. 1985); *United States v. Posnick*, 24 C.M.R. 11 (C.M.A. 1957); *United States v. Bridges*, 25 C.M.R. 383 (C.M.A. 1958). *See also United States v. Traxler*, 39 M.J. 476 (C.M.A. 1994) (finding that missing movement of aircraft and disobedience of an officer's order to board the aircraft were not multiplicious).

2. An AWOL of extended duration is not multiplicious with missing movement. *United States v. Olinger*, 47 M.J. 545 (N-M. Ct. Crim. App. 1997), *aff'd*, 50 M.J. 365 (C.A.A.F. 1999).

3. Failure to repair is a lesser included offense of missing movement. *United States v. Smith*, 2 M.J. 566 (A.C.M.R. 1976), *aff'd*, 4 M.J. 210 (C.M.A. 1978).

IV. DESERTION. UCMJ ART. 85.

A. Types of Desertion. Desertion exists when any member of the armed forces:

1. Without authority, goes or remains absent from his or her unit, organization, or place of duty, with intent to remain away permanently. *United States v. Horner*, 32 M.J. 576 (C.G.C.M.R. 1991); or

2. Quits his or her unit, organization or place of duty with intent to avoid hazardous duty or to shirk important service. *United States v. Hocker*, 32 M.J. 594 (A.C.M.R. 1991); or

3. Without being separated from one of the armed forces, enlists or accepts an appointment in another of the armed forces without fully disclosing the fact that he has not been regularly separated, or enters any foreign armed service except when authorized by the United States.

4. Additionally, a commissioned officer is in desertion if, after tender of a resignation and before its acceptance, he quits his post or proper duties without leave and with intent to remain away permanently.

B. Elements of Desertion with Intent to Remain Away Permanently. (The most common form of desertion). MCM, pt. IV, ¶ 9.b.(1).

1. The accused absented himself from his unit, organization, or place of duty;

2. That the absence was without authority;

3. That the accused, at the time the absence began or at some time during the absence, intended to remain away from his unit, organization, or place of duty permanently; and

4. The accused remained absent until the date alleged.

5. If the absence was terminated by apprehension, that element is added.

C. Less Common Forms of Desertion.

1. Desertion with intent to avoid hazardous duty or to shirk important service. MCM, pt. IV, ¶ 9b(2).

a) Prospective duty as a medic at Fort Sam Houston during Persian Gulf War qualified as important service. *United States v. Swanholm*, 36 M.J. 743 (A.C.M.R. 1992).

b) Thirty-day sentence to brig not important service for purposes of desertion. *United States v. Wolff*, 25 M.J. 752 (N.M.C.M.R. 1987).

c) Being an accused at a special court-martial is not important service. *United States v. Walker*, 26 M.J. 886 (A.F.C.M.R. 1988) (accused still found guilty, however, because he had an intent to remain away permanently). *See* TJAGSA Practice Note, *Being an Accused: "Service," But Not "Important Service,"* ARMY LAW., Apr. 1989, at 55 (discussing *Walker*).

2. Desertion before notice of acceptance of resignation. MCM, pt. IV, ¶ 9.b.(3).

D. Desertion Terminated by Apprehension.

1. In addition to the four elements of desertion listed above, if the accused's absence was terminated by apprehension, the Government may allege termination by apprehension as an aggravating factor.

2. If alleged in the specification and proved beyond a reasonable doubt, termination by apprehension increases the maximum confinement from two years to three years. MCM, pt. IV, ¶ 9.e.(2)(a) and (b).

3. Termination by apprehension may apply to all forms of desertion except absence with intent to avoid hazardous duty or to shirk important service, as the maximum punishment for this latter most serious form of desertion is already a DD and five years. MCM, pt. IV, ¶ 9.e.(1).

4. An accused may be convicted of desertion terminated by apprehension even though he was apprehended by civilian authorities for a civilian offense and thereafter notified the civilian authorities of his AWOL status. *United States v. Fields*, 32 C.M.R. 193 (C.M.A. 1962); *United States v. Babb*, 19 C.M.R. 317 (C.M.A. 1955); *United States v. Northern*, 42 M.J. 638 (N-M. Ct. Crim. App. 1995). Apprehension by civilian authorities and the subsequent return to military authorities for an offense unrelated to one's military status does not in and of itself prove that the return was involuntary. *United States v. Washington*, 24 M.J. 527 (A.F.C.M.R. 1987).

E. Termination Generally. Desertion did not terminate when military authorities requested civilian authorities deny a deserter bail until resolution of civilian charges. *United States v. Asbury*, 28 M.J. 595 (N.M.C.M.R. 1989).

F. Attempted Desertion. Attempted desertion should be charged under Article 85 rather than under Article 80. MCM, pt. IV, ¶ 4c(6)(a).

G. *Mens Rea* for Desertion. The offenses of desertion and absence without leave are similar in most respects, except for the intent element involved in desertion. *See United States v. Horner*, 32 M.J. 576 (C.G.C.M.R. 1991). The remaining elements of desertion are the same as those for AWOL and are discussed *supra*, ¶ II, this chapter.

1. Desertion is a specific intent crime. *United States v. Holder*, 22 C.M.R. 3 (C.M.A. 1956).

2. Evidence of intent may be based upon all the facts and circumstances of the case. Length of absence, actions and statements of the accused, and the method of termination of the absence (apprehension or voluntary surrender) are some factors to be considered. MCM, pt. IV, ¶ 9c(1)(c)(iii). The determination of whether an accused intended to avoid hazardous duty or shirk important service is subjective, and whether the service is "important" is an objective question dependent upon the totality of circumstances. *United States v. Gonzalez*, 42 M.J. 469 (1995).

3. The length of the absence alone is insufficient to establish an intent to desert; however, in combination with other circumstantial evidence, it may be sufficient. *United States v. Care*, 40 C.M.R. 247 (C.M.A. 1969).

4. The totality of circumstances surrounding the offense can negate specific intent to absent oneself permanently. *United States v. Logan*, 18 M.J. 606 (A.F.C.M.R. 1984).

5. Having an understandable or laudable motive to desert is not a defense if the evidence sufficiently establishes the elements. *United States v. Gonzalez*, 39 M.J. 742 (N.M.C.M.R. 1994), *aff'd* 42 M.J. 469 (1995).

6. Evidence of an accused's motive to quit her unit as gesture of protest because of moral or ethical reservations that the unit might commit war crimes is irrelevant to a charge of desertion with intent to avoid hazardous duty or shirk important service. *United States v. Huet-Vaughn* 43 M.J. 105 (C.A.A.F. 1995).

7. Evidence of a 26-month absence while accused was on orders for a war zone and where he was apprehended a long distance from his unit was sufficient to establish intent to desert. *United States v. Mackey*, 46 C.M.R. 754 (N.C.M.R. 1972).

8. Evidence of a two-year absence in vicinity of assigned unit, termination by apprehension, and a previous absence, despite retention of an identification card, was sufficient to show an intent to desert. *United States v. Balagtas*, 48 C.M.R. 339 (N.C.M.R. 1972).

9. The intent to remain away permanently need not coincide with the accused's departure. A person must have had, either at the inception of the absence or at some time during the absence, the intent to remain away permanently. MCM, pt. IV, ¶ 9.c.(1)(c)(i).

10. In a case where desertion with intent to shirk important service was charged, infantry service in Vietnam was held to be "important service." *United States v. Moss*, 44 C.M.R. 298 (A.C.M.R. 1971). *See also United States v. Hocker*, 32 M.J. 594 (A.C.M.R. 1991) (accused's plea provident to desertion with intent to avoid hazardous duty where service was duty in Persian Gulf).

H. Pleading.

1. In view of the three types of intent encompassed in Article 85 (*i.e.*, intent to remain away permanently, intent to avoid hazardous duty, intent to shirk important service), the crime of desertion is not alleged unless the specific form of intent is stated in the specification. *United States v. Morgan*, 44 C.M.R. 898 (A.C.M.R. 1971) (the court found the accused guilty of the lesser included offense of AWOL).

2. "Desert" and "desertion" are terms of art which necessarily and implicitly include the requirement that the absence was without authority. *United States v. Lee*, 19 M.J. 587 (N.M.C.M.R. 1984) (specification that alleges that the service member "did desert" is the equivalent of alleging that the members did without authority and with the intent to remain away permanently absent himself from his unit).

3. AWOL under Article 86 is a lesser included offense of most forms of desertion. MCM, pt. IV, ¶ 9.d.

V. DEFENSES TO UNAUTHORIZED ABSENCE.

A. Introduction. This section treats defenses as they relate to unauthorized absence only. For a complete treatment of defenses to court-martial charges, see *infra*, chapter 5.

B. Statute of Limitations.

1. In time of war, there is no statute of limitations for AWOL and desertion. Article 43(a). For example:

   a) After the armistice on 27 July 1953, hostilities in Korea were no longer "in time of war." *United States v. Shell*, 23 C.M.R. 110 (C.M.A. 1957) (holding that unauthorized absence that began on 4 August 1953 was subject to statute of limitations).

   b) After 10 August 1964, hostilities in Vietnam constituted "in time of war" for suspension of the statute of limitations. *United States v. Anderson*, 38 C.M.R. 386 (C.M.A. 1968). "Time of war" ended 27 January 1973. *United States v. Reyes*, 48 C.M.R. 832 (A.C.M.R. 1974); *see United States v. Robertson*, 1 M.J. 934 (N.C.M.R. 1976).

2. If the unauthorized absence begins in time of peace, the statute of limitations, if raised, will bar prosecution if the offense was committed more than 5 years before receipt of sworn charges by the summary court-martial convening authority. UCMJ art. 43(b). The statute of limitations is tolled while the accused is AWOL, beyond the authority of the United States to apprehend him, in custody of civil authorities, or in the hands of the enemy. However, AWOL is not a continuing offense, so the statute of limitations begins to run as soon as the service member is reported as AWOL. *United States v. Miller*, 38

M.J. 121 (C.M.A. 1993). [Note: Prior to 24 November 1986, the statute of limitations was two years for AWOL and three years for desertion. *See Miller*, 38 M.J. at 122.]

3. Swearing of charges and receipt of the charges by the officer exercising summary court-martial jurisdiction over the unit tolls the statute of limitations for the offenses charged. UCMJ art. 43(b)(1). The critical question is whether the "sworn charges and specifications" are timely received, not whether the same charge sheet received by the summary court-martial convening authority is used at the court-martial. *United States v. Miller*, 38 M.J. 121, 124 (C.M.A. 1993); *United States v. Johnson*, 3 M.J. 623 (N.C.M.R. 1977).

4. Where charges have been preferred and received by the summary court-martial convening authority and the statute of limitations has thus been tolled, minor amendments to the specifications do not void the tolling of the statute. *United States v. Arbic*, 36 C.M.R. 448 (C.M.A. 1966).

5. It is permissible to prefer charges against an accused with an open-ended termination date and forward them to the summary court-martial convening authority (to stop the running of the statute of limitations), and then add a termination date when it is known. *United States v. Reeves*, 49 C.M.R. 841 (A.C.M.R. 1975).

6. Dismissal of charges that are barred by the statute of limitations does not preclude a later trial on a charge sheet that was properly received by the summary court-martial convening authority within the period provided by the statute of limitations. *United States v. Jackson*, 20 M.J. 83 (C.M.A. 1985).

7. Even if the charged offense is not barred by the statute of limitations, the accused cannot be convicted of a lesser included offense that is barred by the statute of limitations, unless there is an affirmative waiver. *United States v. Busbin*, 23 C.M.R. 125 (C.M.A. 1957).

8. If a lesser included offense is barred by the statute of limitations, the military judge must inform the accused and allow the accused to choose between protection under the statute of limitations or the instruction on the lesser included offense. R.C.M. 907(b)(2)(B); *United States v. Cooper*, 37 C.M.R. 10 (C.M.A. 1966); *United States v. Wiedemann*, 36 C.M.R. 521 (C.M.A. 1966).

9. The military judge has a duty to advise the accused of his right to assert the statute of limitations when it appears that the period of time has elapsed. *United States v. Rodgers*, 24 C.M.R. 36 (C.M.A. 1957); *overruled on other grounds by United States v. Miller*, 38 M.J. 121 (C.M.A. 1993); *United States v. Brown*, 1 M.J. 1151 (N.C.M.R. 1977) (no duty to advise the accused where referred charges mirrored the original charges that were timely received by the summary court-martial convening authority within the period provided by the statute of limitations and the original charge sheet was attached to the referred charge sheet).

10. The rights accorded an accused under the statute of limitations may be waived when the accused, with full knowledge of the privilege, fails to plead the statute in bar of the prosecution or sentence. *United States v. Troxell*, 30 C.M.R. 6 (C.M.A. 1960) (permitting an accused, charged with desertion, to plead guilty to AWOL and not assert the statute of limitations, IAW pretrial agreement).

11. When the statutory period has apparently elapsed, the burden of proof of showing timely charges is on the government. *United States v. Morris*, 28 C.M.R. 240 (C.M.A.

1959) (statute of limitations did not toll, because accused was not in territory in which the US had authority to apprehend him).

12. Computation of time. A year is 365 days during regular years and 366 days in leap year. The date of the offense counts as the first day of the running of the statute and the count proceeds forward to the day before receipt by the summary court-martial convening authority. *United States v. Tunnel*, 19 M.J. 819 (N.M.C.M.R. 1984), *aff'd* 23 M.J. 110 (C.M.A. 1986). *Contra United States v. Reed*, 19 M.J. 702 (N.M.C.M.R. 1984) (begins day after offense and concludes on day necessary action is accomplished to toll statute).

C. Former Jeopardy (Article 44, UCMJ).

1. No person may, without his consent, be tried a second time for the same offense. Article 44(a).

2. When jeopardy attaches.

 a) A proceeding which, after introduction of evidence but before a finding, is dismissed or terminated by the convening authority or on motion of the prosecution for failure of available evidence or witnesses without any fault of the accused, is a trial. Article 44(c).

 b) Withdrawal of charges after arraignment but before presentation of evidence does not constitute former jeopardy, and denial of a motion to dismiss charges at a subsequent trial is proper. *United States v. Wells*, 26 C.M.R. 289 (C.M.A. 1958).

 c) Once tried for a lesser offense, accused cannot be tried for a major offense that differs from the lesser offense in degree only. Trial for AWOL bars subsequent trial for desertion. *United States v. Hayes*, 14 C.M.R. 445 (N.B.R. 1953).

 d) "The protection against double jeopardy does not rest upon a surface comparison of the allegations of the charges; it also involves consideration of whether there is a substantial relationship between the wrongdoing asserted in the one charge and the misconduct alleged in the other." *United States v. Lynch*, 47 C.M.R. 498, 500 (C.M.A. 1973) (doctrine of former jeopardy precluded another trial for unauthorized absence from different unit and shorter time period). *But see United States v. Robinson*, 21 C.M.R. 380 (A.B.R. 1956) (permitting, after conviction for an AWOL and after disapproval of findings and sentence by the convening authority, trial for AWOL for the same period but from a different unit than was previously charged); *United States v. Hutzler*, 5 C.M.R. 661, 664 n.3 (A.B.R. 1951).

 e) Double jeopardy does not attach when charges are dismissed for violating the statute of limitations. Thus, the government is not barred from prosecuting the accused on a charge sheet that had properly been received by the summary court-martial convening authority within the period of the statute, following dismissal of charges for the same offense (but on a different charge sheet) that was not received within the period of the statute. However, if evidence was introduced in the first proceeding, the first is considered a trial and jeopardy attaches. *United States v. Jackson*, 20 M.J. 83 (C.M.A. 1985).

 f) Nonjudicial punishment previously imposed under Article 15 for a *minor* offense and punishment imposed under Article 13 for a *minor* disciplinary infraction may be interposed as a bar to trial for the same minor offense or infraction. R.C.M. 907(b)(2)(D)(iv).

(1) "Minor" normally does not include offenses for which the maximum punishment at a general court-martial could be dishonorable discharge or confinement for more than one year. MCM, pt. V, ¶ 1.e.

(2) If an accused has previously received punishment under Article 15 for other than a minor offense, the service member may be tried subsequently by court-martial; however, the prior punishment under Article 15 must be considered in determining the amount of punishment to be adjudged at trial if the accused is found guilty at the court-martial. *United States v. Jackson*, 20 M.J. 83 (C.M.A. 1985); *see* UCMJ art. 15(f); R.C.M. 1001(c)(1)(B); *United States v. Pierce*, 27 M.J. 367 (C.M.A. 1989) (accused must be given complete credit for any and all nonjudicial punishment suffered—day-for-day, dollar-for-dollar, and stripe-for-stripe).

(3) An AWOL of 5 days, which was accused's first offense, was a "minor offense" that should have been dismissed upon motion, after accused had previously been punished for the same offense under Article 15. *United States v. Yray*, 10 C.M.R. 618 (A.B.R. 1953).

D. Jurisdiction.

1. For jurisdiction generally, see DA Pam 27-173, pt. II.

2. The mere fact of expiration of enlistment during a status of unauthorized absence did not terminate jurisdiction or the AWOL. *United States v. Klunk*, 11 C.M.R. 92 (C.M.A. 1953).

3. When unauthorized absence has been alleged, an accused's status as a member of the armed forces must be proved beyond a reasonable doubt. *United States v. Marsh*, 15 M.J. 252 (C.M.A. 1983).

E. Impossibility: The Inability to Return to Military Control.

1. When a service member is, due to unforeseen circumstances, unable to return at the end of authorized leave through no fault of his own, he has not committed the offense of AWOL as the absence is excused. MCM, pt. IV, ¶ 10c(6); *see also United States v. Lee*, 16 M.J. 278 (C.M.A. 1983) (mechanical problems with automobile); *United States v. Calpito*, 40 C.M.R. 162 (C.M.A. 1969).

2. When a service member, *already in an AWOL status*, is unable to return because of sickness, lack of transportation or other disability, he remains in an AWOL status; however, the disability for part of the AWOL should be considered as an extenuating circumstance. MCM, pt. IV, ¶ 10c(6).

3. Types of impossibility in AWOL situations.

a) Impossibility due to physical disability.

(1) Where accused was ill at the end of his authorized leave and where, on medical advice, he remained in bed for several days before turning himself in to military authorities, the military judge should have given instructions on the defense of physical incapacity. *United States v. Amie*, 22 C.M.R. 304 (C.M.A. 1957); *see also United States v. Irving*, 2 M.J.

967 (A.C.M.R. 1976) ("[s]ickness which amounts to physical incapacity to report or otherwise comply with orders, and which is not self-induced, is a legal excuse"); *United States v. Edwards*, 18 C.M.R. 830 (A.F.B.R. 1955) (exceeding territorial limits of pass is not *per se* unauthorized absence).

(2) Evidence of accused's dental problems which went untreated because of a difference of professional opinion did not raise the defense of physical incapacity after the accused went AWOL to receive civilian dental treatment. *United States v. Watson*, 50 C.M.R. 814 (N.C.M.R. 1975).

(3) Evidence raised defense of physical inability where accused, returning to his ship, was robbed and knocked unconscious and, upon regaining consciousness the next day, immediately attempted to return to his ship. *United States v. Mills*, 17 C.M.R. 480 (N.C.M.R. 1954).

(4) The accused was robbed the night before he was due to return to his unit and made no effort to return other than to attempt to borrow money (refusing one offer), although he was aware of his duty to return and was physically able to do so. No defense of impossibility was found. In a footnote, the court wrote that the accused was derelict in his responsibilities, because he did not contact military authorities or seek the aid of any responsible civilian agency. *United States v. Bermudez*, 47 C.M.R. 68 (A.C.M.R. 1973).

b) Impossibility due to transportation misfortune.

(1) Where second lieutenant's car broke down while he was returning from a weekend pass and he elected to remain with his car until it was repaired, the Manual provision concerning "through no fault of his own" does not apply as his decision was for his own convenience. *United States v. Kessinger*, C.M.R. 261 (A.B.R. 1952).

(2) Where a second lieutenant postponed his return from leave to assist a friend in filing an accident report, the absence was not excusable as involuntary as no inability to return existed. *United States v. Scott*, 9 C.M.R. 241 (A.B.R. 1952).

(3) Where a second lieutenant mistakenly took a "hop" to Washington, D.C. rather than to Atlanta, and thereafter had difficulty obtaining transportation back to his unit, no valid defense was found. Rather, the evidence could be considered in extenuation and mitigation. *United States v. Mann*, 12 C.M.R. 367 (A.B.R. 1953).

c) Impossibility due to acts of God (sudden and unexpected floods; snow; storms; hurricanes; earthquakes; or any unexpected, sudden, violent, natural occurrence) can be a defense. If the particular act of nature may be expected to occur, it is not a defense because it is foreseeable (*e.g.*, a snowstorm after repeated snowstorm warnings in Minnesota in January).

d) Impossibility due to wrongful acts of third parties includes train wrecks, plane crashes, and explosions that are not caused by the accused. These situations present a legitimate defense of impossibility.

e) Impossibility due to civilian confinement.

(1) The inability to return to military control depends on the accused's status at time of confinement and on the results of the civilian trial. The table below summarizes the rule. *See generally* MCM, pt. IV, ¶ 10c(5).

Status of Service Member at Time of Confinement	Result of Civilian Trial		Prosecution for AWOL?
	Acquittal	*Conviction*	
(a) Delivery of soldier to civilian authorities under Article 14	X	X	No
(b) AWOL	X	X	Yes
(c) Absent with leave	X		No
(d) Absent with leave		X	Yes*
*AWOL begins at expiration of leave			

(2) Adjudication as a youthful offender is tantamount to a conviction within the meaning of MCM, pt. IV, ¶ 10.c.(5). *United States v. Myhre*, 25 C.M.R. 294 (C.M.A. 1958).

(3) A soldier who voluntarily commits an offense while on authorized leave and is apprehended and detained by civilian authorities may be charged with AWOL for the period after his leave expired until his return to military control. *United States v. Myhre*, 25 C.M.R. 294 (C.M.A. 1958).

(4) Where a service member, while AWOL, is apprehended, detained and acquitted by civilian authorities, absent evidence of an attempt to return to military control, the entire period of time is chargeable as AWOL. *United States v. Grover*, 27 C.M.R. 165 (C.M.A. 1958); *United States v. Bowman*, 49 C.M.R. 406 (A.C.M.R. 1974) (while AWOL, accused was arrested and convicted for a civilian offense; civilian authorities did not make the accused available to return to military control; the AWOL continued through the entire time period he was in civilian control).

(5) Where accused was granted "special leave" to answer civilian charges, he could not later be convicted of AWOL for the time spent in civilian jail if convicted by civilian authorities. *United States v. Northrup*, 31 C.M.R. 73 (C.M.A. 1961); *United States v. Williams*, 49 C.M.R. 12 (C.M.A. 1974).

(6) Absent an arrest on behalf of the military, an offer to turn the service member over to military authorities, or a notification that the civilian authorities are not going to prosecute, the Army does not have an affirmative duty to seek the release to military authorities of an absent soldier held in a civilian jail on civilian charges. *United States v. Bowman*, 49 C.M.R. 406 (A.C.M.R. 1974) (distinguishing *United States v. Keaton*, 40 C.M.R. 212 (C.M.A. 1969)).

F. Mistake of Fact.

1. General intent crime: mistake of fact must be both honest and reasonable to constitute a defense. *United States v. Holder*, 22 C.M.R. 3 (C.M.A. 1956); *United States v. Scheunemann*, 34 C.M.R. 259 (C.M.A. 1964).

2. In specific intent crimes, such as desertion, however, the mistake of fact need only be honest. *United States v. Guest*, 46 M.J. 778 (Army Ct. Crim. App. 1997); R.C.M. 916(j).

3. When the evidence raises the defense of mistake, the government must disprove the defense beyond a reasonable doubt. *United States v. Thompson*, 39 C.M.R. 537 (A.B.R. 1968) (reversing conviction for desertion because the military judge failed to instruct on burden of proof for mistake of fact).

4. Mere speculation by the factfinder as to when an honest and reasonable mistake of fact ended and the unauthorized absence commenced is neither sufficient to sustain a conviction for AWOL nor the basis for a criminal conviction. *United States v. Morsfield*, 3 M.J. 691 (N.C.M.R. 1977).

5. A service member who was ordered to go home to await orders for Vietnam and who waited for 2-1/2 years for the orders that never arrived was not guilty of AWOL. *United States v. Davis*, 46 C.M.R. 241 (C.M.A. 1973); *see also United States v. Hale*, 42 C.M.R. 342 (C.M.A. 1970).

G. Duress.

1. Duress or coercion is a reasonably grounded fear on the part of an actor that he or another innocent person would be immediately killed or would immediately suffer serious bodily injury if he did not commit the act. Duress is a defense to all offenses except where the accused kills an innocent person. R.C.M. 916(h). *United States v. Hullum*, 15 M.J. 261 (C.M.A. 1983) (accused's absence may be excused, if he left because his life was endangered).

2. The defense of duress is not limited to those circumstances where the accused feels that he personally is going to immediately be killed or suffer serious bodily injury. *United States v. Jemmings*, 1 M.J. 414 (C.M.A. 1976) (accused pled guilty to housebreaking and, in the providence inquiry, he testified that he committed the act because he was scared that something would happen to his family if he did not); *see also United States v. Palus*, 13 M.J. 179 (C.M.A. 1982) (reversing conviction, where accused wrote bad checks to cover debts because he feared for his wife's safety, because evidence raised the duress defense).

3. The need of a service member to absent himself from a perilous situation at his duty station in order to find a safer place from threatened injury is not *normally* a good defense to AWOL. *See United States v. Wilson*, 30 C.M.R. 630 (N.B.R. 1960) (accused went AWOL because another service member threatened his life; but Board of Review affirmed the conviction because he did not eliminate the threat by going AWOL). *But see United States v. Hullum*, 15 M.J. 261 (C.M.A. 1983) (accused's absence may be excused, if he left because his life was endangered); *United States v. Roberts*, 15 M.J. 106 (C.M.A. 1983) (summary disposition) (finding that sexual harassment and immediate threat to the physical safety of the accused's wife raised the defense of duress to an unauthorized absence).

4. Although sexual harassment may, in certain circumstances, be a defense to an unauthorized absence, it did not constitute duress when the second lieutenant conceded during the providence inquiry that she did not reasonably fear imminent death or serious

bodily injury of her children when she went AWOL. *United States v. Biscoe*, 47 M.J. 398 (C.A.A.F. 1998).

5. An accused's fear that work to which he was assigned in the mess hall would aggravate his eye injury and commander's causing accused to be evicted forcibly from his off-post residence did not constitute the affirmative defense of duress in an AWOL case, because accused could not reasonably fear death or serious bodily injury. *United States v. Guzman*, 3 M.J. 740 (N.C.M.R.), *rev'd on other grounds*, 4 M.J. 115 (C.M.A. 1977).

6. The accused must reasonably apprehend immediate threat of death or serious bodily harm, and there must not be alternatives. *United States v. Olinger*, 50 M.J. 365 (C.A.A.F. 1999) (finding no "substantial basis" in law to reject the guilty plea, where accused went AWOL and missed a movement because he felt his wife's depression might kill her; during the providence inquiry, the accused failed to provide enough details of immediate threat of death or serious bodily harm and that there were no alternative sources of assistance for his wife other than going AWOL and missing movement).

7. Accused was not entitled to duress defense because he had a reasonable opportunity to avoid going AWOL. *United States v. Riofredo*, 30 M.J. 1251 (N.M.C.M.R. 1990) (finding that accused should have sought the assistance of the command to stop assaults by noncommissioned officer); R.C.M. 916(h); *see generally* TJAGSA Practice Note, *Duress and Absence Without Authority*, ARMY LAW., Dec. 1990, at 34 (discussing *Riofredo*).

8. *United States v. Washington*, 57 M.J. 394 (C.A.A.F. 2002) *aff'd*, 58 M.J. 129 (C.A.A.F. 2003). Accused who was ordered and who refused to receive his sixth and final anthrax vaccination could not raise defense of duress. The defense requires an unlawful threat from a human being. Defense of duress is not raised by a reasonable belief that compliance with a lawful order will result in death or serious bodily injury.

VI. PROTECTED STATUS.

A. General. Articles 89, 90, and 91 cover offenses against superior commissioned officers and noncommissioned and warrant officers in the execution of office. Two conditions—superior status and the performance of the duties of office—provide increased protection to victims and increased punishment to violators of these Articles

B. "Superior Commissioned Officer" Defined. The victim's status as the superior commissioned officer of the accused is an element of crimes involving disrespect (Article 89), disobedience (Article 90(2)), and assault (Article 90(1)) in which the victim's status as a superior officer enhances the penalty. The following rules are applicable to each of the above offenses.

1. Accused & Victim in Same Armed Service. MCM pt. IV, ¶ 13(c)(1)(a).

    a) The victim is the accused's "superior commissioned officer" if the victim is a commissioned officer superior in rank to the accused (not date of rank in the same grade).

    b) The victim is the accused's "superior commissioned officer" if the victim is superior in command to the accused, even if the victim is inferior in grade to the accused.

    c) The victim is not the accused's "superior commissioned officer" if the victim is superior in grade but inferior in command.

2. Accused & Victim in Diff. Armed Services. MCM pt. IV, ¶ 13(c)(1)(b).

a) The victim is the accused's "superior commissioned officer" if the victim is a commissioned officer and superior in the chain of command over the accused.

b) The victim is the accused's "superior commissioned officer" if the victim, not a medical officer nor a chaplain, is senior in grade to the accused and both are detained by a hostile entity so that recourse to the normal chain of command is prevented.

c) The victim is not the accused's "superior commissioned officer" merely because the victim is superior in grade to the accused. In *United States v. Peoples*, 6 M.J. 904, 905 (A.C.M.R. 1979), however, the court cited with approval an Article 15 given under the theory of Article 92(2) (failure to obey) for violating the order of an officer of another armed force who was not in the accused's chain of command.

d) In *United States v. Merriweather*, 13 M.J. 605 (A.F.C.M.R. 1982), the court disapproved the conviction of an airman of disrespect to two Navy medical officers. There was no command relationship where the accused merely spent two hours in a Navy emergency room. The court affirmed a conviction for the lesser included offense of disorderly conduct.

3. Commissioned Warrant Officers.

a) Both trial and defense counsel should be alert as to whether a warrant officer in a particular case is commissioned. Warrant officers are commissioned upon promotion to CW2. 10 U.S.C. § 582. Warrant Officer One (WO1) is not a commissioned officer.

b) "Commissioned officer" includes a commissioned warrant officer. 10 U.S.C. § 101(b)(2). *See also* R.C.M. 103 discussion.

c) In the Navy, a Chief Warrant Officer is a commissioned officer, the disobedience of whose order constitutes a violation of Article 90. *United States v. Kanewske*, 37 C.M.R. 298, 299 (C.M.A. 1967).

C. "Warrant Officer" or "Noncommissioned Officer" Defined. A victim's status as a WO or NCO is an element of those crimes involving insubordinate conduct toward such individuals, to include: disrespect (Article 91(3)), disobedience (Article 91(2)), and assault (Article 91(1)). Warrant or noncommissioned officer victims must be acting in execution of office.

1. Warrant Officers. Those individuals appointed as warrant officers to meet Army requirements for officers possessing particular skills and specialized knowledge. Although warrant officers usually perform specialized duties within the Army, they may under appropriate circumstances serve in command positions. *See* ¶ VI.B.3 above regarding "commissioned warrant officers."

2. Noncommissioned Officers.

a) Those in the rank of corporal (E-4) and above.

b) Not including a specialist (E-4).

c) Not including a victim of the rank of specialist (E-4) or below who is an "acting" NCO. *United States v. Lumbus & Sutton*, 49 C.M.R. 248 (C.M.A. 1974); *United States v. Evans*, 50 C.M.R. 198 (A.C.M.R. 1975). *See also* MCM, pt. IV, ¶ 15.c.(1).

D. "Superior" WO/NCO.

    1. Article 91 protects warrant officers and noncommissioned officers from disrespect, assault, and disobedience when they are in execution of their office. The statute does not require a superior-subordinate relationship. *See United States v. Diggs*, 52 M.J. 251 (2000) (staff sergeant (E-6) that pushed sergeant (E-5) guilty of assaulting an NCO under Article 91).

    2. If pleaded and proven, the fact the victim was superior to the accused and that the accused had knowledge of the victim's superior status is an aggravating factor that exposes the accused a greater maximum punishment. *See* MCM, pt. IV, ¶ 15c analysis. *See also United States v. White*, 39 M.J. 796 (N.M.C.M.R. 1994) (holding that Navy service member's plea of guilty to disrespect toward superior noncommissioned officer, where accused directed obscenities towards Air Force security police NCO apprehending him on an Air Force base, was provident).

E. Divestiture. Misconduct on the part of a superior in dealing with a subordinate may divest the former of his authority and thus destroy his protected status if it was substantial departure from the required standards of conduct. *See* MCM, pt IV, ¶ 13.c.(5).

    1. Conduct amounting to divestiture. *United States v. Diggs*, 52 M.J. 251 (C.A.A.F. 2000) (striking accused); *United States v. Richardson*, 7 M.J. 320 (C.M.A. 1979) (racial slurs; calling accused "boy"); *United States v. Rozier*, 1 M.J. 469 (C.M.A. 1976) (unlawful apprehension coupled with unwarranted physical abuse); *United States v. Hendrix*, 45 C.M.R. 186 (C.M.A. 1972) (officer authorized to search the accused's quarters for narcotics exceeded the scope of his official authority to search and was not in the execution of his office when, over the accused's protests, he proceeded to read a letter found in an envelope which he could see contained no contraband); *United States v. Struckman*, 43 C.M.R. 333 (C.M.A. 1971) (inviting accused to fight); *United States v. Noriega*, 21 C.M.R. 322 (C.M.A. 1956) (officer victim serving as bartender at enlisted men's party); *United States v. Cheeks*, 43 C.M.R. 1013 (A.F.C.M.R. 1971) (sustained verbal abuse of prisoner); *United States v. Revels*, 41 C.M.R. 475 (A.C.M.R. 1969) (use of brute force on accused by confinement officer).

    2. Conduct *not* amounting to divestiture. *United States v. Pratcher*, 17 M.J. 388 (C.M.A. 1984) (involvement in collecting debts contrary to regulation); *United States v. Lewis*, 12 M.J. 205 (C.M.A. 1982) (failure to give proper Article 31(b) warnings); *United States v. Lewis*, 7 M.J. 348 (C.M.A. 1979) (search that was subsequently determined to not be based on probable cause); *United States v. Middleton*, 36 M.J. 835 (A.C.M.R. 1977) (close personal friendship with subordinate); *United States v. King*, 29 M.J. 885 (A.C.M.R. 1989) (striking a prisoner who lunged at a guard); *United States v. Collier*, 27 M.J. 806 (A.C.M.R. 1988) (use of profane language) *rev'd in part on other grounds by,* 29 M.J. 365 (C.M.A. 1990); *United States v. Leach*, 22 M.J. 738 (N.M.C.M.R. 1986) (general allegations of "horseplay"); *United States v. Allen*, 10 M.J. 576 (A.C.M.R. 1980) (addressing accused as "boy" where accused did not regard use of term as racial slur and both the victim and accused were the same race); *United States v. Fetherson*, 8 M.J. 607, 609 (N.M.C.M.R. 1977) (illegal apprehension); *United States v. McDaniel*, 7 M.J. 522 (A.C.M.R. 1979) (sergeant who places drunken and protesting soldier in cold shower); *United States v. Vallenthine*, 2 M.J. 1170 (N.C.M.R. 1974) (escorting with one hand on shirt collar and other on seat of trousers); *United States v. Montgomery*, 11 C.M.R. 308 (A.B.R. 1953) (playing poker with subordinate officers).

3. If an NCO commits misconduct that divests him of his authority as an NCO, he may regain his protected status by desisting in the illegal conduct and attempting to resolve the matter within appropriate channels. *United States v. Diggs*, 52 M.J. 251 (C.A.A.F. 2000).

4. Divestiture is limited to offenses where the protected status of the victim is an element, but it does not necessarily extend to lesser included offenses. Although the accused may not be convicted of an assault upon a superior under Articles 90 or 91 when the victim's conduct divests himself of his status, the accused may be found guilty of the lesser included offense of assault under Article 128. *United States v. Richardson*, 7 M.J. 320 (C.M.A. 1979); *United States v. Johnson*, 43 C.M.R. 604 (A.C.M.R. 1970).

5. Members may find "partial" divestiture. *United States v. Sanders*, 41 M.J. 485 (C.A.A.F. 1995) (members found victim not in execution of office for purposes of assault, but he had not divesting himself of his rank status: "He had left his post, but not his stripes").

6. Divestiture does not apply to disobedience offenses. *See United States v. Cheeks*, 43 C.M.R. 1013 (A.F.C.M.R. 1971). *But see United States v. Collier*, 27 M.J. 806 (A.C.M.R. 1988) *rev'd in part on other grounds by*, 29 M.J. 365 (C.M.A. 1990). *See generally* Major Eugene R. Milhizer, *The Divestiture Defense and United States v. Collier*, ARMY LAW., Mar., 1990, at 3

VII. DISRESPECT.

A. Defined. UCMJ Articles 89 & 91(3).

1. Actions. *United States v. Ferenczi*, 27 C.M.R. 77 (C.M.A. 1958) (subordinate contemptuously turns and walks away from a superior who is talking to him); *United States v. Van Beek*, 47 C.M.R. 98 (A.C.M.R. 1973) (exploding gas grenade in absent officer's quarters – "gravamen of an Article 89 offense is not merely insult, but the undermining of lawful authority.").

2. Words. *United States v. Montgomery*, 11 C.M.R. 308 (A.B.R. 1953) ("Keep your Goddamn mouth shut, you field grade son-of-a-bitch or I'll tear you apart; I'll beat you to death you. . . . I'll bite your. . . off, you punk, you"); *United States v. Dornick*, 16 M.J. 642 (A.F.C.M.R. 1983) ("Hi, sweetheart").

3. Actions & words are not distinct bases—all circumstances of a case may be considered when determining whether disrespectful behavior in violation of Article 89 has occurred. *United States v. Najera*, 52 M.J. 247 (C.A.A.F. 2000).

B. Knowledge. The accused must be aware of the victim's status. *United States v. Payne*, 29 M.J. 899, 900 (A.C.M.R. 1989); MCM, pt. IV, ¶ 13c(2) & 15c(2).

C. Disrespect must be directed *toward* the victim. *United States v. Sorrells*, 49 C.M.R. 44 (A.C.M.R. 1974) (no disrespect when loud profanity was spoken in the presence of the superior but directed toward others present in the room); *see also United States v. Alexander*, 11 M.J. 726 (A.C.M.R. 1981) (accused's plea of guilty to disrespect to his first sergeant was not improvident on ground that his outburst was not directed toward that individual, where facts showed that accused became angry at having to open his locker for the first sergeant to check for contraband and he took his clothes out of his locker and threw them on floor at feet of first sergeant).

D. Pleading.

1. Disrespectful behavior must be alleged. If the words or acts that constitute the disrespectful conduct are innocuous, the pleadings will be fatally defective unless

circumstances surrounding the behavior are alleged to detail the nature of insubordination. *United States v. Barber*, 8 M.J. 153 (C.M.A. 1979) (words, "If you have something to say about me, say it to my face," as spoken by a subordinate to a superior noncommissioned officer in the execution of his office, found to be disrespectful on their face; court read the language to constitute a demand by the subordinate that the superior conform his official conduct to a standard imposed by the subordinate); *United States v. Bartee*, 50 C.M.R. 51 (N.M.C.M.R. 1974) (statement to superior commissioned officer, "Man, I ain't getting no haircut," did constitute disrespect); *United States v. Sutton*, 48 C.M.R. 609 (A.C.M.R. 1974) (specification alleging accused said, "You had better get out of the man's room" held insufficient); *United States v. Smith*, 43 C.M.R. 796 (A.C.M.R. 1971) (specification alleging that accused referred to a male victim as "man" held insufficient); *United States v. Klein*, 42 C.M.R. 671 (A.C.M.R. 1970) (mere utterance of words, "People get hurt like that," did not constitute, per se, disrespectful language).

2. Failure to allege victim's status as "his superior commissioned officer" may be fatal. The omission of the pronoun "his" has been held to destroy a specification's legitimacy. *United States v. Carter*, 42 C.M.R. 898 (A.C.M.R. 1970); *United States v. Showers*, 48 C.M.R. 837 (A.C.M.R. 1974). *Contra United States v. Ashby*, 50 C.M.R. 37 (N.C.M.R. 1974) (failure to allege "his superior commissioned officer" was not fatal where the specification alleged the officer victim's rank and service, and both the enlisted accused and the officer victim were in the same service).

3. Disrespect, under Article 91, and provoking speech and gestures, under Article 117, are separate offenses and not multiplicious. *United States v. McHerrin*, 42 M.J. 672 (Army Ct. Crim. App. 1995).

E. Disrespect as a Lesser included Offense to Other Crimes.

1. Disobedience of a superior. MCM, pt. IV, ¶ 14d(3)(b); *United States v. Virgilito*, 47 C.M.R. 331 (C.M.A. 1973); *United States v. Croom*, 1 M.J. 635 (A.C.M.R. 1975). *But see United States v. Cooper*, 14 M.J. 758 (A.C.M.R. 1982) (disrespect not lesser included offense to disobedience where disrespect subsequent to disobedience).

2. Assault. *United States v. Van Beek*, 47 C.M.R. 98 (A.C.M.R. 1973).

3. Not communicating a threat. *United States v. Ross*, 40 C.M.R. 718 (A.C.M.R. 1969) (holding that disrespect, under Article 89, was not a lesser included offense of communicating a threat under Article 134, because the element "his superior commissioned officer" was not fairly alleged in the threat specification).

F. Additional Requirements for Disrespect to a Noncommissioned, Warrant, or Petty Officer.

1. The offensive words or conduct must be within the hearing or sight of the noncommissioned, warrant, or petty officer victim. This is not required in the case of a commissioned officer victim. MCM, pt. IV, ¶ 15.c.(5); *United States v. Van Beek*, 47 C.M.R. 98, 99 (A.C.M.R. 1973).

2. The noncommissioned, warrant, or petty officer victim, at the time of the offense, must be "in the execution of his office," to include any act or service required or authorized to be done by him because of statute, regulation, order of a superior or military usage. *United States v. Brooks*, 44 C.M.R. 873 (A.C.M.R. 1971) (holding off-duty NCO working at EM Club as sergeant-at-arms in execution of his office); *United States v. Fetherson*, 8 M.J. 607, 610 (N.M.C.M.R. 1977) (holding off-duty NCO quelling disorderly conduct or maintaining order among subordinates in execution of his office).

3. An NCO of one branch of the armed forces is the "superior NCO" of an enlisted accused of another armed force only when the NCO is in a position of authority over the accused. *United States v. White*, 39 M.J. 796 (N.M.C.M.R. 1994).

4. A commissioned officer is protected even if acting in a private capacity and off duty. *United States v. Van Beek*, 47 C.M.R. 98, 99-100 (A.C.M.R. 1973); *United States v. Montgomery*, 11 C.M.R. 308 (A.B.R. 1953) (officer victim involved in poker game).

VIII. DISOBEDIENCE: PERSONAL ORDER. UCMJ ART. 90(2) & 91(2)

A. The Order.

1. The order must be directed to the accused specifically. It does not include violations of regulations, standing orders, or routine duties. MCM, pt. IV, ¶ 14c(2)(b); *United States v. Byers*, 40 M.J. 321 (C.M.A. 1994) (order revoking driving privileges signed by JAG was a routine administrative sanction for traffic offenses and was not a personal order by the post commander); *United States v. Ranney*, 67 M.J. 297 (C.A.A.F. 2009) (revocation of driving privileges issued automatically upon drunk driving arrest was not sufficient for purposes of Art. 90, but did support a conviction under Art. 92); *United States v. Gussen*, 33 M.J. 736 (A.C.M.R. 1991) (evidence that accused disobeyed an order issued by brigade commander to entire brigade, but relayed to the accused through NCOs, only supports finding of violation of orders in violation of Article 92 and not violation of a superior's personal order); *United States v. Selman*, 28 M.J. 627 (A.F.C.M.R. 1989) (letter to all minimum security prisoners setting forth restrictions was not a personal order to the accused).

2. Form of Order. As long as understandable, the form of the order and the method of transmittal are immaterial. MCM, pt. IV, ¶ 14.c.(2)(c); *United States v. McLaughlin*, 14 M.J. 908 (N.M.C.M.R. 1982) (use of the word "please" does not negate the order).

3. Scope of Order. In order to sustain the presumption of lawfulness of an order, the order must have a valid military purpose and must be a clear, narrowly drawn mandate. *United States v. Moore*, 58 M.J. 466 (2003) (rejecting a First Amendment overbroad attack and a Fifth Amendment vagueness attack on an article 90 violation because the order in question had a valid military purpose and was "sufficiently clear, specific, and narrowly drawn.").

a) The order must be a specific mandate to do or not to do a specific act. MCM, pt. IV, ¶ 14.c.(2)(b); *United States v. Womack*, 29 M.J. 88 (C.M.A. 1989) ("safe sex" order for HIV positive airman was "specific, definite, and certain."); *United States v. Warren*, 13 M.J. 160 (C.M.A. 1982) (ambiguous whether statement "settle down and be quiet" was order or mere counseling); *United States v. Mantilla*, 36 M.J. 621 (A.C.M.R. 1992) (order to "double time" to barracks to retrieve gear was positive command rather than advice); *United States v. Claytor*, 34 M.J. 1030 (N.M.C.M.R. 1992) (order to "shut up" on the heels of disrespectful language about a superior commissioned officer was a specific mandate to cease speaking and say nothing further).

b) *But see United States v. Mitchell*, 20 C.M.R. 295 (C.M.A. 1955) ("leave out the Orderly Room because I don't want to have any trouble with you" lacks specificity of meaning and extrinsic evidence can be used to clarify language); *United States v. Beattie*, 17 M.J. 537 (A.C.M.R. 1983) (where superiors of intoxicated accused did not want him at his assigned place of duty, which was the motor pool, unclarified order to "return to his place of duty and go to work" was not a clear mandate).

4. Lawfulness of the order is a question of law that must be decided by the military judge.

    a) *United States v. Diesher*, 61 M.J. 313 (C.A.A.F. 2005) (holding the legality of an order is an issue of law that must be decided by the military judge (citing *United States v. New,* 55 M.J. 95 (C.A.A.F. 2001)).

    b) In 2005, MCM, Part IV, para. 14c(2)(a) was amended to clarify that the determination of lawfulness resides with the military judge, rather than the trier of fact. The analysis cites *United States v. New*, 55 M.J. 95 (C.A.A.F. 2001) as the basis for this change.

B. Knowledge.

1. The prosecution must prove, as an element of the offense, that the accused had actual knowledge of the order. MCM, pt. IV, ¶ 14c(2)(e); *United States v. Shelly*, 19 M.J. 325 (C.M.A. 1985); *United States v. Pettigrew*, 41 C.M.R. 191 (C.M.A. 1970) (although knowledge may be proven by circumstantial evidence, the knowledge must be actual and not constructive).

2. The prosecution must prove that the accused had actual knowledge of the status of the victim. MCM, pt. IV, ¶ 14c(2)(e); *United States v. Young*, 40 C.M.R. 36 (C.M.A. 1060) (voluntary intoxication raised issue of whether accused knew he was dealing with his superior officer); *United States v. Oisten*, 33 C.M.R. 188 (C.M.A. 1963); *United States v. Payne*, 29 M.J. 899 (A.C.M.R. 1989).

C. Willfulness of Disobedience.

1. Disobedience must be intentional defiance of authority. Failure to comply through heedlessness or forgetfulness is not "willful" (but it may violate Article 92). MCM, pt. IV, ¶ 14c(2)(f).

2. Intentional noncompliance, not "flaunting of authority," is required. *United States v. Ferenczi*, 27 C.M.R. 77 (C.M.A. 1958).

3. Voluntary intoxication might prevent the accused from having the willful state of mind required by Article 91. *United States v. Cameron*, 37 M.J. 1042 (A.C.M.R. 1993) (where accused was intoxicated and did not complete the assigned task of cleaning room by proscribed deadline, members should have been instructed on lesser included offense of failing to obey lawful order, under Article 92, which does not require willfulness).

D. Origin of the Order.

1. The alleged victim must be personally involved in the issuance of the order. *United States v. Ranney,* 67 M.J. 297 (C.A.A.F. 2009) (revocation of driving privileges issued without the knowledge or involvement of the Base Traffic Officer was not sufficient for purposes of Art. 90, but did support a conviction under Art. 92).

2. The order must originate from the alleged victim, and not be the order of a superior for whom the alleged victim is a mere conduit. *United States v. Marsh*, 11 C.M.R. 48 (C.M.A. 1953) (specification improperly alleged victim as a captain who was merely transmitting order from the Commanding General); *United States v. Sellers*, 30 C.M.R. 262 (C.M.A. 1961) (major was not a mere conduit, where he passed on order of colonel, threw the weight of his rank and position into the balance, and added additional

requirement); *United States v. Wartsbaugh*, 45 C.M.R. 309 (C.M.A. 1972) (setting aside Article 90 violation where the court characterized the company commander's order as "predicated upon…a battalion directive").

E. Time for Compliance. MCM, pt. IV, ¶ 14c(2)(g).

1. When an order requires immediate compliance, accused's statement that he will not obey and failure to make any move to comply constitutes disobedience. *United States v. Stout*, 5 C.M.R. 67 (C.M.A. 1952) (order to join combat patrol). Time in which compliance is required is a question of fact. *United States v. Cooper*, 14 M.J. 758 (A.C.M.R. 1982) (order to go upstairs and change clothes not countermanded by subsequent order to accompany victim to orderly room, because disobedience to first order already complete); *United States v. McLaughlin*, 14 M.J. 908 (N.M.C.M.R. 1982) (order to produce ID card required immediate compliance).

2. Immediate compliance is required by any order that does not explicitly or implicitly indicate that delayed compliance is authorized or directed. MCM, pt. IV, ¶ 14c(2)(g) (2008 amendment), *United States v. Schwabauer*, 34 M.J. 709 (A.C.M.R. 1992) (direct order to "stop and come back here" clearly and unambiguously required immediate obedience without delay), *aff'd,* 37 M.J. 338 (C.M.A. 1993). However, when time for compliance is not stated explicitly or implicitly, then reasonable delay in compliance does not constitute disobedience. MCM, pt. IV, ¶ 14c(2)(g). *United States v. Clowser*, 16 C.M.R. 543 (A.F.B.R. 1954) (delay resulting from a sincere and reasonable choice of means to comply with order to "go up to the barracks and go to bed" was not a completed disobedience).

3. When immediate compliance is required, disobedience is completed when the one to whom the order is directed first refuses and evinces an intentional defiance of authority. *United States v. Vansant*, 11 C.M.R. 30 (C.M.A. 1953) (order to return to his platoon and be there in one and a half hours necessitated immediate compliance, and refusal to comply constituted disobedience).

4. For orders that require preliminary steps before they can be executed, the recipient must begin the preliminary steps immediately or the disobedience is complete. *United States v. Wilson*, 17 M.J. 1032 (A.C.M.R. 1984) *pet. denied,* 19 M.J. 79 (C.M.A. 1984) (lieutenant's order to "shotgun" a truck, which entailed preparation prior to travel, was disobeyed when accused verbally refused three times and walked out of lieutenant's office).

5. Apprehension of an accused before compliance is due is a legitimate defense to the alleged disobedience. *See United States v. Williams*, 39 C.M.R. 78 (C.M.A. 1968).

6. If an order is to be performed in the future, the accused's present statement of intent to disobey does not constitute disobedience. *United States v. Squire*, 47 C.M.R. 214 (N.C.M.R. 1973).

F. Matters in Defense.

1. The order lacks content/specific mandate. *United States v. Bratcher*, 39 C.M.R. 125 (C.M.A. 1969); *United States v. Oldaker*, 41 C.M.R. 497 (A.C.M.R. 1969) (order "to train" given to basic trainee lacked content); *United States v. Couser*, 3 M.J. 561 (A.C.M.R. 1977) (order to resume training with company was proper); *United States v. Beattie*, 17 M.J. 537 (A.C.M.R. 1983) (order to "follow the instructions of his NCO's" lacked content).

2. "Ultimate offense" doctrine.

   a) The order requires acts already required by law, regulation, standing orders, or routine (pre-existing) duty. *United States v. Bratcher*, 39 C.M.R. 125 (C.M.A. 1969) (order to "perform duties as a duty soldier, the duties to be performed and to be assigned to him by the First Sergeant" was not a specific mandate but rather an exhortation to do his duty as already required by law; order to obey the law can have no validity beyond the limit of the ultimate offense committed); *United States v. Sidney*, 48 C.M.R. 801 (A.C.M.R. 1974) (officer's order to comply with local regulations on registration and safekeeping of personal weapons should have been charged under Article 92(2)); *United States v. Wartsbaugh*, 45 C.M.R. 309 (C.M.A. 1972) (order to comply with battalion uniform directive should have been charged under Article 92(2)); *but cf. United States v. Traxler*, 39 M.J. 476 (C.M.A. 1994) (commander can lift otherwise routine duty "above the common ruck" to ensure compliance but not to merely enhance punishment).

   b) Minor offenses may not be escalated in severity by charging them as violation of orders or willful disobedience of superiors. *United States v. Hargrove*, 51 M.J. 408 (1999); *United States v. Quarles*, 1 M.J. 231 (C.M.A. 1975) (holding maximum punishment cannot be increased by charging disobedience rather than failure to repair); *United States v. Loos*, 16 C.M.R. 52 (C.M.A. 1954) (holding "gravamen" of offense was failure to repair rather than failure to obey lawful order).

   c) Violation of a personal order is punishable as a separate offense if it is given for the purpose of having the full authority of the superior's position and rank to ensure compliance. *United States v. Traxler*, 39 M.J. 476 (C.M.A. 1994) (willful disobedience of superior commissioned officer and missing movement); *United States v. Landwehr*, 18 M.J. 355 (C.M.A. 1984) (willful disobedience of superior commissioned officer and failure to repair); *United States v. Pettersen*, 17 M.J. 69 (C.M.A. 1983) (willful disobedience of superior noncommissioned officer and AWOL); *United States v. Greene*, 8 M.J. 796 (N.C.M.R. 1980); *United States v. United States v. Bethea*, 2 M.J. 892 (A.C.M.R. 1976); *States v. Bivins*, 34 C.M.R. 527 (A.B.R. 1964).

3. Repeated orders.

   a) If the sole purpose of repeated personal orders is to increase the punishment for an offense, disobedience of the repeated order is not a crime. *United States v. Tiggs*, 40 C.M.R. 352 (A.B.R. 1968).

   b) Repeated orders may constitute an unreasonable multiplication of charges. *United States v. Graves*, 12 M.J. 583 (A.F.C.M.R. 1981) (dismissing conviction for willful disobedience of lieutenant's order that immediately followed and was identical to order from sergeant, which was the basis of a separate conviction); *United States v. Greene*, 8 M.J. 796 (N.C.M.R. 1980) (subsequent orders of superior commissioned officers merely reiterating original order of petty officer could not form basis for additional convictions for willful disobedience of superior commissioned officers); *United States v. Bivins*, 34 C.M.R. 527 (A.B.R. 1964).

4. Violation of an order that is part of an apprehension constitutes resisting apprehension rather than disobedience of an order. *United States v. Nixon*, 45 C.M.R. 254 (C.M.A. 1974) (officer's order "to leave the . . . room and get into a jeep" was the initial step of an

apprehension, and disobedience should have been prosecuted under Article 95 rather than Article 90); *United States v. Burroughs*, C.M.R. 404 (A.C.M.R. 1974). *But see United States v. Jessie*, 2 M.J. 573 (A.C.M.R. 1977) (when already in custody, order to remain in building to reinforce status was independent lawful command).

5. The order is inconsistent with a service regulation. *United States v. Roach*, 29 M.J. 33 (C.M.A. 1989) (Coast Guard regulation on drug and alcohol policy).

6. The defense of conflicting orders. *United States v. Clausen*, 43 C.M.R. 128 (C.M.A. 1971); *United States v. Patton*, 41 C.M.R. 572 (A.C.M.R. 1969) ("criminal prosecution for disobedience of an order cannot be based upon a subordinate's election to obey one of two conflicting orders when simultaneous compliance with both orders is impossible"); *but cf. United States v. Hill*, 26 M.J. 876 (N.M.C.M.R. 1988) (no defense where accused obeyed neither of the conflicting orders but rather remained in his "rack").

7. Orders must not conflict with, or detract from, the scope or effectiveness of orders issued by higher headquarters. *United States v. Clausen*, 43 C.M.R. 128 (C.M.A. 1971); *United States v. Green*, 22 M.J. 711 (A.C.M.R. 1986).

8. Conscientious objection is not a defense to disobedience of lawful orders. *United States v. Johnson*, 45 M.J. 88 (C.A.A.F. 1996); *United States v. Walker*, 41 M.J. 462 (1995); *United States v. Austin*, 27 M.J. 227 (C.A.A.F. 1988).

9. State of mind defenses may apply. *United States v. Young*, 40 C.M.R. 36 (C.M.A. 1969).

IX. VIOLATION OF A LAWFUL GENERAL REGULATION / ORDER. UCMJ ART. 92(1).

A. Authority to Issue a General Order. MCM, pt. IV, ¶ 16c(1)(a).

1. President; Secretary of Defense; Secretary of Homeland Security; and Secretaries of the Army, Navy, and Air Force. (NOTE: EO 13397 (14 Oct. 2005) amended the MCM to change authority to issue a general order from the Secretary of Transportation to the Secretary of Homeland Security).

2. A GCM convening authority.

3. A flag or general officer in command.

4. Superiors commanders to (2) and (3) above.

5. To be a lawful general order, the order must be *issued* as the result of the personal decision of the person authorized to issue general orders. *United States v. Townsend*, 49 M.J. 175, 179-80 (C.A.A.F. 1998) (order signed by Acting Chief, Office of Personnel and Training was *issued* by the Commandant of the Coast Guard); *United States v. Bartell*, 32 M.J. 295 (C.M.A. 1991) (general order signed "By Direction"); *United States v. Breault*, 30 M.J. 833 (N.M.C.M.R. 1990) (general order signed by chief of staff).

B. Regulation Defects.

1. The regulation must prohibit conduct of the nature of that attributed to the accused in the specification. *United States v. Baker*, 40 C.M.R. 216 (C.M.A. 1969); *United States v. Sweitzer*, 33 C.M.R. 251 (C.M.A. 1963).

2. The regulation must apply to a group of persons that includes the accused. *United States v. Jackson*, 46 C.M.R. 1128 (A.C.M.R. 1973) (finding that regulation was intended to guide military police rather than the individual soldier).

3. The regulation must purport to establish criminal sanctions against individuals rather than mere guidance. *United States v. Green*, Army 20010446, 2003 Lexis 137 (Army Ct. Crim. App. June 6, 2003)(DoD Directive intended to update policies and responsibilities on drug abuse and prevention held to be general guidance and not punitive in nature); *United States v. Blanchard*, 19 M.J. 196 (C.M.A. 1985) (USAFE customs regulation was directory in nature); *United States v. Scott*, 46 C.M.R. 25 (C.M.A. 1972) (regulation establishing drug suppression policy was not punitive order); *United States v. Nardell*, 45 C.M.R. 101 (C.M.A. 1972) (SOP for club system was predominantly instructional guidance); *United States v. Benway*, 41 C.M.R. 345 (C.M.A. 10970); *United States v. Hogsett*, 25 C.M.R. 185 (C.M.A. 1958) (instruction interpreting postal laws was not general order); *United States v. Hode*, 44 M.J. 816 (A.F. Ct. Crim. App. 1996) (AFI 34-119 on the Alcoholic Beverage Program was not punitive); *United States v. Goodwin*, 37 M.J. 606 (A.C.M.R. 1993) (punitive regulation can refer to provisions in nonpunitive regulation); *United States v. Finsel*, 33 M.J. 739 (A.C.M.R. 1991) (task force commander's "Weapons Safety" letter was punitive in nature), *aff'd*, 36 M.J. 441 (C.M.A. 1993); *United States v. Asfeld*, 30 M.J. 917 (A.C.M.R. 1990) (AR 600-21, including sexual harassment policy provisions, was not a punitive regulation); *United States v. Brunson*, 30 M.J. 766 (A.C.M.R. 1990) (AR 600-15, providing guidance on handling complaints of indebtedness by soldiers, was not punitive); *United States v. Horton*, 17 M.J. 1131 (N.M.C.M.R. 1984) (regulation governing contacts with citizens of communist countries was punitive); *United States v. Stewart*, 2 M.J. 423 (A.C.M.R. 1975) (U.S. Army Japan Regulation 190-6 on control of privately owned weapons was not punitive).

4. It is not a defense that the regulation was superseded before the accused's conduct, if a successor regulation contained the same criminal prohibition and it was in force at the time of the accused's conduct, unless it misled the accused. *United States v. Grublak*, 47 C.M.R. 371 (A.C.M.R. 1973).

5. A regulation that is facially overbroad may be salvaged by including a *scienter* or *mens rea* requirement. *United States v. Bradley*, 15 M.J. 843 (A.F.C.M.R. 1983); *United States v. Cannon*, 13 M.J. 777 (A.C.M.R. 1982).

6. Local regulations must not conflict with or detract from the scope of effectiveness of a regulation issued by higher headquarters. *United States v. Green*, 22 M.J. 711 (A.C.M.R. 1986) (Fort Stewart regulation prohibiting soldiers from "[h]aving any alcohol in their system . . . during duty hours" was not enforceable because it detracted from the effectiveness of Army Regulation 600-85); *see United States v. Garcia*, 21 M.J. 127 (C.M.A. 1985).

7. United States Army, Europe, regulation that prohibited transporting persons without prescribed travel documents on the Helmstadt-Berlin autobahn in a vehicle with United States military registration was a "necessary and reasonable implementation by the United States military of an action required by the treaty and in furtherance of national policy." As such, the regulation could be enforced by criminal sanctions. *United States v. Stockman*, 17 M.J. 530 (A.C.M.R. 1983) (the accused, assigned to duty with the United States Forces in Berlin, violated the regulation by engaged in a conspiracy with two German Nationals to smuggle East German citizens into Berlin).

C. Knowledge.

1. Actual knowledge of the regulation or order is not an element of the crime. *United States v. Tolkach*, 14 M.J. 239 (C.M.A. 1982); *United States v. Tinker*, 27 C.M.R. 366

(C.M.A. 1959); *United States v. Leverette*, 9 M.J. 627 (A.C.M.R. 1980), *aff'd,* 9 M.J. 421 (C.M.A. 1980).

    2. For knowledge to be presumed, a regulation must be properly published. *United States v. Tolkach*, 14 M.J. 239 (C.M.A. 1982) (Eighth Air Force general regulation not properly published because it was never received at base master publications library).

    3. To be enforceable against service members, local regulations need not be published in the Federal Register. *United States v. Tolkach*, 14 M.J. 239 (C.M.A. 1982); *United States v. Academia*, 14 M.J. 582 (N.M.C.M.R. 1982).

D. Pleading.

    1. A specification is defective if it fails to allege that the order or regulation is "general." *United States v. Koepke*, 39 C.M.R. 100 (C.M.A. 1969); *United States v. Baker*, 38 C.M.R. 144 (C.M.A. 1967) (specification alleging violation of a specific Division regulation fails to state offense under Article 92(1)); *but see United States v. Watkins*, 21 M.J. 208 (C.M.A. 1986); *United States v. Watson*, 40 C.M.R. 571 (A.B.R. 1969) (specification alleging violation of a specific "Army" regulation was sufficient; distinguishing *Koepke*).

    2. The specification need not allege that an accused "wrongfully" violated a lawful general regulation, because the allegation of the violation itself implies the unlawful nature of the conduct. *United States v. Torrey*, 10 M.J. 508 (A.F.C.M.R. 1980).

    3. Accused, a recruiter, was charged with violation of a sub-paragraph "6(d)" of lawful general order by providing alcohol to a person enrolled in the Delayed Entry Program (DEP). The panel found him guilty of violating the superior paragraph "6" of the same general order by wrongfully engaging in a non-professional, personal relationship with the same DEP member. Court held this was a fatal variance because the substituted offense was materially different from the one originally charged in the specification, and accused was prejudiced by depriving him the opportunity to defend against the substituted paragraph of the order. *United States v. Teffeau*, 58 M.J. 62 (C.A.A.F. 2003). Additionally, the manner in which the accused violated the regulation *must* be alleged. *United States v. Sweitzer*, 33 C.M.R. 251 (C.M.A. 1963).

E. Proof. At trial, the existence and content of the regulation will not be presumed; it must be proven with evidence or established by judicial notice. *United States v. Williams*, 3 M.J. 155 (C.M.A. 1977). In judge alone trials, failure to prove existence of regulation can be cured by proceeding in revision or by an appellate court taking judicial notice. *United States v. Mead*, 16 M.J. 270 (C.M.A. 1983).

F. Exceptions. The prosecution must prove beyond a reasonable doubt that the accused's conduct did not come within any exceptions to the regulation, once the evidence raises the issue. *United States v. Lavine*, 13 M.J. 150 (C.M.A. 1982); *United States v. Cuffee*, 10 M.J. 381 (C.M.A. 1981).

G. Application. Service member need not be assigned to command of officer issuing general regulation in order to be subject to its proscriptions. *United States v. Leverette*, 9 M.J. 627 (A.C.M.R. 1980) (soldier on leave visiting Fort Campbell convicted of violating local general regulation), *aff'd,* 9 M.J. 421 (C.M.A. 1980).

H. Misconduct Otherwise Proscribed by Punitive Articles. Neither a general regulation nor an order may be used to enhance punishment for misconduct already prohibited by the punitive articles. *United States v. Curry*, 28 M.J. 419 (C.M.A. 1989) (Article 93 preempted conviction under Article 92 for disobedience of an order not to maltreat subordinates). *Cf.* MCM, pt. IV, ¶ 16e(1), (2) Note.

I. Attempts. Attempt to violate a regulation under Article 80 does not require knowledge of the regulation; the accused need only intend to commit the proscribed act. *United States v. Davis*, 16 M.J. 225 (C.M.A. 1983); *United States v. Foster*, 14 M.J. 246 (C.M.A. 1982).

J. Constitutional Rights. Where a regulation is attacked as unconstitutional or violative of a statute, "a narrowing construction" is mandated, if possible, to avoid the problem. *United States v. Williams*, 29 M.J. 112 (C.M.A. 1989) ("show and tell" regulation, narrowly construed to require service member to show physical possession or documentation of lawful disposition of controlled items, did not violate 5th amendment or Article 31).

X. FAILURE TO OBEY LOCAL ORDERS. UCMJ ART. 92(2).

A. The Order. Includes all other lawful orders issued by a member of the armed forces that the accused had a duty to obey. MCM, pt. IV, ¶ 16c(2)(a).

B. Limitation on Maximum Punishment. The maximum punishments set out in MCM, pt. IV, ¶ 16.e. include a dishonorable discharge and confinement for two years for violation of general regulations and a bad-conduct discharge and confinement for six months for disobedience of other lawful orders. A note, however, sets out certain limitations in this regard.

1. A note located after MCM, pt. IV, ¶ 16e(1) and (2) provides that these maximum punishments do not apply in the following cases:

   a) If in the absence of the order or regulation which was violated or not obeyed the accused would on the same facts be subject to conviction for another specific offense for which a lesser punishment is prescribed; or

   b) If the violation or failure to obey is a breach of restraint imposed as a result of an order.

   c) In these instances, the maximum punishment is that prescribed elsewhere for that particular offense.

2. This limitation was commonly known as the "Footnote 5" limitation, because it was Footnote 5 to the Table of Maximum Punishments in older versions of the MCM.

3. This limitation is only operative, however, where the lesser offense is the "gravamen of the offense." *United States v. Timmons*, 13 M.J. 431 (C.M.A. 1982) (gravamen of the offense was not being in the authorized uniform in violation of Article 134 rather than failing to obey order of petty officer); *United States v. Showalter*, 35 C.M.R. 382 (C.M.A. 1965) (gravamen of offense was not being in the authorized uniform in violation of Article 134 rather than failing to obey a general regulation); *United States v. Yunque-Burgos*, 13 C.M.R. 54 (C.M.A. 1953); *United States v. Buckmiller*, 4 C.M.R. 96 (C.M.A. 1952) (seminal case establishing gravamen test and rejecting a "technical and entirely literal interpretation of the footnote").

4. The note's rationale has been applied to offenses other than Articles 92(1) and 92(2). *See United States v. Battle*, 27 M.J. 781 (A.F.C.M.R. 1988); *United States v. Burroughs*, 49 C.M.R. 404 (A.C.M.R. 1974) (using the maximum punishment provided for resisting apprehension under Article 95 rather than that for willful disobedience of a superior commissioned officer under Article 90, of which the accused was convicted).

C. Source of Order. The order may be given by a person not superior to the accused, but the person giving the order must have a special status that imposes upon the accused the duty to obey.

MCM, pt. IV, ¶ 16c(2)(c)(i); *United States v. Stovall*, 44 C.M.R. 576 (A.F.C.M.R. 1971) (security policeman).

D. Actual Knowledge. The accused must have actual knowledge of the order. MCM, pt. IV, ¶ 16c(2)(b); *United States v. Shelly*, 19 M.J. 325 (C.M.A. 1985) (directive by battery commander); *United States v. Curtin*, 26 C.M.R. 207 (C.M.A. 1958) (instruction on constructive knowledge was erroneous); *United States v. Henderson*, 32 M.J. 941 (N.M.C.M.R. 1991) (district order governing use of government vehicles by Marine recruiters), *aff'd*, 34 M.J. 174 (C.M.A. 1992); *United States v. Jack*, 10 M.J. 572 (A.F.C.M.R. 1980) (conviction set aside where accused violated local regulation concerning visiting hours in female barracks where sign posted at building's entrance did not designate issuing authority).

E. Negligent Disobedience Sufficient for Guilt. Failure to comply through heedlessness or forgetfulness can be sufficient for a conviction under Article 92. MCM, pt. IV, ¶ 14c(2)(f); *United States v. Jordan*, 21 C.M.R. 627 (A.F.B.R. 1955).

XI. THE LAWFULNESS OF ORDERS.

A. Presumption of Lawfulness. Orders from superiors requiring the performance of military duties are presumed to be lawful. MCM, pt. IV, ¶ 14c(2)(a)(i); *United States v. McDaniels*, 50 M.J. 407 (C.A.A.F. 1999) (order to not drive personal vehicle after diagnosis of narcolepsy); *United States v. Nieves*, 44 M.J. 96 (C.A.A.F. 1996) (order prohibiting discussions with witnesses); *United States v. New*, 55 M.J. 95 (C.A.A.F. 2001) (order requiring soldier to wear United Nations blue beret and insignia).

B. Disobedience. A superior's order is presumed to be lawful and is disobeyed at the subordinate's peril. To sustain the presumption, the order must relate to military duty, it must not conflict with the statutory or constitutional rights of the person receiving the order, and it must be a specific mandate to do or not to do a specific act. In sum, an order is presumed lawful if it has a valid military purpose and is a clear, specific, narrowly drawn mandate. *United States v. Moore*, 58 M.J. 466 (C.A.A.F. 2003). The dictates of a person's conscience, religion, or personal philosophy cannot excuse disobedience. *United States v. Stockman*, 17 M.J. 530 (A.C.M.R. 1973).

C. Valid Military Purpose. The order must relate to military duty, which includes all activities reasonably necessary to accomplish a military mission, or safeguard or promote the morale, discipline, and usefulness of members of a unit and directly with the maintenance of good order in the armed forces. MCM, pt. IV, ¶ 14c(2)(a)(iii). The order can affect otherwise private activity. *United States v. McDaniels*, 50 M.J. 407 (C.A.A.F. 1999) (order to not drive personal vehicle after diagnosis of narcolepsy); *United States v. Hill*, 49 M.J. 242 (C.A.A.F. 1999) (no-contact order issued by military police had valid military purpose of maintaining good order and discipline in the military community and to protect the alleged victim while during the investigation); *United States v. Padgett*, 48 M.J. 273 (C.A.A.F. 1998) (order requiring 25-year-old service member to terminate his romantic relationship with 14-year-old girl had valid military purpose); *United States v. Milldebrandt*, 25 C.M.R. 139 (C.M.A. 1958) (order to report, while on leave, financial conditions unrelated to the military did not have valid military purpose).

   1. An order that has for its sole object a private end is unlawful, but an order that benefits the command as well as serving individuals is lawful. *United States v. Robinson*, 20 C.M.R. 63 (C.M.A. 1955) (use of enlisted personnel in Officers' Open Mess at Fort McNair).

   2. Punishment.

a) Orders extending punishments beyond those lawfully imposed are illegal. *United States v. McCoy*, 30 C.M.R. 68 (C.M.A. 1960) (order to continue extra duty after punishment imposed under Article 15 already completed).

b) "Extra training" must be oriented to improving the soldier's performance of military duties. Such corrective measures assume the nature of training or instruction, not punishment. MCM, pt. I, ¶ 1g; AR 600-20, ¶ 4-6b (11 Feb 2009); *see United States v. Hoover*, 24 M.J. 874 (A.C.M.R. 1987) (requiring accused to live in pup tent for 3 weeks between the hours of 2200 and 0400 was unlawful punishment).

D. Overly Broad Limitation on Personal Right. An order that is "arbitrary and capricious, overly broad in scope, or to impose an unjust limitation on a personal right" is not lawful. *United States v. Milldebrandt*, 25 C.M.R. 139 (C.M.A. 1958) (order to report, while on leave, financial conditions unrelated to the military was not lawful); *United States v. Spencer*, 29 M.J. 740 (A.F.C.M.R. 1989) (order to turn over all civilian medical records to military clinic by specific date was unlawful, because it was broader and more restrictive of private rights and personal affairs than required by military needs and provided for by service regulation); *United States v. Jeffers*, 57 M.J. 13 (C.A.A.F. 2002) (no social contact order with female in unit with whom accused had adulterous relationship not overbroad).

1. Marriage. Regulations reasonably restricting marriages of foreign-based service personnel to local nationals are legal. *United States v. Wheeler*, 30 C.M.R. 387 (C.M.A. 1961) ("a military commander may, at least in foreign areas, impose reasonable restrictions on the right of military personnel of his command to marry"); *United States v. Nation*, 26 C.M.R. 504 (C.M.A. 1958) (six-month waiting period was unreasonable and arbitrary restraint on the personal right to marry).

2. "Safe sex" order to servicemember infected with HIV is lawful. *United States v. Dumford*, 30 M.J. 137 (C.M.A. 1990); *United States v. Womack*, 29 M.J. 88 (C.M.A. 1989).

3. A service member who violates the terms of a no-contact order is subject to punishment under either Article 90 or Article 92, without the necessity of proof that the contact was undertaken for an improper purpose. Public policy supports a strict reading of a no-contact order. A military commander who has a legitimate interest in deterring contact between a service member and another person is not required to sort through every contact to determine, after the fact, whether there was a nefarious purpose. *United States v. Thompkins*, 58 M.J. 43 (C.A.A.F. 2003).

4. Personal relationships and contacts. *United States v. Hill*, 49 M.J. 242 (C.A.A.F. 1999) (order to have no contact with alleged victim lawful); *United States v. Padgett*, 48 M.J. 273 (C.A.A.F. 1998) (order requiring 25-year-old service member to terminate his romantic relationship with 14-year-old girl lawful); *United States v. Nieves*, 44 M.J. 96 (C.A.A.F. 1996) (order prohibiting discussions with witnesses, during an investigation, was lawful); *United States v. Aycock*, 35 C.M.R. 130 (C.M.A. 1964) (order prohibiting accused from contacting witnesses concerning the charges was unlawful because it interfered with right to prepare a defense); *United States v. Wysong*, 26 C.M.R. 29 (C.M.A. 1958) (order "not to talk to or speak with any of the men in the company concerned with this investigation except in line of duty" was so broad in nature and all-inclusive in scope that it was illegal); *United States v. Mann*, 50 M.J. 689 (A.F. Ct. Crim. App. 1999) (order to "cease and refrain from any and all contact of any nature" with enlisted member with whom the accused allegedly fraternized, which indicated that

accused's counsel had unrestricted access, was lawful); *United States v. Button*, 31 M.J. 897 (A.F.C.M.R. 1990) (order not to go to family quarters, where alleged sexual abuse victim lived, was lawful), *aff'd,* 34 M.J. 139 (C.M.A. 1992); *United States v. Hawkins*, 30 M.J. 682 (A.F.C.M.R. 1990) (order to have no contact with alleged victims and witness, unless by the area defense counsel, was lawful); *United States v. Wine*, 28 M.J. 688 (A.F.C.M.R. 1989) (order to disassociate from neighbor's estranged wife lawful); *United States v. Moore*, 58 M.J. 466 (C.A.A.F. 2003) (order "not to converse with the civilian workers" in the galley was lawful and not over broad when given after the accused violated a policy limiting interaction between civilian employees and servicemembers).

5. Alcohol.

    a) Regulations establishing a minimum drinking age for service personnel in a command abroad are legal. *United States v. Manos*, 37 C.M.R. 274 (C.M.A. 1967).

    b) A military member may also be lawfully ordered not to consume alcoholic beverages as a condition of pretrial restriction, if reasonably necessary to protect the morale, welfare, and safety of the unit or the accused; to protect victims or potential witnesses; or to ensure the accused's presence at the court-martial or pretrial hearings in a sober condition. *United States v. Blye*, 37 M.J. 92 (C.M.A. 1993).

    c) Order not to consume alcohol must have a reasonable connection to military needs; *United States v. Stewart*, 33 M.J. 519 (A.F.C.M.R. 1991) (order not to consume alcoholic beverages to see if the accused was an alcoholic was invalid); *United States v. Kochan*, 27 M.J. 574 (N.M.C.M.R. 1988) (order not to drink alcohol until 21-years old was illegal).

6. Loans. Orders restricting loans between service members may be lawful, if there is a sufficient connection between the military's duty to protect the morale, discipline, and usefulness of its members. *United States v. McClain*, 10 M.J. 271 (C.M.A. 1981) (upholding conviction for violation of a regulation prohibiting loans between permanent party personnel and trainees at Fort Jackson); *United States v. Smith*, 1 M.J. 156 (C.M.A. 1975) (regulation prohibiting all loans for profit or any benefit without consent of commander, without a corresponding military need, was invalid as too restrictive); *United States v. Giordano*, 35 C.M.R. 135 (C.M.A. 1964) (order fixing a maximum legal rate of interest on loans among military members was lawful).

7. Writing checks. *United States v. James*, 52 M.J. 709 (Army Ct. Crim. App. 2000) (order "not to write any more checks" was lawful). *Contra United States v. Alexander*, 26 M.J. 796 (A.F.C.M.R. 1988) (order "not to write any checks" was much too broad to be considered valid).

8. Regulations may proscribe the use of customs-free privileges in Korea for personal gain or profit. *United States v. Lehman*, 5 M.J. 740 (A.F.C.M.R. 1978).

9. As long as not unreasonable and not unduly humiliating or degrading, an order to produce a urine specimen under direct observation is lawful. *Unger v. Ziemniak*, 27 M.J. 349 (C.M.A. 1989).

10. Order to cooks to shower before reporting to work in the galley was lawful. *United States v. Horner*, 32 M.J. 576 (C.G.C.M.R. 1991).

11. Regulation prohibiting transportation of persons without prescribed travel documents on the Helmstadt-Berlin autobahn between former East and West Germany in a vehicle with United States military registration was lawful and was not a violation of human rights or the Thirteenth Amendment. *United States v. Stockman*, 17 M.J. 530 (A.C.M.R. 1983).

12. Regulations requiring members of the service to obtain approval from their commanders before circulating petitions on military installations are lawful. *Brown v. Glines*, 444 U.S. 348 (1979) (Air Force had substantial governmental interest unrelated to the suppression of free expression; while 10 U.S.C. § 1034 ensures that individual servicemen can write to members of Congress without sending the communication through official channels, it does not cover the general circulation of a petition within a military base); *Secretary of the Navy v. Huff*, 444 U.S. 453 (1979) (similar Navy regulation).

E. Litigating the Issue of Lawfulness of the Order. Lawfulness of an order, although an important issue, is not a discrete element of a disobedience offense. Therefore, it is a question of law to be determined by the military judge. MCM pt. IV, ¶ 14c(2)(a). *United States v. Jeffers*, 57 M.J. 13 (C.A.A.F. 2002); *United States v. New*, 55 M.J. 95 (C.A.A.F. 2001); *But see United States v. Mack*, 65 M.J. 108 (C.A.A.F. 2007) (while the lawfulness of an order is a question of law to be determined by the military judge, submitting the question of lawfulness to a panel is harmless error when the accused fails to rebut the presumption of lawfulness).

XII. DERELICTION OF DUTY. UCMJ ART. 92(3).

A. Duty.

1. The duty may be imposed by treaty, statute, regulation, lawful order, SOP, or custom of the service. MCM, pt. IV, ¶ 16c(3)(a); *United States v. Dallamn*, 34 M.J. 274 (C.M.A. 1992) (no duty to perform medical examination prior to prescribing drugs to persons not entitled to military medical services), *aff'd,* 37 M.J. 213 (C.M.A. 1993); *United States v. Dupree*, 24 M.J. 319 (C.M.A. 1987) (Air Force regulation imposed duty to report drug abuse, but dereliction could not be sustained where prisoner's marijuana use was inextricably intertwined with accused guard's misconduct in taking prisoners off-base); *United States v. Heyward*, 22 M.J. 35 (C.M.A. 1986) (although Air Force regulation imposed duty to report drug abuse, the privilege against self-incrimination excuses non-compliance where, at the time the duty to report arose, the accused was already an accessory or principal to the illegal activity); *United States v. Grow*, 11 C.M.R. 77 (C.M.A. 1953) (failure of major general to secure classified information, as required by non-punitive Army regulation, constituted dereliction of duty).

2. "Duty" does not include non-military tasks voluntarily performed after regular duty hours for additional pay. *United States v. Garrison*, 14 C.M.R. 359 (A.B.R. 1954) (secretary/treasurer of NCO club).

3. The evidence must prove the existence of the duty beyond a reasonable doubt. *United States v. Tanksley*, 36 M.J. 428 (C.M.A. 1993) (evidence of duty to "acquire parts and materials necessary to maintain communication equipment" did not establish that accused "had a duty to acquire light sticks or bayonets properly, or indeed, at all").

B. Knowledge.

1. The accused must have known or should have known of the duty. MCM, pt. IV, ¶ 16b(3)(b), 16c(3)(b) (MCM added knowledge as element for negligent dereliction in 1986); *United States v. Pacheco,* 56 M.J. 1, (C.A.A.F. 2001) (accused's knowledge of his duty to safeguard a weapons cache and his willful dereliction of this duty was established

by the taking of weapons as trophies); *United States v. Pratt*, 34 C.M.R. 731 (C.G.B.R. 1963) (evidence insufficient to establish that accused reasonably aware of facts necessitating initiation of rescue procedures).

    2. Willful dereliction, which has a greater maximum punishment, requires actual knowledge of the duty. *United States v. Ferguson*, 40 M.J. 823, 833-34 (N.M.C.M.R. 1994).

    3. There is no requirement that the accused know the source of the duty. *United States v. Markley*, 40 M.J. 581 (A.F.C.M.R. 1993).

C. Standards for Dereliction.

    1. Willful nonperformance of duty. "Willful" means intentional. It requires doing an act knowingly and purposely, specifically intending the natural and probable consequences of the act. MCM, pt. IV, ¶ 16c(3)(c).

    2. Negligent nonperformance of duty. "Negligence" is the lack of that degree of care that a reasonably prudent person would have exercised under the same or similar circumstances, *i.e.* simple negligence. MCM, pt. IV, ¶ 16c(3)(c); *United States v. Lawson*, 36 M.J. 415 (C.M.A. 1993) (improper posting of road guides in pairs and obtaining a roster of individuals to be posted); *United States v. Rust*, 38 M.J. 726 (A.F.C.M.R. 1993); *United States v. Dellarosa*, 30 M.J. 255 (C.M.A. 1990) (weather reporting); *United States v. Kelchner*, 36 C.M.R. 183 (C.M.A. 1966) (evidence insufficient to prove Navy commander negligently failed to supervise and assist subordinate's work); *United States v. Grow*, 11 C.M.R. 77 (C.M.A. 1953) (failure of major general to safeguard classified information); *United States v. Ferguson*, 12 C.M.R. 570 (A.B.R. 1953) (evidence insufficient to prove company commander was derelict in his instructions on safety measures; "in testing for negligence the law does not substitute hindsight for foresight").

    3. Culpable inefficiency. "Culpable inefficiency" is inefficiency in the performance of a duty for which there is no reasonable or just excuse. MCM, pt. IV, ¶ 16c(3)(c); *United States v. Nickels*, 20 M.J. 225 (C.M.A. 1985) (not maintaining proper fiscal control over postal account); *see United States v. Dellarosa*, 30 M.J. 255, 259 (C.M.A. 1990) (finding the distinction between nonperformance and faulty performance no longer significant).

D. Ineptitude as a Defense. A person who fails to perform a duty because of ineptitude rather than by willfulness, negligence, or culpable inefficiency is not guilty of an offense. MCM, pt. IV, ¶ 16c(3)(c); *United States v. Powell*, 32 M.J. 117 (C.M.A. 1991) ("ineptitude as a defense is largely fact-specific, requiring consideration of the duty imposed, the abilities and training of the soldier upon whom the duty is imposed, and the circumstances in which he is called upon to perform his duty").

E. Dereliction of Duty as a Lesser Offense to Other Crimes.

    1. Dereliction of duty, where the duty is premised upon a regulation or custom of the service, is not a lesser included offense of willful disobedience of a superior officer's order. *United States v. Haracivet*, 45 C.M.R. 674 (A.C.M.R. 1972).

    2. Dereliction of duty can be a lesser included offense of failure to obey a general order or regulation or a lawful order, under Article 92. *United States v. Green*, Army 20010446, 2003 Lexis 137 (Army Ct. Crim. App. June 6, 2003)(DoD Directive on possession of drug paraphernalia not punitive, but accused could be guilty of dereliction of duty); *United States v. Shavrnoch*, 49 M.J. 334 (1998) (Air Force regulation on underage drinking not

punitive); *United States v. Bivins*, 49 M.J. 328 (1998) (Air Force regulation on underage drinking not punitive); *United States v. Green*, 47 C.M.R. 727 (A.F.C.M.R. 1973) (finding that dereliction of duty was lesser included offense of failure to obey a lawful order of NCO concerning submitting daily urine specimens at treatment center).

F. Pleading.

1. The specification must spell out the nature of the inadequate performance alleged. *United States v. Kelchner*, 36 C.M.R. 183 (C.M.A. 1966); *United States v. Long*, 46 M.J. 783 (C.M.A. 1997) (misuse of credit card for official government travel).

2. The specification need not set forth the particular source of the duty violated. *United States v. Moore*, 21 C.M.R. 544 (N.B.R. 1956).

3. The specification must allege nonperformance or faulty performance of a specified duty, and a bare allegation that an act was "not authorized" is insufficient. *United States v. Sojfer*, 44 M.J. 603 (N-M. Ct. Crim. App. 1996) (specification alleging that accused corpsman committed acts beyond the scope of his duties, *i.e.* breast and pelvic examinations, failed to state the offense of dereliction), *aff'd*, 47 M.J. 425 (C.A.A.F. 1998).

4. Variance between the nature of the inadequate performance alleged and the nature of the inadequate performance proven at trial may be fatal. *United States v. Smith*, 40 C.M.R. 316 (C.M.A. 1969) (accused charged with dereliction by failure to walk his post by sitting down upon his post, but evidence showed he left his post before being properly relieved, in violation of Article 113, and was found asleep in a building off his post); *United States v. Swanson*, 20 C.M.R. 416 (A.B.R. 1950) (accused charged with dereliction by *failure* to forward funds, but finding was failure to *properly handle* funds).

5. For the enhanced maximum punishment for willful dereliction, the specification must allege willfulness, including actual knowledge of the duty. *United States v. Ferguson*, 40 M.J. 823 (N.M.C.M.R. 1994).

G. Examples of Misconduct Constituting Dereliction of Duty.

1. Poor judgment in performance of duties can constitute dereliction. *United States v. Rust*, 41 M.J. 472 (C.A.A.F. 1995) (failure of on-call obstetrician to come to hospital to examine and admit patient showing signs of premature labor); *United States v. Sievert*, 29 C.M.R. 657 (N.B.R. 1959) (navigator, transiting narrow passage at night, failed to use all radars available to him and failed to react when faced with substantial discrepancies in position of ship).

2. Affirmative criminal acts can support a dereliction of duty offense where those acts fall within the scope of the duty. *United States v. Casey*, 45 M.J. 623, 629 (N-M. Ct. Crim. App. 1996) (theft of monies collected for phone charges); *United States v. Bankston*, 22 M.J. 896 (N.M.C.M.R. 1986) (stealing cash collected from video games); *United States v. Taylor*, 13 C.M.R. 201 (A.B.R. 1953) (lieutenant stole from mess fund, of which he was the custodian); *United States v. Voelker*, 7 C.M.R. 102 (A.B.R. 1953) (lieutenant spent money from special services fund provided to cover costs of transportation, food, and lodging for enlisted men on athletic team).

3. Loss to the Government or some other victim is not required for dereliction. *United States v. Nichels*, 20 M.J. 225 (C.M.A. 1985) (dereliction even though accused repaid or arranged to repay the $3,000 lost due to the accused's failure to maintain proper fiscal control over postal account).

4. Failure to maintain alert and responsible watch supports conviction for dereliction of duty. *United States v. Stuart*, 17 C.M.R. 486 (A.B.R. 1954).

5. Willfully failing to properly use official time and government funds during TDY can constitute dereliction. *United States v. Mann*, 50 M.J. 689 (A.F. Ct. Crim. App. 1999) (during 5 duty days of TDY, the only legitimate business the accused Air Force major accomplished was a 45 minute conversation that could have taken place over the telephone; the accused was derelict in his duty to expend official time and funds only for legitimate governmental purposes by remaining TDY for personal reasons).

6. Failure to report changes in marital status affecting pay and allowances constitutes dereliction of duty. *United States v. Markley*, 40 M.J. 581 (A.F.C.M.R. 1994).

7. Even though civilians may have a First Amendment right to blow their nose on the American flag, the accused doing so while on flag-raising detail constituted dereliction of duty. *United States v. Wilson*, 33 M.J. 797 (A.C.M.R. 1991).

8. Failure to report or prevent crime. *See generally United States v. Thompson*, 22 M.J. 40 (C.M.A. 1986); *United States v. Heyward*, 22 M.J. 35 (C.M.A. 1986).

XIII. ENLISTMENT DEFINED.

A. Enlistment: A Contract that Changes "Status."

1. Valid Enlistments. *In re Grimley*, 137 U.S. 147 (1890) (finding valid enlistment, for jurisdictional purposes, where recruit lied about not being over the statutory maximum age of 35).

   a) A valid contract creates military status, and a breach of the contract does not affect status.

   b) Incapacity to contract and contracting involuntarily may prevent the existence of status.

2. Void Enlistments—No Status Due to Statutory Disqualifications.

   a) Insanity, intoxication. 10 U.S.C. § 504.

   b) Felons, deserters (secretaries may authorize exceptions). 10 U.S.C. § 504.

   c) Age (minimum age - 17). 10 U.S.C. § 505.

   d) Citizenship status. 10 U.S.C. § 3253.

B. Regulatory Enlistment Criteria. Army Regulation 601-210.

1. No prior service applicants - Chapter 2.

2. Prior service applicants - Chapter 3.

C. Regulatory Disqualifications.

1. Old rule: Regulations on enlistment qualifications are not only for the benefit of the service but also for the benefit of the applicant. Where recruiter misconduct amounts to a violation of Article 84, the resulting enlistment is void as contrary to public policy. *United States v. Russo*, 1 M.J. 134 (C.M.A. 1975) (holding enlistment void, where

accused suffered from dyslexia which severely impaired his ability to read and recruiter gave list of answers to qualification test).

2. *Russo* created a prophylactic rule that voided all enlistment contracts where recruiter misconduct existed. This resulted in numerous courts-martial where the accused defended by alleging the government had no jurisdiction over him because of recruiter misconduct. Congress responded by amending Article 2 to establish "constructive enlistments," in order to overrule *Russo* (*see* E. below); *see United States v. Quintal*, 10 M.J. 532 (A.C.M.R. 1980); *United States v. Gibson*, 43 M.J. 343, 346 n.3 (C.A.A.F. 1995).

D. Involuntary Enlistment.

1. *United States v. Catlow*, 48 C.M.R. 758 (C.M.A. 1974) (enlistment was involuntary and void at its inception, where accused entered into it after a civilian judge told him his only choice was between 5 years in jail or enlistment in the Army for 3 years).

2. *United States v. Lightfoot*, 4 M.J. 262 (C.M.A. 1974) (enlistment was voluntary, where accused, on advice of counsel, proposed military service as an alternative to confinement and the recruiter did not know that the criminal proceedings had been dismissed against the accused contingent on his entrance into the military). *See also, United States v. Ghiglieri*, 25 M.J. 687 (A.C.M.R. 1987).

E. The Codification of *In Re Grimley*.

1. In 1979, Article 2 was amended to read as follows:

> "(b) The voluntary enlistment of any person who has the capacity to understand the significance of enlisting in the armed forces shall be valid for purposes of jurisdiction under subsection (a) and a change of status from civilian to member of the armed forces shall be effective upon the taking of the oath of enlistment.
>
> (c) Notwithstanding any other provision of law, a person serving with an armed force who—
>
> (1) submitted voluntarily to military authority;
>
> (2) met the mental competence and minimum age qualifications of sections 504 and 505 of his title at the time of voluntary submission to military authority;
>
> (3) received military pay or allowances; and
>
> (4) performed military duties;
>
> is subject to this chapter until such person's active service has been terminated in accordance with law or regulations promulgated by the Secretary concerned."

2. Recruiter misconduct or intoxication at the time of the oath can be cured by "constructive enlistment." *United States v. Hirsch*, 26 M.J. 800 (A.C.M.R. 1988).

3. "Constructive enlistment" applies to reserve officer on active duty training (ADT). *United States v. Ernest*, 32 M.J. 135 (C.M.A. 1991).

4. A court-martial is competent to determine whether an enlistment was voidable because of misrepresentation. *Woodrick v. Divich*, 24 M.J. 147 (C.M.A. 1987). However, since a federal court *habeas corpus* proceeding was pending, the "demands of comity"

supported abating court-martial proceedings until the proceedings in the District Court were resolved.

XIV. FRAUDULENT ENLISTMENT, APPOINTMENT, OR SEPARATION. UCMJ ART. 83.

A. Nature of The Offense. A fraudulent enlistment, appointment, or separation is one procured by either a knowingly false representation as to any of the qualifications or disqualifications prescribed by law, regulation, or orders for the specific enlistment, appointment, or separation, or a deliberate concealment as to any of those disqualifications. Matters that may be material to an enlistment, appointment, or separation include any information used by the recruiting, appointing, or separating officer in reaching a decision as to enlistment, appointment, or separation in any particular case, and any information that normally would have been so considered had it been provided to that officer. MCM, pt. IV, ¶ 7c(1).

B. Fraudulent Enlistment or Appointment.

1. False Representation or Concealment.

a) Testimony of the accused's recruiters and documentary evidence of his traffic violations proved that the accused willfully concealed offenses, the cumulative number of which would have disqualified him from enlistment, and supported a conviction for fraudulent enlistment. *United States v. Hawkins*, 37 M.J. 718 (A.F.C.M.R. 1993).

b) The accused perpetrated a fraudulent enlistment by enlisting in the Marine Corps using his brother's name. *United States v. Victorian*, 31 M.J. 830 (N.M.C.M.R. 1990) (holding, however, that the statute of limitations barred prosecution for fraudulent enlistment).

c) Falsely misrepresenting educational qualifications and willfully concealing arrest record constituted fraudulent extension of enlistment, which was not preempted by Article 83. *United States v. Weigand*, 23 M.J. 644 (A.C.M.R. 1986).

d) Accused fraudulently entered the Army on several occasions using, at varying times, eleven different names. *United States v. Brown*, 22 M.J. 597 (A.C.M.R. 1986).

2. Receipt of Pay or Allowances. An essential element of the offense of fraudulent enlistment or appointment is that the accused shall have received pay or allowances thereunder. Accordingly, a member of the armed forces who enlists or accepts an appointment without being regularly separated from a prior enlistment or appointment should be charged under Article 83 only if that member has received pay or allowances under the fraudulent enlistment or appointment. Also, acceptance of food, clothing, shelter, or transportation from the government constitutes receipt of allowances. Whatever is furnished the accused while in custody, confinement, or other restraint pending trial for fraudulent enlistment or appointment, however, is not considered an allowance. MCM, pt. IV, ¶ 7c(2).

C. Fraudulent Separation.

1. The accused procured a fraudulent separation from the Army by submitting, as her own, a urine sample obtained from a pregnant servicemember. The separation was invalid, and the accused remained subject to court-martial jurisdiction. *Wickham v. Hall*, 12 M.J. 145 (C.M.A. 1981). The 5th Circuit Court of Appeals affirmed a District Court

ruling, in summary judgment, that Article 3(b) was constitutional. *Wickham v. Hall*, 706 F.2d. 713 (5th Cir. 1983).

2. Court-martial had jurisdiction to try and punish accused for offense of procuring his false separation from the Army. The accused apparently forged the signatures of several NCOs and the post commander in order to fraudulently obtain a DD Form 214 releasing him from active duty. *United States v. Cole*, 24 M.J. 18 (C.M.A. 1987) (upholding the constitutionality of Article 3(b)).

3. Accused was properly convicted, under Article 80, of attempting to procure a fraudulent separation from the Army. *United States v. Marshall*, 40 C.M.R. 138 (C.M.A. 1969); *see also United States v. Horns*, 24 C.M.R. 663 (A.F.B.R. 1957) (accused convicted of attempting to procure a fraudulent separation from the Air Force by making a false sworn statement that he was a homosexual and had engaged in homosexual activities; conviction set aside because of newly discovered psychiatric evidence).

D. One Offense. Procuring one's own enlistment, appointment, or separation by several misrepresentations or concealments as to qualifications for the one enlistment, appointment, or separation is only one offense under Article 83. MCM, pt. IV, ¶ 7c(3).

E. Interposition of the Statute of Limitations.

1. Plea of guilty to fraudulent enlistment was improvident, because prosecution of that offense was barred by the statute of limitations and the record failed to indicate that the accused was aware of the bar. *United States v. Victorian*, 31 M.J. 830 (N.M.C.M.R. 1990).

2. Defense counsel's failure to raise statute of limitations that barred accused's conviction for fraudulent enlistment fell below minimum acceptable level of competence demanded of attorneys. *United States v. Jackson*, 18 M.J. 753 (A.C.M.R. 1984), *aff'd in part, rev'd in part,* 20 M.J. 414 (C.M.A. 1985).

F. Related Offense. Fraudulent extension of enlistment by means of a false official statement, charged as a violation of Article 134, was not preempted by Article 83 nor Article 107. *United States v. Wiegand*, 23 M.J. 644 (A.C.M.R. 1986).

XV. EFFECTING UNLAWFUL ENLISTMENT, APPOINTMENT, OR SEPARATION. UCMJ ART. 84.

A. Text. "Any person subject to this chapter who effects an enlistment or appointment in or separation from the armed forces of any person who is known to him to be ineligible for that enlistment, appointment, or separation because it is prohibited by law, regulation, or order shall be punished as a court-martial may direct." Article 84.

B. Explanation. The enlistment, appointment, or separation must have been prohibited by law, regulation, or order, and the accused must have then known that the person enlisted, appointed, or separated was eligible for the enlistment, appointment, or separation. MCM, pt. IV, para 8c.

C. Examples of Effecting an Unlawful Enlistment.

1. Accused recruiter, who had applicants that failed entrance examinations improperly retake the examinations in other jurisdictions, was guilty of effecting unlawful enlistment, under Article 84. *United States v. Hightower*, 5 M.J. 717 (A.C.M.R. 1978).

2. Accused effected unlawful enlistments and conspired to do so by involvement in a scam that provided ineligible applicants with bogus high school diplomas. *United States v. White*, 36 M.J. 284 (C.M.A. 1993).

XVI. CRUELTY AND MALTREATMENT. UCMJ ART. 93.

A. Introduction.

1. Text. "Any person subject to this chapter who is guilty of cruelty toward, or oppression or maltreatment of, any person subject to his orders shall be punished as a court-martial may direct." Article 93.

2. Elements.

a) That a certain person was subject to the orders of the accused; and

b) That the accused was cruel toward, or oppressed, or maltreated that person. MCM, pt. IV, ¶ 17b.

B. Nature of the Victim. The victim must be subject to the orders of the accused. This includes not only those under the direct or immediate supervision or command of the accused, but also any person (soldier or civilian) who is required by law to obey the lawful orders of the accused. *United States v. Sojfer*, 44 M.J. 603 (N-M. Ct. Crim. App. 1996) (E-3 seeking care at military medical facility could be "subject to the orders of" an E-6 corpsman since there was an important difference in rank which required the victim to obey the accused's orders), *aff'd*, 47 M.J. 425 (C.A.A.F. 1998); *but cf. United States v. Curry*, 28 M.J. 419 (C.M.A. 1989) (requiring more than seniority of rank to implicate Art. 93).

C. Nature of the Act. The cruelty, oppression, or maltreatment, although not necessarily physical, must be measured by an objective standard. Assault, improper punishment, and sexual harassment may constitute this offense. MCM, pt. IV, ¶ 17c(2).

1. Nature of superior's official position could place them in a "unique situation of dominance and control" and therefore bring ostensibly voluntary sexual relationship with a trainee within the definition of oppression and maltreatment, but not all personal relationships between superiors and subordinates, or between drill sergeants and their trainees, necessarily result in physical or mental pain or suffering; and government has the burden of proving that accused's conduct resulted in such physical or mental pain and suffering by an objective standard. *United States v. Johnson*, 45 M.J. 543 (Army Ct. Crim. App. 1997); *but see United States v. Fuller*, 54 M.J. 107 (C.A.A.F. 2000) (comment of sexual nature was not maltreatment by sexual harrassment because prosecution failed to prove that it offended the alleged victim); *U.S. v Goddard*, 54 M.J. 763 (N-.M Ct. Crim. App. 2000).

2. In a prosecution for maltreatment, it is not necessary to prove physical or mental harm or suffering on the part of the victim. It is only necessary to show, as measured from an objective viewpoint in light of the totality of the circumstances, that the accused's actions reasonably could have caused physical or mental harm or suffering. *United States v. Carson*, 57 M.J. 410 (C.A.A.F. 2002) (MP desk sergeant's indecent exposure of his penis to a subordinate female MP constituted maltreatment under Article 93).

D. Select Cases.

1. A consensual sexual relationship between a superior and a subordinate, without more, is not maltreatment. *United States v. Fuller*, 54 M.J. 107 (C.A.A.F. 2000) (even though relationship may have constituted fraternization, evidence did not evince "dominance and control" by the superior).

2. *U.S. v Goddard*, 54 M.J. 763 (N.M. Ct. Crim. App. 2000). A one time consensual sexual encounter with a female subordinate on the floor of the detachment's administrative office will not support a conviction for cruelty and maltreatment.

3. Cruelty, oppression, or maltreatment, although not necessarily physical, must be measured by an objective standard. The imposition of necessary or proper duties and the exaction of their performance does not constitute this offense even though the duties are arduous or hazardous or both. However, the accused's intrusive body searches of female trainees, objectively viewed, reasonably could have caused mental harm or suffering based on testimony that a person subject to an EPW search could feel "violated," and testimony by a victim that she felt humiliated by the search. *United States v. Springer*, 58 M.J. 164 (C.A.A.F. 2003).

XVII. FRATERNIZATION. UCMJ ART. 134.

A. Defining Wrongful Fraternization.

1. Military case law.

a) Military case law suggests that wrongful fraternization is more easily described than defined. Usually, some other criminal offense was involved when officers were tried for this offense. Whatever the nature of the relationship, each case was clearly decided on its own merits with a searching examination of the surrounding circumstances rather than focusing on the act itself.

b) The legal test for describing or defining fraternization is found in *United States v. Free*, 14 C.M.R. 466 (N.B.R. 1953): "Because of the many situations which might arise, it would be a practical impossibility to lay down a measuring rod of particularities to determine in advance what acts are prejudicial to good order and discipline and what are not. As we have said, the surrounding circumstances have more to do with making the act prejudicial than the act itself in many cases. Suffice it to say, then, that each case must be determined on its own merits. Where it is shown that the acts and circumstances are such as to lead a reasonably prudent person, experienced in the problems of military leadership, to conclude that the good order and discipline of the armed forces has been prejudiced by the compromising of an enlisted person's respect for the integrity and gentlemanly obligations of an officer, there has been an offense under Article 134.

2. The Manual for Courts-Martial specifically includes fraternization between officer and enlisted personnel as an offense under UCMJ art. 134. The elements of the offense are:

a) That the accused was a commissioned or warrant officer;

b) That the accused fraternized on terms of military equality with one or more certain enlisted member(s) in a certain manner;

c) That the accused then knew the person(s) to be (an) enlisted member(s);

d) That such fraternization violated the custom of the accused's service that officers shall not fraternize with enlisted members on terms of military equality; and

e) That, under the circumstances, the conduct of the accused was to the prejudice of good order and discipline in the armed forces or was of a nature to bring discredit upon the armed forces. MCM, pt. IV, ¶ 83b.

3. AR 600-20, paras. 4-14 and 4-15 (11 Feb 2009), define improper superior-subordinate relationships, to include several specified prohibited relationships. The regulation is punitive, so violation may be punished under Article 92.

4. Case law and regulatory guidance can assist in developing a template for determining improper superior-subordinate relationships or wrongful fraternization. Additional scrutiny should be given to relationships involving (1) direct command/supervisory authority, or (2) power to influence personnel or disciplinary actions. "[A]uthority or influence . . . is central to any discussion of the propriety of a particular relationship." DA Pam 600-35 (21 Feb 2000). These relationships are most likely to generate adverse effects.

B. Charging Fraternization.

1. Enlisted fraternization may be charged as a violation of UCMJ art. 134. *United States v. Clarke*, 25 M.J. 631 (A.C.M.R. 1987), *aff'd*, 27 M.J. 361 (C.M.A. 1989); *United States v. Carter*, 23 M.J. 683 (N.M.C.M.R. 1986); *United States v. March*, 32 M.J. 740 (A.C.M.R. 1991). Additionally, Article 134 has been successfully used to prosecute instances of officer-officer fraternization, *United States v. Callaway*, 21 M.J. 770 (A.C.M.R. 1986).

2. In addition to AR 600-20, many commands have published regulations and policy letters concerning fraternization. Violations of regulations or policy letters are punishable under Article 92, if:

a) The regulation or policy letter specifically regulates individual conduct without being vague or overbroad. *See United States v. Callaway*, 21 M.J. 770 (A.C.M.R. 1986); *United States v. Adams*, 19 M.J. 996 (A.C.M.R. 1985); *United States v. Moorer*, 15 M.J. 520 (A.C.M.R. 1983), *aff'd in part, rev'd in part,* 16 M.J. 451 (C.M.A. 1983); *United States v. Hoard*, 12 M.J. 563 (A.C.M.R. 1981);

b) The regulation or policy letter indicates that violations of the provisions are punishable under the UCMJ (directory language may be sufficient); and

c) Knowledge: Service members are presumed to have knowledge of lawful general regulations if they are properly published. Actual knowledge of regulations or policy letters issued by brigade-size or smaller organizations must be proven. *See generally United States v. Mayfield*, 21 M.J. 418 (C.M.A. 1981); *United States v. Tolkack*, 14 M.J. 239 (C.M.A. 1982); *see also United States v. Tedder*, 24 M.J. 176, 1981 (C.M.A. 1987).

C. Options Available to Commanders.

1. Counsel the individuals involved.

2. Pursue other non-punitive measures (*e.g.*, reassignment, oral or written admonitions or reprimands, adverse OER/EER, bar to reenlistment, relief, administrative elimination).

3. Consider nonjudicial or punitive action.

a) If the offense amounts to a social relationship between an officer and an enlisted person and violates good order and discipline, it may be charged under UCMJ art. 134.

b) If the relationship violates other offenses such as adultery, sodomy, indecent acts, maltreatment, etc., the conduct should be alleged as such.

c) Other articles may be charged depending upon the specific facts of the case.

d) The conduct may be in violation of a regulation or order and charged under Art 92.

D. Applications.

1. Sexual activity.

a) *United States v. Froehlke*, 390 F. Supp. 503 (D.D.C. 1975). Upheld conviction of warrant officer for undressing and bathing an enlisted woman (not his wife) with whom he had been drinking. Offense of unlawful fraternization held not unconstitutionally vague.

b) *United States v. Hoard*, 12 M.J. 563 (A.C.M.R. 1981). "[W]rongfully socializing, drinking, and engaging in sexual intercourse with female receptees in violation of cadre-trainee regulation."

c) *United States v. Lowery*, 21 M.J. 998 (A.C.M.R. 1986), *aff'd*, 24 M.J. 347 (C.M.A. 1987). Conviction upheld when accused officer had sexual intercourse with enlisted female, formerly under his command, where the female would not have gone to the accused's office to make an appointment but for the superior-subordinate relationship.

d) *United States v. Tedder*, 24 M.J. 176 (C.M.A. 1987). Charges of unbecoming conduct based on officer having sexual relationship with enlisted woman Marine and seeking to have subordinates arrange dates for him with another subordinate Marine were not impermissibly vague.

e) *United States v. Parrillo*, 31 M.J. 886 (A.F.C.M.R. 1990), *aff'd* 34 M.J. 112 (C.M.A. 1992) Sexual relations with enlisted members under the accused officer's supervision violated an Air Force custom against fraternization.

f) *United States v. Sanchez*, 50 M.J. 506 (A. F. Ct. Crim. App. 1998). Accused cannot be convicted of both conduct unbecoming (Art. 133) and fraternization (Art. 134) when the misconduct alleged in the specifications is identical; fraternization gets dismissed. Those fraternization allegations not alleged in conduct unbecoming specifications remain. Court cites *United States v. Harwood*, 46 M.J. 26, 28 (1997) in support.

g) *United States v. Rogers*, 54 M.J. 244 (2000). Evidence legally sufficient to sustain Art. 133 conviction for the offense of conduct unbecoming an officer by engaging in an unprofessional relationship with a subordinate officer in appellant's chain of command. AF Court holds there is no need to prove breach of custom or violation of punitive regulation.

2. Homosexual conduct.

a) *United States v. Lovejoy*, 42 C.M.R. 210 (C.M.A. 1970). Accused convicted of sodomy and fraternization with enlisted member of submarine crew. Sodomy occurred at accused's on-shore apartment, which he had invited enlisted sailor to share.

b) *United States v. Pitasi*, 44 C.M.R. 31 (C.M.A. 1971). Charges of sodomy set aside on appeal as unproven but conviction for fraternization based on same relationship upheld.

c) *United States v. Free*, 14 C.M.R. 466 (N.B.R. 1953). Accused convicted of sharing liquor with enlisted sailor in his quarters; sailor testified that after accepting invitation to spend the night in accused's quarters, he was awakened in night by accused getting into bed with him.

3. Drugs and other illegal activities.

    a) *United States v. Graham*, 9 M.J. 556 (N.C.M.R. 1980). Navy lieutenant convicted under Article 133 for conduct unbecoming an officer for smoking marijuana on shore with members of his ship's crew.

    b) *United States v. Chesterfield*, 31 M.J. 942 (A.C.M.R. 1990). Drinking and smoking hashish with subordinates constituted fraternization.

4. Excessive socializing.

    a) *United States v. Arthur*, 32 M.J. 541 (A.F.C.M.R. 1990). Accused officer's romantic relationship with an enlisted co-worker did not constitute fraternization.

    b) *United States v. McCreight*, 43 M.J. 483 (C.A.A.F. 1996). Conviction for fraternization sustained where 1LT showed partiality and preferential treatment to senior airman; associated with airman on a first name basis at work and during numerous social contacts, including drinking and gambling; repeatedly allowed the same airman to stay in his apartment; and on one occasion drank with same airman under circumstances where the accused was the "designated drunk" and the airman was the designated driver. No sexual aspect alleged or proven. Fraternization does not require sexual conduct. *Accord United States v. Nunes*, 39 M.J. 889 (A.F.C.M.R. 1994) ("That no sexual relationship was alleged is irrelevant. This case is a useful corrective to the common notion that fraternization perforce must include sexual hanky-panky.").

5. Proof of custom and other facts.

    a) *United States v. Wales*, 31 M.J. 301 (C.M.A. 1990). Accused's conviction for fraternization was reversed because the judge did not instruct that the members must find that the accused (an Air Force officer) was the supervisor of the enlisted member at the time of the alleged fraternization, and because the government did not prove that the accused's conduct violated a custom of the service. To prove a custom of the military service, proof must be offered by a knowledgeable witness--subject to cross-examination--about that custom.

    b) *United States v. Appel*, 31 M.J. 314 (C.M.A. 1990). If the government relies on a violation of a custom as fraternization, it must prove the custom (Air Force accused). Proof of a military custom may not be based on judicial notice.

    c) *United States v. Thompson*, 31 M.J. 781 (A.C.M.R. 1990). Military judge is entitled to take judicial notice of a post regulation proscribing fraternization.

d) *United States v. Johanns*, 20 M.J. 155 (C.M.A. 1985), *cert. denied* 474 U.S. 850 (1985). Decision of A.F.C.M.R. that "[C]ustom in the Air Force "against fraternization has been so eroded as to make *criminal prosecution* against an officer for engaging in mutually voluntary, private, non-deviate sexual intercourse with an enlisted member, neither under his command or supervision, unavailable.

e) *United States v. Fox*, 34 M.J. 99 (C.M.A. 1992). Air Force fraternization specification must at least imply existence of a superior-subordinate or supervisory relationship and court members must be instructed that to find the accused guilty they must find the existence of such a relationship.

f) *United States v. Blake*, 35 M.J. 539 (A.C.M.R. 1992). Specification alleging fraternization between Army 1SG and female NCO in his company was fatally defective where it failed to allege a violation of Army custom, which is an essential element.

g) *United States v. Boyett*, 37 M.J. 872 (A.F.C.M.R. 1993), *aff'd* 42 M.J. 150 (1995). Determination in previous case (*Johanns*) that custom against fraternization in the Air Force had been so eroded as to make criminal prosecution against officer for engaging in mutually voluntary, private, nondeviate sexual intercourse with enlisted member, neither under his command nor supervision, unavailable was limited to state of customs reflected in record in that case, and would not preclude every prosecution for fraternization based on such conduct. (Per Heimberg, J., with three Judges concurring and one Judge concurring separately).

h) *United States v. Brown*, 55 M.J. 375 (C.A.A.F. 2001). The military judge did not abuse his discretion when he admitted the nonpunitive Air Force Pamphlet (AFP) 36-2705, Discrimination and Sexual Harassment (28 February 1995) over defense objection. In so ruling, the CAAF agreed with the military judge that the AFP was relevant to establish notice of the prohibited conduct and the applicable standard of conduct in the Air Force community to the appellant. Additionally, the CAAF stated that in cases were evidence of the custom of the service is needed to prove an element of an offense, it is likely that the probative value will out weigh the prejudicial effect.

XVIII. IMPERSONATING AN OFFICER, WARRANT OFFICER, OR NONCOMMISSIONED OFFICER. UCMJ ART. 134.

A. General. The offense does not depend upon the accused deriving a benefit from the deception or upon some third party being misled, but rather upon whether the acts and conduct would adversely influence the good order and discipline of the armed forces. *United States v. Messenger*, 6 C.M.R. 21 (C.M.A. 1952); *United States v. Frisbie*, 29 M.J. 974 (A.F.C.M.R. 1990); WINTHROP, MILITARY LAW AND PRECEDENTS 726 (2d ed., 1920 Reprint); MCM, pt. IV, ¶ 86c(1); TJAGSA Practice Note, *Impersonating an Officer and the Overt Act Requirement*, ARMY LAW., Jul. 1990, at 42 (discussing *Frisbie*).

B. Intent. Intent to defraud may be plead and proven as an aggravating factor. MCM, pt. IV, ¶ 86b.

C. Related Offenses. Impersonating an officer, warrant officer, or noncommissioned officer differs from the offense of impersonating a CID agent or other agent of the federal government, in that the accused is not required to act out the part of the officer. Instead, merely posing as an officer is sufficient. *United States v. Felton*, 31 M.J. 526 (A.C.M.R. 1990); *United States v.*

Wesley, 12 M.J. 886 (A.C.M.R. 1981); *United States v. Reece*, 12 M.J. 770 (A.C.M.R. 1981); *United States v. Adams*, 14 M.J. 647 (A.C.M.R. 1982); *see also* TJAGSA Practice Note, *Impersonating a CID Agent and the Overt Act Requirement*, ARMY LAW., Mar. 1991, at 21 (discusses *Felton*); Cooper, *Persona Est Homo Cum Statu Quodam Consideratus*, ARMY LAW., April 1981, at 17.

XIX. MALINGERING. UCMJ ART. 115.

A. General. The essence of this offense is the design to avoid performance of any work, duty, or service which may properly or normally be expected of one in the military service. Whether to avoid all duty, or only a particular job, it is the purpose to shirk which characterizes the offense. Hence, the nature or permanency of a self-inflicted injury is not material on the question of guilt, nor is the seriousness of a physical or mental disability which is a sham. Evidence of the extent of the self-inflicted injury or feigned disability may, however, be relevant as a factor indicating the presence or absence of the purpose. MCM, pt. IV, ¶ 40c(1).

B. Elements.

1. The accused was assigned to, or was aware of prospective assignment to, or availability for, the performance of work, duty, or service.

    a) All soldiers are inferred to be aware of their general, routine military duties. *United States v. Mamaluy*, 27 C.M.R. 176 (C.M.A. 1959).

    b) With regard to special duties or prospective assignments (*e.g.*, emergency deployment to hostile regions), the government must establish that accused had actual knowledge of such duties.

2. The accused feigned illness, physical disablement, mental lapse or derangement, or intentionally inflicted injury upon himself or herself.

    a) *United States v. Pedersen*, 8 C.M.R. 63 (C.M.A. 1953). Accused was charged with intentionally shooting himself in order to be discharged from the Army but testified at trial that the injury was accidentally inflicted. No one witnessed the shooting, and the government had no admissible evidence with which to impeach the accused. As a result, the court held that the prosecution had failed in its proof and dismissed the charges.

    b) *United States v. Kisner*, 35 C.M.R. 125 (C.M.A. 1964). Accused was charged with deliberately shooting himself in the foot in order to avoid transfer to Korea. After initially declaring that the injury was accidentally incurred, he confessed to intentionally inflicting the wound in order to avoid deployment to Korea. Because the record was devoid of any independent evidence to corroborate the confession, the Court of Military Appeals reversed the conviction and dismissed the charge.

    c) *United States v. Belton*, 36 C.M.R. 602 (A.B.R. 1966). Accused on orders to Vietnam, who refused to eat food over a period of time, resulting in his debility, intentionally inflicted self-injury for purposes of Article 115.

3. The accused's purpose or intent in doing so was to avoid the work, duty or service.

    a) The words "work," "duty," and "service" are not restricted to one context or sense. The breadth of these terms would seem to cover all aspects of a serviceperson's official existence. Unquestionably, what the law intended to proscribe was a self-inflicted injury, which would prevent the injured party from being available for the performance of all military tasks. *See United States v. Mamaluy*, 27 C.M.R. 176 (C.M.A. 1959) (Cutting his wrist to escape confinement was sufficient to allege a purpose to avoid either work, duty, or service.); *United States v. Guy*, 38 C.M.R. 694 (N.B.R. 1967) (Intentional self-injury for the purpose of avoiding disciplinary action was sufficient to avoid either work, duty, or service); *United States v. Johnson*, 28 C.M.R. 629 (N.B.R. 1959) (a sailor who persuaded a friend to cut off his thumb was convicted of conspiracy to maim himself and malingering when the act was done as a means of avoiding further military duty).

b) Intent or purpose may be established by circumstantial evidence, and it may be inferred that a person intended the natural and probable consequences of an act intentionally performed by him. *United States v. Houghton*, 32 C.M.R. 3 (C.M.A. 1962); *but see United States v. Lawrence*, 10 M.J. 752 (A.C.M.R. 1981) (court held that evidence which established only that the accused injured himself in order to halt an investigation into a false report he had filed was insufficient to support a conviction for malingering).

c) Unsuccessfully attempting to commit suicide to avoid prosecution constitutes malingering. *United States v. Johnson*, 26 M.J. 415 (C.M.A. 1988).

d) Evidence of prior misconduct may be admissible against the accused for the limited purpose of establishing his wrongful intent. *See United States v. Brown*, 38 C.M.R. 445 (A.B.R. 1967) (where the accused was charged with malingering by intentionally shooting himself in the foot while on a combat mission in Vietnam, evidence that he had quit as a point man for a patrol the day before the shooting and had skulked in bringing up the rear and wanted to be evacuated and complained of headaches was relevant on the issue of intent).

C. Defense of Accident. *United States v. Harrison*, 41 C.M.R. 179 (C.M.A. 1970). Where an accused charged with malingering by intentionally shooting himself in the foot for the purpose of avoiding duty in the field testified he had a faulty weapon which discharged accidentally while he was dozing, the instructions on the elements of the offense and the defense of accident were prejudicially inconsistent where the court was advised it must find the accused intentionally inflicted injury upon himself by shooting himself in the foot, but the instructions on accident included the statement that even though the act is unintentional, it is not excusable where it was a result of or incidental to an unlawful act.

D. To Avoid Assigned Duty. *See United States v. Yarborough*, 5 C.M.R. 106 (C.M.A. 1952) (malingering to avoid assigned duty while before the enemy constitutes misbehavior punishable under UCMJ art. 99). *See also, United States v. Glover*, 33 M.J. 640 (N.M.C.M.R. 1991) (testimony required from people who knew what restrictions had been placed on accused's activity to show he was attempting to avoid assigned duties.)

E. Without Intent to Avoid Military Duty. *See United States v. Taylor*, 38 C.M.R. 393 (C.M.A. 1968). In *Taylor*, the evidence pertaining to a charge of malingering in violation of UCMJ art. 115 showed that the accused superficially slashed his arms with a razor blade in the presence of two cell mates in the brig, representing at the time that he wanted to outdo the performance of another inmate who had done the same thing earlier. The law officer instructed that intentional injury without a purpose to avoid service but under circumstances to the prejudice of good order and discipline was a lesser included offense, and the court could validly find the accused not guilty of the portion of the specification alleging the purpose of the injury to have been avoiding service and the accused guilty of being disorderly to the prejudice of good order and discipline in the armed forces in violation of Article 134, UCMJ. Held: Article 115 does not pre-empt the spectrum of self-inflicted injuries. *See also United States v. Ramsey,* 40 M.J. 71 (C.M.A. 1994).

XX. LOSS, DAMAGE, DESTRUCTION, OR WRONGFUL DISPOSITION OF MILITARY PROPERTY. UCMJ ART. 108.

A. "Military Property" Defined.

1. "Military property is all property, real or personal, owned, held, or used by one of the armed forces of the United States. It is immaterial whether the property sold, disposed, destroyed, lost, or damaged had been issued to the accused, to someone else, or even issued at all. If it is proved by either direct or circumstantial evidence that items of individual issue were issued to the accused, it may be inferred, depending on all the evidence, that the damage, destruction, or loss proved was due to the neglect of the accused. Retail merchandise of service exchange stores is not military property under this article." MCM, ¶ 32c(1).

2. For purposes of both Article 108 and Article 121, all appropriated funds belonging to the United States are within the meaning of the term "military property of the United States." *United States v. Hemingway,* 36 M.J. 349 (C.M.A. 1993). *See generally* TJAGSA Practice Note, *Defining Military Property,* ARMY LAW., Oct. 1990, at 44.

3. Myriad items can constitute military property, including: Watches, *United States v. Ford,* 30 C.M.R. 3 (C.M.A. 1960); Examinations, *United States v. Reid,* 31 C.M.R. 83 (C.M.A. 1961); Electric Drill, *United States v. Foust,* 20 C.M.R. 907 (A.B.R. 1955); A gate, *United States v. Meirthew,* 11 C.M.R. 450 (A.B.R. 1953); Sheets, mattress, and mattress cover, *United States v. Burrell,* 12 C.M.R. 943 (A.F.B.R. 1953); Sinks, pipes, and window casements, *United States v. Tomasulo,* 12 C.M.R. 531 (A.B.R. 1953); Camera in ship's store, *United States v. Simonds,* 20 M.J. 279 (C.M.A. 1985); Blankets, *United States v. Blevins,* 34 C.M.R. 967 (A.F.B.R. 1964).

4. Military property does not include:

   a) Postal funds. *United States v. Spradlin,* 33 M.J. 870 (N.M.C.M.R. 1991).

   b) Nonappropriated fund organization property, which is not furnished to a military service for use by the military service. *United States v. Geisler,* 37 C.M.R. 530 (A.C.M.R. 1965) (property of officer's club); *see United States v. Ford,* 30 M.J. 871 (A.F.C.M.R. 1990) *(en banc); United States v. Thompson,* 30 M.J. 905 (A.C.M.R. 1990); *see generally* TJAGSA Practice Note, *Appropriated Funds as Military Property,* ARMY LAW., Jan. 1991, at 44.

   c) Army and Air Force Exchange Service (AAFES) property. *United States v. Underwood,* 41 C.M.R. 410 (A.C.M.R. 1969); *United States v. Schelin,* 12 M.J. 575 (A.C.M.R. 1981), *aff'd,* 15 M.J. 218 (C.M.A. 1983). Navy courts have held, however, that property of the Navy Exchange is military property. *United States v. Mullins,* 34 C.M.R. 694 (N.C.M.R. 1964); *United States v. Harvey,* 6 M.J. 545 (N.C.M.R. 1978).

B. **Property Need Not Have Been Personally Issued.** The purpose of Article 108 is to ensure that all military property, however obtained and wherever located, is protected from loss, damage, or destruction. As such, all persons subject to the UCMJ have an affirmative duty to preserve the integrity of military property. *United States v. O'Hara,* 34 C.M.R 721 (N.B.R. 1964).

C. Pleading. The specification must as a whole or directly state that the property was *military* property of the United States. *United States v. Rockey*, 022 C.M.R. 372 (A.B.R. 1956); *United States v. Schiavo*, 14 M.J. 649 (A.C.M.R. 1982).

D. Multiplicity. Larceny and wrongful disposition of the same property are separately punishable. *United States v. West*, 17 M.J. 145 (C.M.A. 1984); *see also United States v. Harder*, 17 M.J. 1058 (A.F.C.M.R. 1983) (larceny and wrongful sale are separately punishable). *But see United States v. Teters*, 37 M.J. 370 (C.M.A. 1993) (holding that the test to be applied to determine whether there are two offenses or only one is whether each provision requires proof of an additional fact which the other does not ("elements test")).

E. Unlawful Sale of Military Property.

    1. "Sale" defined. The term "sale" means an actual or constructive delivery of possession in return for a "valuable consideration," and the passing of such title as the seller may possess, whatever that title may be. *United States v. Blevins*, 34 C.M.R. 967 (A.F.B.R. 1964).

    2. "Sale" distinguished from larceny.

        a) The sale of property implies the transfer of at least ostensible title to a purchaser in return for consideration. When the evidence merely shows that the accused, according to prior arrangements, stole property and delivered it to one or more of his fellow principals in the theft, receiving payment for his services, no sale is made. *United States v. Walter*, 36 C.M.R. 186 (C.M.A. 1966).

        b) Under proper circumstances, one transaction can constitute both a larceny and wrongful sale of the same property. *United States v. Lucas*, 33 C.M.R. 511 (A.C.M.R. 1962) (Accused, without authority and with intent to steal, took automotive parts out of a government salvage yard and later sold them at a civilian junk yard. The larceny was complete when the automotive parts were taken from the salvage yard; and the act of selling such parts did not constitute the final element of the larceny offense.)

        c) Lack of knowledge as defense. Because the offense of wrongful sale of government property involves a general criminal intent, lack of knowledge as to ownership of the property constitutes an affirmative defense provided the accused's actions are based on an honest and reasonable mistake. *United States v. Germak*, 31 C.M.R. 708 (A.F.B.R. 1961); *United States v. Pearson*, 15 M.J. 888 (A.C.M.R. 1983).

        d) Multiplicity. An accused can be separately found guilty of wrongful sale under Article 108 and concealment under Article 134 of the same military property. *United States v. Wolfe*, 19 M.J. 174 (C.M.A. 1985). *But see United States v. Teters*, 37 M.J. 370 (C.M.A. 1993) (holding that the test to be applied to determine whether there are two offenses or only one is whether each provision requires proof of an additional fact which the other does not ("elements test")).

F. Wrongful Disposition of Military Property. Disposing of military property by any means other than sale is an offense under Article 108 if such disposition is made without proper authority. For example, giving military property away without proper authorization constitutes an offense under this article. It makes no difference if the surrender of the property is temporary or permanent. *United States v. Banks*, 15 M.J. 723 (A.C.M.R. 1983), *aff'd*, 20 M.J. 166 (C.M.A. 1985); *See also United States v. Reap*, 43 M.J. 61 (1995) (accused who gave another marine a starlight scope and tool boxes outside of regular supply channels and without receipts was guilty of violating Article 108 when he had no color of authority to distribute the supplies).

G. Damaging, Destroying, or Losing Military Property.

1. Loss, damage, or destruction of military property under this provision may be the result of intentional misconduct or neglect.

2. Damage. Removing the screws that secure the nose landing gear inspection window of a military aircraft was legally sufficient to support the damage element required under Article 108. The word "damage" must be reasonably construed to mean any change in the condition of the property that impairs its operational readiness. The government was not required to prove that the accused had a motive to wrongfully damage military property in order to secure a conviction for the offense. *United States v. Daniels*, 56 M.J. 365 (C.A.A.F. 2002).

3. Willfulness. Willful damage, destruction, or loss is one that is intentionally occasioned. It refers to the doing of an act knowingly and purposely, specifically intending the natural and probable consequences thereof. *United States v. Boswell*, 32 C.M.R. 726 (C.G.B.R. 1962). Willful damage is a lesser included offense of sabotage under 18 U.S.C. § 2155. *United States v. Johnson*, 15 M.J. 676 (A.F.C.M.R. 1983); *see United States v. Washington*, 29 M.J. 536 (A.F.C.M.R. 1989); TJAGSA Practice Note, *Damaging Property and Mens Rea*, ARMY LAW., Feb. 1990, at 66.

   a) *United States v. George*, 35 C.M.R. 801 (A.F.B.R. 1965). Evidence that the accused removed perishable medical serums from a refrigerator in a medical warehouse in the tropics and left them at room temperature was sufficient to establish a willful destruction of government property although the purpose in removing the serums was to steal the refrigerator. The evidence established that the removal was intentional, and showing that the accused had a fully conscious awareness of the probable ultimate consequences of his purposeful act was unnecessary.

   b) *United States v. Creek*, 39 C.M.R. 666 (A.C.M.R. 1967). The evidence was insufficient to sustain a conviction of willfully and wrongfully destroying an M26 fragmentation hand grenade, military property of the United States, where evidence existed that some sort of explosive device was detonated and some witnesses expressed the opinion it was a grenade because of the sound and damage done, when they all admitted it could have been anything else and another witness said it sounded like recoilless rifle fire while others declined to express an opinion.

   c) *United States v. Barnhardt*, 45 C.M.R. 624 (C.G.C.M.R. 1971). Where the accused placed six metal objects in the starboard reduction gear of the cutter on which he was assigned and later, at the suggestion of a petty officer in whom he had confided, removed only the four objects he could see without reporting the remaining two, which he stated he thought might have fallen into the slump, the accused's plea of guilty to willfully damaging military property was provident; the intentional quality of the accused's conduct had not changed to negligence by his removal of some but not all of the foreign, metal objects from the gear.

   d) *United States v. Hendley*, 17 C.M.R. 761 (A.F.B.R. 1954). The accused, who had been drinking, took a military police sedan without authority and was chased at high speed. In trying to evade his pursuers, he weaved in and out of traffic;

narrowly missed one oncoming vehicle; subsequently sideswiped another; and finally went out of control, left the road, and smashed into several trees. The Board of Review only approved negligent damage to military property.

e) *United States v. Peacock*, 24 M.J. 410 (C.M.A. 1987). Placing rivets and nuts in an auxiliary fuel tank, thus temporarily impairing the aircraft's operational readiness, constitutes willful damage to military property.

4. Negligence. Loss, destruction, or damage is occasioned through neglect when it is the result of a want of such attention of the foreseeable consequences of an act or omission as was appropriate under the circumstances.

a) *United States v. Ryan*, 14 C.M.R. 153 (C.M.A. 1954). The doctrine of *res ipsa loquitur* is not applicable to a prosecution for damaging a military vehicle through neglect, and the mere happening of a collision with resulting damage is not in itself sufficient to support a conviction for violation of Article 108. Negligence must be affirmatively established by the prosecution evidence. Here, the accused was found guilty of damaging a government vehicle through neglect. No evidence indicated that the accused was driving at an excessive speed or in any sort of reckless manner, or that he was under the influence of alcohol, or that at the time of the accident he was engaged in the violation of traffic or other safety regulations of any nature. HELD: The evidence was wholly insufficient to support findings of guilt.

b) *United States v. Foster*, 48 C.M.R. 414 (N.C.M.R. 1973). Conviction based on accused's guilty plea set aside and dismissed where providence inquiry established that accused, while on guard, operated a government forklift without permission and that while he was doing so the hydraulic brake line malfunctioned. No evidence of accused's actual negligence was established by the government.

c) *United States v. Stuck*, 31 C.M.R. 148 (C.M.A. 1961). Although evidence was presented that a Navy vehicle turned over to the accused in good condition was damaged, and witnesses testified they saw the vehicle bump and heard a noise as the accused drove it through a gate, and evidence of paint scratches on the vehicle and the gate post indicated he must have struck the gate post, the evidence was insufficient to establish beyond a reasonable doubt that the vehicle was damaged through the accused's negligence. This is because the accused testified he had driven over a rock, evidence indicated that the road approaching the gate was bumpy and full of holes, and the gate was held open by a rock which could have been moved onto the road.

d) *United States v. Lane*, 34 C.M.R. 744 (C.G.B.R. 1963). The evidence was legally and factually sufficient to sustain findings of guilty of damaging and suffering damage to a Coast Guard vessel through neglect where the accused voluntarily and intentionally turned two wheels controlling flood valves on a floating drydock in which the vessel was berthed, thereby consciously setting in motion a sequence of events which a reasonably prudent man would expect to end in some kind of harm; and if, as the court found, the precise form and shape of the injury to the vessel was not specifically intended, then it was the result of a lack of due solicitude on the part of the accused made punishable under Article 108.

e) *United States v. Traweek*, 35 C.M.R. 629 (A.B.R. 1965). Evidence that a government helicopter in operating condition was parked, tied down, and covered and that it was subsequently found untied, uncovered and turned over on its side and wrecked and that the accused, who was on guard at the helicopter site, was lying unconscious a short distance from it was sufficient to corroborate accused's confession that he entered the helicopter to warm himself and caused the damage when he started the motor to generate heat.

    f) *United States v. Miller*, 12 M.J. 559 (A.F.C.M.R. 1981). Article 108 offense made out where accused who had control of a military truck permitted an unlicensed 16-year-old military dependent to operate truck resulting in accident and damage to vehicle.

H. Suffering the Loss, Damage, Destruction, Sale or Wrongful Disposition of Military Property.

    1. The word "suffer," as used in the UCMJ, does not have a meaning other than that accorded to it in the ordinary and general usage, *i.e.*, is to allow, to permit, and not to forbid or hinder; also, to tolerate and to put up with. *United States v. Johnpier*, 30 C.M.R. 90 (C.M.A. 1961).

    2. In charging an accused with the loss of military property, the word "suffer" may properly be used in alleging willful or intentional misconduct by the accused, as well as negligent dereliction on his part. *United States v. O'Hara*, 34 C.M.R. 721 (N.B.R. 1964); *see also* MCM, pt. IV, ¶ 32c(2).

    3. Where a member of the naval service intentionally loses military property by willfully pushing it over the side of his ship, he may be charged under Article 108 of willfully suffering the loss or wrongfully disposing of military property. *United States v O'Hara*, 34 C.M.R. 721 (N.B.R. 1964).

I. Value.

    1. Under all theories of prosecution under Article 108, UCMJ, the government must establish as an element of proof the value of the property destroyed, lost, or sold, or the amount of damage to that property. MCM, pt. IV, para 32b.

    2. "In the case of loss, destruction, sale, or wrongful disposition, the value of the property controls the maximum punishment which may be adjudged. In the case of damage, the amount of damage controls. As a general rule, the amount of damage is the estimated or actual cost of repair by the government agency normally employed in such work, or the cost of replacement, as shown by government price lists or otherwise, whichever is less." MCM, pt. IV, ¶ 32c(3).

    3. In the case of the wrongful sale of stolen military property, it is the time of taking at which value is to be determined and the burden is on the prosecution to establish the property condition as of that time. *United States v. Steward*, 20 C.M.R. 247 (C.M.A. 1955).

    4. Documents such as accounts receivable are not writings representing value. While they may record or even reflect value, they do not represent value as do negotiable instruments or other documents used to acquire goods or services. *United States v. Payne*, 9 M.J. 681 (A.F.C.M.R. 1980) (Accused who destroyed telephone toll records representing money owed to the Government by telephone users could not be convicted of destroying $4,000 in government property represented by the toll tickets. Instead, only a conviction for destruction of property of "some value" could stand).

    5. Various documents have been held to have the value they represent, including checks made out to other payees, *United States v. Windham*, 36 C.M.R. 21 (C.M.A. 1965); money orders, *United States v. Sowards*, 5 M.J. 864 (A.F.C.M.R. 1978); airline tickets, *United*

States v. Stewart, 1 M.J. 750 (A.F.C.M.R. 1975); and gasoline coupons, *United States v. Cook*, 15 C.M.R. 622 (A.F.B.R. 1954).

6. A government price list is competent evidence of value, and may be the best method of proving the market value of government property; however, it is an administrative determination of value, not binding on a court-martial, but entitled to its consideration. Value also may be inferred from the nature of property. A court may properly consider other evidence of value; for example, the property's serviceability. *United States v. Thompson*, 27 C.M.R. 119 (C.M.R. 1958); *United States v. Downs*, 46 C.M.R. 1227 (N.C.M.R. 1973).

PART II: THE GENERAL ARTICLES

I. **CONDUCT UNBECOMING AN OFFICER. UCMJ ART. 133.**

A. Conduct "must offend so seriously against law, justice, morality or decorum as to expose to disgrace, socially or as a man, the offender, and at the same time must be of such a nature or committed under such circumstances as to bring dishonor or disrepute upon the military profession which he represents." William Winthrop, *Military Law and Precedents* 711-12 (2d ed.1920)).

B. All that is required is for the offender's conduct to fall below the level of conduct expected of officers and to seriously expose him to public opprobrium. *United States v. Rogers*, 54 M.J. 244, 256 (C.A.A.F. 2000).

C. Private conduct may constitute an offense under Article 133, UCMJ, and there is no requirement that the conduct be otherwise criminal. United States v. *Moore*, 38 M.J. 490 (C.M.A. 1994); *United States v. Norvell*, 26 M.J. 477, 481 (C.M.A.1988). Conduct constitute an offense elsewhere under the UCMJ. *United States v. Taylor*, 23 M.J. 314, 318 (C.M.A.1987).

D. Applies to female officers. *United States v. Norvell*, 26 M.J. 477 (C.M.A.1988).

E. Acts Covered. Includes acts punishable under other articles of the UCMJ and offenses not so listed, except for minor derelictions that do not satisfy the requirements of Article 133. *United States v. Taylor*, 23 M.J. 314 (C.M.A. 1987) (UCMJ art. 133 conviction affirmed even where misconduct does not violate a punitive article); *United States v. Wolfson*, 36 C.M.R. 722 (A.B.R. 1965) (not every deviation in conduct constitutes unbecoming conduct; to be actionable conduct must be morally unbefitting and unworthy). Examples include:

1. Child Pornography. *United States v. Forney*, 67 M.J. 271 (C.A.A.F. 2009). Conduct involving child pornography, including receipt and possession, can constitute conduct unbecoming an officer. This can include both actual and virtual child pornography. *But see United States v. Amazaki*, 67 M.J. 666 (A. Ct. Crim. App. 2009) (holding that, under the facts, as a matter of due process, the accused was not "on fair notice that his unwitting possession of child pornography . . . was negligent or that his conduct in failing to discover, delete, or secure these images amounted to conduct unbecoming an officer and gentleman.").

2. Drugs. *United States v. Graham*, 9 M.J. 556 (N.C.M.R. 1980); *United States v. Maderia*, 38 M.J. 494 (C.M.A. 1994) (publicly associating with person known by the accused to be a drug smuggler and discussing drug use and possibility of assistance in drug smuggling operations).

3. Sex. *United States v. Coronado*, 11 M.J. 522 (A.F.C.M.R. 1981) (even though the offense occurred off the military installation, jurisdiction was properly exercised by general court-martial which convicted accused of conduct unbecoming an officer and gentleman by performing acts of sodomy on an enlisted man); *United States v. Jefferson*, 21 M.J. 203 (C.M.A. 1986) (adultery and fraternization); *United States v. Shobar*, 26 M.J. 501 (A.F.C.M.R. 1988) (sexual exploitation of civilian waitress under the accused's supervision); *United States v. Frazier*, 34 M.J. 194 (C.M.A. 1992) (officer's engaging in open and intimate relationship with wife of enlisted soldier constituted conduct unbecoming an officer).

4. Indecent language and conduct. *United States v. Parini*, 12 M.J. 679 (A.C.M.R. 1981) (colonel attempted to extract sexual favors from subordinates in return for favorable treatment); *United States v. Hartwig*, 35 M.J. 682 (A.C.M.R. 1992) (officer was properly convicted of conduct unbecoming based on his letter containing sexually suggestive

comments to 14 year-old girl in response to her letter of support for Operation Desert Storm), *aff'd,* 39 M.J. 125 (C.M.A. 1994); *United States v. Moore,* 38 M.J. 490 (C.M.A. 1994) (private remarks to sex partner in adulterous relationship regarding oral and anal sex were indecent and degrading and not protected by First Amendment); *see also United States v. Mazer,* 58 M.J. 691 (N-M. Ct. Crim. App. 2003) (making suggestive, explicit and indecent statements on an internet chat room to someone the accused believed to be a 14-year old girl), *set aside on other grounds, remanded by,* 60 M.J. 344 (C.A.A.F. 2004).

5. Homosexual conduct.

   a) *United States v. Harvey,* 67 M.J. 758 (A.F. Ct. Crim. App. 2009). Conduct that falls within a recognized liberty interest under *Lawrence,* as applied to the military through *Marcum,* may nonetheless be punished under Article 133. Under the circumstances of this case, fellatio between consenting adults "evince[d] . . . a degree of indecorum that disgraced and dishonored the appellant and seriously compromised his standing as an officer."

   b) *United States v. Modesto,* 39 M.J. 1055 (A.C.M.R. 1994) (off-post, off-duty, cross-dressing at gay club was conduct unbecoming); *see generally* TJAGSA Practice Note, *Cross-Dressing as an Offense,* ARMY LAW., Mar. 1991, at 42.

6. Lying and breaches of trust. *United States v. Lindsay,* 11 M.J. 550 (A.C.M.R. 1981) (lying to a criminal investigator about a subject of official investigation is conduct unbecoming an officer and gentleman. Even though making a false statement to a CID agent was, at the time, generally not an offense absent an independent duty to account the special status of an officer and the position of trust he occupies makes the intentional deceit a crime under Article 133); *United States v. Timberlake,* 18 M.J. 371 (C.M.A. 1984) (forging false PCS orders); *United States v. Gunnels,* 21 C.M.R. 925 (A.B.R. 1956) (taking money to procure a discharge); *United States v. Rushatz,* 30 M.J. 525 (A.C.M.R. 1990) (advising junior officers how to overstate rent for off-post housing using backdated receipts), *aff'd,* 31 M.J. 450 (C.M.A. 1990).

7. Financial impropriety. *United States v. Brunson,* 30 M.J. 766 (A.C.M.R. 1990) (failing to pay a just debt); *United States v. Jenkins,* 39 M.J. 843 (A.C.M.R. 1994) (negligently writing 76 dishonored checks and six false letters purportedly from bank officials).

8. Physical contact. *United States v. Isaac,* 59 M.J. 537 (C.G. Ct. Crim. App. 2003) (officer pled guilty to three specifications of Art. 133 for "forcefully" picking up and carrying three different female enlisted personnel on three separate occasions).

9. Obstruction of Justice. Can include obstruction of foreign criminal investigations or proceedings. *United States v. Ashby,* 68 M.J. 108 (C.A.A.F. 2009); *United States v. Schweitzer,* 68 M.J. 133 (C.A.A.F. 2009).

10. Miscellaneous conduct. *United States v. Schumacher,* 11 M.J. 612 (A.C.M.R. 1981) (officer's public intoxication); *United States v. Bonar,* 40 C.M.R. 482 (A.B.R. 1969) (affirming conviction for driving in violation of a state justice of the peace's court order); *United States v. Norvell,* 26 M.J. 477 (C.M.A. 1988) (dishonorable catheterization to avoid giving a valid urine sample, and then informing an enlisted person of this); *see* TJAGSA Practice Note, *Drugs, Sex and Commissioned Officers: Recent Developments Pertaining to Article 133, UCMJ,* ARMY LAW., Feb. 1989, at 62 (discusses *Norvell*); *United States v. Lewis,* 28 M.J. 179 (C.M.A. 1989) (charging a fellow officer for tutoring in leadership); *see* TJAGSA Practice Note, *Charging "Tuition" Can Constitute Conduct*

Unbecoming an Officer and a Gentleman, ARMY LAW., Aug. 1989, at 36 (discusses *Lewis*); *United States v. Bilby*, 39 M.J. 467 (C.M.A. 1994) (soliciting someone to violate a federal statute); *United States v. Miller*, 37 M.J. 133 (C.M.A. 1993) (failing to report child abuse by spouse and failing to obtain necessary medical care for abused child).

11. Conviction reversed for visiting legal brothel with enlisted members where the accused did not seek or engage in sex, *United States v. Guaglione*, 27 M.J. 268 (C.M.A. 1988); *see generally* TJAGSA Practice Note, *Drugs, Sex, and Commissioned Officers: Recent Developments Pertaining to Article 133, UCMJ*, ARMY LAW., Feb. 1989, at 62 (discusses *Guaglione*), and for merely loaning money to a subordinate. *United States v. Smith*, 16 M.J. 694 (A.F.C.M.R. 1983).

F. Article 133 is not unconstitutionally void for vagueness. *Parker v. Levy*, 417 U.S. 733 (1974).

G. Pleadings.

1. Referencing an unconstitutional statutory definition of child pornography in the pleadings and instructing the members using the unconstitutional statutory definition created instructional error in an Article 133 child pornography case. *United States v. Forney*, 67 M.J. 271 (C.A.A.F. 2009) (Effron, C.J., concurring in the result) (Erdmann, J., dissenting).

2. Failing to allege the act was dishonorable or conduct unbecoming an officer is not necessarily fatal. *United States v. Wolfson*, 36 C.M.R. 722 (A.B.R. 1966); *United States v. Wilson*, 14 M.J. 680 (A.F.C.M.R. 1982).

3. Allegations of "undue familiarity" and "excessive social contacts" with married female service members were legally insufficient. *United States v. Kroop*, 38 M.J. 470 (C.M.A. 1993). *But cf. United States v. Boyett*, 42 M.J. 150 (C.A.A.F. 1995) (affirming conviction for unprofessional close personal relationship, including sexual intercourse, with enlisted person not under accused's supervision); *United States v. Rogers*, 54 M.J. 244 (C.A.A.F. 2000) (specification that LTC had "unprofessional relationship of undue familiarity" with LT in his command did state an offense).

4. LIOs.

a) Where the underlying acts of misconduct are the same, a service disorder or discredit under Article 134 is a lesser included offense of conduct unbecoming an officer under Article 133. *United States v. Cherukuri*, 53 M.J. 68 (C.A.A.F. 2000), *aff'd by* 54 M.J. 448 (C.A.A.F. 2001); *see also United States v. Conliffe*, 67 M.J. 127 (C.A.A.F. 2009); *United States v. Harwood*, 46 M.J. 26 (C.A.A.F. 1997); *United States v. Rodriguez*, 18 M.J. 363, 368-369 n. 4 (C.M.A. 1984).

b) Where the underlying act of misconduct is the same, larceny under Article 121 is a lesser included offense of conduct unbecoming an officer under Article 133. *United States v. Frelix-Vann*, 55 M.J. 329 (C.A.A.F. 2001) (Army captain pled guilty to one specification of conduct unbecoming and one specification of larceny for same underlying misconduct), *aff'd by* 56 M.J. 458 (C.A.A.F. 2002). *See also United States v. Timberlake*, 18 M.J. 371 (C.M.A. 1984) (violation of punitive article, such as art. 123, forgery, is lesser included offense of conduct unbecoming when same underlying misconduct at issue).

5. Multiplicity. While any misconduct may be charged as an article 133 offense—even when chargeable as a violation of one of the other punitive articles—findings for both an article 133 offense and the same underlying offense may not stand. *United States v.*

Timberlake, 18 M.J. 371 (C.M.A. 1984). Where service court found conduct unbecoming charge and obstructing justice charge multiplicious, no error in allowing the government to elect which finding to retain. *United States v. Palagar*, 56 M.J. 294 (C.A.A.F. 2002).

    6. Unreasonable Multiplication of Charges (UMC). Four specifications of communicating sexually suggestive and sexually explicit language to a minor via e-mail, in violation of Art. 133, did not represent UMC, because they did not reflect the same act or transaction. Each specification identified a discrete and unique communication. *United States v. Mazer*, 58 M.J. 691 (N-M. Ct. Crim. App. 2003), *set aside on other grounds, remanded by* 60 M.J. 344 (C.A.A.F. 2004).

  H. Punishment.

    1. Maximum punishment is a dismissal, forfeiture of all pay and allowances, and confinement for a period not in excess of that authorized for the most analogous offense for which a punishment is prescribed by the MCM, or, if none is prescribed, for one year. MCM, pt. IV, ¶ 59e.

    2. The maximum sentence that may be adjudged for a dupliciously pled specification under Article 133 will be that imposable for "the most analogous offense" with the greatest maximum punishment. *United States v. Hart*, 32 M.J. 101 (C.M.A. 1991).

II. THE GENERAL ARTICLE. UCMJ ART. 134.

  A. Three Bases of Criminal Liability.

    1. Conduct Prejudicial to Good Order and Discipline.

    2. Conduct of a Nature to Bring Discredit upon the Armed Forces.

    3. Conduct Constituting a Non-capital Crime.

  B. Offenses Listed in MCM, pt. IV, ¶¶ 61-113.

    1. Require proof of prejudice to good order and discipline *or* tendency to bring discredit upon the armed forces.

    2. This list is nonexhaustive. Other novel offenses may be charged, provided the alleged misconduct satisfies the standard in one of the three clauses of Article 134 and the misconduct cannot be prosecuted under another article of the UCMJ.

  C. Conduct Prejudicial to Good Order and Discipline (Clause 1).

    1. Not every irregular, mischievous or improper act is a court-martial offense. MCM, pt. IV, ¶ 60c(2)(a). *United States v. Sadinsky*, 34 C.M.R. 343 (C.M.A. 1964); *United States v. Rowe*, No. 32852, 1999 CCA LEXIS 125 (A.F. Ct. Crim. App. Apr. 7, 1999)(unpublished) (allegation of knowing and willful harassment by repeated contact causing substantial emotional stress and reasonable fear of bodily harm was legally sufficient).

    2. Conduct must be *directly* and *palpably* prejudicial to good order and discipline. *United States v. Sadinsky*, 34 C.M.R. 343 (C.M.A. 1964); *see United States v. Davis*, 26 M.J. 445 (C.M.A. 1988) (cross dressing); *United States v. Woods*, 28 M.J. 318 (C.M.A. 1989) (unprotected sexual intercourse where the accused has the HIV virus).

    3. A breach of custom may result in a violation of clause one of Article 134. MCM, pt. IV, ¶ 60c(2)(b). *United States v. Smart*, 12 C.M.R. 826 (A.F.B.R. 1953). It must satisfy the following requirements: (1) long established practice; (2) common usage attaining the

force of law; (3) not contrary to military law; and (4) ceases when observance has been abandoned.

D. Conduct of a Nature to Bring Discredit upon the Armed Forces (Clause Two).

1. Conduct must have the tendency to bring the service into disrepute or tend to lower it in public esteem. MCM, pt. IV, ¶ 60c(3); *United States v. Sullivan*, 42 M.J. 360 (C.A.A.F. 1995) (any reasonable officer would have known that asking strangers of the opposite sex intimate questions about their sexual activities, while using a false name and a fictional publishing company as a cover, was service discrediting conduct); *United States v. Sanchez*, 29 C.M.R. 32 (C.M.A. 1960) (sex act with chicken; "[W]hen an accused performs detestable and degenerate acts which clearly evince a wanton disregard for the moral standards generally and properly accepted by society, he heaps discredit on the . . . Government he represents.").

2. Conduct must generally be "open and notorious" to be service discrediting. It is not necessary to prove that a third person actually observed the act, but only that it was reasonably likely that a third person would observe it. *United States v. Izquierdo*, 51 M.J. 421 (C.A.A.F. 1999) (sexual intercourse in barracks room while two roommates also in room, even though accused hung sheet that substantially blocked roommates' side of room); *United States v. Sims*, 57 M.J. 419 (2002) (not open and notorious when appellant was in his unlocked private dorm room, with a greater expectation of privacy than a shared room, and neither party had disrobed); *United States v. Carr*, 28 M.J. 661 (N.M.C.M.R. 1989) (intercourse on a public beach at night not likely to be seen).

3. Conduct will be service discrediting where civilians are aware of both the military status and the discrediting behavior. *United States v. Green*, 39 M.J. 606 (A.C.M.R. 1994); *see United States v. Kirksey*, 20 C.M.R. 272 (C.M.A. 1955).

4. Violations of state or foreign law is not *per se* service discrediting. *United States v. Sadler*, 29 M.J. 370 (C.M.A. 1990).

E. Conduct Punishable Under First Two Theories. Prosecutors often charge and courts often affirm various offenses invoking both the language of Clause 1 and of Clause 2. When using the list below, be sure to distinguish whether the specific court treated the conduct as both PGO&D and SD, or exclusively as one or the other.

1. Historically, other offenses have also been prosecuted. *United States v. Light*, 36 C.M.R. 579 (A.B.R. 1965) (borrowing money from subordinates); *United States v. Baur*, 10 M.J. 789 (A.F.C.M.R. 1981) (obstruction of justice); *United States v. Pechefsky*, 13 M.J. 814 (A.F.C.M.R. 1982) (forging credit recommendations).

2. These listings are not exhaustive and other novel offenses may be charged under the first two theories of the article, providing the offenses are not prosecutable elsewhere in the UCMJ. *United States v. Wright*, 5 M.J. 106 (C.M.A. 1978).

a) *United States v. Erickson*, 61 M.J. 230 (C.A.A.F. 2005) (inhalation "huffing" nitrous oxide); *United States v. Glover*, 50 M.J. 476 (C.A.A.F. 1999) (inhaling Dust-Off, a cleaning product).

b) *United States v. Choate*, 32 M.J. 423 (C.M.A. 1991) ("mooning," under some circumstances, can be PGO&D).

c) *United States v. Johnson*, 4 M.J. 770 (A.C.M.R. 1978) (peeping tom).

d) *United States v. Kopp*, 9 M.J. 564 (A.F.C.M.R. 1980) (wrongfully setting off a false alarm in a residential building at Air Force base).

e) *United States v. Woods*, 28 M.J. 318 (C.M.A. 1989) (unprotected sexual intercourse where the accused has the AIDS virus); *see also United States v. Morris*, 30 M.J. 1221 (A.C.M.R. 1990).

f) *United States v. Davis*, 26 M.J. 445 (C.M.A. 1988) (on-post cross-dressing); *United States v. Guerrero*, 33 M.J. 295 (C.M.A. 1991), *cert. denied*, 502 U.S. 1096 (1992) (off-post cross-dressing).

g) *United States v. King*, 34 M.J. 95 (C.M.A. 1992); *United States v. Perez*, 33 M.J. 1050 (A.C.M.R. 1991) (adultery).

h) *United States v. Sullivan*, 42 M.J. 360 (C.A.A.F. 1995) (non-consensual, obscene phone calls).

i) *United States v. Warnock*, 34 M.J. 567 (A.C.M.R. 1991) (photographing nude female officer with her consent and showing negatives to enlisted paramour NOT prejudicial to good order and discipline under the circumstances).

j) *United States v. Henderson*, 32 M.J. 941 (N.M.C.M.R. 1991), *aff'd*, 34 M.J. 174 (C.M.A. 1992) (sexually exploiting recruits).

k) *United States v. Stone*, 40 M.J. 420 (C.M.A. 1994) (falsely claiming during a speech to high school students to have been a special forces leader in Iraq).

l) *United States v. Vaughan*, 58 M.J. 29 (C.A.A.F. 2003) (child neglect where soldier-mom left infant at home, unattended for several hours).

m) *United States v. Saunders*, 59 M.J. 1 (C.A.A.F. 2003) (harassment/stalking). Be cognizant of preemption concerns (Art. 120a, Stalking).

n) *United States v. Farence*, 57 M.J. 674 (C.G. Ct. Crim. App. 2002), *pet. denied*, 58 M.J. 203 (2003) (displaying images depicting bestiality to subordinates while on duty).

o) Child Pornography. See Ch. 3, Part II, Para. II.G.

(1) *United States v. Irvin*, 60 M.J. 23 (C.A.A.F. 2004) (child pornography).

(2) *United States v. Mason*, 60 M.J. 15 (C.A.A.F. 2004) (virtual, as well as actual, child pornography).

(3) *United States v. Brisbane*, 63 M.J. 106 (C.A.A.F. 2006) (knowing possession of images depicting sexually explicit conduct by minors, whether actual or virtual).

3. Speech Offenses.

a) *Parker v. Levy,* 417 U.S. 733 (1974) (upholding application of Article 134 to "a commissioned officer publicly urging enlisted personnel to refuse to obey orders which might send them into combat," and finding that such conduct "was unprotected under the most expansive notions of the First Amendment.")

(1) "While the members of the military are not excluded from the protection granted by the First Amendment, the different character of the military community and of the military mission requires a different application of those protections." *Id.* at 758.

(2) "The fundamental necessity for obedience, and the consequent necessity for imposition of discipline, may render permissible within the military that which would be constitutionally impermissible outside it." *Id.* at 758.

b) *United States v. Priest,* 45 C.M.R. 338 (C.M.A. 1972) (upholding the accused's conviction under Article 134 for making disloyal statements, including statements protesting U.S. involvement in Vietnam, in a publications where copies were made available to servicemembers at the Navy Exchange, the Washington Navy Yard, and at a Pentagon newsstand).

(1) "[T]he right of free speech in the armed services is not unlimited and must be brought into balance with the paramount consideration of providing an effective fighting force for the defense of our Country." *Id.* at 344.

(2) "Our inquiry, therefore, is whether the gravity of the effect of accused's publications on good order and discipline in the armed forces, discounted by the improbability of their effectiveness on the audience he sought to reach, justifies his conviction." *Id.* at 344–45.

c) *United States v. Wilcox,* 66 M.J. 442 (C.A.A.F. 2008). In determining whether speech can be punished under Article 134 as prejudicial to good order and discipline, or service-discrediting, a balance must be struck "between the essential needs of the armed forces and the right to speak out as a free American." Before reaching this balancing test, though, there are two threshold determinations: (1) whether the speech is otherwise protected under the First Amendment, and (2) whether the government proved the elements of the Article 134 offense. In addressing the first prong, certain types of speech lack protection under the First Amendment. They include fighting words, dangerous speech, and obscenity. In the military, dangerous speech is that which "interferes with or prevents the orderly accomplishment of the mission or presents a clear danger to loyalty, discipline, mission, or morale of the troops." *See United States v. Brown,* 45 M.J. 389, 395 (C.A.A.F. 1996). In addressing the second prong, the CAAF stated that in order to prove the element of an Article 134 offense involving speech where the question is whether the conduct is prejudicial to good order and discipline, the government must prove that there is a "direct and palpable connection between speech and the military mission." *See Priest, supra,* at 343. In order to prove that the conduct is service-discrediting, there must be "a direct and palpable connection between [the] speech and the military mission or military environment." In *Wilcox*, the court held that the accused's statements on the Internet were not unprotected speech. The postings were not dangerous speech because the language did not "interfere[ ] with or prevent[ ] the orderly accomplishment of the mission or present[ ] a clear danger to loyalty, discipline, mission, or morale of the troops." Furthermore, the court concluded that the language did not constitute fighting words and was not obscene. As the language was protected speech, the court next addressed the connection between the speech and the military. The court found that the connection between the accused's statements and the military was so "tenuous and speculative as to be legally insufficient to support the conclusion" that his conduct was either prejudicial to good order and discipline or service discrediting. Concluding that the speech is protected and that the government did not prove the elements of an Article 134 charge, the court did not conduct the balancing test between the First Amendment protections and the needs of the military.

    d) *United States v. Blair,* 67 M.J. 566 (C.G. Ct. Crim. App. 2009). Accused, while in civilian clothes, posted Ku Klux Klan recruiting flyers in an airport bathroom. Plea to "wrongfully recruit[ing] for, solicit[ing] membership in, and promot[ing] the activities of the Ku Klux Klan," "while publicly displaying an affiliation with the Armed Services," which conduct was of a nature to bring discredit to the Armed Forces, was provident. The court concluded that "publicly displaying an affiliation with the Armed Services" includes conduct that takes place in an area available to the public, whether or not another person is actually present. In this case, there was a sufficient factual basis for his plea because there was the possibility that a member of the public who knew him to be in the Coast Guard could have readily seen him posting the flyers. Next, the court applied the *United States v. Wilcox,* 66 M.J. 442 (C.A.A.F. 2008), and found that the conviction was warranted despite First Amendment concerns. Considering matters presented at sentencing, including the airport director's testimony that it "made [him] sick" when he found out that the source of the flyers was an active duty Coast Guardsman, the CGCCA found that "the potential effects, both stated and inherent, of [the accused's] conduct on the Coast Guard's reputation outweigh [his] interest in his right to speak out while on government business at the airport."

F. Crimes and Offenses Not Capital (Clause Three).

    1. Specific Federal Statute.

        a) Example: Threat Against the President Under 18 U.S.C. § 871. *United States v. Ogren,* 54 M.J. 481 (C.A.A.F. 2001) (threat made while in pretrial confinement for unrelated charges: " . . . I'm going to find Clinton and blow his f_____ brains out").

        b) The offense must occur in a place where the law in question applies. MCM, pt. IV, ¶ 60c(4)(c)(i); *see United States v. Williams,* 17 M.J. 207 (C.M.A. 1984); *United States v. Clark,* 41 C.M.R. 82 (C.M.A. 1969); *United States v. Kolly,* 48 M.J. 795 (N-M. Ct. Crim. App. 1998) (federal child porn statute applied extraterritorially to offenses servicemember committed in Japan).

        c) Elements of the federal statute are controlling. *United States v. Ridgeway,* 13 M.J. 742 (A.C.M.R. 1982).

        d) A servicemember can be convicted of an attempt to commit a federal offense under clause three, even if the underlying federal statute has no attempt provision. *United States v. Craig,* 19 M.J. 166 (C.M.A. 1985).

        e) A specification containing allegations of fact insufficient to establish a violation of a designated federal statute may nonetheless be sufficient to constitute a violation of either clause one or two, Article 134. *United States v. Mayo,* 12 M.J. 286 (C.M.A. 1982); *United States v. Wagner,* 52 M.J. 634 (N-M. Ct. Crim.

App. 1999); *see also United States v. Robbins*, 48 M.J. 745 (A.F. Ct. Crim. App. 1998), *modified in part*, 52 M.J. 159 (1999)(Sullivan, J. dissenting); *United States v. Gould*, 13 M.J. 734 (A.C.M.R. 1982).

f) Examples.

(1) Soliciting a minor (or not). *United States v. Brooks,* 60 M.J. 495 (C.A.A.F. 2005). Appellant was convicted of violating 18 U.S.C. § 2422(b) under Article 134, Clause 3, for attempting to commit the offense of carnal knowledge with a victim under the age of twelve, and wrongfully soliciting an individual under the age of eighteen to engage in a criminal sexual act. Appellant never communicated directly with a minor or a person he believed was a minor. A conviction under Sec. 2422(b) does not require direct inducement of a minor, nor does it require an actual minor. The relevant intent is the intent to persuade or to attempt to persuade, not the intent to commit the actual sexual act. In this case appellant acted with the intent to induce a minor to engage in unlawful sexual activity, and then completed the attempt with actions that strongly corroborated the required culpability. *See also United States v. Amador,* 61 M.J. 619 (A.F. Ct. Crim. App. 2005).

(2) Storing stolen explosives. *United States v. Disney*, 62 M.J. 46 (C.A.A.F. 2005). Appellant stole ordnance from several military training events. Appellant was convicted of one specification of larceny of military property under Article 121 and one specification of storing stolen explosives in violation of 18 U.S.C. § 842 (h) under clause 3 of Article 134.

2. State Law: Federal Assimilative Crimes Act (FACA). 18 U.S.C. §13.

a) Adopts un-preempted state offenses as the local federal law of application.

b) The purpose of FACA is to fill the gaps left by the patchwork of federal statutes. *United States v. Robbins*, 52 M.J. 159 (C.A.A.F. 1999); *United States v. Picotte*, 30 C.M.R. 196 (C.M.A. 1961).

c) "Offenses" may include any non-regulatory statutory prohibition that provides for some form of punishment if violated. *United States v. White*, 39 M.J. 796 (N.M.C.M.R. 1994) (assimilating provisions of state motor vehicle code denominated as "violations" rather than "crimes", but which provide for penal sanctions). *But cf. United States v. Clinkenbeard*, 44 M.J. 577 (A.F. Ct. Crim. App. 1996) (reaching contrary result).

d) Applies state law whether enacted before or after passage of FACA. *United States v. Rowe*, 32 C.M.R. 302 (C.M.A. 1962).

e) State law may not be assimilated if the act or omission is punishable by any enactment of Congress. *Lewis v. United States*, 523 U.S. 155, 118 S.Ct. 1135 (1998). *Lewis* establishes a two-part test (This test should be applied in conjunction with the related, but similar Article 134 preemption analysis discussed below):

(1) Is the accused's "act or omission…made punishable by any enactment of Congress?" If not, then assimilate. If so, ask:

(2) Do the relevant federal statutes preclude application of the state law? Specifically, would the application of the state law interfere with the achievement of a federal policy, effectively rewrite an offense definition that Congress carefully considered, or run counter to Congressional intent to occupy the entire field under consideration?

f) The FACA may not be used to extend or narrow the scope of existing federal criminal law. *Lewis v. United States*, 523 U.S. 155, 118 S.Ct. 1135 (1998); *United States v. Perkins*, 6 M.J. 602 (A.C.M.R. 1978); see also *United States v. Robbins*, 52 M.J. 159 (1999).

g) Jurisdiction.

(1) The government must establish exclusive or concurrent federal jurisdiction before FACA is applicable. *See United States v. Dallman*, 34 M.J. 274 (C.M.A. 1992), *aff'd*, 37 M.J. 213 (C.M.A. 1993).

(2) A guilty plea may be sufficient to establish jurisdiction required by the Act. *United States v. Kline*, 21 M.J. 366 (C.M.A. 1986); *United States v. Jones*, 34 M.J. 270 (C.M.A. 1992).

G. Child Pornography.

1. There is no enumerated crime addressing child pornography in the UCMJ and the President has not listed a child pornography offense under Article 134. Crimes in the military that involve child pornography must be charged under a general article (Article 133 or Article 134). There are two ways to charge child pornography crimes using Article 134:

a) Charge the criminal conduct using Article 134, clauses 1 and 2.

b) Charge a violation of an applicable federal statute using Article 134, clause 3.

2. Clauses 1 and 2, Article 134.

a) "It is a mystery to me why, after this [c]ourt's ten-year history of invalidating convictions for child pornography offenses under clause 3, and of upholding convictions for such offenses under clause 2, we continue to see cases charged under clause 3." *United States v. Medina*, 66 M.J. 21, 29 n.1 (C.A.A.F. 2008) (Stucky, J., dissenting).

b) Possession of child pornography may be charged as a Clause 1 or Clause 2 offense. *United States v. Irvin*, 60 M.J. 23 (C.A.A.F. 2004).

c) Virtual Child Pornography under Clauses 1 and 2.

(1) *United States v. Mason*, 60 M.J. 15 (C.A.A.F. 2004) ("The receipt or possession of "virtual" child pornography can, like "actual" child pornography, be service-discrediting or prejudicial to good order and discipline.").

(2) *United States v. Brisbane*, 63 M.J. 106 (C.A.A.F. 2006) ("The knowing possession of images depicting sexually explicit conduct by minors, whether actual or virtual, when determined to be service-discrediting conduct or conduct prejudicial to good order and discipline, is an offense under Article 134").

d) Referencing an unconstitutional statutory definition of child pornography in the pleadings and instructing the members using the unconstitutional statutory definition created instructional error in an Article 133 child pornography case. *United States v. Forney,* 67 M.J. 271 (C.A.A.F. 2009) (Effron, C.J., concurring in the result) (Erdmann, J., dissenting). This analysis should also apply if the offense was charged under clauses 1 and 2 of Article 134.

e) The nature of the images is not dispositive as to whether receiving such images is PGO&D or SD. *United States v. O'Connor,* 58 M.J. 450 (C.A.A.F. 2003) (providence inquiry failed to establish whether accused pled guilty to possession of virtual or actual child pornography; no LIO of clause 1 or clause 2 because no discussion of PGO&D or SD).

f) Although *United States v. Medina,* 66 M.J. 21 (C.A.A.F. 2008) provides the current state of the law regarding the relationship between the three clauses of Article 134, the following cases were affirmed under clause 2 of Article 134:

> (1) *United States v. Sapp,* 53 M.J. 90 (C.A.A.F. 2000) (after finding that the military judge failed to adequately advise the accused of the elements of federal offense of possession of child pornography, under 18 U.S.C. § 2252(a)(4)(A), which he was charged with violating under clause 3 of Article 134, the Air Force court did not err by affirming the lesser included offense of service-discrediting conduct, under clause 2 of Article 134.

> (2) *United States v. Augustine,* 53 M.J. 95 (C.A.A.F. 2000) (affirming under clause 2 rather than clause 3 of Article 134).

> (3) *United States v. Hays,* 62 M.J. 158 (C.A.A.F. 2005) (holding the plea inquiry did not implicate the appellant's First Amendment rights, thus placing the analysis under *Sapp* and *Augustine*; although the MJ did not discuss with appellant whether his conduct was service discrediting or prejudicial to good order and discipline, there is no doubt that appellant was aware of the impact of his conduct on the image of the armed forces; affirmed under Clause 2).

3. Clause 3, Article 134.

a) *See generally* MCM, pt. IV, ¶ 60c(4).

b) Key federal statutes. The following federal statutes are available for charging various conduct involving the production, possession, transportation, and distribution of child pornography:

> (1) 18 U.S.C. § 2251, Sexual Exploitation of Children. Among other prohibitions, this provision covers the use of minors in the production of child pornography.

> (2) 18 U.S.C. § 2252, Certain Activities Relating to Material Involving the Sexual Exploitation of Minors. This child pornography provision was the predecessor to the computer-specific 18 U.S.C. § 2252A.

> (3) 18 U.S.C. § 2252A, Certain Activities Relating to Material Constituting or Containing Child Pornography. This is the federal provision that most comprehensively covers the use of computers and the Internet to possess, transport, and distribute child pornography.

(4) Statutory Definitions. 18 U.S.C. § 2256 contains the applicable definitions for child pornography offenses.

c) Recent Amendments.

(1) The Effective Child Pornography Prosecution Act of 2007, Pub. L. No. 110-358 (Oct. 8, 2008) (adds "using any means or facility of interstate or foreign commerce" to several sections in 18 USC 2251, 2251A, 2252, and 2252A).

(2) The Enhancing the Effective Prosecution of Child Pornography Act of 2007, Pub. L. No. 110-358 (Oct. 8, 2008) (adds to 18 USC 2252(a)(4) and 2252A(a)(5) the following language after "possesses": "or knowingly accesses with intent to view").

(3) The Providing Resources, Officer, and Technology to Eradicate Cyber Threats to Our Children Act of 2008 (or The PROTECT Our Children Act of 2008), Pub. L. No. 110-401 (Oct. 13, 2008) (Sec 301 prohibits broadcast of live images of child abuse, Sec. 302 amends the definition of "visual image" under 18 USC 2256(5) by inserting "and data which is capable of conversion into a visual image that has been transmitted by any means, whether or not stored in a permanent format", Sec. 304 prohibits the adaptation or modification of an image of an identifiable minor to produce child pornography).

d) Pleading Child Pornography Offenses Using Clause 3.

(1) *See* MCM, pt. IV, ¶ 60c(6).

(2) *See infra* Chapter 7, Appendix B.

e) Actual versus Virtual Children.

(1) Using the CPPA and Clause 3, Article 134.

(a) In *Ashcroft v. Free Speech Coalition*, 535 U.S. 234 (2002), the U.S. Supreme Court held that specific language within the definition of child pornography in the 1996 Child Pornography Prevention Act (CPPA) was unconstitutional. Specifically, the definition impermissibly prohibited "virtual" child pornography in contravention of the First Amendment. The "virtual image" language was contained in § 2256(8)(B) and § 2256(8)(D).

(b) Following *Ashcroft*, the CAAF made the "actual" character of visual depictions of child pornography a factual predicate for guilty pleas under the CPPA. *United States v. O'Connor*, 58 M.J. 450 (C.A.A.F. 2003).

(c) Either the "appears to be" language or "conveys the impression" language found in the CPPA's unconstitutional definition of child pornography can trigger the requirement to prove an "actual" child was used to make an image of child pornography. *United States v. Wolford*, 62 M.J. 418 (C.A.A.F. 2006).

(2) Using Clauses 1 and 2, Article 134. Child pornography, whether virtual or actual, can be prejudicial to good order and discipline and service-discrediting. *See United States v. Mason*, 60 M.J. 15 (C.A.A.F. 2004); *United States v. Brisbane*, 63 M.J. 106 (C.A.A.F. 2006).

f) Issues.

    (1) Constitutionality of the Federal statute.

        (a) In *Ashcroft v. Free Speech Coalition*, 535 U.S. 234 (2002), the U.S. Supreme Court held that specific language within the definition of child pornography in the 1996 Child Pornography Prevention Act (CPPA) was unconstitutional. Specifically, the definition impermissibly prohibited "virtual" child pornography in contravention of the First Amendment. The "virtual image" language was contained in § 2256(8)(B) and § 2256(8)(D).

        (b) The Prosecutorial Remedies and Other Tools to end the Exploitation of Children Today Act of 2003, Pub. L. No. 108-21, 117 Stat. 650 (Apr. 30, 2003), which amended 18 U.S.C. § 2252A to include a provision that prohibits the solicitation and pandering of child pornography. *United States v. Williams*, 128 S. Ct. 1830, 170 L. Ed. 2d 650 (2008) (holding the Act to be neither impermissibly vague nor overbroad and holding that offers to provide or requests to obtain child pornography are categorically excluded from the First Amendment).

        (c) The Protection of Children Against Sexual Exploitation Act, 18 U.S.C. § 2252. Constitutional because its prohibition against knowing transport, shipment, receipt, distribution, or reproduction of a visual depiction of a minor engaged in sexually explicit conduct requires that the accused know that the performer in the depiction was a minor, thereby satisfying First Amendment concerns. *United States v. X-Citement Video*, 115 S.Ct. 464 (1994); *United States v. Maxwell*, 42 M.J. 568 (A.F. Ct. Crim. App. 1995), *reversed in part United States v. Maxwell*, 45 M.J. 406 (C.A.A.F. 1996) (transmission of visual images electronically through the use of an on-line computer service is "transport in interstate or foreign commerce' in light of legislative intent to prevent the transport of obscene material in interstate commerce regardless of the means used to effect that end and statute is constitutional in light of *United States v. X-Citement Video*, 115 S.Ct. 464 (1994) (statute contains a scienter requirement because the word "knowingly" must be read as applying to the words "use of a minor").

    (2) Extraterritoriality. Practitioners in overseas and deployed locations should ensure that the federal statute is applicable to the conduct at issue.

(a) *United States v. Martinelli*, 62 M.J. 52 (C.A.A.F. 2005). Appellant pled guilty, in relevant part, to sending, receiving, reproducing, and possessing child pornography under Article 134, Clause 3, in violation of the CPPA. The conduct was charged using 18 U.S.C. §2252A(a)(1–3). Appellant's misconduct took place in Germany, both at an off-post internet café, and in his on-post barracks room. HELD: 1) The CPPA is not extraterritorial as there is no evidence of specific congressional intent to extend its coverage; 2) domestic application is possible under a "continuing offense" theory for *sending* material that flowed through servers in the United States; 3) appellant's plea to specification 1 under clause 3 of Article 134 is improvident under *O'Connor* because of the focus on the unconstitutional definition of child pornography and the lack of focus on "actual" vs. "virtual" images; and 4) there was no reference to appellant's conduct as service discrediting or prejudicial to good order and discipline. Strong dissents from both C.J. Gierke and J. Crawford.

(b) *United States v. Reeves*, 62 M.J. 88 (C.A.A.F. 2005). The accused was stationed in Hanau, Germany and used the on-post library computer to receive and print out images of child pornography that had been sent over the Internet. While still in Germany, he also used a videocamera to record sexually explicit imagery of two German girls from about 200 feet away. His conduct was charged using 18 U.S.C. §§ 2251 and 2252A(a)(1–3). Citing *Martinelli*, the court held none of the following acts were continuing offenses with conduct that occurred in the United States, and as such, there could be no domestic application of the CPPA: (1) possession of child pornography at an on-post public library, land used by and under the control of the federal government; (2) receiving child pornography that had been transmitted through the internet; and (3) using minors to engage in sexually explicit conduct for the purpose of producing a visual depiction of such conduct.

(3) Definitions. *United States v. Kuemmerle*, 67 M.J. 141 (C.A.A.F. 2009). The CPPA does not define "distribute." The court looked to three sources for a definition of the term: (1) the plain meaning, (2) the manner Article III courts have interpreted the term, and (3) the guidance that the UCMJ provides through parallel provisions. *See also United States v. Craig*, 67 M.J. 742 (N-M. Ct. Crim. App. 2009) (military judge read part of the definition of "distribute" from Article 112a, stating, "Distribute means to deliver to the possession of another.") .

(4) Method of Distribution.

(a) Yahoo! Briefcase. *United States v. Navrestad*, 66 M.J. 262 (C.A.A.F. 2008). Sending a hyperlink to a Yahoo! Briefcase during an internet chat session, where the

Briefcase contained images of child pornography, does not constitute either distribution of child pornography as defined in the CPPA or possession of child pornography as affirmed by the ACCA under Clauses 1 and 2, where the link itself only provides a roadmap to the child pornography and where the accused did not download or print any of the images to his own computer. The accused was initially charged under Clause 3 of Article 134, but Clause 1 and 2 language was added to both specifications prior to arraignment. Convictions for both possession under Clauses 1 and 2, and distribution under the CPPA were set aside. Note: Yahoo! discontinued its Briefcase service on 30 March 2009.

(b) KaZaA. *United States v. Ober,* 66 M.J. 393 (C.A.A.F. 2008). Using KaZaA to search for and download child pornography from host users over the Internet constituted transportation of child pornography in interstate commerce for purposes of 18 U.S.C. § 2252A(a)(1) because "a user's download caused an upload on the host user's computer."

(c) Peer-to-Peer Software in General. *United States v. Christy,* 65 M.J. 657 (A. Ct. Crim. App. 2007). The accused downloaded peer-to-peer software and set up a "shared files" folder. As part of his licensing agreement with the software company, he agreed to share all files in that folder, i.e., his child pornography, with other users. While the term "distribution" is not defined in the statute, definitions found in federal case law are broad enough to cover the act of posting images in a shared file folder and agreeing to allow others to download from the folder. Additionally, the accused's conduct was "knowing" under the CPPA, as he admitted during his providence inquiry that he knew 1) that he was posting his child pornography images in a shared file folder, and 2) that anyone with the same peer-to-peer software both had his permission and the general ability to download the files he posted.

(5) Lesser included offenses: Clause 1 and Clause 2. The use of Clause 1 and Clause 2 as a LIO to a Clause 3 offense has recently been limited by the CAAF holding in *United States v. Medina,* 66 M.J. 21 (C.A.A.F. 2008). The court holds that in order for either Clause 1 or Clause 2 to be considered as a LIO to a Clause 3 offense, the Clause 3 specification should contain Clause 1 or Clause 2 language. If Clause 1 or Clause 2 language is absent from a Clause 3 offense, the opinion may yet allow for Clause 1 or Clause 2 to operate as a LIO provided the military judge clearly explains Clause 1 and Clause 2 and how they can operate as a LIO to the accused. Prudence, however, dictates that counsel plead the Clause 1 and/or Clause 2 language to avoid the issue at trial.

(6) Evidence to determine age of models. *United States v. Russell,* 47 M.J. 412 (C.A.A.F. 1998) (accused admitted that he guessed the models

were "13 or older"; a pediatrician testified that the females shown in the exhibits were not more than 15.5 years old; and members were able to look at the pictures and use their common sense and experience to conclude that the girls were under age 18); *United States v. Maxwell*, 45 M.J. 406 (C.A.A.F. 1996) (government was only required to prove that accused believed the images depicted minors to support conviction for knowingly transporting or receiving child pornography in interstate commerce (18 U.S.C. § 2252); government was not required to prove that accused had basis for actual knowledge of the subjects' ages). *United States v. Cendejas*, 62 M.J. 334 (C.A.A.F. 2006) (factfinder can make the determination that pornographic images are actual children based upon a review of the images alone).

g) Other Applications.

(1) *United States v. Kuemmerle*, 67 M.J. 141 (C.A.A.F. 2009). As the CPPA does not expressly define "distribute," the court looked to three sources for a definition of the term: (1) the plain meaning, (2) the manner Article III courts have interpreted the term, and (3) the guidance that the UCMJ provides through parallel provisions. Considering these sources, under the CPPA, distribution of child pornography through the Internet consists of two acts: (1) the posting of the image, where the image left the possession of the original user, and (2) the delivery of the image, where another user accessed and viewed the image. Here, the accused posted the image to his Yahoo! profile prior to his entry on active duty. The court reasoned that the profile serves as a "'public bulletin board' such that all Internet users can access information posted by the profile's owner." Although this was done prior to entering active duty, he accessed the account while on active duty and could have removed the image. The offense of distribution occurred while he was on active duty when the ICE agent accessed and viewed the image that he had posted for others to view.

(2) *United States v. Craig*, 67 M.J. 742 (N-M. Ct. Crim. App. 2009). As 18 U.S.C. § 2252A does not define "distribute," the military judge read part of the definition of "distribute" from Article 112a, stating, "Distribute means to deliver to the possession of another." the plain meaning of the term "distribute" includes "the transfer of an item from the possession of one person into the possession of another." The military judge provided a correct statement of the law in defining "distribute."

(3) *United States v. Smith,* 61 M.J. 696 (N-M. Ct. Crim. App. 2005) (Appellant engaged in marketing adult entertainment for profit on the internet, posting hundreds of photos of females engaged in sexually explicit conduct, many of them minors. Among other offenses, appellant ultimately pled guilty to violating 18 U.S.C. § 2257, under Clause 3, Article 134 for managing a website containing these depictions without maintaining proper records of each performer as that section requires. HELD: Appellant's failure to determine the age and record the identity of the child performer bore a direct relationship to the Government's interest in preventing child pornography).

(4) "Lascivious exhibition" category of sexually explicit conduct prohibited by § 2251(a). *United States v. Roderick*, 62 M.J. 425 (C.A.A.F. 2006) (applying the "Dost" factors to determine "lascivious exhibition").

(5) In prosecuting a violation of 18 U.S.C. § 2252 (a)(2) by knowingly receiving sexually explicit depictions of minors that have been transported in interstate commerce, "knowingly" applies to the sexually explicit nature of the materials and the ages of the subjects. The Government does not have to prove that the accused knew that the sexually explicit depictions passed through interstate commerce. The interstate commerce element is merely jurisdictional. *United States v. Murray*, 52 M.J. 423 (C.A.A.F. 2000).

h) Multiplicity/UMC.

(1) *United States v. Purdy*, 67 M.J. 780 (N-M. Ct. Crim. App. 2009). The accused downloaded child pornography from the Internet onto his personal computer while stationed in Belgium. He then downloaded the images from the hard drive onto a compact disk and reformatted the hard drive, but retained the compact disk. He was charged with both receiving and possessing child pornography under Clause 3 of Art. 134. He pled guilty to both offenses under Clauses 1 and 2. In this case, his act of saving the images to the CD-ROM "was a clear exercise of dominion . . . separate and apart" from his receipt of the images at an earlier point in time. The conviction for both offenses was proper and the military judge did not commit plain error.

(2) *United States v. Craig*, 67 M.J. 742 (N-M. Ct. Crim. App. 2009). The accused used "LimeWire," a peer-to-peer file-sharing software program to search for and download child pornography. He downloaded the child pornography into a "share" folder on his hard drive. He kept some of the images in the "share" folder, copied some to compact disks, and deleted others. He pled guilty to both receipt and possession of child pornography under 18 U.S.C. § 2252A using Clause 3 of Art. 134. The court held that these two specifications were not facially duplicative and therefore military judge did not commit plain error in failing to dismiss these specifications as multiplicious. The charges of receipt and possession "address at least two criminal actions by the [accused] each of which occurred at a different time within the charged time period and involved separate media.

H. Limitations on the Use of Article 134, UCMJ.

1. The Preemption Doctrine. MCM, pt. IV, ¶ 60c(5)(a). (See also the discussion of FACA preemption above).

a) Article 134 cannot be used to prohibit conduct already prohibited by Congress in UCMJ arts. 78 & 80-132.

b) Under the test provided in *United States v. Wright*, 5 M.J. 106 (C.M.A. 1978), conduct is already prohibited if:

(1) Congress intended to limit prosecutions for certain conduct to offenses defined in specific articles of the UCMJ, **and**

(2) The offense sought to be charged is composed of a residuum of elements of an enumerated offense under the UCMJ.

c) Applications.

(1) Prosecution under Article 134, Clause 1 for inhalation ("huffing") nitrous oxide is not preempted by Article 112a. *United States v. Erickson*, 61 M.J. 230 (C.A.A.F. 2005).

(2) Federal Statutes: Prosecution of bank fraud under 18 U.S.C. § 1344 is not be preempted by Article 132. *United States v. Tenney*, 60 M.J. 838 (N-M. Ct. Crim. App. 2005); Prosecution under 18 U.S.C. § 842 (h) for possession of stolen explosives is not preempted. *United States v. Canatelli*, 5 M.J. 838 (A.C.M.R. 1978).

(3) State Statutes: State statute prohibiting wrongfully eluding a police officer is not preempted. *United States v. Kline*, 21 M..J. 366 (C.M.A. 1986); State auto burglary statute is not preempted. *United States v. Sellars*, 5 M.J. 814 (A.C.M.R. 1978); State statute prohibiting hunting at night is not preempted. *United States v. Fishel*, 12 M.J. 602 (A.C.M.R. 1981); State statute prohibiting the unlawful termination of another's pregnancy is not preempted by Articles 118 and 119. *United States v. Robbins*, 52 M.J. 159 (C.A.A.F. 1999); State child abuse statute is not preempted *per se*; however, evidence establishes no more than assault under article 128. *United States v. Irvin*, 21 M.J. 184 (C.M.A. 1985), *cert. denied*, 479 U.S. 852 (1986); *see also United States v. Wallace*, 49 M.J. 292 (C.A.A.F. 1998).

(4) Preempted Statutes: State statute prohibiting false reports of crimes is preempted. *United States v. Jones*, 5 M.J. 579 (A.C.M.R. 1978); Prosecution of cable television fraud using Hawaii statute is preempted by an applicable federal statute on cable television fraud, 47 U.S.C. § 553 (a) & (b). *United States v. Mitchell*, 36 M.J. 882 (N.M.C.M.R. 1993), *aff'd*, 40 M.J. 270 (C.M.A. 1994), *cert. denied* 513 U.S. 1041 (1994).

2. The Capital Crime Exception. MCM, pt. IV, ¶ 60c(5)(b).

a) Capital crimes are those crimes made punishable by death under the common law or by statute of the United States.

b) Capital crimes may not be tried under Article 134. Only non-capital offenses may be prosecuted under article 134. *United States v. French*, 27 C.M.R. 245 (C.M.A. 1959).

3. Crimes Punishable under Article 92. MCM, pt. IV, ¶ 60c(2)(b).

a) Violations of "customs of the service" that are now contained in regulations should be charged as violations of Article 92, if the regulation is punitive.

b) *United States v. Caballero*, 49 C.M.R. 594 (C.M.A. 1975) (setting aside a conviction under Art. 134 for possession of drug paraphernalia, holding that possession of drug paraphernalia is properly prosecuted under Art. 92, where an order or regulation proscribing such possession exists).

c) *United States v. Borunda*, 67 M.J. 607 (A.F. Ct. Crim. App. 2009). The AFCCA interpreted *Caballero* "to mean that when a lawful general order or regulation proscribing the possession of drug paraphernalia exists, an order which by definition is punitive," the offense must be charged under Art. 92(1), UCMJ, and not Art. 134. In the absence of a lawful general order or regulation, the Government is at liberty to charge the conduct under another theory of Article 92 or Article 134.

I. Pleading Considerations.

1. Under Clauses One and Two.

a) The form specification should be used if the alleged misconduct falls under any offense listed in MCM, pt. IV, paras. 61-113.

b) Generally, no specific allegation is required that the conduct at issue is a disorder or neglect. MCM, pt. IV, ¶ 60c(6)(a); *United States v. Williams*, 24 C.M.R. 135 (C.M.A. 1957).

c) However, when drafting novel specifications, it may be necessary to allege wrongfulness of the act if it would be otherwise innocent conduct. *United States v. Regan*, 11 M.J. 745 (A.C.M.R. 1981) (specification dismissed for failure to state an offense that alleged that the accused "threw butter on the ceiling in the dining facility of the 30th Engineer Battalion").

2. Clause Three.

a) Each element of the federal or assimilated statute must be alleged expressly or by necessary implication. MCM, pt. IV, ¶ 60c(6)(b).

b) The federal or assimilated state statute *should* be identified. MCM, pt. IV, ¶ 60c(6)(b).

c) After *United States v. Medina*, 66 M.J. 21 (C.A.A.F. 2008), it is prudent to add language to the Clause 3 specification alleging that the conduct was prejudicial to good order and discipline and/or service discrediting.

d) Sample specifications. *See* Chapter 7, Appendix B.

3. Applying *United States v. Foster*, 40 M.J. 140 (C.M.A. 1994), *United States v. Medina*, 66 M.J. 21 (C.A.A.F. 2008), and *United States v. Miller*, 67 M.J. 385 (C.A.A.F. 2009), practitioners should use extreme care when the Manual *for Courts-Martial* suggests that offenses under Article 134 are lesser included offenses of offenses arising under the enumerated articles of the UCMJ. *See* Chapter 7 for pleading considerations.

J. Punishment.

1. For the offenses listed in MCM, pt. IV, paras. 61-113, the specified punishments control. R.C.M. 1003(c)(1)(A).

2. For other offenses, the following rules apply:

   a) If the offense is either included in, or closely related to, an offense listed in paras. 61-113, then the penalty provided in the MCM for the listed offense applies. *United States v. Sellars*, 5 M.J. 814 (A.C.M.R. 1978) (state auto burglary statute was closely related to Article 130 housebreaking and should therefore be punished consistent with article 130 punishments); R.C.M. 1003(c)(1)(B)(i).

   b) If an unlisted offense is included in a listed crime and is closely related to another, or is equally related to two or more listed offenses, the lesser punishment of the related crimes shall apply. R.C.M. 1003(c)(1)(B)(i). This is the opposite rule from that of Article 133, where the greater punishment applies. *See* section XXII.D.2., *supra*.

   c) If the punishment for an unlisted offense cannot be determined by applying the above tests (a & b), which is usually the case, then the punishment is that provided by the civilian statute or authorized by the custom of the service. R.C.M. 1003(c)(1)(B)(ii).

      (1) The accused was charged with and knowingly receiving visual depictions of minors engaging in sexually explicit conduct under Clauses 1 and 2 of Article 134. The military judge did not err in referencing the analogous federal statute, 18 USC § 2252(a)(2) to determine the maximum punishment, "when every element of the federal crime, except the jurisdictional element, was included in the specification." *United States v. Leonard*, 64 M.J. 381 (C.A.A.F. 2007).

      (2) Prosecution under 18 U.S.C. § 842 (h), for possession of stolen explosives, is punished under penalties provided in the federal statute. *United States v. Canatelli*, 5 M.J. 838 (A.C.M.R. 1978).

      (3) Prosecution under 4 U.S.C. § 3, for wrongfully and dishonorably defiling the American flag, is punished under the penalties provided in the statute. *United States v. Cramer*, 24 C.M.R. 31 (C.M.A. 1957).

PART III: WARTIME-RELATED OFFENSES AND ESPIONAGE

I. **WARTIME-RELATED OFFENSES.**

   A. Offenses Available.

      1. Desertion. UCMJ art. 85.

      2. Assaulting or Willfully Disobeying Superior Commissioned Officer. UCMJ art. 90.

      3. Misbehavior Before the Enemy. UCMJ art. 99.

      4. Subordinate Compelling Surrender. UCMJ art. 100.

      5. Improper Use of a Countersign. UCMJ art. 101.

      6. Forcing A Safeguard. UCMJ art. 102.

      7. Captured or Abandoned Property. UCMJ art. 103.

8. Aiding the Enemy. UCMJ art. 104.

9. Misconduct as a Prisoner. UCMJ art. 105.

10. Spies. UCMJ art. 106.

11. Espionage. UCMJ art. 106a.

12. Misbehavior of a Sentinel or Lookout. UCMJ art. 113.

13. Malingering. UCMJ art. 115.

14. Straggling. UCMJ art. 134.

15. Offenses by a Sentinel. UCMJ art. 134.

16. Other Offenses.

    a) Failure to Obey Lawful General Regulation. UCMJ art. 92.

    b) Dereliction of Duty. UCMJ art. 92.

    c) Violation of Federal Statutes. UCMJ art. 134.

B. The "Triggers". Typically the offenses listed above can occur or become aggravated only when one of the two triggers below exist.

1. Time of War.

2. Before the Enemy.

C. Time Of War.

1. Definition. "Time of war" means a period of war declared by Congress or the factual determination by the President that the existence of hostilities warrants a finding that time of war exists. R.C.M. 103(19).

    a) Definition applies only to R.C.M. 1004(c)(6) and to Parts IV and V of the Manual.

    b) The UCMJ does not define "time of war." R.C.M. 103(19), analysis.

    c) The Court of Military Appeals (now Court of Appeals for the Armed Forces) has held that "time of war," as used in the UCMJ, does not necessarily mean declared war. Whether a time of war exists depends on the purpose of the specific article in which the phrase appears.

    d) For purposes of Art. 2a(10), "time of war" means a war formally declared by Congress. *United States v. Avarette*, 41 C.M.R. 363 (C.M.A. 1970).

    e) Vietnam conflict was time of war for purposes of suspension of the statute of limitations under Article 43. *United States v. Anderson*, 38 C.M.R. 386 (C.M.A. 1968).

2. The court has examined the following circumstances to determine if time of war exists:

    a) The nature of the conflict, *i.e.* there must exist armed hostilities against an organized enemy. *United States v. Shell*, 23 C.M.R. 110, 114 (C.M.A. 1957);

    b) The movement and numbers of United States forces in the combat area;

c) The casualties involved;

d) Legislation, executive orders or proclamations concerning the hostilities. *United States v. Bancroft*, 11 C.M.R. 3 (C.M.A. 1953).

3. Geographical limitation of time of war.

   a) Not limited with respect to Article 43, UCMJ. *United States v. Anderson*, 38 C.M.R. 386 (C.M.A. 1968).

   b) May be limited for other purposes. *See United States v. Taylor*, 15 C.M.R. 232 (C.M.A. 1954); *United States v. Ayers*, 15 C.M.R. 220 (C.M.A. 1954).

4. For a more broad discussion of the impact of "time of war" on offenses for purposes of Article 43, *see infra* Chapter 5, para. XVI.F.

D. Applications.

   1. Offenses which can occur only in time of war.

      a) Improper use of a countersign. UCMJ art. 101.

      b) Misconduct as a prisoner. UCMJ art. 105.

      c) Spies. UCMJ art. 106.

   2. Offenses which are capital offenses in time of war.

      a) Desertion. UCMJ art. 85.

      b) Willful Disobedience of a Superior Commissioned Officer's Order. UCMJ art. 90.

      c) Misbehavior As A Sentinel. UCMJ art. 113.

      d) Rape/Homicide. *See* R.C.M. 1004(c)(6).

   3. Offenses where time of war is an aggravating factor.

      a) Drug offenses. UCMJ art. 112a.

      b) Malingering. UCMJ art. 115.

      c) Offenses by a Sentinel. UCMJ art. 134.

II. **MISBEHAVIOR BEFORE THE ENEMY. UCMJ ART. 99.**

A. Enemy Defined. Organized forces in time of war or any hostile body, including civilians, that may oppose U.S. forces. *United States v. Monday*, 36 C.M.R. 711 (A.B.R. 1966), *pet. denied*, 37 C.M.R. 471 (C.M.A. 1969).

B. Before The Enemy.

   1. A question of tactical relation not of distance. A reasonable possibility of being called into action is sufficient. *United States v. Sperland*, 5 C.M.R. 89 (C.M.A. 1952).

   2. Subsequent enemy contact may not be used to establish misconduct before the enemy. *United States v. Terry*, 36 C.M.R. 756 (N.B.R. 1965), *aff'd*, 36 C.M.R. 348 (C.M.A. 1966).

C. Nine Forms of the Offense.

   1. Running away.

2. Shamefully abandoning, surrendering, or delivering up command, unit, place, ship or military property.

3. Endangering safety.

4. Casting away arms or ammunition.

5. Cowardly conduct.

6. Quitting place of duty to plunder or pillage.

7. Causing false alarms.

8. Willfully failing to do utmost to encounter the enemy.

9. Failure to afford relief and assistance.

D. Elements. Each form has its own set of elements. An example, Article 99(5), is below:

1. That the accused committed an act of cowardice;

2. That this conduct occurred while the accused was before the enemy; and

3. That this conduct was the result of fear.

E. Applications.

1. Cowardice is misbehavior motivated by fear. Fear is the natural feeling of apprehension when going into battle. *United States v. Smith*, 7 C.M.R. 73 (C.M.A. 1953).

2. The mere display of apprehension does not constitute the offense. *United States v. Barnett*, 3 C.M.R. 248 (A.B.R. 1951).

3. An intent to avoid combat does not in itself justify an inference of fear. *United States v. Yarborough*, 5 C.M.R. 106 (C.M.A. 1952).

4. Refusal to proceed against the enemy because of illness is not cowardice unless motivated by fear. *United States v. Presley*, 40 C.M.R. 186 (C.M.A. 1969).

5. Article 99 covers the area of misbehavior before the enemy offenses. Art. 134 is not a catch-all. *United States v. Hamilton*, 15 C.M.R. 383 (C.M.A. 1954).

III. WAR TROPHIES.

A. Captured Or Abandoned Property. UCMJ art. 103.

1. Soldiers must give notice and turn over to the proper authorities without delay all captured or abandoned enemy property.

2. Soldiers can be punished for:

a) Failing to carry out duties described in ¶ 1 above.

b) Buying, selling, trading or in any way disposing of captured or abandoned public or private property.

c) Engaging in looting or pillaging.

B. Unlawful Importation, Transfer, and Sale of a Dangerous Firearm. 26 U.S.C. §§ 5844, 5861.

IV. STRAGGLING. UCMJ ART. 134.

A. Elements.

1. That the accused, while accompanying the accused's organization on a march, maneuvers, or similar exercise, straggled.

2. That the straggling was wrongful, and

3. That under the circumstances, the conduct of the accused was to the prejudice of good order and discipline in the armed forces or was of a nature to bring discredit upon the armed forces.

B. Explanation.

1. "Straggle" means to wander away, to stray, to become separated from, or to lag or linger behind.

2. Must plead specific mission or maneuver. *See* MCM, pt. IV, ¶ 107(c).

V. ESPIONAGE. UCMJ ART. 106A.

A. Nature of the Offense. Article 106a establishes a peace time espionage offense which is different from spying, another wartime offense, under Article 106, UCMJ.

B. Three Theories for Espionage Cases.

1. Violation of general regulations;

2. Assimilation of federal statutes under Article 134, clause 3;

3. Violation of Article 106 or 106a. *See United States v. Baba*, 21 M.J. 76 (C.M.A. 1985).

C. Elements of Art 106a.

1. The accused communicated, delivered, or transmitted information relating to the national defense;

2. Information was communicated and delivered to a foreign government;

3. That the accused did so with the intent or reason to believe that such matter would be used to the injury of the United States or to the advantage of a foreign nation. MCM, pt. IV, ¶ 30b(1).

D. Attempted Espionage. Unlike most UCMJ offenses, Article 106a covers both espionage and any attempted espionage.

1. Accused's actions in enlisting aid of fellow sailor en route to delivering material to foreign embassy, removing classified documents from ship's storage facility and converting them to his own personal possession, and traveling halfway to embassy to deliver went beyond "mere preparation" and guilty plea to charge of attempted espionage was provident. *United States v. Schoof*, 37 M.J. 96 (C.M.A. 1993).

2. Where accused took several classified radio messages to Tokyo in order to deliver them to a Soviet agent named "Alex," his conduct was more than mere preparation and constituted attempted espionage in violation of article 106a, UCMJ. *United States v. Wilmouth*, 34 M.J. 739 (N.M.C.M.R. 1991).

E. Espionage as a Capital Offense.

1. Accused must commit offense of espionage or attempted espionage; and

2. The offense must concern:

    a) Nuclear weaponry, military spacecraft or satellites, early warning systems, or other means of defense retaliation against large scale attack;

    b) War plans;

    c) Communications intelligence or cryptographic information; or

    d) Major weapons system or major elements of defense strategy. MCM, pt. IV, ¶ 30b(3).

F. Applications.

1. *United States v. Richardson*, 33 M.J. 127 (C.M.A. 1991) (case reversed because MJ erred in instructing panel that intent requirement for offense of attempted espionage would be satisfied if accused acted in bad faith "or otherwise without authority" in disseminating information).

2. *United States v. Peri*, 33 M.J. 927 (A.C.M.R. 1993) (accused's conscious, voluntary act of conveying defense information across the East German border and then intentionally delivering himself and the information into custody and control of East German authorities constituted "delivery," as required to prove espionage).

3. *United States v. Wilmoth*, 34 M.J. 739 (N.M.C.M.R. 1991) (Art. 106a includes both espionage and attempted espionage and an essential element of attempted espionage is an act that amounts to more than mere preparation).

4. *United States v. Schoof*, 37 M.J. 96 (C.M.A. 1993) (accused's actions in enlisting aid of fellow sailor en route to delivering material to foreign embassy, removing classified documents from ship's storage facility and converting them to his own personal possession, and traveling halfway to embassy to deliver went beyond "mere preparation" and guilty plea to charge of attempted espionage was provident).

5. *United States v. Sombolay*, 37 M.J. 647 (A.C.M.R. 1993) (to be convicted of espionage, information or documents passed by accused need not be of the type requiring a security classification, but gravamen of offense is the *mens rea* with which accused has acted, not impact or effect of act itself, *i.e.*, did accused intend to harm the United States or have reason to believe that his conduct would harm the United States).

CHAPTER 4: CONVENTIONAL OFFENSES

I. **OFFENSES AGAINST THE PERSON. UCMJ ARTS. 128, 120A, 134**

   A. Simple Assault / Battery. MCM, pt. IV, ¶ 54; UCMJ art. 128.

   Under the UCMJ, assault is defined as an attempt or offer with unlawful force or violence to do bodily harm to another, whether or not the attempt or offer is consummated. An assault can therefore be committed in one of three separate ways: **by offer, by attempt, or by battery**. UCMJ art. 128.

   1. Assault by Offer.

      a) An act or omission that foreseeably puts another in reasonable apprehension that force will immediately be applied to his person is an assault by offer provided the act or omission involved is either intentional or culpably negligent. The gravamen of this offense is the placing of the victim in reasonable apprehension of an immediate unlawful touching of his person. The fact that the offered touching cannot actually be accomplished is no defense provided the victim is placed in reasonable apprehension. MCM, pt. IV, ¶ 54d.

      b) Victim's apprehension of harm.

         (1) The ability to inflict injury need not be real but only reasonably apparent to the victim. For example, pointing an unloaded pistol at another in jest constitutes an assault by intentional offer if the victim is aware of the attack and is placed in reasonable apprehension of bodily injury. *United States v. Bush*, 47 C.M.R. 532 (N.C.M.R. 1973).

         (2) The victim's belief that the accused does not intend to inflict injury vitiates the offense under the theory of offer. *United States v. Norton*, 4 C.M.R. 3 (C.M.A. 1952).

         (3) The victim's apprehension of impending harm must be reasonable. *See United States v. Hernandez*, 44 C.M.R. 500 (A.C.M.R. 1971).

      c) Mere words or threats of future violence are insufficient to constitute an offer-type assault. *United States v. Hines*, 21 C.M.R. 201 (C.M.A. 1956) (working the bolt of a loaded weapon so that it was ready for instant firing, coupled with a statement indicating a present intent to use the weapon, was more than mere preparation and constituted an act of assault); *see also United States v. Milton*, 46 M.J. 317 (C.A.A.F. 1997) (holding that words alone are generally not sufficient to constitute an assault by offer, but assault may occur where circumstances surrounding threat may constitute assault if victim feels "reasonable apprehension").

      d) An accused who tries but fails to offer violence to frighten a victim may be guilty of an attempt to commit an assault by offer under UCMJ art. 80. *United States v. Locke*, 16 M.J. 763 (A.C.M.R. 1983). Whether an "attempted offer to batter" is an offense under the UCMJ remains an open question. *See United States v. Anzalone*, 41 M.J. 142 (C.M.A. 1994). *Cf. United States v. Williamson*, 42 M.J. 613 (N-M. Ct. Crim. App. 1995).

      e) The culpably negligent offer. Culpable negligence is defined in MCM, pt. IV, ¶ 44c(2)(a)(i) as a degree of carelessness greater than simple negligence. It is a negligent act or omission accompanied by a culpable disregard for the foreseeable consequences to others of that act or omission. *United States v. Pittman*, 42 C.M.R. 720 (A.C.M.R. 1970); *United States v. Gibson*, 39 M.J. 1043 (A.C.M.R. 1994), *aff'd*, 43 M.J. 343 (1995). "The actor need not actually intend or foresee those consequences: it is only necessary that a reasonable person in such circumstances would have realized the substantial and unjustified danger created by his act." *United States v. Baker*, 24 M.J. 354, 356 (C.M.A. 1987). The absence of intent to do bodily harm is not a defense. *United States v. Redding*, 34 C.M.R. 22 (C.M.A. 1963). An example of such an assault would be a situation wherein the accused knowingly conducts rifle target practice in a built up area and thus frightens innocent bystanders into a reasonable belief of imminent injury.

2. Assault by Attempt.

   a) An overt act that amounts to more than mere preparation and is done with apparent present ability and with the specific intent to do bodily harm constitutes an assault by attempt. MCM, pt. IV, ¶ 54c.

   b) More than mere preparation to inflict harm is required. *United States v. Crocker*, 35 C.M.R. 725 (A.F.B.R. 1965) (where the accused with open knife advances towards his victim at the time when an affray is impending or is in progress and comes within striking distance, this amounts to more than mere preparation and is sufficient to complete the offense).

   (1) Words alone, or threats of future harm, are insufficient. *United States v. Hines*, 21 C.M.R. 201 (C.M.A. 1956).

   (2) An apparent ability to inflict bodily harm must exist. *United States v. Hernandez*, 44 C.M.R. 500 (A.C.M.R. 1971) (no offense where Government failed to prove that instrument used under the circumstances was likely to result in harm); *United States v. Smith*, 15 C.M.R. 41 (C.M.A. 1954) (accused need not be within actual striking distance of victim to constitute apparent ability to inflict harm).

   c) *Mens Rea*. Attempt-type assault requires a specific intent to inflict bodily harm upon the victim. MCM, pt. IV, ¶ 54c.

   (1) Victim's apprehension of impending harm is unnecessary. MCM, pt. IV, ¶ 54c(1)(b)(i). *See United States v. Anzalone*, 41 M.J. 142 (C.M.A. 1994); *United States v. Van Beek*, 47 C.M.R. 99 (A.C.M.R. 1973).

   (2) *United States v. Davis*, 49 C.M.R. 463 (A.C.M.R. 1974). Firing pistol over the heads of victims, without the intent to injure them, is insufficient for assault by attempt.

3. Battery.

   a) An intentional or culpably negligent application of force or violence to the person of another by a material agency constitutes a battery. *See generally United States v. Schoolfield*, 40 M.J. 132 (C.M.A. 1994) (discussing alternative theories of battery in the context of an HIV case).

   b) Any offensive touching will suffice. *See United States v. Sever*, 39 M.J. 1 (C.M.A. 1994) (nonconsensual kiss); *United States v. Bonano-Torres*, 29 M.J. 845 (A.C.M.R. 1989), *aff'd*, 31 M.J. 175 (C.M.A. 1990) (nonconsensual kiss and touching buttons on blouse); *United States v. Madigar*, 46 M.J. 802 (C.G. Ct. Crim. App. 1997) (unnecessary exposure to X-ray radiation was sufficient physical touching); *United States v. Banks*, 39 M.J. 571 (N.M.C.M.R. 1993), *aff'd*, 40 M.J. 320 (C.M.A. 1994) (smoke inhalation).

c) *Mens Rea.*

(1) Unlawful touching must be the result of an intentional or culpably negligent act. A culpably negligent act requires a negligent act/omission coupled with a culpable disregard for the foreseeable consequences to others. *See United States v. Turner*, 11 M.J. 784 (A.C.M.R. 1981) (contrasting an intentional battery with a culpably negligent battery; the court agreed that the accused who threw a rake at an MP, hitting him on the arm, had in fact committed a battery, but it split on whether the violent act was intentional or culpably negligent).

(2) *United States v. Gibson*, 43 M.J. 343 (C.A.A.F. 1995) (playing with and dropping a 40mm grenade round was a culpably negligent act sufficient to support a charge of aggravated assault (by battery); a reasonable soldier should have known what the object was and that dropping it would create a substantial and unjustified danger to bystanders).

(3) *United States v. Banks*, 39 M.J. 571 (N.M.C.M.R. 1993) (finding the accused was culpably negligent when he consumed alcohol while cooking and passed out, thereby causing stove to catch fire and causing smoke inhalation injury to his infant son), *aff'd*, 40 M.J. 320 (C.M.A. 1994).

(4) *United States v. Mayo*, 50 M.J. 473 (C.A.A.F. 1999) (intentionally throwing a 19-month-old child, while playing, with sufficient force and from sufficient height to fracture the child's femur may be a culpably negligent act).

d) Consent is not always a defense. *United States v. Arab*, 55 M.J. 508 (A. Ct. Crim. App. 2001) (consent not a defense to assault consummated by battery arising from sadomasochistic activities involving an accused's wife, where the nature of injuries and means used suggested the wife was subjected to extreme pain); *United States v. Dumford*, 28 M.J. 836 (A.F.C.M.R. 1989), *aff'd*, 30 M.J. 137 (C.M.A. 1990), *cert. denied*, 498 U.S. 854 (1990) (consent not a defense to assault for sexual activity where the accused has the AIDS virus); *United States v. Bygrave*, 46 M.J. 491 (1997) (victim's informed consent is no defense to a charge of aggravated assault for unprotected intercourse by HIV-infected accused); *United States v. Brantner*, 28 M.J. 941 (N.M.C.M.R. 1989) (consent not a defense to assault by using unsterilized needles); *United States v. O'Neal*, 36 C.M.R. 189 (C.M.A. 1966) (both parties to a mutual affray are guilty of assault); *United States v. Holmes*, 24 C.M.R. 762 (A.F.B.R.) (consent not a defense if the injury more than trifling or there is a breach of public order); *cf. United States v. Rath*, 27 M.J. 600 (A.C.M.R. 1988) (child may consent to some types of assault); *United States v. Serrano*, 51 M.J. 622 (N.-M. Ct. Crim. App. 1999) (act likely to produce grievous bodily harm or death); *United States v. Booker*, 25 M.J. 114 (C.M.A. 1987) & *United States v. Outhier*, 45 M.J. 326 (C.A.A.F. 1996) (consent invalid where obtained by fraud).

e) Notice of Lack of Consent. *United States v. Johnson*, 54 M.J. 67 (2000) (where there was a friendly relationship involving touchings that were not offensive and the victim never protested against backrubs, the government had to prove that the accused was on notice of lack of consent), *aff'd by* 55 M.J. 243 (C.A.A.F. 2001).

    f) Justification. *See also* Chapter 5, Defenses.

        (1) Certain persons may be justified in touching others even without their permission. *See, e.g., United States v. McDaniel*, 7 M.J. 522 (A.C.M.R. 1979) (no assault for NCO to place drunk and protesting soldier in a cold shower to sober him up). *See* R.C.M. 916(c).

        (2) Parental discipline defense. *See generally United States v. Rivera*, 54 M.J. 489 (2001); *United States v. Robertson*, 36 M.J. 190 (C.M.A. 1991); *United States v. Brown*, 26 M.J. 148 (C.M.A. 1988). Requirements:

            (a) Proper parental purpose. Force used for safeguarding or promoting the welfare of the minor, including prevention or punishment of misconduct.

            (b) Reasonable force. Force must not be intended, or known to create a substantial risk of, serious bodily injury, disfigurement, extreme pain or mental distress, or gross degradation.

B. Aggravated Assault With a Dangerous Means, Weapon or Force. UCMJ art. 128(b)(1).

    1. Aggravated assault with a dangerous weapon, means, or force includes the assault theories of offer, attempt, and battery. MCM, pt. IV, ¶ 54b(4)(a).

    2. Dangerous. A means/force/weapon is dangerous when used in a manner likely to produce grievous bodily harm. *United States v. Hernandez*, 44 C.M.R. 500 (C.M.A. 1971) (claymore mine, under the circumstances, not used as a dangerous weapon). The offense is not established by the subjective state of mind of the victim but by an objective test as to whether the instrument is used as a dangerous weapon. *United States v. Cato*, 17 M.J. 1108 (A.C.M.R. 1984). The mere use of a weapon in the course of an assault is sufficient whether or not the accused actually intended to employ the weapon to accomplish the assault. *United States v. Griffin*, 50 M.J. 480 (C.A.A.F. 1999).

        a) Government must prove natural and probable consequence of means or force used would be death or grievous bodily harm. *United States v. Outhier*, 45 M.J. 326 (C.A.A.F. 1996); Whether a particular means is a "means likely" depends on two findings: 1) the risk of harm must be more than fanciful, speculative, or remote possibility; and 2) the natural and probable consequence of inflicting injury by such means must be death or grievous bodily harm. *United States v. Weatherspoon*, 49 M.J. 209 (C.A.A.F. 1998).

        b) Firearms. An unloaded firearm is not a dangerous weapon within the meaning of Article 128 in an offer-type assault, even if the victim reasonably believed the weapon was capable of inflicting imminent death or grievous bodily harm. *United States v. Davis*, 47 M.J. 484 (C.A.A.F. 1998). *Cf. United States v. Smith*, 2 C.M.R. 256 (A.B.R. 1951) (pistol as bludgeon is a dangerous weapon); *United States v. Lamp*, 44 C.M.R. 504 (A.C.M.R. 1971) (functional carbine with rounds in magazine but not chambered is a dangerous weapon); *United States v. Bean*, 62 M.J. 264 (C.A.A.F. 2006) (engaging the safety of a loaded, operable firearm does not remove its character as a dangerous weapon). *United States v. Cato*, 17 M.J. 1108 (A.C.M.R. 1984) (jammed rifle a dangerous weapon). [*Note*:

Under UCMJ art. 134, a person can be convicted for carrying a concealed weapon provided it is shown that the weapon was "dangerous." *United States v. Thompson*, 14 C.M.R. 38 (C.M.A. 1954). The term "dangerous weapon" has a different meaning in connection with the art. 134 offense than it does in connection with the offense of aggravated assault. Under UCMJ art. 134, the term "dangerous weapon" includes an unloaded pistol. *United States v. Ramsey*, 18 C.M.R. 588 (A.F.B.R. 1954); *United States v. Brungs*, 14 C.M.R. 851 (A.F.B.R. 1954).]

c) Fists. *United States v. Kenne*, 50 C.M.R. 217 (A.C.M.R. 1975); *United States v. Saunders*, 25 C.M.R. 89 (C.M.R. 1958); *United States v. Vigil*, 13 C.M.R. 30 (C.M.A. 1953); *United States v. Whitfield*, 35 M.J. 535 (A.C.M.R. 1992); *United States v. Debaugh*, 35 M.J. 548 (A.C.M.R. 1992).

d) Belt buckle. *United States v. Patterson*, 21 C.M.R. 135 (C.M.A. 1956).

e) Beer bottle. *United States v. Straub*, 30 C.M.R. 156 (C.M.A. 1961).

f) Butter knife. *United States v. Lewis*, 34 C.M.R. 980 (A.B.R. 1964).

g) Stick. *United States v. Ealy*, 39 C.M.R. 313 (A.B.R. 1967).

h) CS/riot grenade. *United States v. Aubert*, 46 C.M.R. 848 (A.C.M.R. 1972); *United States v. Schroder*, 47 C.M.R. 430 (A.C.M.R. 1973).

i) AIDS (HIV) virus.

(1) *United States v. Dacus*, 66 M.J. 235 (C.A.A.F. 2008). In a guilty plea to aggravated assault, a medical doctor provided sentencing evidence for the accused that his viral load was very low and when combined with the use of a condom, the likelihood of transmission of HIV was very low. Under *United States v. Witherspoon*, 49 M.J. 208 (C.A.A.F. 1998), whether the means is "likely" has two prongs: "(1) the risk of harm and (2) the magnitude of the harm." As the court stated in *Witherspoon*, "Where the magnitude of harm is great, there may be an aggravated assault even though the risk of harm is statistically low." Citing *United States v. Joseph*, 37 M.J. 392 (C.M.A. 1993), the court stated that "[T]he question is not the statistical probability of HIV invading the blood, but rather the likelihood of the virus causing death or serious bodily harm *if* it invades the body." Additionally, "the probability of infection need only be more than merely a fanciful, speculative, or remote possibility." Assessing the second *Witherspoon* prong, the court found that the evidence in this case did not conflict with the accused's plea to aggravated assault because death or grievous bodily harm is a natural and probable consequence if HIV were transmitted by sexual intercourse. Moving to the first *Witherspoon* prong, the court concluded that the risk of HIV transmission in this case was low and remote, but more than fanciful or speculative. Considering both prongs, the court concluded that while the risk may have been low, the magnitude of harm was significant.

(2) Other Cases: *United States v. Joseph*, 37 M.J. 392 (C.M.A. 1993); *United States v. Johnson*, 30 M.J. 53 (C.M.A. 1990); *United States v. Stewart*, 29 M.J. 92 (C.M.A. 1989); *United States v. Bygrave*, 46 M.J. 491 (1997) (consent no defense); *United States v. Schoolfield*, 36 M.J. 545 (A.C.M.R. 1992), *aff'd*, 40 M.J. 132 (C.M.A. 1994); *United States v.*

Klauck, 47 M.J. 24 (C.A.A.F. 1997). *But see United States v. Perez*, 33 M.J. 1050 (A.C.M.R. 1991) (unprotected sexual intercourse by HIV infected soldier did not constitute an assault by battery where the evidence indicated that the accused's vasectomy prevented transfer of the virus).

j) Other sexually transmitted diseases. *United States v. Reister*, 40 M.J. 666 (N.M.C.M.R. 1994) (genital herpes).

k) Tent pole. *United States v. Winston*, 27 M.J. 618 (A.C.M.R. 1988).

l) Bed extender. *United States v. Wilson*, 26 M.J. 10 (C.M.A. 1988).

m) Unsterilized needle. *United States v. Brantner*, 28 M.J. 941 (N.M.C.M.R. 1989).

3. Grievous bodily harm is defined as serious bodily injury such as broken bones and deep cuts. MCM, pt. IV, ¶ 54c.

4. An assault and threat, which occur at the same time, are multiplicious for sentencing. *United States v. Morris*, 41 C.M.R. 731 (A.C.M.R. 1970); *United States v. Metcalf*, 41 C.M.R. 574 (A.C.M.R. 1969).

5. LIOs: Assault with a dangerous weapon. Where the evidence shows that an intoxicated accused pointed a loaded firearm at others, having first threatened them verbally and with a knife, and assuming a firing position, the lesser included offense of simple assault is not reasonably raised, whether the safety is engaged or not. *United States v. Bean*, 62 M.J. 264 (C.A.A.F. 2005).

C. Aggravated Assault By Intentionally Inflicting Grievous Bodily Harm. UCMJ art. 128(b)(2).

1. Requires non-negligent battery resulting in grievous bodily harm.

2. Specific intent to inflict grievous bodily harm is necessary. *United States v. Groves*, 10 C.M.R. 39 (C.M.A. 1953) (error not to instruct on defense of intoxication).

3. Aggravated assault by intentionally inflicting grievous bodily harm is multiplicious with maiming under Article 124 when the same actions give rise to both convictions. *United States v. Allen*, NMCM 9800849, 2003 Lexis 169 (N-M. Ct. Crim. App. July 30, 2003).

D. Assault and Communication of Threat Distinguished. An assault (UCMJ art. 128) is an attempt or offer to do bodily harm with unlawful force or violence. Communication of a threat (UCMJ art. 134) embraces a declaration or intent to do bodily harm. Both offenses therefore relate to infliction of physical injury. When committed simultaneously upon the same victim, they are properly a single offense for punishment purposes. *United States v. Lockett*, 7 M.J. 753 (A.C.M.R. 1979); *United States v. Morris*, 41 C.M.R. 731 (A.C.M.R. 1970); *United States v. Conway*, 33 C.M.R. 903 (A.F.C.M.R. 1963).

E. Stalking, UCMJ art. 120a.

1. Implementing Executive Order signed 18 April 2007 (E.O. 13430). ISSUES:

a) The criminal act is a "course of conduct," defined by the statute as:

(1) A repeated maintenance of visual or physical proximity to a specific person, or

(2) A repeated conveyance of verbal threat, written threats, or threats implied by conduct, or a combination of such threats, directed at or towards a specific person.

b) "Repeated," in the definition of "course of conduct," means two or more occasions.

c) Be alert to the implications of these statutory definitions for conduct occurring in barracks, or on a ship, or in a deployed environment where soldiers are compelled to be in close visual or physical proximity to one another.

d) Note that threats conveyed by computer are not expressly incorporated in the statutory definition. To prosecute a course of conduct based on threats conveyed by computer, consider litigating whether computer-conveyed threats are "written" for purposes of the statute. In the alternative, assimilate a state or federal offense to prosecute computer-conveyed threats. Be cognizant of the preemption doctrine (*see* discussion on Preemption, Chapter 3, The General Article, *supra*).

2. There are no reported cases under this article.

F. Child Endangerment. MCM, pt. IV, ¶ 68a, UCMJ art. 134.

1. This is a new offense as of October 2007. *See* Executive Order 13447, dated 28 September 2007.

2. There are no reported cases under this article, however, as the Analysis states, child neglect was recognized in *United States v. Vaughn*, 58 M.J. 29 (2003) (in light of service custom, norms of states, and service-discrediting nature of offense, child neglect is punishable under Article 134, even if no harm results to the child).

3. Elements:

a) That the accused had a duty of care of a certain child;

b) That the child was under the age of 16 years;

c) That the accused endangered the child's mental or physical health, safety, or welfare through design or culpable negligence; and

d) That, under the circumstances, the conduct of the accused was to the prejudice of good order and discipline in the armed forces or was of a nature to bring discredit upon the armed forces.

4. Issues.

a) Culpable negligence is more than simple negligence and is a negligent act accompanied by a culpable disregard for the forseeable consequences to others of that act or omission. MCM, pt. IV, ¶ 68a(c)(3).

b) As in *Vaughn, supra*, there is no requirement of actual physical or mental harm to the child. MCM, pt. IV, ¶ 68a(c)(4).

c) Age of the victim is a factor in determining the quantum of negligence. The explanation provides several examples of acts to assist in determining whether an act is negligent, and if so, whether the negligence rises to the level of culpable negligence. *See* MCM, pt. IV, ¶ 68a(c)(6).

II. **HOMICIDES. UCMJ ARTS. 118, 119, & 134.**

A. Common Law Classifications.

1. At common law, homicides are classified as justifiable, excusable, or criminal. Justifiable homicides are those commanded or authorized by law; they are not punishable. Excusable homicides are those in which the killer is to some extent at fault but where circumstances do not justify infliction of full punishment for criminal homicide; *i.e.*, the killing remains criminal but the penalty is reduced. Any killing that is not justifiable or excusable is criminal homicide -- either murder, manslaughter, or negligent homicide.

2. "Born Alive" Rule. *United States v. Nelson*, 53 M.J. 319 (C.A.A.F. 2000). The UCMJ does not define "human being" for the purposes of Articles 118 and 119, but Congress intended those articles to be construed with reference to the common law. A child is "born alive" if it: (1) was wholly expelled from its mother's body, and (2) possessed or was capable of an existence by means of a circulation independent of that of the mother. Even if the child never took a breath of air from its own lungs, the child's capability to do so is sufficient. *But see* UCMJ, Article 119a, Death or Injury to an Unborn Child.

B. Causation.

1. Generally. *See also* Chapter 5, Defenses.

2. Death From Multiple Causes.

a) *United States v. Gomez*, 15 M.J. 954 (A.C.M.R. 1982) (adopts two-part time of death standard: either irreversible cessation of circulatory and respiratory functions, or irreversible cessation of total brain functions).

b) *United States v. Schreiber*, 18 C.M.R. 226 (C.M.A. 1955) (accused held responsible for death even if his gunshot wound, following a severe beating of the victim by another, only contributed to the death by causing shock).

c) *United States v. Houghton*, 32 C.M.R. 3 (C.M.A. 1962) (in child abuse death, contributing to or accelerating the death of the victim sufficient to establish responsibility).

3. The Fragile Victim. If the wound, though not ordinarily fatal, causes the death of the victim, the accused is responsible. *United States v. Eddy*, 26 C.M.R. 718 (A.B.R. 1958).

4. Negligent or improper medical treatment of the victim will not excuse the accused unless it constitutes gross negligence or intentional malpractice. *United States v. Baguex*, 2 C.M.R. 424 (A.B.R. 1952) (death by asphyxiation from aspiration into lungs of blood from facial injuries); *United States v. Eddy*, 26 C.M.R. 718 (A.B.R. 1958).

5. Accused's act need not be the sole cause of death, or the latest/most immediate cause of death. *United States v. Romero*, 1 M.J. 227 (C.M.A. 1975) (accused guilty of negligent homicide in overdose death after helping victim position syringe); *see also United States v. Mazur*, 13 M.J. 143 (C.M.A. 1982) (accused guilty of involuntary manslaughter by culpable negligence when assisted victim who could no longer inject self with heroin).

6. Accused is responsible if his act caused the victim to kill herself unintentionally or by her negligence. *See United States v. Schatzinger*, 9 C.M.R. 586 (N.B.R. 1953).

7. Intervening cause.

a) An unforeseeable, independent, intervening event that causes the victim's death may negate causation by the accused. *See United States v. Riley*, 58 M.J.

305 (2003) (holding doctors' failure to diagnose appellant's pregnancy was not an intervening cause of the baby's death sufficient to relieve appellant of criminal liability (negligent birthing of child)).

b) Contributory negligence by the victim must loom so large in comparison to the accused's conduct as to be an intervening cause. *United States v. Oxendine*, 55 M.J. 323 (2001) (victim's voluntary participation in a dangerous joint venture, being held outside a third-story window by his ankles, was not an intervening cause).

c) When an accused's wrongful acts set in motion an unbroken, foreseeable chain of events resulting in another's death, his conduct is the proximate cause of the death. *United States v. Stanley*, 60 M.J. 622 (A.F. Ct. Crim. App. 2004) (accused violently shook a 6-week old infant, who was resuscitated at the emergency room but remained in a persistent vegitative state; infant died upon removal of life support; the decision to remove life support did not "loom so large" as to relieve the accused of criminal liability); *see also United States v. Markert*, 65 M.J. 677 (N-M. Ct. Crim. App. 2007) (weapon horseplay resulted in Marine being shot in head; removal of life support was not an intervening cause).

C. Premeditated Murder. UCMJ art. 118(1).

1. Intent. Requires a specific intent to kill *and* consideration of the act intended to bring about death. The intent to kill need not be entertained for any particular or considerable length of time and the existence of premeditation may be inferred from the circumstances surrounding the killing. MCM, pt. IV, ¶ 43c(2)(a). *See generally United States v. Eby*, 44 M.J. 425 (1996).

   a) The "premeditated design to kill" does not have to exist for any particular or measurable length of time. *United States v. Sechler*, 12 C.M.R. 119 (C.M.A. 1953).

   b) Intent only to inflict grievous bodily harm is insufficient. *United States v. Mitchell*, 7 C.M.R. 77 (C.M.A. 1953).

   c) The distinction between premeditated murder and unpremeditated murder is sufficiently clear to withstand constitutional challenge. *United States v. Curtis*, 44 M.J. 106, 147 (C.A.A.F. 1996); *United States v. Loving*, 41 M.J. 213 at 279-80 (C.M.A. 1994), *aff'd*, 517 U.S. 748 (1996).

   d) Premeditation is not a question of time but of reflection. *United States v. Cole*, 54 M.J. 572 (Army Ct. Crim. App. 2000), *aff'd*, 55 M.J. 466 (C.A.A.F. 2001).

   e) Instructions. Because of the potential confusion to panel members in making the distinction between premeditated and unpremeditated murder, counsel should consider requesting instructions in addition to the pattern instruction in the *Military Judges Benchbook*. *See United States v. Eby*, 44 M.J. 425 (C.A.A.F. 1996); *United States v. Hoskins*, 36 M.J. 343 (C.M.A. 1993), *cert. denied*, 513 U.S. 809 (1994).

2. Proof of Premeditation.

   a) The existence of premeditation may be inferred from the circumstances. MCM, pt. IV, ¶ 43c(2)(a).

b) Inferred from the viciousness of the assault. *United States v. Ayers*, 34 C.M.R. 116 (C.M.A. 1964).

c) Inferred from the number of blows and the nature and location of injuries. *United States v. Teeter*, 12 M.J. 716 (A.C.M.R. 1981), *aff'd in part*, 16 M.J. 68 (C.M.A. 1983); *United States v. Williams*, 39 M.J. 758 (A.C.M.R. 1994).

d) Inferred from prior anger and threats against the victim. *United States v. Bullock*, 10 M.J. 674 (A.C.M.R. 1981), *aff'd*, 13 M.J. 490 (C.M.A. 1982).

e) Inferred from the fact that the weapon was procured before killing. *United States v. Mitchell*, 2 M.J. 1020 (A.C.M.R. 1976).

f) Inferred from accused's elaborate preparations preceding the murder, elaborate precautions to avoid detection, and brutal nature of the attack on the victim. *United States v. Matthews*, 13 M.J. 501 (A.C.M.R. 1982), *rev'd as to sentence*, 16 M.J. 354 (C.M.A. 1983).

g) Inferred from lack of provocation; disadvantage of victim; and nature, extent and duration of attack. *United States v. Viola*, 26 M.J. 822 (A.C.M.R. 1988), *cert. denied*, 490 U.S. 1020 (1989).

h) Other circumstances. *United States v. Curtis*, 44 M.J. 106 (C.A.A.F. 1996) (after clearly premeditated murder of first victim accused stabbed victim's wife who came to his aid and then indecently assaulted her); *United States v. Curry*, 31 M.J. 359 (C.M.A. 1990) (violent shaking of child victim, coupled with the accused's demeanor at hospital, prior abuse of child, and incredible explanation of injuries); *United States v. Levell*, 43 M.J. 847 (N-M. Ct. Crim. App. 1996) (opening gun case, walking to victim laying on the ground, saying "what do you think of this," then firing fatal shots showed accused reflected with a cool mind on killing victim); *United States v. Shanks*, 13 M.J. 783 (A.C.M.R. 1982) (homicidal act part of conspiracy); *see also United States v. Cooper*, 28 M.J. 810 (A.C.M.R. 1989), *aff'd*, 30 M.J. 201 (C.M.A. 1990); *United States v. Nelson*, 28 M.J. 553 (A.C.M.R. 1989).

3. Transferred Intent. *See* MCM, pt. IV, ¶ 43c(2)(b).

   a) *United States v. Black*, 11 C.M.R. 57 (C.M.A. 1953) (where the accused shot first victim with intent to murder and the bullet passed through his body striking a second, unintended victim, the accused was properly convicted of murder as to both victims).

   b) *United States v. Willis*, 46 M.J. 258 (C.A.A.F. 1997) (accused's act of pulling trigger three times at nearly point blank range, moving the pistol between each shot with the evident intent of covering small area occupied by intended victim and her husband was sufficient to infer accused's intent to kill intended victim's husband under doctrine of transferred intent).

4. State of Mind Defenses. All state of mind defenses apply to reduce premeditated murder to unpremeditated murder; however,

   a) Voluntary intoxication may reduce premeditated murder to unpremeditated murder or murder by murder by inherently dangerous act, but it may not reduce premeditated or unpremeditated murder to manslaughter or any other lesser offense. *United States v. Morgan*, 37 M.J. 407 (C.M.A. 1993); M.C.M. pt. IV, ¶ 43c(2)(c). Accused can still be convicted of premeditated murder even though accused drank alcohol if his behavior clearly established that he fully appreciated what he was doing before, during, and after the murder. *United States v. Glover*, No. 9901132 (Army Ct. Crim. App. Nov. 7, 2002) (unpublished).

    b) Rage or personality disorder do not necessarily reduce to unpremeditated murder. *United States v. Roukis*, 60 M.J. 925 (Army Ct. Crim. App. 2005) *aff'd*, 62 M.J. 212 (2005) ("The fact that appellant may have been enraged at the time of the killing, whether as a result of his particular personality disorder or the circumstances of his marriage, 'does not necessarily mean that he was deprived of the ability to premeditate or that he did not premeditate.'").

5. Punishment.

    a) Maximum: Death. Capital case procedures are set forth in R.C.M. 1004. The M.C.M. capital procedures were held to be constitutional in *Loving v. United States*, 517 U.S. 748 (1996).

    b) Mandatory Minimum: Imprisonment for life with eligibility for parole. M.C.M., pt. IV, ¶ 43d(2)(e).

D. Unpremeditated Murder. UCMJ art. 118(2).

1. Nature of Act. The offense can be based on an act or omission to act where there is a duty to act; *United States v. Valdez*, 35 M.J. 555 (A.C.M.R. 1992) (parent's deliberate failure to provide medical and other care to his child which resulted in child's death supported charge of murder), *aff'd*, 40 M.J. 491 (C.M.A. 1994). *See also United States v. Nelson*, 53 M.J. 319 (C.A.A.F. 2000)(holding that a mother who chose to give birth without medical assistance and failed to check on the health of her newborn for over an hour, resulting in the child's death, could be guilty of involuntary manslaughter based on culpable negligence in her duty to care for the child); *but see United States v. Riley*, 47 M.J. 603 (A.F. Ct. Crim. App. 1997) (murder conviction set aside and finding of involuntary manslaughter of an accused who sought no medical attention during pregnancy or delivery), *modified and aff'd*, 58 M.J. 305 (C.A.A.F. 2003) (involuntary manslaughter conviction set aside in favor of negligent homicide conviction because accused's failure to seek medical care was not culpably negligent).

2. Intent. Accused must have either a specific intent to kill or inflict great bodily harm.

    a) The inference of intent. A permissive inference is recognized that a person intends the natural and probable consequences of an act purposely done by him. *United States v. Owens*, 21 M.J. 117 (C.M.A. 1985); *United States v. Varraso*, 21 M.J. 129 (C.M.A. 1985); *see United States v. Wilson*, 26 M.J. 10 (C.M.A. 1988).

    b) Great bodily harm. A serious injury not including minor injuries such as a black eye or bloody nose, but includes fractured or dislocated bones, deep cuts, torn members of the body, serious damage to internal organs, and other serious bodily injury. MCM, pt. IV, ¶ 43c(3)(b).

    c) All state of mind defenses apply except voluntary intoxication. MCM, pt. IV, ¶ 43c(2)(c). Voluntary intoxication cannot defeat capacity of accused to entertain intent to kill or inflict great bodily harm required for unpremeditated murder; one who voluntarily intoxicates himself or herself cannot be heard to complain of being incapable, by virtue of that intoxication, of intentionally committing acts leading to death of another person. *United States v. Morgan*, 37 M.J. 407 (C.M.A. 1993).

3. Heat of passion defense reduces unpremeditated murder to voluntary manslaughter. See paragraph H, below.

   a) Heat of passion must be caused by adequate provocation. The provocation must be adequate to excite uncontrollable passion in a reasonable person. MCM, pt. IV, ¶44c(1)(b).

4. Transferred intent also applies to unpremeditated murder. MCM. pt. IV, ¶ 43c(3)(a) ("The intent need not be directed toward the person killed"). *See United States v. Willis*, 43 M.J. 889 (A.F. Ct. Crim. App. 1996), *aff'd,* 46 M.J. 258 (C.A.A.F. 1997).

5. Maximum Punishment: Life imprisonment, with or without eligibility for parole. MCM, pt. IV, ¶ 43e(2). RCM 1003(b)(7).

E. Murder While Doing An Inherently Dangerous Act. UCMJ art. 118(3).

   1. In General. Alternative theory to unpremeditated murder.

   2. Intent.

      a) Specific intent not required. *United States v. McMonagle*, 38 M.J. 53 (C.M.A. 1993) (firing a weapon indiscriminately in an inhabited area during a sham firefight in Panama during Operation JUST CAUSE).

      b) Knowledge. Accused must have known that the probable consequence of his act would be death or great bodily harm. *United States v. Berg*, 30 M.J. 195 (C.M.A. 1990), *aff'd on reconsideration*, 31 M.J. 38 (C.M.A. 1990). MCM, pt. IV, ¶ 43c(4)(b).

      c) Death-causing act must be intentional. *United States v. Hartley*, 36 C.M.R. 405 (C.M.A. 1966).

      d) The act must evidence wanton heedlessness of death or great bodily harm. MCM, pt. IV, ¶ 43c(4)(a).

   3. Nature of Act. The conduct of the accused must be inherently dangerous to "another", *i.e.*, at least one other person. This is a change Congress made in the law pursuant to the National Defense Authorization Act for Fiscal Year 1993 in response to *United States v. Berg*, 31 M.J. 38 (C.M.A. 1990), in which the Court of Military Appeals required the accused's conduct to endanger more than one other person.

   4. Malice Requirement. For a discussion of the malice required, see *United States v. Vandenack*, 15 M.J. 230 (C.M.A. 1983) (no defense that accused did not intend to cause death or great bodily injury, provided the act showed wanton disregard of human life).

   5. Voluntary intoxication not a defense. MCM, pt. IV, ¶ 43c(3)(c).

   6. Examples of Inherently Dangerous Conduct.

      a) *United States v. McMonagle*, 38 M.J. 53 (C.M.A. 1993) (firing a weapon indiscriminately in an inhabited area during a sham firefight in Panama during OPERATION JUST CAUSE).

      b) *United States v. Hartley*, 36 C.M.R. 405 (C.M.A. 1966) (shooting into a crowded room).

      c) *United States v. Judd*, 27 C.M.R. 187 (C.M.A. 1959) (shooting into a house trailer with two others present).

d) *United States v. Vandenack*, 15 M.J. 230 (C.M.A. 1983) (speeding and intentionally running red light after a prior accident).

F. Felony Murder. UCMJ art. 118(4).

1. Statutory Penalty: death or life imprisonment.

2. In General. Homicide must be committed during the perpetration or attempted perpetration of burglary, sodomy, rape, robbery, or aggravated arson. *United States v. Jefferson*, 22 M.J. 315 (C.M.A. 1986).

3. Intent. No specific intent required, except that of underlying felony. *United States v. Hamer*, 12 M.J. 898 (A.C.M.R. 1982).

4. Causation. Causal relationship between felony and death must be established. *United States v. Borner*, 12 C.M.R. 62 (C.M.A. 1953).

5. Multiplicity. Felony murder is multiplicious with premeditated murder, *United States v. Teeter*, 16 M.J. 68 (C.M.A. 1983), and with unpremeditated murder. *United States v. Hubbard*, 28 M.J. 27 (C.M.A. 1989).

6. Capital Punishment.

a) In *Enmund v. Florida*, 458 U.S. 782 (1982), the Supreme Court held that to impose the death penalty for felony murder the accused must have killed or have had the intent to kill.

b) *Tison v. Arizona*, 481 U.S. 137 (1987) (expands *Enmund*, holding that the Eighth Amendment does not prohibit the death penalty where the accused is a major participant in a felony that results in murder and "the mental state is one of reckless indifference").

c) R.C.M. 1004(c)(8) allows the death penalty only if the accused was the actual perpetrator of the killing. CAAF has held that this factor requires proof of an intent to kill or reckless indifference to human life. *Loving v. Hart*, 47 M.J. 438 (C.A.A.F. 1998).

d) Accused's pleas of guilty to unpremeditated murder and robbery by means of force and violence were, in context, pleas to the capital offense of felony murder. *United States v. Dock*, 28 M.J. 117 (C.M.A. 1989).

7. Instructions. Where members could have reasonably found that accused formed the intent to steal from victim either prior to the infliction of the death blows or after rendering him helpless, he was not entitled to an instruction that, to be convicted of felony-murder he had to have the intent to commit the felony at the time of the actions which caused the killing. *United States v. Fell*, 33 M.J. 628 (A.C.M.R. 1991).

G. Attempted Murder. UCMJ art. 80. Attempted murder requires a specific intent to kill.

1. Although a service member may be convicted of murder if he commits homicide without an intent to kill, but with an intent to inflict great bodily harm (UCMJ art. 118(2)) or while engaged in an act which is inherently dangerous to others and evinces a wanton disregard of human life (UCMJ art. 118(3)), those states of mind will not suffice to establish attempted murder. *United States v. Roa*, 12 M.J. 210 (C.M.A. 1982).

2. Beyond mere preparation. Where the purported co-conspirator was acting as a government agent at all relevant times, the court would consider only the acts of the accused in determining whether the planned murder-for-hire went beyond mere

preparation, so as to constitute attempted murder. *United States v. Owen*, 47 M.J. 501 (Army Ct. Crim. App. 1997).

H. Voluntary Manslaughter. UCMJ art. 119(a).

    1. Defined. An unlawful killing done with an intent to kill or inflict great bodily harm but done in the heat of sudden passion caused by adequate provocation.

        a) Article 119(a) as a lesser-included offense. When the evidence places heat of passion and adequate provocation at issue in the trial, the military judge must instruct the members, *sua sponte*, on the lesser included offense of voluntary manslaughter. *United States v. Wells*, 52 M.J. 126 (C.A.A.F. 1999).

        b) Objective requirements.

            (1) Adequate provocation so as to excite uncontrollable passion in a reasonable man. Adequate provocation is an objective concept. *United States v. Stark*, 17 M.J. 519 (A.C.M.R. 1984) (insulting, teasing, and taunting remarks are inadequate provocation). *But cf. United States v. Saulsberry*, 43 M.J. 649 (Army Ct. Crim. App. 1995) (finding adequate provocation after sustained taunting and simple assault), *aff'd*, 47 M.J. 493 (C.A.A.F. 1998).

            (2) Provocation not sought or induced.

            (3) Unspent at moment killing occurs. *United States v. Bellamy*, 36 C.M.R. 115 (C.M.A. 1966) (whether a particular provocation has spent its force & what constitutes a reasonable time for cooling off are questions of fact for the panel/fact-finder). The rage must continue throughout the attack. *United States v. Seeloff*, 15 M.J. 978 (A.C.M.R. 1983).

        c) Subjective requirements. The accused must in fact have been acting under such a heat of passion, fear, or rage. *See United States v. Staten*, 6 M.J. 275 (C.M.A. 1979); *United States v. Jackson*, 6 M.J. 261 (C.M.A. 1979).

        d) Sufficiency of proof. Despite defense claim that accused acted in sudden heat of passion, conviction of premeditated murder of wife's lover was supported by sufficient evidence, including the obtaining of a special knife, decapitation of the victim, and comment to onlookers that "this is what happens when you commit adultery." *United States v. Schap*, 44 M.J. 512 (Army Ct. Crim. App. 1996), *aff'd*, 49 M.J. 317 (C.A.A.F. 1998) (once raised at trial, Gov't must disprove its existence beyond a reasonable doubt).

        e) Marital infidelity *alone* is not enough to justify voluntary manslaughter, still need to show accused was deprived of ability to premeditate or that the accused did not premeditate. *United States v. Roukis*, 60 M.J. 925 (Army Ct. Crim. App. 2005) *aff'd*, 62 M.J. 212 (2005).

    2. Attempted Voluntary Manslaughter. The offenses of *attempted* voluntary manslaughter and assault with intent to commit voluntary manslaughter require a showing of accused's specific intent to kill. A showing only of a specific intent to inflict great bodily harm will be insufficient to establish these offenses. *United States v. Barnes*, 15 M.J. 121 (C.M.A. 1983).

I. Involuntary Manslaughter Resulting From A Culpably Negligent Act. UCMJ art. 119(b)(1).

    1. Intent. The standard of culpable negligence applies. MCM, pt. IV, ¶ 44c(2).

2. Culpable negligence. "A degree of carelessness greater than simple negligence. It is a negligent act or omission accompanied by a culpable disregard for the foreseeable consequences to others." MCM, pt. IV, ¶ 44c(2)(a)(i).

    a) Consequences are "foreseeable" when a reasonable person, in view of all the circumstances, would have realized the substantial and unjustifiable danger created by his acts. *United States v. Oxendine*, 55 M.J. 323 (2001) (holding a drunk victim by his ankles out of a third-story window without safety devices as part of a game of trust).

    b) Applications:

        (1) Horseplay with Weapon. *United States v. Markert*, 65 M.J. 677 (N-M. Ct. Crim. App. 2007).

        (2) Drug overdose death of another. *United States v. Henderson*, 23 M.J. 77 (C.M.A. 1986) (providing drug, encouraging use, providing private room, presence); *United States v. Mazur*, 13 M.J. 143 (C.M.A. 1982) (assisting fellow soldier to inject heroin into his vein); *see generally* Milhizer, *Involuntary Manslaughter and Drug Overdose Death: A Proposed Methodology*, ARMY LAW., Mar. 1989, at 10.

        (3) Child Abuse. *United States v. Stanley*, 60 M.J. 622 (A.F. Ct. Crim. App. 2004) (accused violently shook a 6-week old infant, who was resuscitated at the emergency room but remained in a persistent vegitative state; infant died upon removal of life support; the decision to remove life support did not "loom so large" as to relieve the accused of criminal liability); *United States v. Brown*, 26 M.J. 148 (C.M.A. 1988) (violently shaking a child); *United States v. Baker*, 24 M.J. 354 (C.M.A. 1987) (violently throwing child to an unpadded floor); *United States v. Mitchell*, 12 M.J. 1015 (A.C.M.R. 1982) (beating a child who would not stop crying).

        (4) Participating in a dangerous joint venture. *United States v. Oxendine*, 55 M.J. 323 (C.A.A.F. 2001) (accused helped hang drunk Marine out of a third story window during thrill-seeking game with other Marines; drunk Marine fell to his death).

        (5) Giving car keys to a drunk. *United States v. Brown*, 22 M.J. 448 (C.M.A. 1986).

        (6) Failing to follow safety rules and driving after brakes failed. *United States v. Cherry*, 22 M.J. 284 (C.M.A. 1986).

        (7) Culpably negligent surgical procedures. *United States v. Ansari*, 15 M.J. 812 (N.M.C.M.R. 1983); *but see United States v. Billig*, 26 M.J. 744 (N.M.C.M.R. 1988).

        (8) Failure of parent to seek medical care for child. *United States v. Martinez*, 48 M.J. 689 (Army Ct. Crim. App. 1998), *aff'd*, 52 M.J. 22 (1999); *United States v. Nelson*, 53 M.J. 319 (C.A.A.F. 2000); *but see United States v. Riley*, 58 M.J. 305 (2003) (intentionally unassisted delivery of a baby where medical care was readily available was not culpably negligent so as to support a finding of involuntary manslaughter; found negligent homicide).

3. Proximate Causation.

   a) "To be proximate, an act need not be the sole cause of death, nor must it be the immediate cause--the latest in time and space preceding the death. But a contributing cause is deemed proximate only if it plays a material role in the victim's [death]." *United States v. Cooke*, 18 M.J. 152, 154 (C.M.A. 1984) (quoting *United States v. Romero*, 24 C.M.A. 39, 1 M.J. 227, 230, 51 C.M.R. 133 (C.M.A. 1975)).

   b) *United States v. Stanley*, 60 M.J. 622 (A.F. Ct. Crim. App. 2004) (accused violently shook a 6-week old infant, who was resuscitated at the emergency room but remained in a persistent vegitative state; infant died upon removal of life support; the decision to remove life support did not "loom so large" as to relieve the accused of criminal liability).

4. Effect of Contributory Negligence. The deceased's or a third party's contributory negligence may exonerate the accused if it "looms so large" in comparison with the accused's negligence that the accused's negligence is no longer a substantial factor in the final result. *United States v. Cooke*, 18 M.J. 152 (C.M.A. 1984).

5. Charge of involuntary manslaughter based upon culpably negligent failure to act requires, as a threshold matter, proof of a legal duty to act. *United States v. Cowan*, 42 M.J. 475 (C.A.A.F. 1995).

6. Involuntary manslaughter by culpable negligence <u>not</u> raised when death is the result of an intentional assault. *United States v. Wilson*, 26 M.J. 10 (C.M.A. 1988).

7. Pleading. When charged under a culpable negligence theory, an involuntary manslaughter specification must allege that death was a reasonably foreseeable consequence of the accused's misconduct. *United States v. McGhee*, 29 M.J. 840 (A.C.M.R. 1989); *see generally* TJAGSA Practice Note, *The Scope of Assault*, ARMY LAW., Apr. 1990, Oct. 67, 68-70 (discusses *McGhee*).

J. Involuntary Manslaughter While Perpetrating An Offense Directly Affecting The Person Of Another. UCMJ art. 119(b)(2).

   1. Requires an act affecting some particular person as distinguished from an offense affecting society in general. MCM, pt. IV, ¶ 44c(2)(b).

   2. Applications.

      a) Assault. *United States v. Jones*, 30 M.J. 127 (C.M.A. 1990); *United States v. Wilson*, 26 M.J. 10 (C.M.A. 1988); *United States v. Madison*, 34 C.M.R. 435 (C.M.A. 1964); *see generally* TJAGSA Practice Note, *Involuntary Manslaughter Based Upon an Assault*, ARMY LAW., Aug. 1990, at 32 (discusses *Jones*); *but see United States v. Richards*, 56 M.J. 282 (2002) (insufficient evidence to necessitate involuntary manslaughter instruction).

      b) Drug Overdose Death of Another. *United States v. Sargent*, 18 M.J. 331 (C.M.A. 1984) (mere sale of drugs is not an offense "directly affecting the person of another"); *see also United States v. Dillon*, 18 M.J. 340 (C.M.A. 1984); *see generally* Milhizer, *Involuntary Manslaughter and Drug-Overdose Deaths: A Proposed Methodology*, ARMY LAW., Mar. 1989, at 10.

K. Death or Injury to an Unborn Child. UCMJ Article 119a.

1. Implementing Executive Order signed 18 April 2007. ISSUES:

    a) Article 119a exempts the following individuals from prosecution:

        (1) Any person authorized by state or federal law to perform abortions for conduct relating to an abortion for which the consent of the pregnant woman, or a person authorized by law to act on her behalf, has been obtained or for which such consent is implied by law;

        (2) Any person for any medical treatment of the pregnant woman or her unborn child; or

        (3) Any woman with respect to her unborn child.

    b) Intentional Killing of an Unborn Child or Attempts. UCMJ art. 119a specifically states that an individual who intentionally kills an unborn child or attempts to kill an unborn child will be punished under Articles 80, 118, or 119. Nonetheless, Part IV, ¶ 44a.b.(3) & (4) provide elements for an offense involving the intentional killing of an unborn child as well as elements for an offense involving attempts to do so. These elements require the specific intent to kill the unborn child.

    c) Scienter. For injuring or killing an unborn child, the government need not prove: 1) that the accused knew the victim was pregnant, nor 2) that the accused should have known that the victim was pregnant. Additionally, for these two offenses, the government need not prove that the accused specifically intended to cause the death of, or bodily injury to, the unborn child.

    d) Punishment. Such punishment, other than death, as a court-martial may direct, but shall be consistent with the offense had it occurred to the unborn child's mother.

2. No reported cases on this offense. *But see United States v. Robbins*, 52 M.J. 159 (1999) (prosecuting accused for involuntary manslaughter by terminating the pregnancy of his wife, in violation of § 2903.04 of the Ohio Revised Code, as assimilated by the Assimilative Crimes Act (ACA)).

L. Negligent Homicide. UCMJ art. 134.

  1. Intent. The standard is simple negligence—the absence of due care. An intent to kill or injure is not required. MCM, pt. IV, ¶ 85c(1).

  2. Simple Negligence Standard.

      a) *See generally United States v. Gargus*, 22 M.J. 861 (A.C.M.R. 1986).

      b) *United States v. Riley*, 58 M.J. 305 (C.A.A.F. 2003) (giving birth in hospital bathroom in a manner creating an unreasonable risk of injury, resulting in the death of the newborn). The *Riley* case demonstrates the comparison between involuntary manslaughter (culpable negligence) and negligent homicide (simple negligence). An inexperienced, immature lay person, giving birth for the first time, could not foresee the potential for explosive and unexpected birth and the likelihood of the baby's resultant *death*. Nevertheless, the appellant's simple negligence was the proximate cause of the baby's death and was sufficient to sustain a conviction for negligent homicide because *some* injury was foreseeable.

  3. Relationship with Other Homicide Offenses.

a) Negligent homicide is a lesser included offense of unpremeditated murder and involuntary manslaughter, because negligence is a "legally less serious" element. *United States v. Davis*, 53 M.J. 202 (C.A.A.F. 2000) (reversing conviction because military judge failed to sua sponte instruct on negligent homicide, where evidence raised possibility that the accused killed his daughter through mere negligence). **Note:** consider the impacts of *United States v. Miller*, 67 M.J. 385 (C.A.A.F. 2009) on this holding.

b) Relationship to Involuntary Manslaughter. Negligent homicide is a lesser included offense of involuntary manslaughter. *United States v. McGhee*, 32 M.J. 322 (C.M.A. 1991), *aff'd without opinion*, 35 M.J. 194 (C.M.A. 1991).

4. Applications.

a) *United States v. McDuffie*, 65 M.J. 631 (A.F. Ct. Crim. App. 2007) (accused diagnosed with sleep apnea, drove vehicle, fell asleep, and drifted into oncoming traffic; involuntary manslaughter conviction set aside and affirmed as negligent homicide).

b) *United States v. Martinez*, 42 M.J. 327 (C.A.A.F. 1995) (allowing fellow soldier to drive accused's vehicle while under the influence of alcohol).

c) *United States v. Robertson*, 37 M.J. 432 (C.M.A. 1993) (failure to obtain medical treatment for child).

d) *United States v. Spicer*, 20 M.J. 188 (C.M.A. 1985) and *United States v. Romero*, 1 M.J. 227 (C.M.A. 1975) (conviction affirmed where accused helped another "shoot up" with heroin, resulting in that person's death by overdose).

e) *United States v. Greenfeather*, 32 C.M.R. 151 (C.M.A. 1962) (vehicle homicide).

f) *United States v. Cuthbertson*, 46 C.M.R. 977 (A.C.M.R. 1972) (aircraft homicide).

g) *United States v. Zukrigl*, 15 M.J. 798 (A.C.M.R. 1983) (failure to check on safety measures for a water crossing exercise).

h) *United States v. Perez*, 15 M.J. 585 (A.C.M.R. 1985) (negligently entrusting child to a babysitter who had a history of assaulting the child).

i) *United States v. Gordon*, 31 M.J. 30 (C.M.A. 1990) (horseplay on a rowboat with a nonswimmer); *see generally* TJAGSA Practice Note, *Negligent Homicide and a Military Nexus*, ARMY LAW., Mar. 1991, at 28 (discusses *Gordon*).

j) *United States v. Billig*, 26 M.J. 744 (N.M.C.M.R. 1988) (offense may not be available for negligent surgical procedures).

k) *United States v. Kick*, 7 M.J. 82 (C.M.A. 1979) (offense of negligent homicide is a proper basis for criminal liability. Furthermore, it has not been preempted by other specified punitive articles, *i.e.*, UCMJ arts. 118 and 119).

5. Military courts have so far refused to use *res ipsa loquitur* to prove negligence in criminal cases. *United States v. Ryan*, 14 C.M.R. 153 (C.M.A. 1954); *United States v. Bryan*, 41 C.M.R. 184 (C.M.A. 1970); *United States v. Thomas*, 11 M.J. 315, 317 n. 2 (C.M.A. 1982).

6. Proximate Cause. The negligence must be the proximate cause of the death. Although proximate cause does not mean sole cause, it does mean a material and foreseeable cause. *United States v. Perez*, 15 M.J. 585 (A.C.M.R. 1983) (death of child foreseeable where mother left child with boyfriend who had twice previously seriously injured child).

III. KIDNAPPING. UCMJ ART. 134.

A. Elements.

1. That the accused seized, confined, inveigled, decoyed, or carried away a certain person;

2. That the accused then held such person against that person's will;

3. That the accused did so willfully and wrongfully; and

4. That, under the circumstances, the conduct of the accused was to the prejudice of good order and discipline in the armed forces or was of a nature to bring discredit upon the armed forces.

B. Theories of Prosecution.

1. If the misconduct occurred in an area over which the United States exercises exclusive or concurrent jurisdiction, the accused may be charged with violating state penal law as assimilated into federal law by the Assimilative Crimes Act, 18 U.S.C. § 13, which, in turn, is incorporated into military law under the Clause 3 of Article 134.

2. If it meets the jurisdictional requirements of the Federal Kidnapping Act, 18 U.S.C. § 1201, which is also assimilated into military law by Clause 3 of Article 134, the crime may be prosecuted under that statute.

3. Kidnapping may be charged as conduct which is service-discrediting or prejudicial to good order and discipline, in violation of Article 134. *United States v. Jeffress*, 28 M.J. 409 (C.M.A. 1989).

C. Nature of Detention. In order to convict accused of kidnapping, there must be more than "incidental" detention.

1. Factors to consider in determining whether the detention was incidental include:

a) Whether there was confinement or carrying away and holding for a period of time;

b) The duration of detention;

c) Whether the detention occurred during the commission of a separate offense;

d) The character of any separate offense;

e) Whether the detention or asportation exceeded that which was inherent in any separate offense and, in the circumstances, showed a voluntary and distinct intention to move/detain the victim beyond that necessary to commit the separate offense at the place where the victim was first encountered; and

f) Whether there was any additional risk to victim beyond that inherent in commission of any separate offense. *United States v. Barnes*, 38 M.J. 72 (C.M.A. 1993) (evidence that victim was locked in room and detained for over two hours against her will during the commission of multiple assaults was more than incidental detention).

2. *United States v. Seay*, 60 M.J. 73 (C.A.A.F. 2004). Accused and accomplice removed victim from his home, strangled, and pinned victim to ground before stabbing victim to death. These acts of restraint and asportation (removing the victim from his home) occurred prior the actual murder and exceeded the acts inherent to the commission of the murder.

3. *United States v. Newbold*, 45 M.J. 109 (C.A.A.F. 1996) (victim was moved no more than 12 feet and was detained only long enough to complete the multiple indecent and aggravated assaults; however, movement of the victim limited the possibility of escape, and once the detention began, the subsequent offenses necessarily were "fed" by the increasingly more heinous actions of the assailants; thus, asportation was not merely incidental to other charged offenses, and evidence was sufficient to sustain guilty plea).

4. *United States v. Jeffress*, 28 M.J. 409 (C.M.A. 1989) (detention of victim consisted of moving her some 15 feet; she was moved from traveled area into greater darkness; there was increased risk of harm to the victim; dragging victim away from beaten path was not inherent in offense of forcible sodomy; factually sufficient to sustain a guilty plea to kidnapping).

5. *United States v. Broussard*, 35 M.J. 665 (A.C.M.R. 1992) (accused grabbed his wife from behind, dragged her into the bedroom, bound her arms and legs to furniture, and held her for a sufficient period of time).

6. *United States v. Caruthers*, 37 M.J. 1006 (A.C.M.R. 1993) (accused's asportation and holding of his wife were more than incidental; accused conceded his wife was seized or held when she was grabbed from behind, gagged, tied and dragged short distance away where she was held for two to three-hour period during commission of sexual assaults).

D. Inveigling. "Inveigle" means to lure, lead astray, or entice by false representations or other deceitful means. MCM, pt. IV, ¶ 92.c.(1).

1. *United States v. Blocker*, 32 M.J. 281 (C.M.A. 1991) (kidnapping conviction affirmed where accused inveigled 17-year-old victim to remain in car when he drove off highway and down dirt hiking path before raping her).

2. *United States v. Mathai*, 34 M.J. 33 (C.M.A. 1992) (NCO accused inveigled victim into his office by stating, "Follow me, Private," after which he prevented her from leaving the room several times and held her against her will).

E. The involuntariness of the seizure and detention is the essence of the offense of kidnapping. Once the offense is complete, the duration of the restraint is not germane, except for sentencing purposes. *United States v. Bailey*, 52 M.J. 786 (A.F. Ct. Crim. App. 1999) (victim did not tell the accused she wanted to go home, and after initially getting out of the accused's truck and being carried back, she did not try to get out of the truck again; however, a victim is not required to voice lack of consent under the law; once the accused carried the unwilling victim back to his truck, the offense of kidnapping was complete), *aff'd*, 55 M.J. 38 (C.A.A.F. 2001).

F. Lesser Included Offenses. Reckless engangerment is not a lesser included offense of kidnapping. *United States v. Thompson*, 67 M.J. 106 (C.A.A.F. 2009).

IV. MAIMING. UCMJ ART. 124.

A. Elements.

1. That the accused inflicted a certain injury upon a certain person;

2. That this injury seriously disfigured the person's body, destroyed or disabled an organ or member, or seriously diminished the person's physical vigor by the injury to an organ or member; and

3. That the accused inflicted this injury with an intent to cause some injury to a person.

B. Nature of Offense. The disfigurement, diminishment of vigor, or destruction or disablement of any member or organ must be a serious injury of a substantially permanent nature. However, the offense is complete if such an injury is inflicted even though there is a possibility that the victim may eventually recover the use of the member or organ, or that the disfigurement may be cured by surgery. MCM, pt. IV, ¶ 50.c.(1).

C. Intent. Maiming is a specific intent crime. The government must prove a specific intent to injure a person, **not** the specific intent to maim or inflict grievous bodily harm.

1. The 1969 Manual described maiming as a general intent crime. MCM, 1969, ¶ 203. This interpretation was based on *United States v. Hicks*, 20 C.M.R. 337 (C.M.A. 1956). *See also United States v. Tua*, 4 M.J. 761 (A.C.M.R. 1977).

2. The 1984 Manual, however, also relying on *Hicks*, describes maiming as requiring a specific intent to injure generally, not a specific intent to maim. MCM, pt. IV, ¶ 50c, analysis. *See United States v. Berri*, 33 M.J. 337 (C.M.A. 1991).

3. When grievous bodily harm has been inflicted by means of intentionally using force in a manner likely to achieve that result, it may be inferred that grievous bodily harm was intended. MCM, pt. IV, ¶ 54.c.(4)(b)(ii); *United States v. Allen*, 59 M.J. 515 (N-M. Ct. Crim. App. 2003) (circumstantial evidence of injury to infant victim sufficient to support inference of accused's intent to injure; affirmed conviction for maiming), *aff'd*, 59 M.J. 478 (C.A.A.F. 2004). [NOTE: Intent to inflict grievous bodily harm is not required for maiming, but the facts of this case supported that finding].

D. Injury.

1. Must be a serious injury of a substantially permanent nature.

2. Maiming may exist even if the injury can be cured by surgery, or if the disfigurement would not be visible under everyday circumstances. *United States v. Spenhoff*, 41 M.J. 772 (A.F. Ct. Crim. App. 1995) (scar on victim's buttocks). *But see United States v. McGhee*, 29 M.J. 840 (A.C.M.R. 1989) (where the scars to the victim's face and body, predominately on the buttocks, were not easily detectable to the casual observer, the injury was insufficient to support a maiming charge), *rev'd in part on other grounds*, 32 M.J. 322 (C.M.A. 1991).

3. Disfigurement need not mutilate an entire body part, but it must cause visible bodily damage and significantly detract from the victim's physical appearance. *United States v. Outin*, 42 M.J. 603 (N-M. Ct. Crim. App. 1995) (scars sustained by child victim who was immersed in scalding water were clearly visible at trial and substantially permanent in nature supported conviction for maiming, even though doctor testified that scars would become less visible with passage of time); *United States v. Morgan*, 47 M.J. 644 (Army Ct. Crim. App. 1997) (permanent scarring and de-pigmentation of the infant victim's groin and buttocks, caused by the accused's immersing him in scalding water, was "perceptible and material" disfigurement within the meaning of Article 124, even though the injury would normally be covered from public view by clothing and affected a relatively small area of the child's skin).

V. SEXUAL OFFENSES.

A. Based on the revision to Article 120 (effective 1 October 2007), this section divides treatment of sexual offenses under the UCMJ. Paragraph V(B) addresses the "new" Article 120, Rape, Sexual Assault, and Other Sexual Offenses. Paragraph V(C) addresses the "old" Article 120, Rape. Beginning with paragraph V(D), the range of other sexual offenses—some of which survive the "new" Article 120 and some of which do not—are developed in sequence. As practitioners navigate this section, they should remain cognizant of 1) the date the offense occurred, and 2) the statute of limitations when deciding which offenses to research.

B. "New Article 120" Rape, Sexual Assault, and Other Sexual Offenses (post-1 October 2007). MCM, pt. IV, ¶ 45; UCMJ art. 120 (2008).

1. Effective date: 1 October 2007. Implementing Executive Order signed 28 September 2007 (E.O. 13447).

2. Statute best considered in three parts: the "Big Four" offenses, the child sexual abuse offenses, and the remaining sexual offenses:

a) The "Big Four" offenses: rape, aggravated sexual assault, aggravated sexual contact, and abusive sexual contact.

(1) By adding "w/ a child" to each of these four, the titles for eight of the statute's fourteen offenses emerge.

(2) Consent and mistake of fact as to consent are affirmative defenses only available to these "Big Four" offenses.

(3) Statutory definitions for "sexual act" and "sexual contact," along with the set of attendant circumstances identified in the statute, combine to define each of the four offenses.

b) The Child Sexual Abuse Offenses: rape of a child, aggravated sexual assault of a child, aggravated sexual abuse of a child, aggravated sexual contact with a child, abusive sexual contact with a child, and indecent liberty with a child.

c) The four remaining sexual offenses include: indecent act, forcible pandering, wrongful sexual contact, and indecent exposure.

3. The "Big Four" offenses:

- by Force

- by Causing GBH

- by Threatening Death / GBH   - by Causing Bodily Harm

- by Rendering Unconscious   - by Threatening (< Death / GBH)

- by Administering Intoxicant   - by Taking Advantage of Incapacity

▼   ▼

Sexual Act ▶   **RAPE**   **AGG. SEXUAL ASSAULT**

Sexual Contact ▶ **AGG. SEXUAL CONTACT**   **ABUSIVE SEXUAL CONTACT**

4. The "Big Four" offenses defined. As the chart above indicates, start with defining whether or not a "sexual act" or a "sexual contact" has been committed, then determine which set of attendant circumstances apply to arrive at the proper offense. The following notes regarding the definitions and attendant circumstances are intended to assist in navigating the chart.

    a) "Sexual Act". (MCM, pt. IV, ¶ 45a(t)(1)).

        (1) The penetration described by "sexual act" excludes male-on-male sexual activity.

        (2) Broader conduct than merely sexual intercourse.

        (3) If penetration accomplished by hand, finger, or any object, specific intent requirement that must be alleged and proved: "with an intent to abuse, humiliate, harass, or degrade any person or to arouse or gratify the sexual desire of any person."

    b) "Sexual Contact". (MCM, pt. IV, ¶ 45a(t)(2)).

        (1) May encompass same conduct proscribed by Article 125, Sodomy, including male-on-male sexual activity.

        (2) Specific intent requirement for all sexual contacts that must be alleged and proved: "with an intent to abuse, humiliate, or degrade any person or to arouse or gratify the sexual desire of any person."

    c) "Lewd Act". (MCM, pt. IV, ¶ 45a(t)(10)).

        (1) Requires intentional "skin-to-skin contact" with the genitalia of another person.

        (2) Requires the specific intent "to abuse, humiliate, or degrade any person or to arouse or gratify the sexual desire of any person."

        (3) Applies only to Aggravated Sexual Abuse of a Child (Art. 120(f)).

    d) "Force". (MCM, pt. IV, ¶ 45a(t)(5)).

        (1) While "without consent" is no longer an element of any of the "Big Four" offenses, "force" is defined using terms that nonetheless invoke the concept of "consent." Specifically, the statute says force means action *to compel submission* of another or *to overcome or prevent another's resistance*. (emphasis added). These emphasized phrases may cause the government to prove lack of consent as part of its "force" proof.

        (2) The concept of "constructive force," developed by case law prior to the revision of Article 120, is defined out of the new Article 120's definition of "force" and appears elsewhere in other statutory definitions.

    e) At this time, the difference between "rendering" another person unconscious or "administering" an intoxicant to another person (for purposes of establishing rape or aggravated sexual contact) and taking advantage of incapacitation (for purposes of establishing an aggravated sexual assault or abusive sexual contact) appears to be the extent to which the principal caused the victim's incapacitation.

    f) "Threatening or placing that other person in fear" of anything less than death or grievous bodily harm is defined at MCM, pt. IV, ¶ 45a(t)(7) and National

Defense Authorization Act, FY2006, PL 109-163, 119 Stat. 3260-1. This definition includes classic examples of the "old" Article 120's doctrine of constructive force. By statutory definition, "threatening" for purposes of establishing an aggravated sexual assault or an abusive sexual contact includes: A threat:

(1) To accuse a person of a crime;

(2) To expose a secret or publicize an asserted fact, whether true or false, tending to subject some person to hatred, contempt, or ridicule; or

(3) Through the use or abuse of military position, rank, or authority, to affect or threaten to affect, either positively or negatively, the military career of some person.

g) The Military Judge's Benchbook now contains a definition for "substantially incapacitated." *See* DA Pam 27-9, Military Judges' Benchbook, ¶ 3-45-5, subpara. d and ¶ 3-45-6, subpara. d.

5. Child Sexual Abuse Offenses.

a) The six child sexual abuse offenses are: rape of a child (Art. 120(b)), aggravated sexual assault of a child (Art. 120(d)), aggravated sexual abuse of a child (Art. 120(f)), aggravated sexual contact with a child (Art. 120(g)), abusive sexual contact with a child (Art. 120(i)), and indecent liberty with a child (Art. 120(j)).

b) Practitioners can best navigate the child sexual abuse framework by using the facts of the case to answer the following three questions:

(1) How old is the child (under 12, between 12 and 16, or over 16)?

(2) What type of sexual touching occurred (sexual act, sexual contact, lewd act, or some other type)?

(3) What type of inducement was employed (none, "rape-level," "aggravated sexual assault-level")?

Once answers to these three questions are obtained, the practitioner can then navigate the elements of the six child abuse offenses in order of severity.

c) Aggravated Sexual Abuse of a Child. MCM, pt. IV, ¶ 45a(f).

(1) Requires a "Lewd Act" as defined at MCM, pt. IV, ¶ 45a(t)(10).

(2) Specific intent requirement for all lewd acts that must be alleged and proved: "with an intent to abuse, humiliate, or degrade any person or to arouse or gratify the sexual desire of any person."

d) Indecent Liberty with a Child. (MCM, pt. IV, ¶ 45a(j)).

(1) Requires specific intent "to arouse, appeal to, or gratify the sexual desire of any person" or "to abuse, humiliate, or degrade any person."

(2) Physical touching is not required. *See* MCM, pt. IV, ¶ 45a(t)(11).

(3) May include communication of indecent language and exposure of one's genitalia, anus, buttocks, or female areola or nipple to a child. *See* MCM, pt. IV, ¶ 45a(t)(11).

(4) Requires "Physical Presence" with the child. *See* MCM, pt. IV, ¶ 45a(j), (t)(11); *United States v. Miller*, 67 M.J. 87 (2008) (applying old Indecent Liberties with a Child provision in Art. 134, constructive presence through webcam is insufficient).

6. The remaining four offenses. The following notes are intended to alert the practitioner to issues involved with litigating these last four offenses.

   a) Wrongful Sexual Contact. MCM, pt. IV, ¶ 45a(l).

   (1) Relies on the same definition of "Sexual Contact" employed by the "Big Four" offenses.

   (2) Sexual contact occurs "without that other person's permission." This language may impose an affirmative consent requirement on the principal. In other words, the statutory language seems to suggest that a principal must ask for affirmative consent from the other party to engage in the conduct that might amount to sexual contact.

   (3) The statutory language for this offense is taken directly from 18 U.S.C. § 2244(b).

   b) The following three offenses were all Article 134 offenses before the statutory change. As such, the implementing executive order, signed 28 October 2007, deleted these offenses from Article 134. In removing these offenses from Article 134, the requirement that the conduct be either prejudicial to good order and discipline or service discrediting has been eliminated.

   (1) Indecent Act. MCM, pt. IV, ¶ 45a(k). Proscribes "indecent conduct," which is defined by statute. Contains no specific intent requirement. The statutory language specifies "voyeurism"-types of offenses, but the *Benchbook* instruction also imports traditional concepts of "open and notorious" sexual behavior. *See* DA Pam 27-9, Military Judges' Benchbook, ¶ 3-45-9, note 2.

   (2) Forcible Pandering. MCM, pt. IV, ¶ 45a(l). Replaces only the "compel" portion of Article 134, Pandering.

   (3) Indecent Exposure. MCM, pt. IV, ¶ 45a(n). Proscribes exposure which occurs in an "indecent manner." "Indecent" is defined at MCM, pt. IV, ¶ 45c(3).

7. A listing of lesser included offenses for the Article 120 offenses may be found both in paragraph (d) and (e) of the implementing executive order. *See* MCM, pt. IV, ¶ 45d & e. Practitioners should be aware that this list is neither exclusive, nor all-inclusive. *See* MCM, App. 23, ¶ 45d; MCM, pt. IV, ¶ 3b(4) ("Specific lesser included offenses, if any, are listed for each offense discussed in this Part, but the lists are not all-inclusive.").

   a) *United States v. Alston*, No. 20080504 (A. Ct. Crim. App. Nov. 19, 2009) (unpub.) (finding that aggravated sexual assault by causing bodily harm is a lesser included offense of rape by force and that the military judge did not err in providing the instruction, even though neither party requested it).

b) *United States v. Bailey*, No. 200800897 (N-M. Ct. Crim. App. Sep. 29, 2009) (unpub.). In a single incident, the accused engaged in various acts of sexual physical contact. He was charged with three specifications under Art. 120. Specification 1 alleged "sexual contact causing bodily harm," Specification 2 alleged abusive sexual contact, and Specification 3 alleged wrongful sexual contact. The accused pled guilty to Specification 3 (wrongful sexual contact), and not guilty to the other two specifications. The military judge accepted his plea to Specification 3, but also convicted him of abusive sexual contact, finding that "the previously pleaded-to wrongful sexual contact was committed by placing the victim in fear of physical injury or other harm, constituting abusive sexual contact." The military judge considered the two offenses "multiplicious for sentencing." The N-MCCA held that the two specifications were multiplicious for findings and the military judge erred in not dismissing the wrongful sexual contact specification upon finding the accused guilty of the "more aggravated abusive sexual contact" specification. The MCM lists wrongful sexual contact as an LIO of abusive sexual contact "depending on the factual circumstances." *See* 2008 MCM, pt. IV, ¶ 45.e.(8). The court reasoned that "the only significant difference between the specifications [is] the additional element of placing the victim in fear," which was proven in the contested portion of the trial. As such, the military judge erred and there was prejudice in the form of an additional conviction, as well as increased punitive exposure. The court also found that the conviction for the specification constituted an unreasonable multiplication of charges. Although the specifications were merged for sentencing, corrective action with respect to the findings was necessary.

8. Affirmative Defenses.

   a) The new Article 120 assigns burdens for all affirmative defenses raised in the context of an Article 120 prosecution:

   (1) "The accused has the burden of proving the affirmative defense by a preponderance of evidence. After the defense meets this burden, the prosecution shall have the burden of proving beyond a reasonable doubt that the affirmative defense did not exist."

   (2) According to one view, this provision improperly assigns two separate burdens of persuasion to two separate parties on a single issue. *See* Major Howard H. Hoege, III, *Overshift: The Unconstitutional Double Burden-Shift on Affirmative Defenses in the New Article 120*, ARMY LAW., May 2007, at 2; *Texas Dep't of Cmty. Affairs v. Burdine*, 450 U.S. 248, 253 (1981) (citing 9 J. WIGMORE, EVIDENCE § 2489 (3d ed. 1940)(stating, "the burden of persuasion 'never shifts.'").

   (3) In the MJ Benchbook (DA Pam 27-9), the Army Trial Judiciary has taken the approach of treating affirmative defenses which will arise under Article 120 prosecutions just like the majority of other affirmative defenses recognized by the MCM and case law. In other words, "some evidence" will raise a defense and once the defense is raised, the government will have the burden of proving beyond a reasonable doubt that the affirmative defense does not exist. *See, e.g.,* DA Pam 27-9, para. 3-45-3, note 10. While this is a workable means to implement the

statutory scheme, practitioners must be aware that this is a departure from the plain language of the statute.

(4) Whatever the approach taken at trial to affirmative defenses, the new Article 120 creates an internal inconsistency within the UCMJ. Article 50a shifts the burden to the accused to prove lack of mental responsibility by clear and convincing evidence. Both Article 120's double burden-shift and the MJ Benchbook instructions apparently apply to all affirmative defenses that arise under Article 120 prosecutions. Neither document explains whether Article 50a or Article 120 procedures will govern the defense of lack of mental responsibility.

(5) For an in-depth discussion of this burden shift and its issues, see Major Howard H. Hoege, III, *Overshift: The Unconstitutional Double Burden-Shift on Affirmative Defenses in the New Article 120*, ARMY LAW., May 2007, at 2.

b) Facial Challenges.

1. *United States v. Neal*, 68 M.J. 289 (C.A.A.F. 2010). In a prosecution of an aggravated sexual contact involving force under Art. 120(e), the trial judge dismissed the charge, finding that consent was an "implied element" and concluding that Article 120 unconstitutionally shifted the burden of proof on an element from the Government to the defense. This occurred after the defense case in chief, before instructions and findings. The government appealed under Article 62 and the N-MCCA reversed, holding that, under the facts of the case, proof of the element of force does not require proof of lack of consent and the affirmative defense of consent does not unconstitutionally shift the burden of proof to the defense. The CAAF, in a 3-2 decision, affirmed the N-MCCA's decision, and remanded the record of trial to the military judge. The court made two key interpretations of the language of the new Article 120: (1) absence of consent is not a fact necessary to prove the crime of aggravated sexual assault, and (2) the words "consent is not an issue" in Article 120(r) do not prohibit the factfinder from considering evidence of consent when determining whether the prosecution has proved the element of force beyond a reasonable doubt (*see also Martin v. Ohio*, 480 U.S. 228 (1987)). Next, the court confirmed the interlocutory posture of the case, noting that there were no instructions, no closing arguments, and no findings. The court then found that the military judge erred in treating lack of consent as an element of the offense and in concluding that the affirmative defense scheme is unconstitutional. Although the court did not rule on the constitutionality of the statute as applied to the accused in this case due to its interlocutory nature, the court cautioned that the constitutionality may be affected by the content of instructions, the sequence of the instructions, and any waiver of instructions. In a dissenting opinion, which Judge Erdmann joined, Judge Ryan concludes that "' [force' and 'consent' . . . are two sides of the same coin," and "making consent an affirmative defense . . . relieves the government of

[the burden of proof as to an element] and unconstitutionally requires the defendant to disprove force."

2. *United States v. Crotchett,* 67 M.J. 713 (N-M. Ct. Crim. App. 2009) (holding that a facial challenge to Art. 120(c), Aggravated Sexual Assault, fails because the court's "construction of the statute leads to the conclusion that Article 120(c)(2)(C) does not mandate a shift to the defense of the burden of proof as to any element).

3. *United States v. Medina,* No. 200900053, 2009 WL 4857364 (N-M. Ct. Crim. App. Dec. 17, 2009). In a prosecution of an aggravated sexual assault involving an incapacitated victim under Art. 120(c), the N-MCCA rejected a facial challenge to Article 120(c), holding that the statute "requires no assignment of burdens that would deprive an accused of his right to due process under the Fifth Amendment." The court did, however, find that, "As a matter of law, the affirmative defense of consent is unavailable where the putative victim is "substantially incapacitated."

4. *United States v. Rozmus,* No. 200900052, 2009 WL 2893176 (N-M. Ct. Crim. App. Sep. 10, 2009) (unpub.) (facial challenge fails because court extends the holding of *Crotchett* to Article 120(c)(2)(b)).

5. *United States v. Prather,* No. 37329 (A.F. Ct. Crim. App. Jan. 25, 2010)(unpub.) (rejecting a facial challenge to Art. 120, citing *Crotchett, supra*).

c) Instructions.

(1) *United States v. Neal,* 68 M.J. 289 (C.A.A.F. 2010). The constitutionality of the statute may be affected by the content of instructions, the sequence of the instructions, and any waiver of instructions. "A properly instructed jury may consider evidence of consent at two different levels: (1) as raising a reasonable doubt as to whether the prosecution has met its burden on the element of force; and (2) as to whether the defense hasestablished an affirmative defense."

(2) *United States v. Medina,* 68 M.J. 587 (N-M. Ct. Crim. App. 2009). In a prosecution of an aggravated sexual assault involving an incapacitated victim under Art. 120(c), the trial judge gave instructions for consent that mirrored the model instructions provided in the Military Judges' Benchbook and departed from the plain language from the statute regarding the assignment of burdens regarding the affirmative defense of consent. Specifically, the military judge instructed the members that "The prosecution has the burden to prove beyond a reasonable doubt that consent did not exist." The panel convicted the accused. On appeal, the N-MCCA noted that the military judge's instructions omitted the accused's burden of proving the affirmative defense of consent by a preponderance of the evidence. However, without deciding whether the instructions constituted error or an abuse of discretion, the court concluded that any error failed to prejudice the accused, and "actually inured to his benefit by alleviating him of any burden of production or proof with respect to the affirmative defense of consent."

(3) *United States v. Prather*, No. 37329 (A.F. Ct. Crim. App. Jan. 25, 2010) (unpub.). After evidence was presented, the military judge informed the parties that he intended to instruct on the affirmative defenses of consent and mistake of fact as to consent. The military judge's instructions were crafted using the statutory language. The defense objected and requested alternate instructions based on those recommended in the *Military Judges' Benchbook*. The military judge overruled the defense objection, and gave the panel instructions based on the wording of the statute, rather than the *Benchbook*. Additionally, the court found that any deviation from the *Benchbook* instruction was to ensure that the instructions implemented the statutory language. As such, the court concluded that the instructions were constitutional and Art. 120 does not violate an accused's right to due process. The court summarily rejected the accused's argument that, due to a general verdict, the AFCCA could not determine whether the members employed the statutory scheme correctly.

(4) *United States v. Rozmus*, No. 200900052, 2009 WL 2893176 (N-M. Ct. Crim. App. Sep. 10, 2009) (unpub.) (facial challenge fails because court extends the holding of *Crotchett* to Article 120(c)(2)(b), as applied challenge fails because no evidence of consent or mistake of fact as to consent raised at trial).

d) Multiplicity and UMC.

(1) *United States v. Oliva*, No. 20080774 (A. Ct. Crim. App. Feb. 24, 2009) (unpublished). The accused, a drill sergeant, was charged with two specifications of aggravated sexual assault under Art. 120. Specification 1 alleged that he "caused the victim . . . to engage in a sexual act, i.e., penetration of her genital opening with [his] finger, by causing bodily harm in the form of bruises on her arm." Specification 2 alleged that he "engaged in a sexual act, i.e., penetration of [the victim's] genital opening with his finger, by placing her in fear of [his] abuse of his military position to affect negatively her career." He pled not guilty to these offenses, however, he pled guilty to two specifications of the lesser included offense of wrongful sexual contact by "placing his finders in [her] vagina without legal justification or authorization and without her consent." He "pled guilty to the *identical* criminal conduct and acts for both specifications." the two specifications were multiplicious for findings and dismissed Specification 2. The accused pled guilty to two specifications of wrongful sexual contact for the exact same underlying conduct.

(2) *United States v. Bailey*, No. 200800897 (N-M. Ct. Crim. App. Sep. 29, 2009) (unpub.). In a single incident, the accused engaged in various acts of sexual physical contact. He was charged with three specifications under Art. 120. Specification 1 alleged "sexual contact causing bodily harm," Specification 2 alleged abusive sexual contact, and Specification 3 alleged wrongful sexual contact. The accused pled guilty to Specification 3 (wrongful sexual contact), and not guilty to the other two specifications. The military judge accepted his plea to Specification 3, but also convicted him of abusive sexual contact, finding that "the previously pleaded-to

wrongful sexual contact was committed by placing the victim in fear of physical injury or other harm, constituting abusive sexual contact." The military judge considered the two offenses "multiplicious for sentencing." The N-MCCA held that the two specifications were multiplicious for findings and the military judge erred in not dismissing the wrongful sexual contact specification upon finding the accused guilty of the "more aggravated abusive sexual contact" specification. The MCM lists wrongful sexual contact as an LIO of abusive sexual contact "depending on the factual circumstances." *See* 2008 MCM, pt. IV, ¶ 45.e.(8). The court reasoned that "the only significant difference between the specifications [is] the additional element of placing the victim in fear," which was proven in the contested portion of the trial. As such, the military judge erred and there was prejudice in the form of an additional conviction, as well as increased punitive exposure. The court also found that the conviction for the specification constituted an unreasonable multiplication of charges.

(3) *United States v. Marshall,* No. 200900533 (N-M. Ct. Crim. App. Feb. 10, 2010) (unpub.). Accused engaged in sexual intercourse with an incapacitated victim. When victim awoke and tried to get him to stop, he withdrew, began masturbating over top of her, and ejaculated onto her hair, stomach, and shirt. The accused was convicted of both aggravated sexual assault and an indecent act, both under Art. 120. Charges were neither multiplicious nor an unreasonable multiplication of charges.

(4) *United States v. Swemley*, No. 200900359 (N-M. Ct. Crim. App. Apr. 29, 2010) (unpub.). Accused was charged with aggravated sexual assault of an incapacitated victim, but the panel convicted of the LIO of assault consummated by a battery by touching the victim and removing her clothing while she was asleep. The N-MCCA found that the military judge did not err in instructing on assault consummated by battery as an LIO of aggravated sexual assault and the accused received the requisite notice that he could be convicted of this lesser offense.

C. "Old Article 120" Rape (pre-1 October 2007). MCM, App. 27, ¶ 45.

1. Elements.

   a) That the accused committed an act of sexual intercourse; and

   b) That the act of sexual intercourse was done by force and without consent.

2. Article 120 has no spousal exemption and is gender-neutral.

3. Any penetration, however slight, is sufficient. *United States v. Aleman*, 2 C.M.R. 269 (A.B.R. 1951).

4. In determining whether force and lack of consent occurred, a totality of the circumstances must be considered. *See United States v. Webster,* 40 M.J. 384, 386 (C.M.A. 1994).

5. Lack of Consent.

   a) Competence to consent.

(1) No consent exists where victim is incompetent, unconscious, or sleeping. *United States v. Booker*, 25 M.J. 114 (C.M.A. 1987); *United States v. Robertson*, 33 C.M.R. 828 (A.F.B.R. 1963); *United States v. Maithai*, 34 M.J. 33 (C.M.A. 1992); *United States v. Grier*, 53 M.J. 30 (C.A.A.F. 2000).

(2) A child of tender years is incapable of consent. *United States v. Aleman*, 2 C.M.R. 269 (A.B.R. 1951); *United States v. Thompson*, 3 M.J. 168 (C.M.A. 1977); *see United States v. Huff*, 4 M.J. 816 (A.C.M.R. 1978) (because victim is under 16, proof of age is proof of nonconsent allowing fresh complaint evidence).

b) Resistance by Victim.

(1) The lack of consent required is more than mere lack of acquiescence. If a victim in possession of his or her mental faculties fails to make lack of consent reasonably manifest by taking such measures of resistance as are called for by the circumstances, the inference may be drawn that the victim did consent. *See* MCM, pt. IV, ¶ 45.c.(1)(b).

(2) If victim is capable of resistance, evidence must show more than victim's lack of acquiescence. *United States v. Bonano-Torres*, 31 M.J. 175 (C.M.A. 1990) (acquiescence to intercourse with accused so the "victim" could go to sleep is insufficient for rape).

(3) Consent may be inferred unless victim makes her lack of consent "reasonably manifest by taking such measures of resistance as are called for by the circumstances." *United States v. Tollinchi*, 54 M.J. 80 (C.A.A.F. 2000) (holding successful resistance by intoxicated seventeen-year-old victim to oral sodomy, followed by lack of resistance to intercourse, rendered rape conviction legally insufficient).

(4) *United States v. Briggs*, 46 M.J. 699 (A.F. Ct. Crim App. 1997) (victim's passive acquiescence did not constitute consent where accused admitted he was not sure she was conscious), *aff'd,* 48 M.J. 143 (C.A.A.F. 1998); *United States v. Hughes*, 48 M.J. 214 (C.A.A.F. 1998) (where accused entered victim's room at night while she was sleeping and had intercourse with her while she was not fully awake, where she called out her boyfriend's name several times during intercourse and only noticed the accused was not her boyfriend after intercourse was completed, there was no consent).

(5) Verbal protest may be sufficient to manifest a lack of consent sufficient to support rape. *United States v. Webster*, 40 M.J. 384 (C.M.A. 1994) (evidence of unwavering and repeated verbal protest in context of a surprise nonviolent sexual aggression by boyfriend was considered reasonable resistance).

c) Resistance by Victim Not Required.

(1) Consent may not be inferred if resistance would have been futile, where resistance is overcome by threats of death or great bodily harm, or where the victim is unable to resist because of the lack of mental or

physical faculties. All the surrounding circumstances are to be considered in determining whether a victim gave consent, or whether he or she failed or ceased to resist only because of a reasonable fear of death or grievous bodily harm. *See* MCM, pt. IV, ¶ 45.c.(1)(b).

(2) Proof of rape of a daughter by her father may not require physical resistance if intercourse is accomplished under long, continued parental duress. *United States v. Dejonge*, 16 M.J. 974 (A.F.C.M.R. 1983); *see United States v. Palmer*, 33 M.J. 7 (C.M.A. 1991); *see United States v. Davis*, 52 M.J. 201 (1999); *United States v. Young*, 50 M.J. 717 (Army Ct. Crim. App. 1999) (compulsion may apply even when child is not a minor); *see generally* TJAGSA Practice Note, *Proving Lack of Consent for Intra-Family Sex Crimes*, ARMY LAW., Jun. 1990, at 51.

(3) Cooperation with assailant after resistance is overcome by numbers, threats, or fear of great bodily harm is not consent. *United States v. Burt*, 45 C.M.R. 557 (A.F.C.M.R. 1972); *United States v. Evans*, 6 M.J. 577 (A.C.M.R. 1978); *United States v. Lewis*, 6 M.J. 581 (A.C.M.R. 1978).

(4) Whether the rape victim was justified in resisting by words alone involves a factual issue whether she viewed physical resistance as impractical or futile. *United States v. Burns*, 9 M.J. 706 (N.C.M.R. 1980).

d) Mistake as to Consent. An honest and reasonable mistake of fact to the victim's consent is a defense. *United States v. Hibbard*, 58 M.J. 71 (2003); *United States v. Taylor*, 26 M.J. 127 (C.M.A. 1988); *United States v. Carr*, 18 M.J. 297 (C.M.A. 1984); *United States v. Davis*, 27 M.J. 543 (A.C.M.R. 1988); *United States v. True*, 41 M.J. 424 (1995) (mistake of fact as to victim's consent to intercourse cannot be predicated upon accused's negligence; mistake must be honest and reasonable); *United States v. Traylor*, 40 M.J. 248 (C.M.A. 1994) (mistake of fact as to consent is not reasonable when based upon belief by accused that victim would consent to intercourse with anyone); *United States v. Parker*, 54 M.J. 700 (Army Ct. Crim. App. 2000) (evidence factually insufficient to sustain conviction where accused claimed he mistakenly believed that the victim consented to intercourse and sodomy where she and the accused engaged in a consensual relationship for several months before the first alleged rape, she sent mixed signals to the accused about their relationship and the relationship included consensual sexual acts).

e) Consent Obtained by Fraud. Consent obtained by fraud in the inducement (*e.g.*, lying about marital status or desire to marry, a promise to pay money or to respect sexual partner in the morning) will not support a charge of rape. Consent obtained by fraud in factum (*i.e.*, a misrepresentation of act performed or some aspects of identity) can support a rape charge. *United States v. Booker*, 25 M.J. 114 (C.M.A. 1987).

f) Identity of partner. The victim's consent is not transferable to other partners. *United States v. Traylor*, 40 M.J. 248 (C.M.A. 1994) (victim consented to sexual intercourse with one soldier but during intercourse, another soldier, the accused, penetrated the victim without first obtaining her consent and victim was not aware of the accused's presence until he had already penetrated her without consent).

6. Relationship Between Elements of Lack of Consent and Force. Although force and lack of consent are separate elements, there may be circumstances in which the two are so

closely intertwined that both elements may be proved by the same evidence. Consent induced by fear, fright, or coercion is equivalent to physical force. Such constructive force may consist of expressed or implied threats of bodily harm. *United States v. Simpson*, 58 M.J. 368, 377 (C.A.A.F. 2003).

7. Force.

   a) When constructive force is not at issue and the victim is capable of resisting, some force more than that required for penetration is necessary; persistent sexual overtures are not enough. *United States v. Bonano-Torres*, 31 M.J. 175 (C.M.A. 1990).

   b) If a victim is incapable of consenting, no greater force is required than that necessary to achieve penetration. *United States v. Grier*, 53 M.J. 30 (C.A.A.F. 2000).

   c) *United States v. Cauley*, 45 M.J. 353 (C.A.A.F. 1996) (sufficient force where victim testified that she accompanied the accused without protest to his private quarters knowing that the accused intended to engage in sexual intercourse and offered no physical resistance as the accused removed her clothing and positioned her on the bed, but further testified that before sexual intercourse she told accused "no" several times and that she did "not want to do this" and "wanted to go home", that she turned her face when he attempted to kiss her and that he used his legs to pry her legs open). *But see United States v. King*, 32 M.J. 558 (A.C.M.R. 1991) (evidence insufficient to show requisite force).

   d) Constructive Force.

   (1) If resistance would have been futile, where resistance is overcome by threats of death or great bodily harm, or where the victim is unable to resist because of the lack of mental or physical faculties, there is no consent and the force involved in penetration will suffice. *See* MCM, pt. IV, ¶ 45.c.(1)(b).

   (2) Constructive force, as a substitute for actual force, may consist of express or implied threats of bodily harm. *United States v. Bradley*, 28 M.J. 197 (C.M.A. 1989) (threat of imprisoning husband); *United States v. Hicks*, 24 M.J. 3 (C.M.A. 1987); *United States v. Palmer*, 33 M.J. 7 (C.M.A. 1991) (parental figure can exert a psychological force over child that is constructive force).

   (3) Force can be subtle and psychological, and need not be overt or physically brutal. *United States v. Torres*, 27 M.J. 867 (A.F.C.M.R. 1989) *clarified*, 1989 CMR LEXIS 1042 (A.F.C.M.R. Nov. 15, 1989); *United States v. Sargent*, 33 M.J. 815 (A.C.M.R. 1991), *aff'd*, 36 M.J. 14 (C.M.A. 1992).

   (4) Constructive force in the form of parental compulsion is not limited to cases in which the victim is under 16 years of age. Age is one factor to consider in determining whether victim's resistance was overcome by parental compulsion. *United States v. Young*, 50 M.J. 717 (Army Ct. Crim. App. 1999) (accused started to "groom" and "condition" his stepdaughter when she was five years old; sexual intercourse started when she was 11 years old; accused was convicted of raping his stepdaughter from when she was 16 to 20 years old).

(5) Rank disparity alone is not sufficient to show constructive force. Other factors are relevant. *United States v. Simpson*, 58 M.J. 368, 377 (C.A.A.F. 2003) (accused was in a power relationship, not a dating one, with the trainees he was accused of raping and the court noted: (1) the accused's physically imposing size; (2) his reputation in the unit for being tough and mean; (3) his position as a noncommissioned officer; (4) his actual and apparent authority over each of the victims in matters other than sexual contact; (5) the location and timing of the assaults, including his use of his official office and other areas within the barracks in which the trainees were required to live; (6) his refusal to accept verbal and physical indications that his victims were not willing participants; and (7) the relatively diminutive size and youth of his victims, and their lack of military experience; and finally, the accused's abuse of authority in ordering the victims to isolated locations where the charged offenses occurred).

(6) *United States v. Leak*, 61 M.J. 234 (C.A.A.F. 2005). Appellant was a small group leader and member of the cadre at the NCO academy where the victim was enrolled. The ACCA concluded that it was not convinced beyond a reasonable doubt that the sexual intercourse on one of those dates was done by force and without consent, and affirmed the lesser included offense of indecent assault. The Government certified the question of whether the ACCA applied a higher standard for constructive force than the CAAF held appropriate in *United States v. Simpson*, 58 M.J. 368 (2003). HELD: The ACCA did not err in their interpretation of constructive force, but the case is remanded for clarification of the basis for their findings. The ACCA did not confuse the requisite standard of physical apprehension addressed to the element of consent with the lesser apprehension of physical injury necessary to demonstrate constructive force. However, certain findings regarding lack of consent and the requisite resistance require clarification.

(7) *United States v. Bright*, 66 M.J. 359 (C.A.A.F. 2008). The accused was a drill sergeant and was convicted of raping a female trainee on three separate occasions. The court concluded there was insufficient evidence, based on totality of circumstances, regarding lack of consent. First, the court observed that the record is devoid of any evidence that PVT W manifested a lack of consent or took any measures to resist sexual intercourse. She made arrangements to meet him at a hotel knowing that sex would occur and she made her own way to the hotel to meet him. On two occasions, she arrived at the hotel first and waited for him. Additionally, even though she resisted sodomy on one occasion, there is no evidence that she resisted "normal sexual intercourse" in any way, verbal or physical. The court next concluded that there is no evidence to support the inference that resistance would have been futile or that he resistance would have been overcome by threats of death or grievous bodily harm. The accused never threatened her physically—the only threat was to take away her pass status. Finally, the court distinguished PVT W's perceived futility of resistance from the facts in *United States v. Simpson*, 58 M.J. 368 (C.A.A.F. 2003) (where the accused ordered his victims into isolated areas, initiated sexual activity, and then refused to

accept "verbal and physical indications that his victims were not willing participants") and *United States v. Clark*, 35 M.J. 432 (C.M.A. 1992) (where the accused cornered the victim in a "small shed with brick walls and a metal door and . . . positioned himself between the door and the victim").

8. Lesser Included Offenses. With the change to Article 120 in 2007, it is important to note that several sexual offenses that were enumerated under Article 134 prior to October 2007 are now incorporated into Article 120. As such, when considering the lesser included offenses under the "old Article 120," it is important to use the lesser included offenses as they existed prior to October 2007. Appendix 27 of the 2008 MCM contains the "old Article 120" offenses as well as the "old Article 134" offenses.

    a) Carnal knowledge. Carnal knowledge is a lesser included offense of rape when the pleading alleges that the victim has not yet attained the age of 16 years. *See infra* ¶ VI.D, this chapter.

    b) Indecent assault. *See infra* ¶ VI.F, this chapter.

    c) Indecent acts with another. *See infra* ¶ VI.I, this chapter.

    d) Sexual intercourse in presence of a third party is an indecent act, a lesser-included offense of rape. *United States v. Tollinchi*, 54 M.J. 80 (C.A.A.F. 2000); *United States v. Berry*, 20 C.M.R. 325, 330 (C.M.A. 1956) (sexual intercourse is "open and notorious," "flagrant," and "discrediting" when participants know a third person is present).

    e) Indecent acts or liberties with a child. *See infra* ¶ VI.J, this chapter.

    f) Attempted rape.

        (1) Accused who was dissuaded by the victim from completing the rape and abandoned the act could be found guilty of attempted rape. *United States v. Valenzuela*, 15 M.J. 699 (A.C.M.R. 1983), *aff'd in part, rev'd in part on multiplicity grounds,* 16 M.J. 305 (C.M.A. 1983). *But see United States v. Byrd*, 24 M.J. 286 (C.M.A. 1987) (voluntary abandonment is a defense to attempted rape, but evidence insufficient to establish defense in this case). *See* MCM, pt. IV, ¶ 4.c.(4); *supra*, ch. 2, ¶ I.E.

        (2) *United States v. Polk*, 48 C.M.R. 993 (A.F.C.M.R. 1974) (gross and atrocious attempt to persuade the victim to consent to intercourse is not attempted rape but may be indecent assault).

9. Multiplicity.

    a) Rape and aggravated assault are multiplicious for findings. *United States v. Sellers*, 14 M.J. 211 (C.M.A. 1982) (summary disposition); *see United States v. DiBello*, 17 M.J. 77 (C.M.A. 1983).

    b) Rape and communication of a threat are multiplicious for findings. *United States v. Hollimon*, 16 M.J. 164 (C.M.A. 1983).

    c) Two rapes of same victim are not multiplicious for any purpose where first rape completely terminated before second rape began. *United States v. Ziegler*, 14 M.J. 860 (A.C.M.R. 1982); *accord United States v. Turner*, 17 M.J. 997 (A.C.M.R. 1984).

d) Rape and extortion are not multiplicious for findings or sentence. *United States v. Hicks*, 24 M.J. 3 (C.M.A. 1987).

e) Rape and adultery charges are not multiplicious for findings. *United States v. Hill*, 1997 CAAF LEXIS 1093 (Sept. 30, 1997); *United States v. Mason*, 42 M.J. 584 (Army Ct. Crim. App. 1995).

f) Rape, sodomy, and indecent acts or liberties with a child are separate offenses. *United States v. Cox*, 42 M.J. 647 (A.F. Ct. Crim. App. 1995), *aff'd*, 45 M.J. 153 (C.A.A.F. 1996).

g) Assault with intent to rape (art. 134) is a lesser included offense to rape where both charges arise out of the same criminal act against the same victim. *United States v. Britton*, 47 M.J 195 (C.A.A.F. 1997). *But see United States v. Miller*, 67 M.J. 385 (C.A.A.F. 2009).

10. Punishment.

    a) *United States v. Stebbins*, 61 M.J. 366 (C.A.A.F. 2005). Appellant pled guilty to rape and sodomy of a child under the age of twelve. LWOP is an authorized punishment for rape after November 18, 1997 (extending the reasoning of *United States v. Ronghi*, 60 M.J. 83 (C.A.A.F. 2004)).

    b) Capital Punishment.

        (1) Although UCMJ art. 120(a) authorizes the death penalty for rape, a plurality of the Supreme Court in *Coker v. Georgia*, 433 U.S. 584 (1977) held that the death penalty for the rape of an adult woman was cruel and unusual punishment regardless of aggravating circumstances. R.C.M. 1004(c)(9), revised to account for *Coker*, limits the death penalty for rape to cases where the victim is under the age of 12 or where the accused maimed or attempted to kill the victim. *See generally United States v. Straight*, 42 M.J. 244, 247 (C.A.A.F. 1995).

        (2) In 2008, the Supreme Court held that the death penalty for the rape of a child is unconstitutional where the child was not killed. In *Kennedy v. Louisiana*, 128 S. Ct. 2641, 171 L. Ed. 2d 525 (2008), the Court held that a Louisiana statute authorizing the imposition of the death penalty for the rape of a child under the age of 12 is prohibited by the Eighth Amendment and Fourteenth Amendments and is unconstitutional. The holding states specifically that "a death sentence for one who raped but did not kill a child, and who did not intend to assist another in killing the child, is unconstitutional." Slip Opinion at 10. The case does not include the UCMJ in its survey of jurisdictions that provide death as the maximum punishment for the rape of a child under 12 years of age. In denying a petition for rehearing based on the exclusion of the military from the survey of jurisdictions retaining the death penalty for child rape, the Court stated that the fact that the Manual for Courts-Martial "retains the death penalty for rape of a child or an adult . . . does not draw into question our conclusions that there is a consensus against the death penalty for the crime in the civilian context. . . ." Suggesting, perhaps, that there may be facts, circumstances, or policy reasons justifying death as a punishment for child rape when committed by a member of the military, the court declined to "decide whether certain considerations

might justify differences in the application of the Cruel and Unusual Punishments Clause to military cases . . . ." *See Kennedy v. Louisiana*, No. 07-343 (U.S. Oct. 1, 2008) (statement accompanying denial of petition for rehearing).

D. Carnal Knowledge. MCM, pt. IV, ¶ 45; UCMJ art. 120(b).

1. Elements.

    a) That the accused committed an act of sexual intercourse with a certain person;

    b) That the person was not the accused's spouse; and

    c) That at the time of the sexual intercourse the person was less than 16 years of age.

2. This offense is gender-neutral.

3. Article 120(d), UCMJ, provides special defense to carnal knowledge based upon mistake of fact as to the age of the victim.

    a) The accused bears both the burden of production and persuasion for this defense.

    b) The defense applies only if the victim has attained the age of 12.

    c) The accused must establish by a preponderance of the evidence that the mistake by the accused as to the age of the victim was both honest and reasonable.

4. Honest and reasonable mistake as to identity of accused's sexual partner constitutes a legal defense. *United States v. Adams*, 33 M.J. 300 (C.M.A. 1991).

5. The victim is not an "accomplice" for purposes of a witness credibility instruction. *United States v. Cameron*, 34 C.M.R. 913 (A.F.B.R. 1964).

6. Marriage.

    a) Government may prove that the accused and the prosecutrix were not married without direct evidence on the issue. *United States v. Wilhite*, 28 M.J. 884 (A.F.C.M.R. 1989).

    b) Carnal knowledge form specification is sufficient even though it does not expressly allege that the accused and his partner were not married. *United States v. Osborne*, 31 M.J. 842 (N.M.C.M.R. 1990).

7. Multiplicity. Carnal knowledge and adultery are not multiplicious for findings. *United States v. Booker*, No. 97-0913, 1999 CAAF LEXIS 637 (C.A.A.F. Feb. 19, 1999)(unpublished).

8. Statute of Limitations. *United States v. McElhaney*, 54 M.J. 120 (C.A.A.F. 2000) (statute of limitations codified at 18 U.S.C. § 3283, which permits prosecution for offenses involving sexual or physical abuse of children under the age of 18 until the child reaches the age of 25, does not apply to courts-martial as UCMJ Article 43 provides the applicable statute of limitations for courts-martial). *Willenbring v. Neurauter*, 48 M.J. 152 (C.A.A.F. 1998) (statute of limitations under Article 43 does not bar trial for rape, as any offense "punishable by death" may be tried at any time without limitation, even if it is referred as a noncapital case), *aff'd*, 57 M.J. 321 (C.A.A.F. 2002).

9. Lesser Included Offenses. *United States v. Holland*, 68 M.J. 576 (C.G. Ct. Crim. App. 2009). Plea provident where accused pled guilty indecent cts with a child as a lesser included offense to carnal knowledge. The court noted that the accused chose to plead guilty to this lesser offense based on a pretrial agreement and waived any objection to the amended specification as a "major amendment." Furthermore, he did so "after thorough consultation with [his] defense counsel." Finally, this offense is listed as an LIO to carnal knowledge in the MCM.

E. Sodomy. MCM, pt. IV, ¶ 51; UCMJ art. 125.

1. Elements.

   a) That the accused engaged in unnatural carnal copulation with a certain other person or with an animal.

   b) (If applicable) That the act was done with a child under the age of 16.

   c) (If applicable) That the act was done by force and without the consent of the other person.

2. Constitutionality.

   a) Before *Lawrence v. Texas*, 123 S.Ct. 2472 (2003), it was clear that Article 125 was constitutional, even as applied to private, consensual sodomy between spouses.

   b) *United States v. Allen*, 53 M.J. 402 (C.A.A.F. 2000) (Constitutional right to privacy (engaging in sexual relations within a marital relationship) must bear a reasonable relationship to activity that is in furtherance of the marriage. As part of a pattern of abuse, the accused beat his wife, solicited her to prostitute herself, and anally sodomized her. Prior to the assaults, she had refused anal sodomy, because she was forcibly sodomized as a teenager).

   c) United *States v. Thompson*, 47 M.J. 378 (C.A.A.F. 1997) (accused could not claim that an act of consensual sodomy with his wife was protected by the constitutional right to privacy, where his wife performed fellatio on him in an attempt to divert his attention away from reloading a pistol which had misfired moments before when he put it against her head and pulled the trigger).

   d) Article 125's prohibition of "unnatural carnal copulation" is not unconstitutionally vague. *United States v. Scoby*, 5 M.J. 160 (C.M.A. 1978).

   e) <u>Lawrence</u>: However, in *Lawrence v. Texas*, 539 U.S. 558 (2003), the Supreme Court overruled as unconstitutional a Texas law criminalizing consensual homosexual sodomy. In that case the Court stated that "[t]he State cannot demean a homosexual person's existence or control their destiny by making their private sexual conduct a crime. Their right to liberty under the Due Process Clause gives them the full right to engage in their conduct without intervention of the government. It is a promise of the Constitution that there is a realm of personal liberty which the government may not enter."

   f) Post-<u>Lawrence</u> cases:

      (1) *United States v. Marcum*, 60 M.J. 198 (C.A.A.F. 2004). Appellant was an NCO supervisor of junior airmen newly assigned to his flight. He regularly socialized with his subordinates, who often spent the night at his off-post home after parties. Appellant was charged, *inter alia*, with

forcible sodomy under Art. 125 but was convicted of the lesser included offense of non-forcible sodomy. The CAAF affirmed Marcum's conviction, holding that as applied to appellant and in the context of his conduct, Art. 125 is constitutional. The court assumed without deciding that appellant's conduct involved private sodomy between consenting adults, appellant's conduct was nevertheless outside the liberty interest recognized in *Lawrence*. Specifically, appellant was the airman's supervising NCO and knew his behavior was prohibited by service regulations concerning improper senior-subordinate relationships. Here, the situation involved a person "who might be coerced" and a "relationship where consent might not easily be refused," facts the Supreme Court specifically identified as not present in *Lawrence*. The CAAF explicitly did not decide whether Art. 125 would be constitutional in other settings.

(2) *Marcum* 3-Part Test for determining when the Constitution allows the prohibition of sodomy:

> (a) Is the accused's conduct within the liberty interest identified by the Supreme Court in *Lawrence*?
>
> (b) Does the conduct encompass any behavior or factors identified as outside the analysis in *Lawrence* (i.e., public acts, prostitution, minors, persons who might be injured or coerced or who might not easily refuse consent)?
>
> (c) Are there additional factors relevant solely in the military environment that affect the reach of the *Lawrence* liberty interest?

(3) *United States v. Stirewalt*, 60 M.J. 297 (C.A.A.F. 2004) (non-forcible sodomy that violated service regulations prohibiting improper relationships between members of different ranks; citing *Marcum*, his conduct fell outside any liberty interest recognized in *Lawrence*).

(4) *United States v. Christian*, 61 M.J. 560 (N-M. Ct. Crim. App. 2005) (consensual sodomy between accused, a recruiter, and "RW," originally a volunteer ASVAB tutor at the accused's recruiting office; although private and not specifically excepted under *Lawrence*, appellant's conduct implicated military-specific interests described in the third prong of the *Marcum* framework. Specifically, his role as a Marine recruiter & his violation of a recruit depot general order). *United States v. Bart*, 61 M.J. 578 (N-M. Ct. Crim. App. 2005) (consensual sodomy between co-workers in violation of SecNavy Instruction, involved adultery, and one partner murdered a spouse to continue the relationship combined to violate *Marcum* third prong).

(5) *United States v. Smith*, 66 M.J. 556 (C.G. Ct. Crim. App. 2008). Assuming *arguendo* that the conduct was not the result of extortion, the sodomy in this case was between two consenting first-class cadets in different chains of command. As such, the court observed that the conduct appeared to fall within the *Lawrence* liberty interest. However, addressing the *Marcum* factors, the court found that Coast Guard Academy regulations prohibit sexual activities between cadets on board

military installations, even if consensual. As there is a regulation prohibiting the behavior, the court held that the conduct constituting sodomy fell outside the protected liberty interest recognized in *Lawrence v. Texas*.

(6) *United States v. Harvey*, 67 M.J. 758 (A.F. Ct. Crim. App. 2009). In a prosecution of sodomy under Art. 133 as conduct unbecoming, military judge did not err in failing to instruct the members on the *Marcum* factors. "Whether an act comports with law, that is, whether it is legal or illegal [in relation to a constitutional or statutory right of an accused] is a question of law, not an issue of fact for determination by the triers of fact."

3. Acts Covered.

   a) "Unnatural carnal copulation" includes both fellatio and cunnilingus. *United States v. Harris*, 8 M.J. 52 (C.M.A. 1979).

   b) Some penetration, however, is required. UCMJ art. 125; *United States v. Barrow*, 42 M.J. 655 (A.F. Ct. Crim. App. 1995) (holding "intercourse" is a synonym for "copulation" and connotes act of penetration that the term "oral sex" does not), *aff'd*, 45 M.J. 478 (C.A.A.F. 1997); *United States v. Deland*, 16 M.J. 889 (A.C.M.R. 1983) *aff'd in part, rev'd in part on multiplicity grounds*, 22 M.J. 70 (C.M.A. 1986). Penetration, however slight, by male genital into orifice of human body except the vagina is sufficient. *United States v. Cox*, 23 M.J. 808 (N.M.C.M.R. 1986). Specification alleging "licking the genitalia" was not inconsistent with the penetration required for sodomy. *United States v. Cox*, 18 M.J. 72 (C.M.A. 1984); *United States v. Green*, 52 M.J. 803 (N-M. Ct. Crim. App. 2000) (victim's testimony that the accused's head was between her legs, his hands were on her thighs, her legs were spread apart, his mouth was on her vagina, he performed "oral sex," and he "was in between" her was sufficient to prove penetration). However, proof of licking, without proof of penetration, is insufficient for guilt. *United States v. Milliren*, 31 M.J. 664 (A.F.C.M.R. 1990); *see generally* TJAGSA Practice Note, *Sodomy and the Requirement for Penetration*, ARMY LAW., Mar. 1991, at 30 (discussing *Milliren*).

4. Evidence is sufficient to prove forcible sodomy where the child victim submitted under compulsion of parental command. *United States v. Edens*, 29 M.J. 755 (A.C.M.R. 1989), *aff'd*, 31 M.J. 267 (C.M.A. 1990). Evidence of a threat by the accused to impose nonjudicial punishment upon the victim, under the circumstances, was not sufficient to prove forcible sodomy. *United States v. Carroway*, 30 M.J. 700 (A.C.M.R. 1990).

5. The defense is entitled to an accomplice instruction when the victim participates voluntarily in the offense. *United States v. Goodman*, 33 C.M.R. 195 (C.M.A. 1963).

6. Multiplicity.

   a) Attempted rape and forcible sodomy or rape and forcible sodomy arising out of the same transaction are separately punishable. *United States v. Dearman*, 7 M.J. 713 (A.C.M.R. 1979); *accord United States v. Rogan*, 19 M.J. 646 (A.F.C.M.R. 1984) (Burglary, rape, and sodomy were all separately punishable offenses since different societal norms were violated in each instance. Burglary is a crime against the habitation, rape an offense against the person, and sodomy an offense against morals); *United States v. Rose*, 6 M.J. 754 (N.C.M.R. 1978).

b) Despite unity of time, offenses of sodomy and indecent liberties with a child were separate for findings and sentencing. *United States v. Cox*, 18 M.J. 72 (C.M.A. 1984). *Accord United States v. Cox*, 42 M.J. 647 (A.F. Ct. Crim. App. 1995), *aff'd* 45 M.J. 153 (C.A.A.F. 1996).

F. "Old" Indecent Assault. MCM, App. 27, ¶ 63.

1. Under the National Defense Authorization Act, FY2006, PL 109-163, 119 Stat. 3261, as of 1 October 2007, Indecent Assault was incorporated into Article 120. The discussion that follows pertains to Indecent Assault as it existed under Article 134 prior to October 2007.

2. Elements.

a) That the accused assaulted a certain person not the spouse of the accused in a certain manner;

b) That the acts were done with the intent to gratify the lust or sexual desire of the accused; and

c) That, under the circumstances, the conduct of the accused was to the prejudice of the good order and discipline in the armed forces or was of a nature to bring discredit upon the armed forces.

3. Nonconsensual offense requiring assault or battery. The assault or battery need not be inherently indecent, lewd, or lascivious but may be rendered so by accompanying words and circumstances. *United States v. Wilson*, 13 M.J. 247 (C.M.A. 1982). *See United States v. Hester*, 44 M.J. 546 (Army Ct. Crim. App. 1996) (victim was a virtual stranger to accused and the two of them were engaged in official business of processing victim into the unit, touching of victim's thigh was an offensive touching which, when done with specific intent to gratify the accused's lust, was an indecent assault).

4. Intent.

a) Requires accused's specific intent to gratify his lust or sexual desires. *United States v. Jackson*, 31 C.M.R. 738 (A.B.R. 1962); *see also United States v. Birch*, 13 M.J. 847 (C.G.C.M.R. 1982) (kissing victim against her will without evidence of specific intent to gratify lust or sexual desires was only a battery); *United States v. Campbell*, 55 M.J. 591 (C.G. Ct. Crim. App. 2001) (although male accused's tickling and similar touchings of female shipmates was unwelcome, boorish, and improper, the court could not reasonably describe the actions as indecent); *United States v. Proper*, 56 M.J. 717 (C.G. Ct. Crim. App. 2002) (pulling coveralls of a female subordinate away from her chest factually insufficient to prove that accused acted with intent to gratify his sexual lusts or desires even though he made comments about her breasts).

b) The assault or battery must be committed with a prurient state of mind. *United States v. Arviso*, 32 M.J. 616 (A.C.M.R. 1991) (evidence established specific intent of accused to gratify his lust or sexual desires when he inserted his finger into anus of female patients after examination by physicians); *United States v. Hoggard*, 43 M.J. 1 (1995) (holding evidence of attempted kiss legally insufficient to establish indecent intent); *United States v. Hester*, 44 M.J. 546 (Army Ct. Crim. App 1996).

5. Can be committed by a male on a woman not his spouse or by a female on a male not her spouse. *United States v. Johnson*, 17 M.J. 251 (C.M.A. 1984).

6. An accused can be found guilty of indecent assault and not guilty of rape even though both the victim and the accused acknowledge that intercourse occurred. *United States v. Watson*, 31 M.J. 49 (C.M.A. 1990); *United States v. Wilson*, 13 M.J. 247 (C.M.A. 1982).

7. Lack of consent.

   a) Unlike rape, mere lack of acquiescence is sufficient lack of consent for indecent assault; actual resistance is not required.

   b) If accused stops advances after he knows of lack of consent, evidence is legally insufficient for indecent assault. *United States v. Ayers*, 54 M.J. 85 (C.A.A.F. 2000) (government failed to prove lack of consent as there was no unwanted sexual touching as she was a "willing participant" when the accused touched her and kissed her, but when the accused tried to progress to sexual intercourse the 'victim' drew the line, and the accused did not cross that line, the 'victim' continued the relationship by calling the accused after the initial incident and agreed to meet him; during subsequent incident, accused stopped advances after 'victim' demonstrated lack of consent), *aff'd by* 55 M.J. 243 (C.A.A.F. 2001).

8. Mistake of fact defense. Accused's plea of guilty to indecent assault was provident even when accused stated during providency that "I personally just thought [at the time] that she was [consenting] and that it wasn't unreasonable;" statement failed to raise mistake of fact defense and was not in substantial conflict with plea. *United States v. Garcia* 44 M.J. 496 (1996), *aff'd,* 48 M.J. 5 (C.A.A.F. 1997).

9. Indecent assault is lesser included offense of indecent acts with child. *United States v. Kibler*, 43 M.J. 725 (Army Ct. Crim. App. 1995), *aff'd,* 46 M.J. 160 (C.A.A.F. 1996), *cert. denied* 523 U.S. 1011 (1998).

G. Assault With Intent to Commit Rape, Sodomy, or Specified Felony. MCM, pt. IV, ¶ 64; UCMJ art. 134.

   1. Elements.

      a) That the accused assaulted a certain person;

      b) That, at the time of the assault, the accused intended to kill (as required for murder or voluntary manslaughter) or intended to commit rape, robbery, sodomy, arson, burglary, or housebreaking; and

      c) That, under the circumstances, the conduct of the accused was to the prejudice of the good order and discipline in the armed forces or was of a nature to bring discredit upon the armed forces.

   2. Specific intent offense. *United States v. Rozema*, 33 C.M.R. 694 (A.F.B.R. 1963). An intent to seduce is not a defense to an assault with intent to commit consensual sodomy. *United States v. Davis*, 15 M.J. 567 (A.C.M.R. 1983); *United States v. Marcey*, 25 C.M.R. 444 (C.M.A. 1958).

   3. Consent may be a defense to assault with intent to commit a sexual offense. *United States v. Davis*, 15 M.J. 567 (A.C.M.R. 1983).

4. Multiplicity.

   a) Offenses of assault with intent to commit rape and attempted rape are one and the same and should not be charged separately. *United States v. Gibson*, 11 M.J. 435 (C.M.A. 1981); *United States v. Edwards*, 35 M.J. 351 (C.M.A. 1992) (assault with intent to commit rape is multiplicious for findings with charge of attempted rape).

   b) Assault with intent to commit rape and assault with intent to commit sodomy, upon the same victim during the same transaction, were not multiplicious for any purpose. *United States v. Flynn*, 28 M.J. 218 (C.M.A. 1989).

   c) Assault with intent to rape (article 134) is a lesser included offense of rape where both charges arise out of the same criminal act against the same victim. *United States v. Britton*, 47 M.J. 195 (C.A.A.F. 1997).

5. For a good explanation of historical underpinnings of this offense, see *United States v. Weymouth*, 43 M.J. 329, 338 (C.A.A.F. 1995).

H. Adultery. MCM, pt. IV, ¶ 62; UCMJ art. 134.

   1. Elements.

      a) That the accused wrongfully had sexual intercourse with a certain person;

      b) That, at the time of intercourse, the accused or the other person was married to someone else; and

      c) That, under the circumstances, the conduct of the accused was to the prejudice of good order and discipline in the armed forces or was of a nature to bring discredit upon the armed forces. *See United States v. Melville*, 25 C.M.R. 101 (C.M.A. 1958); *United States v. Butler*, 5 C.M.R. 213 (A.B.R. 1952).

   2. Prejudicial conduct. *United States v. Green*, 39 M.J. 606 (A.C.M.R. 1994) (NCO's adultery committed in the unit barracks were prejudicial to good order and discipline in that such conduct would tend to reduce other soldiers' confidence in the accused's integrity, leadership, and respect for law, as well as setting a bad example for other soldiers that would tend to cause them to be less likely to conform their conduct to the rigors of military discipline); *See also United States v. Poole*, 39 M.J. 819 (A.C.M.R. 1994).

   3. Specification charging that accused had sexual intercourse with "a woman not his wife" did not allege necessary element of adultery, *i.e.*, that one party to the sexual intercourse was married to a third person. Consistent with this specification, both of the participants could have been single. *United States v. Clifton*, 11 M.J. 842 (A.C.M.R. 1981), *rev'd on other grounds,* 15 M.J. 26 (C.M.A. 1983); *United States v. King*, 34 M.J. 95 (C.M.A. 1992) (defective pleadings legally insufficient even under greater tolerance test).

   4. Adultery is not a lesser included offense to rape. *United States v. Hill*, 1997 CAAF LEXIS 1093 (Sept. 30, 1997); *United States v. Mason*, 42 M.J. 584 (A. Ct. Crim. App. 1995).

   5. Fornication. Private, noncommercial, heterosexual intercourse between unmarried persons is generally not punishable. *United States v. Hickson*, 22 M.J. 146 (C.M.A. 1986); *see United States v. Izquierdo*, 51 M.J. 421 (1999); *United States v. Carr*, 28 M.J. 661 (N.M.C.M.R. 1989).

I. "Old" Indecent Acts With Another. MCM, App. 27 ¶ 90.

1. Under the National Defense Authorization Act, FY 2006, Pub. L. No. 109-163, 119 Stat. 3261, as of 1 October 2007, Indecent Acts With Another was incorporated into Article 120. The discussion that follows pertains to Indecent Acts With Another as it existed under Article 134 prior to October 2007.

2. Elements.

   a) That the accused committed a certain wrongful act with a certain person;

   b) That the act was indecent; and

   c) That, under the circumstances, the conduct of the accused was to the prejudice of good order and discipline in the armed forces or was of a nature to bring discredit upon the armed forces.

3. An indecent act is defined as "that form of immorality relating to sexual impurity which is not only grossly vulgar, obscene and repugnant to common propriety, but which tends to excite lust and deprave the morals with respect to sexual relations." MCM, App. 27 ¶ 90c.

4. Physical touching not required, but participation of another is required.

   a) *United States v. McDaniel*, 39 M.J. 173 (C.M.A. 1994) (accused's instructions to female recruits to disrobe, change positions, and bounce up and down while videotaping them without their knowledge was sufficient participation).

   b) *United States v. Brown*, 39 M.J. 688 (N.M.C.M.R. 1993) (some minimal observation or actual participation by another person is required for the offense to lie; a victim who is asleep while the accused masturbates in her presence will not suffice). *See also United States v. Thomas*, 25 M.J. 75 (C.M.A. 1987); *United States v. Murray-Cotto*, 25 M.J. 784 (A.C.M.R. 1988). *Contra United States v. Jackson*, 30 M.J. 1203 (A.F.C.M.R. 1990); *United States v. Kenerson*, 34 M.J. 704, (A.C.M.R. 1992); *United States v. Proctor*, 58 M.J. 792 (A.F. Ct. Crim. App. 2003); *but see United States v. Jackson*, 30 M.J. 1203 (A.F.C.M.R. 1990) (holding victim provided "inspiration," not participation).

   c) *United States v. Rollins*, 61 M.J. 338 (2005). Appellant was convicted of several 134 offenses, including an indecent act with JG, "by giving him a pornographic magazine and suggesting that they masturbate together." HELD: The indecent act specification is affirmed. A reasonable factfinder could conclude that appellant committed a service discrediting indecent act "with" another by giving a person under the age of eighteen a pornographic magazine to stimulate mutual masturbation while in a parking lot open to the public.

   d) *United States v. Johnson*, 60 M.J. 988 (N-M. Ct. Crim. App. 2005). Appellant pled guilty, in relevant part, to indecent acts with another HELD: The indecent act specification is affirmed. Here, appellant's conduct in watching and encouraging his friend's sexual encounter constituted active participation, citing *United States v. McDaniel*, 39 M.J. 173 (C.M.A. 1994).

5. No specific intent is required. *United States v. Brundidge*, 17 M.J. 536 (A.C.M.R. 1983); *United States v. Jackson*, 31 C.M.R. 738 (A.B.R. 1972).

6. Acts covered.

   a) Acts not inherently indecent may be rendered so by the surrounding circumstances. *United States v. Proctor*, 34 M.J. 549 (A.F.C.M.R. 1992) (spanking young boys on the bare buttocks found to be indecent under the circumstances), *aff'd,* 37 M.J. 330 (C.M.A. 1993).

   b) Private, heterosexual, oral foreplay between two consenting adults that does not amount to sodomy is not an indecent act. *United States v. Stocks*, 35 M.J. 366 (C.M.A. 1992).

   c) Not limited to female victim.

   (1) *United States v. Annal*, 32 C.M.R. 427 (C.M.R. 1963) (crime was committed when Army captain forcefully grabbed another male and tried to embrace him).

   (2) *United States v. Holland*, 31 C.M.R. 30 (C.M.A.1961) (officer was convicted of indecent act by grabbing certain parts of the anatomy of another male officer).

   (3) *United States v. Moore*, 33 C.M.R. 667 (C.G.B.R.1963) (consensual homosexual acts may constitute the offense of indecent acts with another).

   d) Consensual intercourse in the presence of others can constitute an indecent act. *United States v. Tollinchi*, 54 M.J. 80 (C.A.A.F. 2000); *United States v. Brundidge*, 17 M.J. 586 (A.C.M.R. 1983).

   e) Indecent acts, charged as a violation of UCMJ art. 134, need not involve another person. *United States v. Sanchez*, 29 C.M.R. 32 (C.M.A. 1960) (chicken); *United States v. Mabie*, 24 M.J. 711 (A.C.M.R. 1987) (corpse).

   f) Physically restraining victims in public restroom while accused masturbated is an indecent act. *United States v. Eberle*, 44 M.J. 374 (C.A.A.F. 1996).

   g) Fornication. Purely private sexual intercourse between unmarried persons is normally not punishable. *United States v. Hickson*, 22 M.J. 146 (C.M.A. 1986), *overruled on other grounds by United States v. Hill,* 48 M.J. 352 (C.A.A.F. 1997). Context in which the sex act is committed may constitute an offense (*e.g.,* public fornication, fraternization, etc.). *See United States v. Berry*, 20 C.M.R. 325 (C.M.A. 1956) (two soldiers took two girls to a room where each soldier had intercourse with each of the girls in open view; such "open and notorious" conduct was service discrediting). *See also, United States v. Woodard*, 23 M.J. 514 (A.F.C.M.R. 1986) *vacated and remanded on other grounds*, 23 M.J. 400 (C.M.A. 1987), *findings set aside on other grounds*, 24 M.J. 514 (A.F.C.M.R. 1987) (private, consensual, intimate contact between a married officer and a 16-year-old babysitter was, under the circumstances, an indecent act).

   h) "Open and notorious" fornication between consenting adults was an offense under Article 134 prior to October 2007. The act is open and notorious when the participants know that a third party is present or when performed in such a place and under such circumstances that it is reasonably likely to be seen by others, even though others actually do not view the acts. Sexual intercourse in a barracks room behind a pinned up sheet, while two roommates were awake and suspicious, was open and notorious. *United States v. Izquierdo*, 51 M.J. 421 (C.A.A.F. 1999); *see United States v. King*, 29 M.J. 901 (A.C.M.R. 1989).

(1) Consensual fondling of a female soldier's breasts was not "open and notorious" conduct when it occurred in the accused's private bedroom with the door closed but unlocked. The accused was holding a promotion party with about forty attendees in a room next to his bedroom. Although there was a possibility that someone from the party would enter the bedroom and observe the sexual activity, the accused's plea to indecent acts was improvident because it was not reasonably likely that a third person would observe the conduct. *United States v. Sims*, 57 M.J. 419 (C.A.A.F. 2002).

(2) The accused's plea of guilty to committing an indecent act by videotaping intercourse and sodomy with his future wife was provident. The potential that the videotape would be viewed by others, together with the salacious effect on the person doing the taping and viewer alike, contributed to the conclusion that the act of videotaping was indecent. *United States v. Allison*, 56 M.J. 606 (C.G. Ct. Crim. App. 2001).

i) Webcam cases. Broadcasting live sexual images to a child over the Internet via webcam may constitute indecent acts with another under Article 134. *See United States v. Parker*, No. 20080579 (A. Ct. Crim. App. Aug. 31, 2009) (unpub.). Where the child victim is actually a law enforcement officer, the courts have affirmed attempted indecent acts with another. *See United States v. Lorenz*, No. 20061071 (A. Ct. Crim. App. Apr. 20, 2009) (unpub.); *United States v. Miller*, No. 36829, 2009 WL 1508494 (A.F. Ct. Crim. App. Apr. 30, 2009) (unpublished).

7. Consent is not a defense. *United States v. Carreiro*, 14 M.J. 954 (A.C.M.R. 1982); *United States v. Johnson*, 4 M.J. 770 (A.C.M.R. 1978); *United States v. Woodard*, 23 M.J. 514 (A.C.M.R. 1986), *set aside on other grounds*, 24 M.J. 514 (A.F.C.M.R. 1987); *United States v. Thacker*, 37 C.M.R. 28 (C.M.A. 1966) (dicta).

8. Fornication. Not a per se UCMJ violation. *United States v. Snyder*, 4 C.M.R. 15 (C.M.A. 1952). *See also United States v. Blake*, 33 M.J. 923 (A.C.M.R. 1991) (fornication, in and of itself, is not a crime in military law).

9. Lesser included offenses.

a) Lesser included offense of indecent assault. *United States v. Carter*, 39 C.M.R. 764 (A.C.M.R. 1967).

b) Lesser included offense of attempted rape. *United States v. Anderson*, 10 M.J. 536 (A.C.M.R. 1980).

J. "Old" Indecent Acts or Liberties with a Child. MCM, App. 27, ¶ 87.

1. Under the National Defense Authorization Act, FY2006, Pub. L. No. 109-163, 119 Stat. 3261, as of 1 October 2007, Indecent Acts or Liberties with a Child was incorporated into Article 120. The discussion that follows pertains to Indecent Acts or Liberties with a Child as it existed under Article 134 prior to October 2007.

2. Elements.

a) Physical contact.

(1) That the accused committed a certain act upon or with the body of a certain person;

(2) That the person was under 16 years of age and not the spouse of the accused.

(3) That the act of the accused was indecent;

(4) That the accused committed the act with intent to arouse, appeal to, or gratify the lust, passions, or sexual desires of the accused, the victim, or both; and

(5) That, under the circumstances, the conduct of the accused was to the prejudice of good order and discipline in the armed forces or was of a nature to bring discredit upon the armed forces.

    b) No physical contact.

(1) That the accused committed a certain act;

(2) That the act amounted to the taking of indecent liberties with a certain person;

(3) That the accused committed the act in the presence of this person.

(4) That the person was under 16 years of age and not the spouse of the accused.

(5) That the accused committed the act with intent to arouse, appeal to, or gratify the lust, passions, or sexual desires of the accused, the victim, or both; and

(6) That, under the circumstances, the conduct of the accused was to the prejudice of good order and discipline in the armed forces or was of a nature to bring discredit upon the armed forces.

3. Not limited to female victim.

4. Consent is no defense as a child of tender years is incapable of consent. However, factual consent of an alleged victim is relevant on the issue of indecency. Consensual petting between an eighteen-year-old and a fifteen-year-old is not necessarily outside the scope of the offense of indecent acts with a child, but it is a question for the members under proper instructions. Here, the military judge committed plain error when she failed to provide adequately tailored instructions on the issue of indecency after a court-martial member asked for such instructions. *United States v. Baker*, 57 M.J. 330 (C.A.A.F. 2002).

5. Requires evidence of a specific intent to gratify the lust or sexual desires of the accused *or* the victim. *United States v. Johnson*, 35 C.M.R. 587 (A.B.R. 1965); *see United States v. Robertson*, 33 M.J. 832 (A.C.M.R. 1991) (absent a specific intent to gratify lust, accused's act of buying 14 year-old daughter a penis shaped vibrator and "motion lotion" did not amount to an indecent act), *rev'd on other grounds,* 37 M.J. 432 (C.M.A. 1993).

6. Physical presence required; constructive presence insufficient. *See United States v. Miller,* 67 M.J. 87 (C.A.A.F. 2008) (constructive presence through web-cam and Yahoo! chatroom insufficient for an attempted indecent liberties charge).

7. Application.

a) Indecent acts.

(1) Physical contact is required. *United States v. Payne*, 41 C.M.R. 188 (C.M.A. 1970) (accused placed hand between child's legs); *United States v. Sanchez*, 29 C.M.R. 32 (C.M.A. 1960) (accused exposed his penis to child while cradling child in his arms.); *see United States v. Rodriguez*, 28 M.J. 1016 (A.F.C.M.R. 1989), *aff'd*, 31 M.J. 150 (C.M.A. 1990) (rubbing body against female patients); *United States v. Cottril*, 45 M.J. 485 (C.A.A.F. 1997) (accused touching child's vaginal area to the point of pain while bathing her was indecent, regardless of child's purported enjoyment of touchings, given accused's admissions that his acts excited his lust to point of masturbation).

(2) Offense of indecent acts or liberties with a child is not so continuous as to include all indecent acts or liberties with a single victim, without regard to their character, their interrupted nature, or different times of their occurrences, and accused may be charged with more than one offense as a result of one act with a single victim. *United States v. Neblock*, 45 M.J. 191 (C.A.A.F. 1996).

b) Indecent liberties.

(1) No physical contact is required, but act must be done within the physical presence of the child. *United States v. Miller*, 67 M.J. 87 (C.A.A.F. 2008) (constructive presence through web-cam and Yahoo! chatroom insufficient for an attempted indecent liberties charge); *United States v. Brown*, 13 C.M.R. 10 (C.M.A. 1953) (accused's exposure of his penis to two young girls constituted an indecent liberty); *see United States v. Thomas*, supra at ¶ G.3. (participation of the child required); *see United States v. Robba*, 32 M.J. 771 (A.C.M.R. 1991) (victims presence implied); *see also United States v. Brown*, 39 M.J. 688 (N.M.C.M.R. 1993) (holding that a person sleeping in the room did not participate in accused's masturbation, and thus charge of indecent acts with another could not lie).

(2) Indecent liberties with a child can include displaying nonpornographic photographs if accompanied by the requisite intent. *United States v. Orben*, 28 M.J. 172 (C.M.A. 1989); *see* TJAGSA Practice Note, *Displaying Nonpornographic Photographs to a Child Can Constitute Taking Indecent Liberties*, ARMY LAW., Aug. 1989, at 40 (discusses *Orben*); *United States v. Marrie*, 39 M.J. 993 (A.F.C.M.R. 1994) (showing victim material that, while not legally pornographic, is accompanied by behavior or language that demonstrates his intent to arouse his own sexual passions, those of the child, or both), *aff'd*, 43 M.J. 35 (C.A.A.F. 1995).

(3) Multiple acts of indecent liberties may occur simultaneously. *United States v. Lacy*, 53 M.J. 509 (N-M. Ct. Crim. App. 2000) (accused exposed his genitals, masturbated, and showed a pornographic video to two children simultaneously; the court adopted a "different victims" standard for indecent liberties, because the purpose of the offense is the protection of the individual person).

(4) Indecent liberties and indecent exposure are not necessarily multiplicious. *United States v. Rinkes*, 53 M.J. 741 (N-M. Ct. Crim. App. 2000) (accused's convictions of indecent liberties with a child and indecent exposure before an adult did not constitute an unreasonable multiplication of charges as considering the differing societal goals and victims, the specifications were aimed at distinctly separate criminal acts).

K. "Old" Indecent Exposure. MCM, App. 27, ¶ 88.

1. Under the National Defense Authorization Act, FY2006, Pub. L. No. 109-163, 119 Stat. 3261, as of 1 October 2007, Indecent Exposure was incorporated into Article 120. The discussion that follows pertains to Indecent Exposure with a Child as it existed under Article 134 prior to October 2007.

2. Elements.

   a) That the accused exposed a certain part of the accused's body to public view in an indecent manner;

   b) That the exposure was willful and wrongful; and

   c) That, under the circumstances, the conduct of the accused was to the prejudice of good order and discipline in the armed forces or was of a nature to bring discredit upon the armed forces.

3. Negligent exposure is insufficient; "willfulness" is required. *United States v. Manos*, 25 C.M.R. 238 (C.M.A. 1958) (law enforcement officer viewed exposure through accused's window); *United States v. Stackhouse*, 37 C.M.R. 99 (C.M.A. 1967) (evidence was insufficient to sustain the accused's conviction of three specifications of indecent exposure where, in each instance, the accused was observed nude in his own apartment by passersby in the hallway looking in the partly open door of the apartment; such evidence is as consistent with negligence as with purposeful action and negligence is an insufficient basis for a conviction of indecent exposure); *accord United States v. Ardell*, 40 C.M.R. 160 (C.M.A. 1969); *United States v. Burbank*, 37 C.M.R. 955 (A.F.B.R. 1967) (plea of guilty to indecent exposure was not rendered improvident by stipulated evidence that the accused did nothing to attract attention to himself and may not even have been aware of the presence of the young females who saw him, where the accused admitted he had exposed himself in the children's section of the base library, a place so public an intent to be seen must be presumed); *United States v. Shaffer*, 46 M.J. 94 (1997) (evidence supported the conclusion that accused's exposures were "willful" so as to sustain conviction for indecent exposure where, on each occasion of exposure, accused was naked, facing out of his open garage, towards the street, in unobstructed view, during daylight hours and never made an attempt to cover himself or remove himself from view when seen).

4. "Public" exposure is required. To be criminal the exposure need not occur in a public place, but only be in public view. *United States v. Moore*, 33 C.M.R. 667 (C.G.B.R. 1963) (accused, who exposed his penis and made provocative gestures while joking with fellow seamen on board ship, was guilty of indecent exposure). "Public view" occurs when the exposure is done in a place and in a manner that is reasonably expected to be viewed by another. *United States v. Graham*, 56 M.J. 256 (2002) (accused exposed himself to his 15-year-old baby-sitter in the bedroom of his home by inviting her into the bedroom and then allowing his towel to drop in front of her. The accused's actions caused

a normally private place, *i.e.*, the bedroom, to become public, as he reasonably expected the babysitter to view his naked body), *aff'd,* 56 M.J. 266 (C.A.A.F. 2002).

5. Exposure must be "indecent." Nudity per se is not indecent; thus, an unclothed male among others of the same sex is generally neither lewd nor morally offensive. *United States v. Caune*, 46 C.M.R. 200 (C.M.A. 1973).

6. *United States v. Jackson*, 30 M.J. 1203 (A.F.C.M.R. 1990) (rejecting indecent acts with another and affirming indecent exposure instead).

7. Indecent exposure via webcam. *United States v. Ferguson,* No. 10-0020 (C.A.A.F. Mar. 22, 2010) (accused admitted sufficient facts to affirm conviction for indecent exposure via Internet webcam to a law enforcement agent posing as a teenager).

L. Voyeurism/Peeping Tom.

1. Under the new Article 120, voyeurism clearly falls under the definition of indecent conduct for purposes of indecent acts. *See* MCM, pt. IV, ¶ 45(t)(12).

2. Prior to the new Article 120, these offenses were not enumerated under the UCMJ and were considered a form of disorderly conduct punishable under UCMJ art. 134.

   a) Voyeurism. *United States v. Johnson*, 4 M.J. 770 (A.C.M.R. 1978) (accused's act of voyeurism by secreting himself in a women's restroom at the post cafeteria and peering over toilet stalls at unsuspecting victims constituted service discrediting conduct under UCMJ art. 134, not an indecent act with another).

   b) Window Peeping.

      (1) Peeping is disorderly conduct under Article 134 and may be pleaded as service discrediting or as prejudicial to good order and discipline. *United States v. Foster*, 13 M.J. 789 (A.C.M.R. 1982).

      (2) The gravamen of the offense is invading the privacy of other persons by spying upon them without their consent in their premises whether or not they are actually in view. *United States v. Foster*, 13 M.J. 789 (A.C.M.R. 1982); *see also United States v. Clark*, 22 C.M.R. 888 (A.F.B.R. 1956); *United States v. Manos*, 24 C.M.R. 626 (A.F.B.R. 1957).

      (3) Evidence that accused secreted himself in storage room with view of shower room and female officer's billet during early morning hours without any apparent lawful purpose, and that he knocked down and fled from female officer who accidentally discovered him, was legally sufficient to prove offense of housebreaking with intent to peep. *United States v. Webb*, 38 M.J. 62 (C.M.A. 1993).

M. Pandering. MCM, pt. IV, ¶ 97; UCMJ art. 134.

1. Pandering requires at least three parties to the transaction. *United States v. Miller*, 47 M.J. 352 (C.A.A.F. 1997).

2. Pandering does not require, although it can involve, the exchange of valuable consideration. *United States v. Gallegos*, 41 M.J. 446 (C.A.A.F. 1995).

3. Forcible pandering is now an offense under UCMJ art. 120. *See* MCM, pt. IV, ¶ 45(l).

N. Bigamy. MCM, pt. IV, ¶ 65; UCMJ art. 134.

    1. Elements.

        a) That the accused had a living lawful spouse;

        b) That while having such spouse the accused wrongfully married another person; and

        c) That, under the circumstances, the conduct of the accused was to the prejudice of good order and discipline in the armed forces or was of a nature to bring discredit upon the armed forces.

    2. A single service member who knowingly enters into a marriage with a person already married can be prosecuted for conduct of a service-discrediting nature under Article 134 either as an aider and abettor to bigamy under Article 77 or directly as a perpetrator of an offense. *United States v. Bivins*, 49 M.J. 328 (C.A.A.F. 1998).

    3. Defense of duress was not raised by evidence that the accused committed bigamy in order to avoid threatened prosecution of himself and his Turkish friends where there was no reasonable apprehension of immediate harm since accused failed to avail himself of legal counsel and did not commit the offense of bigamy until three days after he was warned about possible criminal liability under Turkish law for his relationship with a Turkish woman. *United States v. Vasquez* 48 M.J. 426 (C.A.A.F. 1998).

O. Indecent Language. MCM, pt. IV, ¶ 89; UCMJ art. 134.

    1. Elements.

        a) That the accused orally or in writing communicated to another person certain language;

        b) That such language was indecent;

        c) That, under the circumstances, the conduct of the accused was to the prejudice of good order and discipline in the armed forces or was of a nature to bring discredit upon the armed forces.

        d) (If applicable) That the person to whom the language was communicated was a child under the age of 16.

    2. Explanation.

        a) "Indecent" language is that which is grossly offensive to modesty, decency, or propriety, or shocks the moral sense, because of its vulgar, filthy, or disgusting nature, or its tendency to incite lustful thought. Language is indecent if it tends reasonably to corrupt morals or incite libidinous thoughts. The language must violate community standards.

        b) In determining adequacy of an indecent language specification, factors to consider include fluctuating community standards, personal relationship existing between speaker and listener, and probable effect of communication as taken from four corners of the specification; another factor when a child is involved is the age of the child. *United States v. Dudding*, 34 M.J. 975 (A.C.M.R. 1992), *aff'd,* 37 M.J. 429 (C.M.A. 1993).

    3. Aggravating Factor. If the communication is made in the physical presence of a child under the age of 16 years it will increase the maximum punishment from a bad conduct

discharge and confinement for six months to a dishonorable discharge and confinement for two years. MCM, pt. IV, ¶ 89e(1).

4. Conviction for uttering indecent language requires proof that the language was calculated to corrupt morals or excite libidinous thoughts. Vulgar, coarse, or profane language is not per se indecent, but must be evaluated in context. *United States v. Negron*, 60 M.J. 136 (C.A.A.F. 2004) (appellant's letter to a credit union that rejected his loan application that contained profanity including sexual acts was an expression of outrage and not calculated to corrupt moral or excite libidinous thoughts, *citing*, *United States v. Brinson*, 49 M.J. 360 (C.A.A.F. 1998) (accused's extreme profanity toward military policemen while being apprehended was disorderly conduct, not indecent language, since it was manifestly calculated to express rage rather than to excite immoral thoughts)); *United States v. French*, 31 M.J. 57 (C.M.A. 1990) (asking stepdaughter under age of 16 for permission to climb into bed with her communicated indecent language; question conveyed message as equally libidinous and obscene as telling stepdaughter that accused had been fantasizing about having sex with her); *United States v. Dudding*, 34 M.J. 975 (A.C.M.R. 1992) (indecent language specifications alleging that accused called a seven or eight-year-old female child "a bitch" and "a cunt" were sufficient to state an offense), *aff'd,* 37 M.J. 429 (C.M.A. 1993); *United States v. Maxwell*, 42 M.J. 568 (A.F. Ct. Crim. App. 1995) (evidence that accused sent anonymous, consensual, non-commercial, but admittedly indecent, e-mail messages via America On Line (AOL) is legally sufficient to support conviction of service-discrediting indecent language) *aff'd in part, rev'd in part, remanded by,* 45 M.J. 406 (C.A.A.F. 1996).

5. While a request for sexual intercourse could be indecent, a general expression of sexual desire falls short of a request for sexual intercourse. Words suggesting heterosexual intercourse between consenting adults are not intrinsically indecent, even if such intercourse would be illegal adultery. *United States v. Coleman*, 48 M.J. 420 (C.A.A.F. 1998); *United States v. Hullett*, 40 M.J. 189 (C.M.A. 1994) (request to engage in sexual intercourse is not per se a violation of the military community's standards of decency, nor is it prejudicial to the good order and discipline of the unit in which it is uttered when even the putative victim is not offended or shocked).

6. "Offensive language" which is not technically "indecent" may be charged as service discrediting conduct under some circumstances. Evidence that accused made phone calls in which he disguised his identity and asked questions of a sexual nature as a part of a fictional survey was sufficient to support a finding that such conduct was service discrediting even though the women thought that the calls were from a legitimate researcher and the accused did not solicit "phone sex" or other sexual activities. *United States v. Sullivan*, 38 M.J. 746 (A.C.M.R. 1993), *aff'd*, 42 M.J. 360 (v1995). *But see United States v. Herron*, 39 M.J. 860 (N.M.C.M.R. 1994) (uttering profanity in loud and angry manner in public setting was not "general disorder" and could not be prosecuted as such; there is no generic "offensive language" offense under the UCMJ).

P. Obscenity. UCMJ art. 134.

1. *United States v. Gallo*, 53 M.J. 556 (A.F. Ct. Crim. App. 2000), *aff'd,* 55 M.J. 418 (C.A.A.F. 2001). The proper community standard by which to determine if the materials the accused received via the Internet, by using his Air Force computer, were obscene, under 18 U.S.C. § 1462(a), was an Air Force community standard.

2. Nationwide community as a whole was not the relevant community for purposes of obscenity prosecution regarding obscene materials transmitted through a computer

service, but rather the Air Force community was the most appropriate community or the entire community of subscribers to service or members of service who used specific bulletin board. *United States v. Maxwell*, 45 M.J. 406 (C.A.A.F. 1996).

VI. OFFENSES AGAINST PROPERTY.

A. Larceny and Wrongful Appropriation. MCM, pt. IV, ¶ 46; UCMJ art. 121.

1. Elements.

    a) Larceny.

    (1) That the accused wrongfully took, obtained, or withheld certain property from the possession of the owner or of any other person;

    (2) That the property belonged to a certain person;

    (3) That the property was of a certain value, or of some value; and

    (4) That the taking, obtaining, or withholding by the accused was with the intent *permanently* to deprive or defraud another person of the use and benefit of the property or permanently to appropriate the property for the use of the accused or for any person other than the owner.

    (5) [If the property is alleged to be military property, add the following element:] That the property was military property.

    b) Wrongful appropriation.

    (1) That the accused wrongfully took, obtained, or withheld certain property from the possession of the owner or of any other person;

    (2) That the property belonged to a certain person;

    (3) That the property was of a certain value, or of some value; and

    (4) That the taking, obtaining, or withholding by the accused was with the intent *temporarily* to deprive or defraud another person of the use and benefit of the property or temporarily to appropriate the property for the use of the accused or for any person other than the owner.

2. Types of Property Covered.

    a) Must be tangible personal property. Article 121 lists the objects which can be the subject of larceny as "any money, personal property, or article of value of any kind."

    b) Intangible items cannot be the subject of an Article 121 violation. *United States v. Mervine*, 26 M.J. 482 (C.M.A. 1988) (debt); *United States v. Dunn*, 27 M.J. 624 (A.F.C.M.R. 1988) (administrative costs).

    c) Article 121 does not cover theft of services. Theft of taxicab services, phone services, use and occupancy of government quarters, and use of a rental car cannot be the subject of larceny under Article 121. *United States v. Abeyta*, 12 M.J. 507 (A.C.M.R. 1981); *United States v. Case*, 37 C.M.R. 606 (A.B.R. 1966); *United States v. Jones*, 23 C.M.R. 818 (A.F.B.R. 1956); *United States v. McCracker*, 19 C.M.R. 876 (A.F.B.R. 1955).

    d) Theft of services may be prosecuted in any of the following ways: (1) under Article 134, UCMJ, as obtaining services under false pretenses or as dishonorably failing to pay just debts; (2) under 18 U.S.C. § 641 as assimilated into military law by Article. 134(3), UCMJ, if the services taken are property of the United States; (3) as a violation of a state statute assimilated through 18 U.S.C. § 13. *See United States v. Wright*, 5 M.J. 106 (C.M.A. 1978), and *United States v. Herndon*, 36 C.M.R. 8 (C.M.A. 1965); *see also United States v. Hitz*, 12 M.J. 695 (N.M.C.M.R. 1981) (accused was properly charged with and convicted of unlawfully obtaining telephone services of the U.S. Navy in violation of UCMJ art. 134); *United States v. Roane*, 43 M.J. 93 (C.A.A.F. 1995); *United States v. Green*, 44 M.J. 631 (C.G. Ct. Crim. App. 1996) (obtaining services by false pretenses).

e) Larceny can be used to cover credit card misuse. *See generally United States v. Christy*, 18 M.J. 688 (N.M.C.M.R. 1984).

3. Element 1: That the accused wrongfully took, obtained, or withheld property (not services) from another. The drafters intended to codify only common law larceny, larceny by false pretenses, and larceny by conversion. *United States v. Mervine*, 26 M.J. 482 (C.M.A. 1988); *United States v. Tenney*, 15 M.J. 779 (A.C.M.R. 1983); *United States v. Herndon*, 36 C.M.R. 8 (C.M.A. 1965); *United States v. Dean*, 33 M.J. 505 (A.F.C.M.R. 1991).

a) Wrongful taking. Requires dominion, control, and asportation. *See generally United States v. Carter*, 24 M.J. 280 (C.M.A. 1987); *United States v. Smith*, 33 M.J. 527 (A.F.C.M.R. 1991), *aff'd*, 35 M.J. 138 (C.M.A. 1992); *United States v. Pacheco*, 56 M.J. 1 (C.A.A.F. 2001) (stealing war trophies). The taking, obtaining or withholding is wrongful if done without the knowing consent of the owner or other lawful authority. MCM, pt. IV, ¶ 46c(1)(d).

(1) *United States v. Sneed*, 38 C.M.R. 249 (C.M.A. 1968). Where accused's accomplices were government agents, larceny of government property could not stand as no taking ever occurred, *i.e.*, articles were never out of government control. *See United States v. Cosby*, 14 M.J. 3 (C.M.A. 1982) (accused can be guilty of wrongful taking even though property was released to him by competent authority); *see also United States v. Cassey*, 34 C.M.R. 338 (C.M.A. 1964) (OSI authorized accomplices to proceed with delivery of government property and then apprehended accused after delivery as he attempted to leave base).

(2) Asportation.

(a) Larceny by taking continues as long as asportation of the property continues. The original asportation continues as long as the perpetrator is not satisfied with the location of the goods and causes the flow of their movement to continue relatively uninterrupted. An accused's actions in joining an ongoing conspiracy to steal a duffel bag before two co-conspirators completed asportation of the property was legally sufficient to sustain convictions of conspiracy to commit larceny and larceny. *United States v. Whitten*, 56 M.J. 234 (C.A.A.F. 2002).

(b) Larceny continues as long as the asportation continues. *United States v. Escobar*, 7 M.J. 197 (C.M.A. 1979) (considering duration of larceny/asportation in context of establishing court-martial jurisdiction; accused stole jacket off post and carried it onto post, thus providing court-martial jurisdiction over the offense); *see also United States v. Henry*, 18 M.J. 773 (N.M.C.M.R. 1984) (accused's mistaken claim-of-right defense negated during asportation phase) *aff'd in part, rev'd in part on multiplicity grounds*, 21 M.J. 172 (C.M.A. 1985).

(c) Because the crime of larceny continues through the asportation phase, anyone who *knowingly* assists in the actual movement of the stolen property is a principal in the larceny. No distinction is made whether the continuation of the asportation by one other than the actual taker was prearranged or the result of decisions made on the spur of the moment. *United States v. Escobar*, 7 M.J. 197 (C.M.A. 1979).

(d) Person who participates in on-going larceny may simply be an accessory after the fact, not a principal, depending upon the purpose of his participation. If participant's motive is to secure the fruits of the crime, the aider becomes a participant in the larceny and is chargeable with larceny; but if his motive is to assist the perpetrator to escape detection and punishment, he is properly charged as an accessory after the fact. *United States v. Manuel*, 8 M.J. 823 (A.F.C.M.R. 1979).

(e) Larceny complete when soldier having custody over items moved them to another part of central issue facility with felonious intent. As such, when accused received the property it was already stolen and his actions did not make him a principal to larceny but rather only a receiver of stolen property under Article 134. *United States v. Henderson*, 9 M.J. 845 (A.C.M.R. 1980).

(f) The assistance need not be prearranged. *United States v. Cannon*, 29 M.J. 549 (A.C.M.R. 1989). *See generally* TJAGSA Practice Note, *Larceny and Proving Asportation*, ARMY LAW., Feb. 1990, at 67 (discusses *Cannon*).

(g) Asportation was ongoing when the accused helped the perpetrator of a larceny; therefore, the accused is guilty of larceny as an aider or abettor. *United States v. Keen*, 31 M.J. 1108 (N.M.C.M.R. 1989). *See generally* TJAGSA Practice Note, *Aiding and Abetting Larceny*, ARMY LAW., Nov. 1990, at 40 (discussing *Keen*).

(3) Lost property. Taking an unexpired credit card found on a public sidewalk was larceny of lost property by wrongful taking since the card contained a clue as to the identity of the owner. *United States v. Wiederkehr*, 33 M.J. 539 (A.F.C.M.R. 1991); *but see United States v. Meeks*, 32 M.J. 1033 (A.F.C.M.R. 1991) (keeping a t-shirt found mixed in

with accused's laundry where there was no clue as to the owner was not a larceny).

(4) Electronic transfers as a "taking."

(a) *United States v. Meng*, 43 M.J. 801 (A.F. Ct. Crim. App. 1995), *rev. denied*, 44 M.J. 47 (C.A.A.F. 1996) (data entries made by accused in his computerized finance records to pay himself more BAS than he was eligible for was larceny).

(b) Where accused never took, obtained, withheld, or possessed the fees, guilty pleas to so much of larceny specifications as pertained to credit card and automatic teller machine (ATM) processing fees were legally improvident. *United States v. Sanchez*, 54 M.J. 874 (A. Ct. Crim. App. 2001) (court notes in dicta that the appellant would have been provident to obtaining services under false pretenses as to the bank processing fees).

b) Obtaining by false pretenses. A false pretense is a false representation of past or existing fact, which may include a person's power, authority or intention. Although the pretense need not be the sole cause inducing the owner to part with the property, it must be an effective and intentional cause of the obtaining. MCM, pt. IV, ¶ 46c(1)(e).

(1) Debit Card and ATM Transactions. *United States v. Lubasky*, 68 M.J. 260 (C.A.A.F. 2009) (accused obtained access to account by false pretenses, representing that he would use the funds only for the purposes victim authorized; evidence was legally sufficient to support a larceny).

(2) In loan application, false promises to repay may support larceny by false pretenses. *United States v. Cummins*, 26 C.M.R. 449 (C.M.A. 1958).

(3) Knowledge of fraud not imputed between government agents. *United States v. Williams*, 3 M.J. 555 (A.C.M.R. 1977), *rev'd on other grounds*, 4 M.J. 336 (1978).

(4) Insurance fraud larceny not complete until accused cashed settlement check. *United States v. Seivers*, 8 M.J. 63 (C.M.A. 1979), *aff'd*, 9 M.J. 397 (C.M.A. 1980).

(5) Sham marriage to obtain monetary benefits may support larceny by false pretenses. *United States v. Bolden*, 28 M.J. 127 (C.M.A. 1989).

(6) Obtaining services by false pretenses (long-distance telephone services) is charged under Article 134. *United States v. Flowerday*, 28 M.J. 705 (A.F.C.M.R. 1989); *United States v. Perkins*, 56 M.J. 825 (A. Ct. Crim. App. 2001).

(7) False pretenses and unauthorized pay/allowances.

(a) When Congress authorized basic allowance for housing for service members with "dependents," it did not intend to include a person linked to a service member only by a sham marriage. A marriage, as intended by Congress, is an undertaking by two parties to establish a life together and assume certain duties and obligations. A marriage entered into solely for the purpose of obtaining government benefits is a sham marriage and not entitled to BAH. *United States v. Phillips*, 52 M.J. 268 (C.A.A.F. 2000).

(b) A false pretense may exist by one's silence or by a failure to correct a known misrepresentation. The accused obtained use of government quarters at Fort Stewart, Georgia between 4 November 1994 and 14 January 1998 by misrepresenting that he was married, when in fact he was divorced. Even though he made no affirmative misrepresentation, his silence when his divorce became final and subsequent failure to correct a known misrepresentation constituted false representation sufficient to establish that he wrongfully obtained services under false pretenses, an Article 134 offense. The court specifically analogized obtaining services by false pretenses (Article 134) with larceny by false pretenses (Article 121). *United States v. Perkins*, 56 M.J. 825 (A. Ct. Crim. App. 2001) (ACCA formally adopted the position already taken by NMCCA and AFCCA).

(c) Procuring casual pay by misrepresentation or failing to inquire into legitimacy of casual pay does not amount to larceny by false pretenses. *United States v. Johnson*, 30 M.J. 930 (A.C.M.R. 1990).

(d) *United States v. Johnson*, 39 M.J. 707 (N.M.C.M.R. 1993), *aff'd*, 40 M.J. 318 (C.M.A. 1993) (larceny of BAQ and VHA by false pretenses when accused divorced his wife, knew that he was under a duty to report his change in marital status, but remained silent and exploited government reliance on his previous statement of marital status in order to continue receiving pay).

(e) *United States v. Bulger*, 41 M.J. 194 (C.M.A. 1994) (evidence that accused falsely declared his wife as a dependent and entered a false address for her in order to obtain increased BAQ and VHA allowances and had not paid support to her since their separation several years earlier, sufficiently established that accused misrepresented existing intention in applying for benefits to support larceny conviction of obtaining by false pretenses).

(8) Defrauding insurance company by killing insured or intentionally destroying property in order to collect insurance proceeds is larceny by false pretenses. *United States v. Garner*, 43 M.J. 435 (C.A.A.F. 1996).

(9) *United States v. Fenner*, 53 M.J. 666 (A.F. Ct. Crim. App. 2000) (sole lessee collected $225 from his 3 roommates for rent and utilities. After his roommates paid him one month, he told them that someone had stolen

all the money, which was a lie. Each of the roommates agreed to pay an extra $75 per month for the next three months to replace the stolen money. The court affirmed the part of a specification that alleged larceny of $75 that one of the roommates paid the accused toward the supposedly stolen rent as the roommate paid the accused $75 under the false pretense that the money had been stolen).

c) Withholding. A "withholding" may arise as a result of a failure to return, account for, or deliver property to its owner when a return, accounting, or delivery is due, even if the owner has made no demand for the property; or it may arise as a result of devoting property to a use not authorized by its owner. Generally this is so whether the person withholding the property acquired it lawfully or unlawfully. MCM, pt. IV, ¶ 46c(1)(b). This theory encompasses the common law offenses of embezzlement and conversion.

(1) *United States v. Moreno*, 23 M.J. 622 (A.F.C.M.R.), *pet. denied*, 24 M.J. 348 (C.M.A. 1986) (accused wrote checks against money erroneously deposited in his account; intent to steal (withholding) may be formed after the property is obtained).

(2) Embezzlement requires a fiduciary relationship and a lawful holding. *United States v. Castillo*, 18 M.J. 590 (N.M.C.M.R. 1984); *see also United States v. McFarland*, 23 C.M.R. 266 (C.M.A. 1957).

(3) Intent to permanently deprive must be concurrent with the taking/withholding. *United States v. Sicley*, 20 C.M.R. 118 (C.M.A. 1955).

(4) Wrongful conversion requires an accounting to the owner. *United States v. Paulk*, 32 C.M.R. 456 (C.M.A. 1963).

(5) *United States v. Head*, 6 M.J. 840 (N.C.M.R. 1979) (larceny by withholding when a victim mistook accused to be a robber and handed his wallet to the accused who, at that time, formed the intent and took money from the wallet. Though he abandoned the wallet, the accused was responsible for larceny of the sum he took).

(6) Neither a receiver of stolen property nor an accessory after the fact can be convicted of larceny on the theory that, with knowledge of the identity of the owner, he withheld the stolen property from the owner. *United States v. Sanderson*, CM 438057 (A.C.M.R. 29 Jun. 79) (unpub.); *see also United States v. Jones*, 33 C.M.R. 167 (C.M.A. 1963).

(7) *United States v. Bilbo*, 9 M.J. 800 (N.C.M.R. 1980). Accused who lawfully obtained loans from fellow Marines but then failed to repay those loans was found guilty of wrongful appropriation, not larceny. N.C.M.R. further held that the Article 134 offense of dishonorable failure to pay just debts was supported by the evidence.

(8) *United States v. Hale*, 28 M.J. 310 (C.M.A. 1989). Retention of rental car beyond period contemplated by rental contract constitutes wrongful appropriation (unless intent to permanently deprive the owner of the property can be proven).

(9) Withholding of unauthorized pay or allowances. These cases differ from the cases annotated above in which unauthorized pay and allowances are *obtained* by false pretenses. The withholding cases discussed here involve either government error or a change in the serviceman's status, which effects his continued entitlement to the pay or allowance. The property is obtained lawfully.

> (a) In the absence of a fiduciary duty to account, a withholding of funds otherwise lawfully obtained is not larcenous. *United States v. Watkins*, 32 M.J. 327 (A.C.M.R. 1990); *United States v. Johnson*, 39 M.J. 707 (N.M.C.M.R. 1993); *but see United States v. Thomas*, 36 M.J. 617 (A.C.M.R. 1992)(accused had a duty to inform government of change in circumstances, failing to do so he is guilty of larceny of funds); *cf. United States v. Markley*, 40 M.J. 581 (A.F.C.M.R. 1994) (failure of duty to report change in marital status effecting entitlement to allowances may support conviction for dereliction of duty); *United States v. Antonelli*, 43 M.J. 183 (C.A.A.F. 1995) (allowances, including BAQ and VHA, remain the property of the United States unless they are used for their statutory or regulatory purposes), *aff'd,* 45 M.J. 12 (C.A.A.F. 1996).

> (b) Once service member realizes that he or she is erroneously receiving pay or allowances and forms the intent to steal that property, the service member has committed larceny even without an affirmative act of deception or a duty to account for the funds. *United States v. Helms*, 47 M.J. 1 (C.A.A.F. 1997) (unanimously resolving issue left open in *United States v. Antonelli*, 43 M.J. 183 (C.A.A.F. 1995), *aff'd,* 45 M.J. 12 (C.A.A.F. 1996)); *United States v. Perkins*, 56 M.J. 825 (Army Ct. Crim. App. 2001).

> (c) *United States v. Gray*, 44 M.J. 585 (N-M. Ct. Crim. App. 1996) (accused's silence after he discovered error of housing office and finance to continue his BAQ and VHA payments after government quarters were assigned was insufficient to support conviction for larceny by wrongful withholding absent any affirmative steps by accused to ensure that he would continue to be overpaid. Further, the accused fully expected the Navy to recoup overpayments eventually, without disciplinary action, as it had done in the past).

> (d) *United States v. Stadler*, 44 M.J. 566 (A.F. Ct. Crim. App. 1996) (larceny of OHA and COLA allowances where accused continued to collect these allowances after his family returned to CONUS and he moved into government quarters), *aff'd,* 47 M.J. 206 (C.A.A.F. 1997).

(e) Evidence insufficient to establish that accused's spouse had possessory or ownership rights to BAQ at w/dep rate and thus failed to establish that accused had stolen BAQ from his wife. *United States v. Evans*, 37 M.J. 468 (C.M.A. 1993).

(f) Excess BAQ was "military property of the United States." *United States v. Dailey*, 37 M.J. 463 (C.M.A. 1993).

(10) Conversion. An unauthorized assumption and exercise of the right of ownership over goods or personal chattels belonging to another, to the alteration of their condition or the exclusion of the owner's rights. BLACK'S LAW DICTIONARY (5th Ed. 1979).

(a) *United States v. Cahn*, 31 M.J. 729 (A.F.C.M.R. 1990). Accused was guilty of larceny by conversion when he retained an ATM card lended to him for withdrawing $20 as a loan, used the card to withdraw $500, and then destroyed it.

(b) *United States v. Antonelli*, 35 M.J. 122 (C.M.A. 1992). Conversion theory of larceny may apply to accused who receives BAQ and VHA allowances to support his dependents, but who does not actually provide support.

4. Element 2: That the property described belonged to a person other than the accused.

a) The "owner" is the person or entity with the superior right to possession. MCM, pt. IV, ¶ 46c. *See United States v. Evans*, 37 M.J. 468 (C.M.A. 1993) (evidence insufficient to establish that accused's spouse had possessory or other ownership right to BAQ and, thus, failed to establish that accused stole BAQ from his spouse); *United States v. Cohen*, 12 M.J. 573 (A.F.C.M.R. 1981) (even though the checks were intended for various banks and credit unions, the United States had possession of the checks while they were in the mail; thus the charge of larceny from the United States was proper); *United States v. Jett*, 14 M.J. 941 (A.C.M.R. 1982) (victim is anyone with a superior right of possession to the accused, regardless of who has title); *United States v. Meadows*, 14 M.J. 1002 (A.C.M.R. 1982) (can commit larceny or wrongful appropriation by taking military equipment from one unit to another); *United States v. Leslie*, 13 M.J. 170 (C.M.A. 1982) (United States had a possessory interest in C.O.D. funds that postal clerk stole instead of forwarding to senders of C.O.D. parcels; therefore, charge of larceny from the United States was proper); *United States v. Lewis*, 19 M.J. 623 (A.C.M.R. 1984) (government retains ownership in TDY advance).

b) Debts or the administrative costs associated with a larceny are not the proper subjects of a larceny. *United States v. Mervine*, 26 M.J. 482 (C.M.A. 1988); *United States v. Dunn*, 27 M.J. 624 (A.F.C.M.R. 1988); TJAGSA Practice Note, *Larceny of a Debt: United States v. Mervine Revisited*, ARMY LAW., Dec. 1988, at 29; TJAGSA Practice Note, L*arceny of Administrative Costs: United States v. Dunn*, ARMY LAW., Mar. 1989, at 32.

c) Erroneous allegation of ownership not a fatal defect. *United States v. Craig*, 24 C.M.R. 28 (C.M.A. 1957).

d) To be guilty of larceny, accused must take property from one having a superior possessory interest. *United States v. Faircloth*, 45 M.J.172 (C.A.A.F. 1996) (accused forged endorsement in financing company's behalf on insurance check issued to accused and financing company as co payees to auto damage; during providency, accused admitted financing company had superior possessory interest).

5. Element 3: That the property in question was of a value alleged, or of some value.

    a) Legitimate (retail) market value at time and place of theft must be established. *United States v. Lewis*, 13 M.J. 561 (A.F.C.M.R. 1982) (accused properly convicted of full value of item where he switched price tags and paid the lower price).

    b) Government item. Government price lists can be used to establish value. *See* M.R.E 803(17).

    c) Non-government item. Average retail selling price established by recent purchase price of like item, testimony of market expert, testimony of owner's opinion as to value, etc.

    d) Value tokens. Writings representing value may be considered to have the value which they represent, even though contingently, at the time of the theft. MCM, pt. IV, ¶ 46c(1)(g)(iii). *See United States v. Windham*, 36 C.M.R. 21 (C.M.A. 1965); *United States v. Riverasoto*, 29 M.J. 594 (A.C.M.R. 1989) (drafted check—face value);*United States v. Cook*, 15 C.M.R. 622 (A.F.B.R. 1954) (gasoline coupons—face value); *United States v. Frost*, 46 C.M.R. 233 (C.M.A. 1973) (blank check—nominal value); *see also United States v. Falcon*, 16 M.J. 528 (A.C.M.R. 1983); *United States v. Stewart*, 1 M.J. 750 (A.C.M.R. 1973) (airline ticket—face value); *United States v. Tucker*, 29 C.M.R. 790 (A.B.R. 1960) (credit card—nominal value); *United States v. Payne*, 9 M.J. 681 (A.F.C.M.R. 1980) (accounts receivable—nominal value); *United States v. Sowards*, 5 M.J. 864 (A.F.C.M.R. 1978) (money orders—face value); *but see United States v. McCollum*, 13 M.J. 127 (C.M.A. 1982) (value can include what items might bring in illegal channels—"thieves value").

    e) Value of property must reasonably approximate the loss. *United States v. Eggleton*, 47 C.M.R. 920 (C.M.A. 1973).

    f) In *United States v. Batiste*, 11 M.J. 791 (A.F.C.M.R. 981), the court held that urine, which was to be sent to the laboratory for testing, was an article of value for purposes of larceny prosecution and the immediate substitution by accused of a like quantity of urine did not diminish the offense of wrongful appropriation.

6. Element 4: That the taking, obtaining, or withholding by the accused was with the intent [permanently/temporarily] to deprive or defraud another person of the use and benefit of the property or [permanently/temporarily] to appropriate the property for the use of the accused or for any other person other than the owner.

    a) Concurrence of intent and wrongful act. The wrongful taking, obtaining or withholding must be accompanied by the intent to steal or wrongfully appropriate the property. Although a person gets property by a taking or obtaining which was not wrongful or which was without a concurrent intent to steal, a larceny is nevertheless committed if an intent to steal is formed after the taking or obtaining and the property is wrongfully withheld with that intent. MCM, pt. IV, ¶ 46c(1)(f)(i).

b) Intent may be proved by circumstantial evidence. *United States v. Zaiss*, 42 M.J. 586 (Army Ct. Crim. App. 1995) (intent to steal may be inferred when accused secretly takes property, hides it, and denies knowing anything about it).

c) Wrongful appropriation of government property requires a specific intent to deprive the government or a unit thereof of more than mere possession of its property. *United States v. McGowan*, 41 M.J. 406 (C.A.A.F. 1995). Taking military equipment for maintenance does not constitute wrongful appropriation. *United States v. Taylor*, 44 C.M.R. 274 (C.M.A. 1972). Similarly, the incidental use of a government vehicle for private purposes does not constitute misappropriation, provided the vehicle is also used for authorized purposes without diversion or deviation. *United States v. Lutgert*, 40 C.M.R. 94 (C.M.A. 1969).

d) Mere borrowing without consent is not always an offense. *United States v. Harville*, 14 M.J. 270 (C.M.A. 1982); *United States v. Thomas*, 34 C.M.R. 3 (C.M.A. 1963) (borrowing clothes from barracks occupant can be defense to wrongful appropriation).

e) There may be a limited right of self-help to seize another's property in order to satisfy a debt or acquire security for it, if there is a prior agreement between the parties providing for such recourse, or if the soldier takes property honestly believing he has a superior claim of right to that specific property. *United States v. Jackson*, 50 M.J. 868 (Army Ct. Crim. App. 1999), *aff'd*, 53 M.J. 220 (C.A.A.F. 2000); *United States v. Gunter*, 42 M.J. 292 (C.A.A.F. 1995); *United States v. Smith*, 14 M.J. 68 (C.M.A. 1982).

(1) Self-help is not justified where the debt is uncertain; and the value of the property taken must reasonably approximate the loss. *United States v. Cunningham*, 14 M.J. 539 (A.C.M.R. 1982), *rev'd and remanded on other grounds*, 15 M.J. 282 (C.M.A. 1983); *United States v. Kelley*, 39 M.J. 1011 (A.C.M.R. 1994); *see also United States v. Eggleton*, 47 C.M.R. 920 (C.M.A. 1973).

(2) Honest mistake of fact by accused that he was entitled to receive property may be a defense to larceny. *United States v. Turner*, 27 M.J. 217 (C.M.A. 1988).

(3) "Claim of Right." A defense exists for a soldier who takes property from another honestly believing that he has a superior claim of right to that specific property. *United States v. Gunter*, 42 M.J. 292 (1995); *United States v. Jackson*, 50 M.J. 868 (Army Ct. Crim. App. 1999) (engagement ring and exercise bike given to fiancé).

(4) No right of retrieval is recognized for contraband. *United States v. Petrie*, 1 M.J. 333 (C.M.A. 1976).

(5) No right of accused to unilaterally elevate himself to position of secured creditor by grabbing at will chattels belonging to service member. *United States v. Martin*, 37 M.J. 546 (N.M.C.M.R. 1993)(taking of ring from service member who owed money as security for debt was wrongful taking).

f) Motive does not negate intent. For example, if the accused took an item as a joke or to teach the owner a lesson about security, the taking is nonetheless wrongful if, viewed objectively, harm was caused (*i.e.*, the owner is permanently or temporarily deprived of the use or benefit of the property). MCM, pt. IV, ¶ 46c(1)(f)(iii); *United States v. Kastner*, 17 M.J. 11 (C.M.A. 1983); *United States v. Johnson*, 17 M.J. 140 (C.M.A. 1984).

g) An accused that believes property to be abandoned lacks the *mens rea* required for larceny. *United States v. Malone*, 14 M.J. 563 (N.M.C.M.R. 1982); *see also* MCM, pt. IV, ¶ 46c(1)(h)(i); *see also United States v. Turner*, 27 M.J. 217 (C.M.A. 1988); *United States v. Jones*, 26 M.J. 1009 (A.C.M.R. 1988).

h) Intent to pay for, replace, or return property is not a defense. MCM, pt. IV, ¶ 46c(1)(f)(iii)A)(B); *see United States v. Brown*, 30 M.J. 693 (A.C.M.R. 1990); *United States v. Woodson*, 52 M.J. 688 (C.G. Ct. Crim. App. 2000). *But see United States v. Boddie*, 49 M.J. 310 (C.A.A.F. 1998) (in dicta, the CAAF states that an intent to pay for property *may* be a defense if there is "a substantial ability to do so").

i) Intent to pay for, replace, or return money or a negotiable instrument having no special value above its face value, with the intent to return an equivalent amount, is a defense to larceny. *United States v. Hegel*, 52 M.J. 778 (C.G. Ct. Crim. App. 2000) (accused stole CityBank Visa card and used it, but because the accused claimed he intended to pay the bill in full when due, the plea of guilty to larceny of funds from CityBank was improvident).

j) Overdraft protection may negate intent to steal in cases of larceny by false pretenses involving bad checks. *United States v. McCanless*, 29 M.J. 985 (A.F.C.M.R. 1990); *see United States v. McNeil*, 30 M.J. 648 (N.M.C.M.R. 1990); *see generally* TJAGSA Practice Note, *Overdraft Protection and Economic Crimes*, ARMY LAW., Jul. 1990, at 45.

k) Where transfer of possession occurred prior to act of accused, no wrongful taking or withholding has occurred. *United States v. Hughes*, 45 M.J. 137 (C.A.A.F. 1996)(accused merely placed lock on his assigned wall locker which contained property belonging to another soldier that was stored there without the permission of the accused).

7. Multiplicity.

a) When a larceny of several articles is committed at substantially the same time and place, it is a single larceny, even though the articles belong to different persons. MCM, pt. IV, ¶ 46c(1)(h)(ii); *United States v. Warner*, 33 M.J. 522 (A.F.C.M.R. 1991); *United States v. Ruiz*, 30 M.J. 867 (N.M.C.M.R. 1990); *United States v. Huggins*, 12 M.J. 657 (A.C.M.R. 1981), *aff'd in part, rev'd in part on multiplicity grounds,* 17 M.J. 345 (C.M.A. 1984); *United States v. Gutierrez*, 42 C.M.R. 521 (A.C.M.R. 1970); *United States v. Miller*, 2000 C.A.A.F. LEXIS 207 (Feb. 24, 2000) (contemporaneous theft of two different victims' checks, which the accused found in one victim's drawer, constituted a single larceny); *United States v. LePresti*, 52 M.J. 644 (N-M. Ct. Crim. App. 1999).

b) *United States v. Florence*, 5 C.M.R. 48 (C.M.A. 1952). Without evidence to justify joining larcenies into one specification and thereby increasing the penalty, the Government should have charged separately.

c) *United States v. Gillingham*, 1 M.J. 1193 (N.C.M.R. 1976). Theft of calculator from one office was not multiplicious with theft of second calculator, moments later, from adjoining office.

d) *United States v. Alvarez*, 5 M.J. 762 (A.C.M.R. 1978). Housebreaking and larceny in the same transaction were not multiplicious.

e) *United States v. Burney*, 44 C.M.R. 125 (C.M.A. 1971). Larceny and wrongful appropriation of a truck to transport stolen goods were not multiplicious.

f) *United States v. Harrison*, 4 M.J. 332 (C.M.A. 1978). Six larcenies and six facilitating false official statements were not multiplicious for sentencing purposes.

8. Divisible Property. *United States v. Pardue*, 35 C.M.R. 455 (C.M.A. 1965). Where the accused is charged only with larceny of an automobile, he may not be found not guilty of wrongful appropriation of the automobile but guilty of larceny of an essential part (*i.e.*, the tires). *See also United States v. Jones*, 13 M.J. 761 (A.F.C.M.R. 1982).

9. Permissive Inferences.

a) Inference of wrongfulness arising out of possession of recently stolen property. If the facts establish that property was wrongfully taken from the possession of the owner and that shortly thereafter the property was discovered in the knowing, conscious, exclusive, and unexplained possession of the accused, the fact-finder at trial may infer that the accused took the property. *United States v. Pasha*, 24 M.J. 87 (C.M.A. 1987); *United States v. Hairston*, 26 C.M.R. 334 (C.M.A. 1958); *United States v. Morton*, 15 M.J. 850 (A.F.C.M.R. 1983).

b) Passing cash register without offering to pay for an item concealed in the accused's pocket creates a permissive inference of intent to steal. *United States v. Wynn*, 23 M.J. 726 (A.F.C.M.R. 1986), *sentence vacated and remanded by*, 26 M.J. 232 (C.M.A. 1988).

c) A power of attorney is not a license to embezzle. *United States v. Willard*, 48 M.J. 147 (1998).

10. Variance.

a) Because the identity of the victim is not an essential element of either larceny or wrongful appropriation, a variance in establishing ownership of the item taken will not always be fatal to the government's case. *United States v. Craig*, 24 C.M.R. 28 (C.M.A. 1957) (variance regarding victim in larceny case not prejudicial error); *United States v. Davis*, 31 C.M.R. 486 (C.G.B.R. 1962) (identity of victim of wrongful appropriation not an essential element); *United States v. Roberto*, 31 C.M.R. 349 (A.B.R. 1961) (variance as to ownership of funds in larceny case not fatal).

b) Variance in the date of the larceny may be fatal when the theory of larceny also changes. *United States v. Wray*, 17 M.J. 735 (C.M.A. 1984) (change of dates and theory from taking to taking and withholding was fatal variance).

11. Larceny of Mail Matter. Theft of misaddressed mail is included within the offenses of stealing mail under Article 134. MCM, pt. IV, ¶ 93; UCMJ art. 134; *United States v. Fox*, 50 M.J. 444 (C.A.A.F. 1999).

12. Credit Card/Automatic Teller Machine Offenses.

   a) "Wrongfully engaging in a credit, debit, or electronic transaction to obtain goods or money is an obtaining-type larceny by false pretense. Such use to obtain goods is usually a larceny of those goods from the merchant offering them." *See* 2008 MCM, pt. IV, ¶ 46.c(1)(h)(vi).

   b) *United States v. Lubasky*, 68 M.J. 260 (C.A.A.F. 2009). The accused, under the guise of assisting the elderly victim with her finances, used her credit cards, ATM cards, and debit cards, for his own benefit.

   (1) Credit card transactions. Under the facts of the case, the unauthorized use of credit cards to obtain cash advances and unspecified goods of a certain value, was not a larceny from the cardholder herself. In using the credit cards in this case, the accused did not obtain anything from the cardholder, but instead obtained items of value from other entities. As such, the court concluded that the proper subject of the credit-card-transaction larcenies in this case was not the cardholder.

   (2) Debit/ATM Transactions. The accused obtained access to the victim's account by false pretenses, representing that he would use the funds only for the purposes she authorized. Any authority he had to access the victim's funds was limited by his "beneficiary status and [the accused's] fiduciary role." Although he had access to the account, his authority to use funds from the account was limited to purchasing items for the cardholder's benefit. Therefore, the evidence was legally sufficient to show that the accused wrongfully obtained money from her with the intent to permanently deprive her of it.

   c) Any theory under Article 134 or Article 121 can support a conviction for credit card offenses. *United States v. Christy*, 18 M.J. 688 (N.M.C.M.R. 1984).

   d) Larceny of another soldier's ATM card and the use of the card to make withdrawals are separate crimes and are separately punishable. *United States v. Garner*, 28 M.J. 634 (A.F.C.M.R. 1989); *United States v. Abendschein*, 19 M.J. 619 (A.C.M.R. 1984); *United States v. Jobes*, 20 M.J. 506 (A.F.C.M.R. 1985).

   e) Withdrawals from several different accounts using one banking machine are separate crimes. *United States v. Aquino*, 20 M.J. 712 (A.C.M.R. 1985).

   f) Defense contention that bank consented to withdrawals by not programming ATM to prevent withdrawals from accounts having insufficient funds was rejected. *United States v. Buswell*, 22 M.J. 617 (A.C.M.R. 1986).

   g) Misuse of Gov't travel card.

   (1) Dereliction of duty. Article 92(3). *United States v. Long*, 46 M.J. 783 (Army Ct. Crim. App. 1997).

   (2) Violation of general regulation. Article 92(1). *United States v. Hughey*, 46 M.J. 152 (1997) (Air Force base regulation restricting use of

government charge cards and establishing payment requirements was lawful general regulation).

13. Military Property As An Aggravating Factor For Larceny. *See supra* discussion of military property under Article 108, ch. 3, ¶ XX).

14. *See* Captain David O. Anglin, *Service Discrediting: Misuse, Abuse, and Fraud in the Government Purchase Card Program*, ARMY LAW., August 2004, at 1.

B. Receiving Stolen Property. MCM, pt. IV, ¶ 106; UCMJ art. 134.

1. Charged as a violation of Article 134. *United States v. Wolfe*, 19 M.J. 174 (C.M.A. 1985).

2. The actual thief cannot be a receiver of the goods he has stolen. MCM, pt. IV, ¶ 106(c)(1); *United States v. Ford*, 30 C.M.R. 3 (C.M.A. 1960); *United States v. Henderson*, 9 M.J. 845 (A.C.M.R. 1980). Thus, the original asportation (carrying away) of the property must be completed by the thief before another can be found guilty of receiving stolen property. *United States v. Graves*, 20 M.J. 344 (C.M.A. 1985).

3. The soldier who receives stolen property innocently and later discovers that it is stolen cannot be guilty of receiving stolen property. *United States v. Rokoski*, 30 C.M.R. 433 (A.B.R. 1960). "Receive" means to accept custody of; one cannot "receive" that which is already in his possession. *United States v. Lowery*, 19 M.J. 754 (A.C.M.R. 1984).

4. Although a principal who is not the actual thief may be liable as a principal or receiver of stolen property, he may not be found guilty of both. *United States v. Cartwright*, 13 M.J. 174 (C.M.A. 1982); MCM, pt. IV, ¶ 106(c)(1).

5. A conspirator to the larceny may not be found guilty of being an accessory after the fact or a receiver of the stolen property. *United States v. Lampani*, 14 M.J. 22 (C.M.A. 1982).

C. Robbery. MCM, pt. IV, ¶ 47; UCMJ art. 122.

1. Elements.

a) That the accused wrongfully took certain property from the person or from the possession and in the presence of a person named or described;

b) That the taking was against the will of that person;

c) That the taking was by means of force, violence, or force and violence, or putting the person in fear of immediate or future injury to that person, a relative, a member of the person's family, anyone accompanying the person at the time of the robbery, the person's property, or the property of a relative, family member, or anyone accompanying the person at the time of the robbery.

d) That the property belonged to a person named or described;

e) That the property was of a certain or of some value; and

f) That the taking of the property by the accused was with the intent permanently to deprive the person robbed of the use and benefit of the property;

g) [If the robbery was committed with a firearm, add the following element:] That the means of force or violence or of putting the person in fear was a firearm.

2. Pleading.

a) Failure to allege ownership of the property. *United States v. Smith*, 40 C.M.R. 432 (A.B.R. 1968) (no error); *United States v. Goudeau*, 44 C.M.R. 438 (A.C.M.R. 1971) (implied from allegation that item was taken from the purse of a named victim).

b) Failure to allege a taking from the person or in the presence of the victim is fatal, but the specification may be sufficient to allege larceny. *United States v. Rios*, 15 C.M.R. 203 (C.M.A. 954); *United States v. Dozier*, 38 C.M.R. 507 (A.B.R. 1967).

c) Failure to allege a taking "against his or her will." *United States v. Smith*, 40 C.M.R. 432 (A.B.R. 1968) (no defect; implied from allegation that taking was by means of force and violence).

3. Robbery has two theories: taking by force and/or violence, *or* taking by putting in fear. The alleged theory must be proved; evidence of the non-alleged theory will not suffice. *See United States v. Hamlin*, 33 C.M.R. 707 (A.F.B.R. 1963). Consequently, most prosecutors allege both theories.

   a) <u>Theory 1</u>: Taking by force and/or violence.

   (1) Victim's fear unnecessary.

   (2) Amount of force required:

   (a) Overcomes actual resistance, or

   (b) Puts victim in a position not to resist, or

   (c) Overcomes the restraint of a fastening (*e.g.*, in snatching purse the thief breaks strap of purse).

   (3) The sequence and relationship of application of force and the intent to steal. Force and intent must be contemporaneous, but need not be simultaneous. If the accused's force and violence place the victim in vulnerable circumstances, this is sufficient for robbery if thereafter, while the victim is still vulnerable, the accused formulates the intent and takes the property. *United States v. Chambers*, 12 M.J. 443 (C.M.A. 1982); *United States v. Washington*, 12 M.J. 1036 (A.C.M.R. 1982).

   (4) Picking a victim's pocket by stealth is not sufficient force for robbery; however, jostling a victim in conjunction with picking his pocket is sufficient force for robbery. *United States v. Reynolds*, 20 M.J. 118 (C.M.A. 1985).

   b) <u>Theory 2</u>: Taking by putting in fear.

   (1) Demonstration of force or menaces.

   (2) Victim placed in fear of death or bodily injury in the present or future to himself, relative, or anyone in his company at the time.

   (a) Reasonable fear. The test for its existence is objective. *United States v. Bates*, 24 C.M.R. 738 (A.F.B.R. 1957).

   (b) Sufficient to warrant giving up property.

   (c) Sufficient to warrant making no resistance.

(3) Taking while fear exists.

4. Wrongful taking must be from the person or in the presence of the victim.

    a) "Presence" for purposes of robbery means that possession or control is so imminent that force or intimidation is required to remove the property. *United States v. Cagle*, 12 M.J. 736 (A.F.C.M.R. 1982).

    b) "In the presence" is satisfied where victim held by force while his property is secured from another building and destroyed before him. *United States v. Maldonado*, 34 C.M.R. 952 (A.B.R.), *rev'd on other grounds*, 35 C.M.R. 257 (C.M.A. 1964).

    c) Property taken need not be from person of victim, but may be from victim's immediate control. *United States v. Hamlin*, 33 C.M.R. 707 (A.F.B.R. 1963).

    d) No fatal variance exists between specification and proof where the former alleges "from the person" but evidence shows "in the presence." *United States v. McCray*, 5 M.J. 820 (A.C.M.R. 1978).

5. Robbery is a composite offense combining larceny with assault. *United States v. Chambers*, 12 M.J. 443 (C.M.A. 1982) (force applied after taking effected sufficient for robbery); *United States v. Brown*, 33 C.M.R. 17 (C.M.A. 1963).

6. Robbery requires a larceny by wrongful taking. The other theories of larceny, wrongful withholding or obtaining, will not suffice. *United States v. Brazil*, 5 M.J. 509 (A.C.M.R. 1978).

7. The intent to rob need not be focused upon specific property. An intent to deprive the victim of whatever is in a pocket or purse is sufficient. *United States v. Davis*, 6 M.J. 669 (A.C.M.R. 1978).

8. The intent to rob need not precede or be simultaneous with the taking of the property. It must only be contemporaneous with such taking. *United States v. Fell*, 33 M.J. 628 (A.C.M.R. 1991); *see also United States v. Washington*, 12 M.J. 1036 (A.C.M.R. 1982); *United States v. Henry*, 18 M.J. 773 (N.M.C.M.R. 1984) (intent to steal formulated during asportation phase) *aff'd in part, rev'd in part on multiplicity grounds*, 21 M.J. 172 (C.M.A. 1985).

9. Forcible taking of property belonging to one entity from multiple persons constitutes one robbery. *United States v. Szentmiklosi*, 55 M.J. 487 (2001), *aff'd*, 57 M.J. 103 (C.A.A.F. 2002).

10. Lesser included Offenses. Under the "elements test," the federal offense of bank larceny was not a lesser included offense of the federal offense of bank robbery, so the defendant was not entitled to a jury instruction on it. A textual comparison of the elements of the two offenses in 18 U.S.C. § 2113 demonstrates that bank larceny requires three elements not required for bank robbery: (1) intent to steal; (2) asportation; and (3) value exceeding $1,000. *Carter v. United States*, 120 S.Ct. 2159 (2000) (although larceny is a lesser included offense of robbery under the UCMJ, the significance of this 5-4 decision is how a majority of the Court mechanically applied the "elements test" by comparing the statutory text).

D. Waste, Spoil, or Destruction of Non-Military Property. MCM, pt. IV, ¶ 33; UCMJ art. 109.

    1. Elements.

a) Wasting or spoiling of non-military property.

> (1) That the accused willfully or recklessly wasted or spoiled certain real property in a certain manner;
>
> (2) That the property was that of another person;
>
> (3) That the property was of a certain value.

b) Destroying or damaging non-military property.

> (1) That the accused willfully and wrongfully destroyed or damaged certain personal property in a certain manner;
>
> (2) That the property was that of another person;
>
> (3) That the property was of a certain value or the damage was of a certain amount.

2. Scope of UCMJ art. 109. All property, both real and personal, which is not military property of the United States.

> a) Avis rental car, two passenger cars, a fence owned by a German corporation, and a German road marker. *United States v. Valadez*, 10 M.J. 529 (A.C.M.R. 1980).
>
> b) Privately owned passenger car. *United States v. Bernacki*, 33 C.M.R. 175 (C.M.A. 1963).
>
> c) Privately owned boat. *United States v. Priest*, 7 M.J. 791 (N.C.M.R. 1979).
>
> d) Real and personal property belonging to officers' club. *United States v. Geisler*, 37 C.M.R. 530 (A.C.M.R. 1965).
>
> e) Real and personal property belonging to post exchange. *United States v. Underwood*, 41 C.M.R. 410 (A.C.M.R. 1969); *United States v. Schelin*, 12 M.J. 575 (A.C.M.R. 1981), *aff'd*, 15 M.J. 210 (C.M.A. 1983); *contra United States v. Mullins*, 34 C.M.R. 694 (N.C.M.R. 1964) and *United States v. Harvey*, 6 M.J. 545 (N.C.M.R. 1978).

3. Real Property. This portion of Article 109 proscribes the willful or reckless waste or spoliation of the real property of another.

> a) Real property is defined as land, and generally whatever is erected on or growing on or affixed to land. BLACK'S LAW DICTIONARY 1096 (5th ed. 1979).
>
> b) The term "wastes" and "spoils", as used in this article, refers to such wrongful acts of voluntary destruction of or permanent damage to real property as burning down buildings, burning piers, tearing down fences, or cutting down trees. MCM, pt. IV, ¶ 33c(1).
>
> c) To be punishable the destruction must be done either willfully, that is intentionally, or recklessly, that is through the culpable disregard of the foreseeable consequences of some voluntary act. For examples of both willful and reckless conduct see previous discussion of UCMJ art. 108.

4. Personal Property. This portion of Article 109 proscribes the willful and wrongful injury to non-military personal property.

a) Violation of this punitive article exists when personal, non-military property is either destroyed or damaged. To be destroyed, the property need not be completely demolished or annihilated, but need only be sufficiently injured to be useless for the purpose for which it was intended. Damage consists of any physical injury to the property. MCM, pt. IV, ¶ 33c(2).

b) Mere negligent or reckless conduct does not satisfy the specific intent necessary to constitute this offense.

    (1) Offense of willful and wrongful damage to private property requires proof of an actual intent to damage, as distinguished from a reckless disregard of property. *United States v. Bernacki*, 33 C.M.R. 175 (C.M.A. 1963); *see also United States v. Valadez*, 10 M.J. 529 (A.C.M.R. 1980). Regardless of the intentional nature of the cause precipitating damage to personal, non-military property, in the absence of evidence that the destruction or damage was the intended result of the accused, a conviction under this portion of Article 109 is not supported. *United States v. Jones*, 50 C.M.R. 724 (A.C.M.R. 1975).

    (2) *United States v. Priest*, 7 M.J. 791 (N.C.M.R. 1979)(accused's admission that he acted in grossly negligent or reckless manner in operating a privately owned boat in shallow water was an insufficient basis for conviction of willfully damaging private personal property of another, in that such an offense must be committed "willfully").

    (3) *United States v. Youkum*, 8 M.J. 763 (A.C.M.R. 1980) (evidence that accused got into his vehicle in a highly angered, vengeful state of mind, revved engine causing wheels to spin, reached high rate of speed in a short distance, aimed vehicle unerringly at victim as well as at parked vehicle from which victim had dismounted, and made no effort to stop until after he had damaged all three was sufficient circumstantial evidence to sustain conviction of willfully and wrongfully damaging vehicles).

    (4) *United States v. Garcia*, 29 M.J. 721 (C.G.C.M.R. 1989). The accused must intend to cause the destruction or damage. Unintentionally breaking a jewelry case to take the contents is insufficient for guilt. *See* TJAGSA Practice Note, *Damaging Property and Mens Rea*, ARMY LAW., Feb. 1990, at 66 (discusses *Garcia*).

    (5) *United States v. White*, 61 M.J. 521 (N-M. Ct. Crim. App. 2005) (insufficient proof of *mens rea* in a willful damage to nonmilitary property case where accused threw himself in front of a vehicle driven by a Japanese national; he denied any intention of damaging the property, but rather claimed his purpose in jumping in front of the vehicle was to injure himself).

5. Pleading the offense. When charged with damage or destruction of non-military personal property, the government should allege that the accused acted in a "willful" manner. *But see United States v. Valadez*, 10 M.J. 529 (A.C.M.R. 1980) (inartfully drawn specification alleging the willful and wrongful damage of a private automobile by operating it in a reckless manner was not fatal).

6. Value. In the case of *destruction*, the value of the property destroyed controls the limit of punishment that may be adjudged, but in the case of *damage*, the amount thereof

instead of the value of the property damaged is controlling. As a general rule, the amount of damage is the estimated or actual cost of repair by artisans employed in this work who are available to the community wherein the owner resides, or the replacement cost, whichever is less. See also the discussion of value pertaining to Article 108, UCMJ.

E. Crimes Violating Protected Places: Burglary, Housebreaking, and Unlawful Entry.

1. Elements.

    a) Burglary. MCM, pt. IV, ¶ 55; UCMJ art. 129.

        (1) That the accused unlawfully broke and entered the dwelling house of another;

        (2) That both the breaking and entering were done in the nighttime; and

        (3) That the breaking and entering were done with the intent to commit an offense punishable under Article 118 through Article 128, except Article 123a.

    b) Housebreaking. MCM, pt. IV, ¶ 56; UCMJ art. 130.

        (1) That the accused unlawfully entered a certain building or structure of a certain other person; and

        (2) That the unlawful entry was made with the intent to commit a criminal offense therein.

    c) Unlawful entry. MCM, pt. IV, ¶ 111; UCMJ art. 134.

        (1) That the accused entered the real property of another or certain personal property of another which amounts to a structure usually used for habitation or storage;

        (2) That such entry was unlawful; and

        (3) That, under the circumstances, the conduct of the accused was to the prejudice of good order and discipline in the armed forces or was of a nature to bring discredit upon the armed forces.

2. Protected Places.

    a) Burglary.

        (1) "Occupied" dwelling includes houses, apartments, hotel rooms, barracks rooms, but not tents. MCM, pt. IV, ¶ 55c(5).

        (2) *United States v. Bailey*, 23 C.M.R. 862 (A.F.B.R. 1957) (affirming burglary conviction for breaking into barracks building to victimize occupant where the victim's room was not broken into).

        (3) *United States v. Norman*, 16 M.J. 937 (A.C.M.R. 1983) (hotel room was dwelling place; specification was sufficient despite failing to allege occupancy of room by the victim).

        (4) *See also United States v. Slovacek*, 24 M.J. 140 (C.M.A. 1984); *United States v. Fagan*, 24 M.J. 865 (N.M.C.M.R. 1987), *aff'd,* 28 M.J.

64 (C.M.A. 1989); *United States v. Thompson*, 32 M.J. 65 (C.M.A. 1991).

b) Housebreaking.

(1) Building or structure: room, shop, store, office, apartment, stateroom, ship's hold, compartment of a vessel, inhabitable trailer, enclosed goods truck or freight car, tent, houseboat. MCM, pt. IV, ¶ 56c(4); *see generally* TJAGSA Practice Note, *Housebreaking Includes More Than Breaking Into a House*, ARMY LAW., Apr. 1989, at 56.

(2) *United States v. Sutton*, 45 C.M.R. 118 (C.M.A. 1972) (inapplicable to track vehicle).

(3) *United States v. Hall*, 30 C.M.R. 374 (C.M.A. 1961) (protects railroad freight car used to store goods).

(4) *United States v. Scimeca*, 12 M.J. 937 (N.M.C.M.R. 1982) (protects walk-in freezer).

(5) *United States v. Cahill*, 23 M.J. 544 (A.C.M.R. 1986) (protects AAFES delivery van used for storage).

(6) *United States v. Demmer*, 24 M.J. 731 (A.C.M.R. 1987) (protects AAFES snack truck used for storage).

(7) *United States v. Davis*, 56 M.J. 299 (C.A.A.F. 2002). Although the accused had authorized access to the key to a government warehouse where his unit's equipment was stored, his entry into the warehouse to steal items belonging to another unit, without any official or authorized purpose, was legally sufficient to prove the "unlawful entry" element of housebreaking. Factors to consider in determining whether or not the entry was with proper authority include: (1) the nature and function of the building involved; (2) the character, status, and duties of the entrant, and even at times his identity; (3) the conditions of the entry, including time, method, ostensible purpose; (4) the presence or absence of a directive; (5) the presence or absence of an explicit invitation to the visitor; (6) the invitational authority of any purported host; and (7) the presence or absence of a prior course of dealing, if any, by the entrant with the structure, and its nature.

c) Unlawful entry.

(1) Dwelling house, garage, warehouse, tent, vegetable garden, orchard, stateroom.

(2) *United States v. Breen*, 36 C.M.R. 156 (C.M.A. 1966) (does not protect service member's barracks locker).

(3) *United States v. Gillin*, 25 C.M.R. 173 (C.M.A. 1958) (inapplicable to an automobile); *see also United States v. Reese*, 12 M.J. 770 (A.C.M.R. 1981).

(4) *United States v. Taylor*, 30 C.M.R. 44 (C.M.A. 1960) (inapplicable to troop aircraft used as a conveyance).

(5) *United States v. Love*, 15 C.M.R. 260 (C.M.A. 1954) (protects troop billeting tent).

(6) *United States v. Wickersham*, 14 M.J. 404 (C.M.A. 1983) (protects fenced storage area).

(7) *United States v. Fayne*, 26 M.J. 528 (A.F.C.M.R. 1988) (showing that accused's estranged wife granted him permission to take water bed precluded conviction for unlawful entry of wife's residence).

(8) *United States v. Jordan*, 57 M.J. 236 (2002). The accused's guilty plea to unlawful entry was improvident because it did not establish a basis for concluding that the accused's conduct was prejudicial to good order and discipline or was of a nature to bring discredit upon the armed forces. Boarding a sailboat without the permission of the owner could constitute the offense of unlawful entry under Article 134. However, the factual circumstances revealed in the providence inquiry did not objectively support the third element of the offense.

3. The government must allege that the place violated was owned by one other than the accused. *See generally United States v. Norman*, 16 M.J. 937 (A.C.M.R. 1983).

4. "Breaking" requirement applies only to burglary.

a) Burglary requires that a "breaking" occur. This element demands a substantial and forcible act. More than the passing of an imaginary line is required. A breaking, removing, or putting aside of something material constituting a part of a dwelling house and relied on as a security against invasion is required. *United States v. Hart*, 49 C.M.R. 693 (A.C.M.R. 1975). A breaking may be either actual or constructive. A constructive breaking occurs when the entry is gained by trick, false pretense, or by intimidating the occupants through violence or threats. MCM, pt. IV, ¶ 55c(2).

b) Pushing aside closed Venetian blinds and entering through an otherwise open window constitutes a breaking. *United States v. Thompson*, 29 M.J. 609 (A.C.M.R. 1989), *aff'd*, 32 M.J. 65 (C.M.A. 1991); *see generally* TJAGSA Practice Note, *Burglary and the Requirement for a Breaking*, ARMY LAW., Jan. 1990, at 32 (discussing the A.C.M.R. opinion in *Thompson*).

c) Specification failing to allege "break and" prior to "enter" was fatally defective. *United States v. Hoskins*, 17 M.J. 134 (C.M.A. 1984).

d) No such breaking is required for either housebreaking or unlawful entry. An unauthorized entry of the protected area is sufficient.

5. Intent requirements.

a) None for unlawful entry. *United States v. Gillin*, 25 C.M.R. 173 (C.M.A. 1958).

b) Housebreaking.

(1) This offense requires a specific intent to commit crime within. *United States v. Walsh*, 5 C.M.R. 793 (A.F.B.R. 1952) (intoxication a defense to housebreaking). Intent to commit a criminal offense, which

was element of housebreaking, had to refer to intent to commit the crime stated in the specification, not merely intent to commit "some crime." *United States v. Webb*, 38 M.J. 62 (C.M.A. 1993).

(2) The offense cannot be a purely military offense. *See* MCM, pt. IV, ¶ 56c(3). "Purely military offenses" are those that "by [their] express terms . . . appl[y] only to a 'member of the armed forces.'" *See United States v. Marsh,* 15 M.J. 252, 254 (C.M.A. 1983). Conduct unbecoming of an officer and a gentleman is a purely military offense for purposes of Article 130. *See United States v. Conliffe*, 67 M.J. 127 (C.A.A.F. 2009).

c) Burglary requires that at the time of the breaking the accused possess the specific intent to commit an offense described in Articles 118-128. An intent to commit a different offense will sustain a guilty finding of housebreaking only. *United States v. Kluttz*, 25 C.M.R. 282 (C.M.A. 1958); *see also United States v. Garcia*, 15 M.J. 685 (A.F.C.M.R. 1983).

d) Intent to commit criminal offense at time unlawful entry was made may be inferred from the time and manner that the entry was made and the conduct of the accused after entry. *United States v. Carter*, 39 M.J. 754 (A.F.C.M.R. 1994).

6. Multiplicity. Housebreaking with intent to commit larceny and larceny therein are not multiplicious. *United States v. Alvarez*, 5 M.J. 726 (A.C.M.R. 1978).

F. Arson. MCM, pt. IV, ¶ 52; UCMJ art. 126.

1. Elements.

    a) Aggravated arson.

        (1) Inhabited dwelling.

            (a) That the accused burned or set on fire an inhabited dwelling;

            (b) That this dwelling belonged to a certain person and was of a certain value; and

            (c) That the act was willful and malicious.

        (2) Structure.

            (a) That the accused burned or set on fire a certain structure;

            (b) That the act was willful and malicious;

            (c) That there was a human being in the structure at the time;

            (d) That the accused knew that there was a human being in the structure at the time; and

            (e) That this structure belonged to a certain person and was of a certain value.

    b) Simple arson.

        (1) That the accused burned or set fire to certain property of another;

(2) That the property was of a certain value; and

(3) That the act was willful and malicious.

2. *Mens Rea.*

a) All degrees of arson require proof of willfulness and maliciousness; that is, not merely negligence or accident. MCM, pt. IV, ¶ 52c. Specific intent is not an element of aggravated or simple arson. *United States v. Acevedo-Velez*, 17 M.J. 1 (C.M.A. 1983) (intent requirement for aggravated arson met where accused set fire to a coat where there was a great possibility the building would catch on fire even though accused did not intend to burn the building); *see United States v. Marks*, 29 M.J. 1 (C.M.A. 1989); *United States v. Banta*, 26 M.J. 109 (C.M.A. 1988) (voluntary intoxication is not a defense); *United States v. Acevedo-Velez*, 17 M.J. 1 (C.M.A. 1983); *United States v. Caldwell*, 17 M.J. 8 (C.M.A. 1983).

b) In the offense of aggravated arson by setting fire to an inhabited dwelling, the accused's knowledge of the type or purpose of structure is not required. *United States v. Duke*, 37 C.M.R. 80 (C.M.A. 1966) (intoxication no defense). Accused properly convicted of aggravated arson for burning his own residence that he intended to abandon and from which his family had moved. *United States v. Dasha*, 23 M.J. 66 (C.M.A. 1986).

c) Intentionally starting a fire and negligently failing to ensure it is extinguished is arson. *United States v. Crutcher*, 49 M.J. 236 (C.A.A.F. 1998) (accused made some effort to put out the fire he had started).

3. Actual burning or charring of alleged property or structure is required, and mere scorching or discoloration is insufficient. MCM, pt. IV, ¶ 52c(2)(c); *United States v. Littrell*, 46 C.M.R. 628 (A.B.R. 1972) (burning of desk within building insufficient to prove aggravated arson; affirmed lesser included offense of attempted aggravated arson).

4. Disorderly conduct as lesser included offense. *United States v. Evans*, 10 M.J. 829 (A.C.M.R. 1981) (accused could be convicted of disorderly conduct as a lesser included offense of arson where specification alleged that accused was disorderly in quarters by setting fire to commode seat in latrine of his billets room and proof reasonably established all elements of disorderly conduct).

5. Simple arson is a lesser included offense of attempted aggravated arson. *United States v. Dorion*, 17 M.J. 1064 (A.F.C.M.R. 1984).

6. Burning with intent to defraud is a violation of UCMJ art. 134. *See generally United States v. Banta, supra* at H.2.a.; *United States v. Fuller*, 25 C.M.R. 405 (C.M.A 1958); *United States v. Snearley*, 35 C.M.R. 434 (C.M.A. 1965); *United States v. Colyon*, 35 C.M.R. 870 (A.F.C.M.R. 1965).

G. Bad Check Offenses.

1. Introduction.

a) Two Offenses.

(1) Making, Drawing, or Uttering a check, Draft, or Order Without Sufficient Funds. MCM, pt. IV, ¶ 49; UCMJ art. 123a.

(2) Making and Uttering a Worthless Check by Dishonorably Failing to Maintain Funds. MCM, pt. IV, ¶ 68; UCMJ art. 134.

b) See generally Richmond, Bad Check Cases: A Primer for Trial and Defense Counsel, ARMY LAW., Jan. 1990, at 3.

2. Article 123a: Making, drawing or uttering check, draft or order with intent to defraud or deceive. MCM, pt. IV, ¶ 49.

a) Elements:

(1) The accused makes, draws, utters or delivers a check/draft/order for payment of money upon a bank/depository.

(2) The above act is made while accused harbors either of the following specific intents:

(a) the *intent to defraud* by the procurement of an article or thing of value, or

(b) the *intent to deceive* for payment of any past due obligation, or for any other purpose.

(3) The accused knew at the time of committing the illegal act that he did not or would not have sufficient funds/credit in the bank/depository for payment in full upon presentment.

(4) For a good discussion and application of these elements, see *United States v. Carter*, 32 M.J. 522 (A.C.M.R. 1990).

b) Definitions. MCM, pt. IV, ¶ 49c.

(1) Written instruments covered. Includes any check, draft, or order for payment or money drawn upon any bank or other depository. *See, e.g., United States v. Palmer*, 14 M.J. 731 (A.F.C.M.R. 1982) (union share drafts).

(2) "Bank" or "other depository". Includes any business regularly but not exclusively engaged in public banking activities.

(3) "Making" and "drawing." Synonymous words and refer to act of writing and signing instrument.

(4) "Uttering" and "delivering." Both mean transferring instrument to another, but "uttering" includes offering to transfer.

(5) "For the procurement." Means for purpose of obtaining any article or thing of value.

(6) "For the payment." Means for purpose of satisfying in whole or part any past due obligation.

(7) "Sufficient funds." Means account balance at presentation is not less than face amount of check.

(8) "Upon its presentment." The time the demand for payment is made upon presentation of the instrument to the depository on which it was drawn.

c) *Mens Rea.*

(1) "Intent to defraud" (UCMJ art. 123a(1)). An intent to obtain through misrepresentation, an article or thing of value with intent permanently or temporarily to apply it to one's own use or benefit. MCM, pt. IV, ¶ 49c(14). *See United States v. Sassaman*, 32 M.J. 687 (A.F.C.M.R. 1991).

(2) "Intent to deceive" (UCMJ art. 123a(2)). An intent to mislead, cheat, or trick another by means of a misrepresentation made for the purpose of gaining an advantage or of bringing about a disadvantage to another. MCM, pt. IV, ¶ 14c(15).

(3) "Intent to deceive" is not the same as "intent to defraud." *United States v. Wade*, 34 C.M.R. 287 (C.M.A. 1964) (specification fails to state offense which alleges "making a check with intent to deceive for the purpose of obtaining lawful currency").

d) Articles or thing of value.

(1) Need not actually be obtained. *United States v. Cordy*, 41 C.M.R. 670 (A.C.M.R. 1967).

(2) Includes every right or interest in property or contract, including intangible, contingent, or future interests. *United States v. Ward*, 35 C.M.R. 834 (A.F.B.R. 1965) (check used to procure auto insurance).

(3) Includes checks given as a gift. *United States v. Woodcock*, 39 M.J. 104 (C.M.A. 1994) (only advantage secured by accused was temporary aggrandizement in the eyes of the person to whom the checks were given).

e) "Past due obligation" or "any other purpose".

(1) "Past due obligation." Obligation to pay money which has legally matured prior to the making or uttering.

(2) "Any other purpose."

(a) Includes all purposes other than payment of past due obligation or the procurement of any article or thing of value, *e.g.*, paying an obligation not yet past due.

(b) Excludes checks made for the purpose of obtaining any article or thing of value covered by Article 123a(1), UCMJ. *United States v. Wade*, 34 C.M.R. 287 (C.M.A. 1964).

f) Knowledge.

(1) Requires present knowledge that bank account is presently, or will be, insufficient at time of presentment. *See United States v. Crosby*, 22 M.J. 854 (A.F.C.M.R. 1986); *United States v. Matthews*, 15 M.J. 622 (N.M.C.M.R. 1982).

(2) "Sufficient funds" relates to time of presentment.

(3) Neither proof of presentment nor refusal of payment is necessary, if it can otherwise be shown that accused had requisite intent and knowledge at time of making or uttering. For example: (a) drawn on nonexistent bank or (b) drawn on overdrawn or closed account.

(4) Conviction does not require proof that the accused knew that the account holders (from whom accused had stolen and used starter checks) had insufficient funds in their bank account. Proof of the accused's knowledge that he was not the owner of the account satisfies the knowledge requirement. *United States v. Guess*, 48 M.J. 69 (C.A.A.F. 1998).

(5) Past "floating" of checks several days before payday does not negate proof of intent. *United States v. Smith*, 49 M.J. 279 (C.A.A.F. 1998).

g) Post-dated check. *Compare United States v. Hodges*, 35 C.M.R. 867 (A.F.B.R. 1965) (check made with requisite knowledge and intent; conviction affirmed), *with United States v. Birdine*, 31 M.J. 674 (C.G.C.M.R. 1990) (post-dated check did not support conviction, because no intent to deceive by accused; accused believed the checks would be covered).

h) Statutory 5-day notice. MCM, pt. IV, ¶ 49c(17).

(1) Failure of maker to pay holder within 5 days after notice of non-payment is prima facie evidence that:

(a) Maker had intent to defraud or deceive.

(b) Maker had knowledge of insufficiency of funds.

(2) The above inference is only permissive and is rebuttable.

(3) Either failure to give notice or payment by accused within 5 days precludes prosecution use of inference, but it does not preclude conviction if elements are otherwise proved.

(4) Notice. *United States v. Jarrett*, 34 C.M.R. 652 (A.B.R. 1964) (reading of bad check charges to an account drawer by his detachment commander does not fulfill the statutory requirement of notice of dishonor); *United States v. Cauley*, 9 M.J. 791 (A.C.M.R. 1980), *rev'd on other grounds*, 12 M.J. 484 (C.M.A. 1982) (introduction at trial of letter from bank to accused's CO seeking his assistance in effecting payment of accused's dishonored checks did not alone constitute proper notice even though letter contained a notation indicating that a copy was to be forwarded to the accused).

(5) Period of redemption. The 5-day redemption period means 5 calendar days and is not limited to ordinary business days, at least when the terminal date is not a Sunday or holiday. Days are computed by excluding the first day and including the last day. *United States v. O'Briant*, 32 C.M.R. 933 (A.F.B.R. 1963).

i) Pleading check offenses.

(1) Specification charging that the accused, on divers occasions, uttered worthless checks was legally sufficient to protect the accused from subsequent prosecutions. *United States v. Carter*, 21 M.J. 665 (A.C.M.R. 1985); *see also United States v. Krauss*, 20 M.J. 741 (N.M.C.M.R. 1985).

(2) "Mega-specs" permitted, and maximum punishment is determined by the number and amount of the checks as if they had been charged

separately. *United States v. Mincey*, 42 M.J. 376 (C.A.A.F. 1995) (*overruling United States v. Poole*, 26 M.J. 272 (C.M.A. 1988)).

(3) Failure to object to duplicitous pleading of bad-check offenses waives any complaint that accused might have had about the pleadings. *United States v. Mincey*, 42 M.J. 376 (C.A.A.F. 1995).

j) Defenses.

(1) Honest mistake of fact. *United States v. Callaghan*, 34 C.M.R. 11 (C.M.A. 1963) (belief funds credited to account a legitimate defense).

(2) Redemption beyond 5-day period. *United States v. Broy*, 34 C.M.R. 199 (C.M.A. 1964) (no defense).

(3) "The Gambler's Defense." The Gambler's Defense is no longer recognized for check offenses arising under UCMJ art. 123a. *United States v. Falcon*, 65 M.J. 386 (C.A.A.F. 2008) (declining to apply *United States v. Allbery*, 44 M.J. 226 (C.A.A.F. 1996) and *United States v. Wallace*, 36 C.M.R. 148 (C.M.A. 1966) to the Article 123a line of cases which held 1) that transactions designed to facilitate gambling are against public policy and 2) that courts will not enforce obligations arising therefrom).

(4) Overdraft protection, relied upon by the accused without false pretenses, constitutes a defense to larceny and related bad check offenses. *United States v. McCanless*, 29 M.J. 985 (A.F.C.M.R. 1990); *see United States v. Crosby*, 41 C.M.R. 927 (A.F.C.M.R. 1969). Unilateral action by a bank in honoring checks, unknown to the accused, does not constitute a defense. *United States v. McNeil*, 30 M.J. 648 (N.M.C.M.R. 1990); *see generally* TJAGSA Practice Note, *Overdraft Protection and Economic Crimes*, ARMY LAW., Jul. 1990, at 45.

(5) Reasonable expectation of payment. *United States v. Webb*, 46 C.M.R. 1083 (A.C.M.R. 1972) (accused who writes overdrafts but reasonably expects to have funds to deposit before presentment has a legitimate defense).

(6) Compulsive gambling not a defense where accused hoped to win large sums to redeem worthless checks. *United States v. Zojak*, 15 M.J. 845 (A.F.C.M.R. 1983).

3. Article 134: Worthless check by dishonorably failing to maintain sufficient funds. MCM, pt. IV, ¶ 68.

a) Elements.

(1) That the accused made and uttered to a certain party a check for the alleged purpose.

(2) That the accused did thereafter fail to place or maintain sufficient funds in or credit with the bank for payment of such check in full upon its presentment for payment.

(3) That such failure was dishonorable.

(4) That such failure was prejudicial to good order and discipline or was service discrediting.

b) "Dishonorable" failure to maintain sufficient funds.

(1) Bad faith, gross indifference, fraud or deceit is necessary. *United States v. Brand*, 28 C.M.R. 3 (C.M.A. 1959).

(2) Negligent failure insufficient. *United States v. Kess*, 48 C.M.R. 108 (A.F.B.R. 1973).

(3) Redemption negates evidence of dishonorableness. *United States v. Groom*, 30 C.M.R. 11 (C.M.A. 1960).

(4) Evidence sufficient. *United States v. Silas*, 31 M.J. 829 (N.M.C.M.R. 1990).

(5) May occur after initial presentment. *United States v. Call*, 32 M.J. 873 (N.M.C.M.R. 1991).

c) Defenses.

(1) Lack of sophistication regarding checking insufficient for guilt under either an Article 123a or Article 134 theory. *United States v. Elizondo*, 29 M.J. 798 (A.C.M.R. 1989); *see generally*, TJAGSA Practice Note, *Mens Rea and Bad Check Offenses*, ARMY LAW., Mar. 1990, at 36 (discusses *Elizondo*).

(2) Honest mistake, not a result of bad faith or gross indifference, is a legitimate defense. *United States v. Connell*, 22 C.M.R. 18 (C.M.A. 1956).

(3) Bad checks written to satisfy gambling debts not enforceable on public policy grounds. *United States v. Allberry*, 44 M.J. 226 (C.A.A.F. 1996); *United States v. Wallace*, 36 C.M.R. 148 (C.M.A. 1966). *But see United States v. Green*, 44 M.J. 828 (Army Ct. Crim. App. 1996) (public policy defense applies only when there is a direct connection between the check cashing service and the gambling activity).

d) A lesser included offense to Article 123a, UCMJ. *United States v. Bowling*, 33 C.M.R. 378 (C.M.A. 1963). *But see United States v. Miller*, 67 M.J. 385 (C.A.A.F. 2009).

4. Larceny or wrongful appropriation by check. UCMJ art. 121.

a) Utilizes the theory of larceny by false pretenses. *United States v. Culley*, 31 C.M.R. 290 (C.M.A. 1962).

b) Intent required.

(1) Intent to deprive or defraud permanently or temporarily. *United States v. Cummins*, 26 C.M.R. 449 (C.M.A. 1958).

(2) Carelessness or negligence in bookkeeping insufficient. *United States v. Bull*, 31 C.M.R. 100 (C.M.A. 1961).

(3) Restitution is no defense, except as it is evidence tending to disprove the accused's alleged intent.

c) Money, personal property, a thing of value must be obtained. Payment of past due obligation insufficient.

d) Defenses.

(1) All state of mind defenses apply. *United States v. Rowan*, 16 C.M.R. 4 (C.M.A. 1954) (honest mistake).

(2) Gambling losses unenforceable. *United States v. Walter*, 23 C.M.R. 274 (C.M.A. 1957).

5. Evidentiary matters. In *United States v. Dean*, 13 M.J. 676 (A.F.C.M.R. 1982), the court held that checks and the notations thereon were admissible as business records under MRE 803(6). The court further held, after judicially noticing U.C.C. § 3-510(b), that the checks were self-authenticating under M.R.E 902(b)(9). *Cf. United States v. Matthews*, 15 M.J. 622 (N.M.C.M.R. 1982) (notations that checks were stolen not admissible under U.C.C. § 3-510).

6. Multiplicity. Uttering check with intent to defraud under Article 123a, UCMJ, and larceny of currency by the checks under Article 121 were multiplicious for findings. *United States v. Ward*, 15 M.J. 377 (C.M.A. 1983) (summary disposition); *see also United States v. Allen*, 16 M.J. 395 (C.M.A. 1983).

H. Forgery. MCM, pt. IV, ¶ 48; UCMJ art. 123.

1. Elements.

a) Forgery: making or altering.

(1) That the accused falsely made or altered a certain signature.

(2) That the signature or writing was of a nature which would, if genuine, apparently impose a legal liability on another or change another's legal rights or liabilities to that person's prejudice; and

(3) That the false making or altering was with the intent to defraud.

b) Forgery: uttering.

(1) That a certain signature or writing was falsely made or altered;

(2) That the signature or writing was of a nature which would, if genuine, apparently impose a legal liability on another or change another's legal rights or liabilities to that person's prejudice;

(3) That the accused uttered, offered, issued, or transferred the signature or writing;

(4) That at such time the accused knew that the signature or writing had been falsely made or altered; and

(5) That the uttering, offering, issuing or transferring was with the intent to defraud.

2. Two distinct types: making or altering, and uttering. MCM, pt. IV, ¶ 48b.

a) Falsely making checks is a separate offense from uttering them; these actions are not alternative methods of committing the forgery, but distinct types of forgery. *United States v. Albrecht*, 43 M.J. 65 (C.A.A.F. 1995).

3. For either type, the document must have legal efficacy. *United States v. Hopwood*, 30 M.J. 146 (C.M.A. 1990); *United States v. Thomas*, 25 M.J. 396 (C.M.A. 1988); MCM, pt. IV, ¶ 48c(4); *see United States v. James*, 42 M.J. 270 (1995) (leave form has "legal efficacy"); *United States v. Ivey*, 32 M.J. 590 (A.C.M.R. 1991) (checking account application), *aff'd*, 35 M.J. 62 (C.M.A. 1992); *United States v. Victorian*, 31 M.J. 830 (N.M.C.M.R. 1990); *United States v. Johnson*, 33 M.J. 1030 (N.M.C.M.R. 1991) (urinalysis report message from drug lab was not a "document of legal efficacy" and as such could not be subject of forgery).

4. *See generally* TJAGSA Practice Note, *Court Strictly Interprets Legal Efficacy*, ARMY LAW., Aug. 1990, at 35; TJAGSA Practice Note, *Legal Efficacy as a Relative Concept*, ARMY LAW., Jan. 1990, at 34; TJAGSA Practice Note, *Forgery and Legal Efficacy*, ARMY LAW., Jun. 1989, at 40.

5. The instrument "tells a lie about itself." *United States v. Blackmon*, 39 M.J. 705 (N.M.C.M.R. 1993) (signing another's name to "starter" checks from the accused's checking account appeared to impose liability upon the third party whose name was being signed) *aff'd*, 41 M.J. 67 (C.M.A. 1994).

6. Significant injury need not result. *United States v. Faircloth*, 45 M.J. 172 (C.A.A.F. 1996) (accused forged endorsement in financing company's behalf on insurance check, issued to accused and financing company as copayees to auto damage); *United States v. Sherman*, 52 M.J. 856 (Army Ct. Crim. App. 2000) (where the accused and co-conspirator opened savings accounts by falsely and fraudulently signing signature cards, the general bookkeeping, security, and insurance functions inherent in agreeing to maintain a bank account imposed sufficient legal liability on the banks to warrant forgery convictions, even where there was no initial deposit).

7. Maximum Punishment. In cases where multiple, discrete instances of check forgery are pled in one "mega-spec," the maximum punishment is calculated as if they had been charged separately, extending analysis of *United States v. Mincey*, 42 M.J. 376 (C.A.A.F. 1995) (maximum punishment of a bad-check "mega-spec" is calculated by the number and amount of the checks as if they had been charged separately) to check forgery. *United States v. Dawkins*, 51 M.J. 601 (C.A.A.F. 1999).

8. A credit application itself is not susceptible of forgery under Article 123, because it, if genuine, would not create any legal right or liability on the part of the purported maker. *United States v. Woodson*, 52 M.J. 688 (C.G. Ct. Crim. App. 2000).

9. "Double forgery." Forgery of an endorsement is factually and legally distinct from forgery of the check itself, because the acts impose apparent legal liability on two separate victims; thus, the government may charge the "double forgery" in two separate specifications. *United States v. Pauling*, 60 M.J. 91 (C.A.A.F. 2004).

I. Failure to Pay Just Debt. MCM, pt. IV, ¶ 71; UCMJ art. 134.

　　1. Elements.

　　　　a) That the accused was indebted to a certain person or entity in a certain sum;

　　　　b) That this debt became due and payable on or about a certain date;

　　　　c) That while the debt was still due and payable the accused dishonorably failed to pay this debt; and

d) That, under the circumstances, the conduct of the accused was to the prejudice of good order and discipline in the armed forces or was of a nature to bring discredit upon the armed forces.

2. Evidence was legally sufficient to support conviction for dishonorable failure to pay a just debt where accused failed to make an arrangement for payment, had made late payments before, failed to contact rental agent even after formal notice, and surreptitiously vacated the apartment without paying, cleaning, or repairing damage. *United States v. Polk*, 47 M.J. 116 (C.A.A.F. 1997).

Guilty plea to offense was improvident where the military judge failed to define dishonorable conduct with respect to an AAFES debt, failed to elicit a factual predicate for dishonorable conduct regarding the debt, and failed to resolve inconsistencies which indicated an inability to pay the debt and a lack of deceit or evasion. A mere failure to pay a debt does not establish dishonorable conduct. Even a negligent failure to pay a debt is not dishonorable. The term "dishonorable" connotes a state of mind amounting to gross indifference or bad faith, and is characterized by deceit, evasion, false promises, denial of indebtedness, or other distinctly culpable circumstances. *United States v. Bullman*, 56 M.J. 377 (C.A.A.F. 2002), *aff'd*, 57 M.J. 478 (C.A.A.F. 2002); *United States v. Burris*, 59 M.J. 700 (C.G. Ct. Ctim. App. 2004).

J. Altering a Public Record. MCM, pt. IV, ¶ 99; UCMJ art. 134.

Mere completion of a blank form indicating graduation for an Army school and presentment of that document to Army officials was not "wrongful alteration of public record," absent additional evidence of intent or attempt to use the document to alter the integrity of official Army record. *United States v. McCoy*, 47 M.J. 653 (Army Ct. Crim. App. 1997).

K. Frauds Against The United States. MCM, pt. IV, ¶ 58; UCMJ art. 132.

Submission of a travel voucher for a TDY trip "concocted" to primarily conduct personal business is a false claim under Article 132. *United States v. Mann*, 50 M.J. 689 (A.F. Ct. Crim. App. 1999).

VII. OFFENSES AGAINST THE ADMINISTRATION OF JUSTICE.

A. Resistance, Breach of Arrest, and Escape. MCM, pt. IV, ¶ 19; UCMJ art. 95.

1. Elements.

    a) Resisting apprehension.

    (1) That a certain person attempted to apprehend the accused;

    (2) That said person was authorized to apprehend the accused; and

    (3) That the accused actively resisted the apprehension.

    b) Flight from apprehension.

    (1) That a certain person attempted to apprehend the accused;

    (2) That said person was authorized to apprehend the accused; and

    (3) That the accused fled from the apprehension.

    c) Breaking arrest.

(1) That a certain person ordered the accused into arrest;

(2) That said person was authorized to order the accused into arrest; and

(3) That the accused went beyond the limits of arrest before being released from that arrest by proper authority.

d) Escape from custody.

(1) That a certain person apprehended the accused;

(2) That said person was authorized to apprehend the accused; and

(3) That the accused freed himself or herself from custody before being released by proper authority.

e) Escape from confinement.

(1) That a certain person ordered the accused into confinement;

(2) That said person was authorized to order the accused into confinement; and

(3) That the accused freed himself or herself from confinement before being released to proper authority.

(4) [If the escape was from post-trial confinement, add the following element:] That the confinement was the result of a court-martial conviction.

2. Applications.

a) Resisting Apprehension.

(1) Article 95 now includes a prohibition against flight from apprehension, but prior to offenses occurring on 10 February 1996 (the FY 96 amendment to art. 95), subject's flight from apprehension, by itself, was insufficient to constitute resisting apprehension under Article 95, UCMJ. *United States v. Pritt*, 54 M.J. 47 (C.A.A.F. 2000); *United States v. Harris*, 29 M.J. 169 (C.M.A. 1989); *United States v. Burgess*, 32 M.J. 446 (C.M.A. 1991).

(2) *United States v. Malone*, 34 M.J. 213 (C.M.A. 1992) (attempt to prevent apprehension by accelerating stolen vehicle, driving around a police barricade, swerving to avoid another vehicle placed in his path, and scattering sentries posted at the gate constituted "active resistance" sufficient to satisfy Article 95).

(3) *United States v. Webb*, 37 M.J. 540 (A.C.M.R. 1993) (acts were sufficient to constitute the offense of resisting apprehension where he temporarily terminated his flight, turned, faced his pursuer, and adopted a "fighting stance," and allowed pursuer to approach within five feet before resuming flight).

(4) *United States v. Rhodes*, 47 M.J. 790 (Army Ct. Crim. App. 1998) (resistance of apprehension by civilian law enforcement officers with no military affiliation was not an offense under Article 95, because the apprehending officers were not within any category of individuals authorized to apprehend under R.C.M. 302).

(5) The prosecution must prove that the accused had "clear notice of the apprehension." *United States v. Diggs*, 52 M.J. 251 (C.A.A.F. 2000).

b) Escape.

(1) *United States v. Standifer*, 35 M.J. 615 (A.F.C.M.R. 1992) (unauthorized visits with wife did not constitute the offense of escape from confinement where the visits occurred with the consent of accused's escorts and accused did not "cast off" his moral suasion), *aff'd in part, rev'd in part on other grounds,* 40 M.J. 440 (C.M.A. 1994).

(2) *United States v. Felix*, 36 M.J. 903 (A.F.C.M.R. 1993) (plea of guilty to escape from correctional custody was provident where accused knowingly and freely admitted to status of physical restraint by being in correctional custody and stating that he avoided a monitor in order to depart) *aff'd*, 40 M.J. 356 (C.M.A. 1994)).

(3) *United States v. Anderson*, 36 M.J. 963 (A.F.C.M.R. 1993) (conviction for escape was not supported by evidence that accused was allowed to go off base with escort, that escort left accused at accused's apartment, intending that accused would return to base with his wife, and that accused then killed his wife and fled) *aff'd,* 39 M.J. 431 (C.M.A. 1994).

(4) Where soldier is placed in confinement and is then temporarily removed from confinement facility while remaining under guard of another soldier, prisoner remains in confinement status, for purposes of escape charge, regardless of whether guard is armed or otherwise has physical prowess to subdue prisoner. *United States v. Jones*, 36 M.J. 1154 (A.C.M.R. 1993).

(5) Once lawfully ordered into confinement, unless released by proper authorities, a soldier may be convicted of escape from confinement, regardless of the nature of the facility in which he is held. *United States v. McDaniel*, 52 M.J. 618 (Army Ct. Crim. App. 1999) (accused was under physical restraint, as required for escape under Article 95, and the escape was from confinement rather than custody because of the accused's status at the time).

B. False Official Statement. MCM, pt. IV, ¶ 31; UCMJ art. 107.

1. Elements.

a) That the accused signed a certain official document or made a certain official statement;

b) That the document or statement was false in certain particulars;

c) That the accused knew it to be false at the time of signing it or making it; and

d) That the false document or statement was made with the intent to deceive.

2. Relation to Federal Statute. Congress intended Article 107 to be construed *in pari materia* with 18 U.S.C. § 1001. *United States v. Jackson*, 26 M.J. 377 (C.M.A. 1988); *United States v. Aronson*, 25 C.M.R. 29 (C.M.A. 1957). The purpose of Article 107 is to protect governmental departments and agencies from the perversion of its official functions which might result from deceptive practices. *United States v.* Jackson, supra;

United States v. Hutchins, 18 C.M.R. 46, 51 (C.M.A. 1955); *see generally*, TJAGSA Practice Note, *The Court of Military Appeals Expands False Official Statement Under Article 107, UCMJ*, ARMY LAW., Nov. 1988, at 37. However, Article 107 is more expansive than 8 U.S.C. § 1001 "because the primary purpose of military criminal law—to maintain morale, good order, and discipline—has no parallel in civilian criminal law." See *United States v. Teffeau*, 58 M.J. 62 (C.A.A.F. 2003) *United States v. Day*, 66 M.J. 172 (C.A.A.F. 2008).

3. Relation to Perjury. The offense of false official statement differs from perjury in that a false official statement may be made outside a judicial proceeding and materiality is not an essential element. MCM, pt. IV, ¶ 3c(3). Materiality may, however, be relevant to the intent of the party making the statement. *Id.*; *see also United States v. Hutchins*, 18 C.M.R. 46 (C.M.A. 1955) (accused made a false official statement in connection with a line of duty investigation). Making a false official statement is not a lesser included offense of perjury. *United States v. Warble*, 30 C.M.R. 839 (A.F.C.M.R. 1960).

1. Meaning of "False." *United States v. Wright*, 65 M.J. 373 (C.A.A.F. 2007). While loading equipment for a deployment, the accused and another soldier stole four government computers. An officer investigating the theft of the computers interviewed the accused, who stated: "While loading up the connex's [sic], I noticed that four of the computers weren't on top of the box anymore." During the providence inquiry, the accused admitted that his statement was false because it meant that he did not know where the computers went. In fact, the accused knew exactly where the computers were located. The court found that the statement was false for purposes of Article 107 even though it was misleading, but true. The statement falsely implied that he had no explanation for the absence of the computers. The statement also falsely implied that the computers went missing while he was loading up the connex boxes.

2. Independent Duty to Account and the Meaning of Officiality.

    a) Formerly, a false statement to an investigator, made by a suspect who had no independent duty to account or answer questions, was not official within the purview of Article 107. *United States v. Osborne*, 26 C.M.R. 235 (C.M.A. 1958); *United States v. Aronson*, 25 C.M.R. 29 (C.M.A. 1957); *see also United States v. Davenport*, 9 M.J. 364, 367-68 (C.M.A. 1980).

    b) Later, the Court of Military Appeals determined that no independent duty to account was required if the accused falsely reported a crime. *United States v. Collier*, 48 C.M.R. 789 (C.M.A. 1974).

    c) More recently, the court determined that officiality was not dependent upon an independent duty to account or initiation of a report. The focus is on the officiality of the statement—whether an official governmental function was perverted by a false or misleading statement.

        (1) *United States v. Harrison*, 26 M.J. 474 (C.M.A. 1988) (accused's false statement to battalion finance clerk in order to obtain an appointment for payment violates Article 107).

        (2) *United States v. Jackson*, 26 M.J. 377 (C.M.A. 1988) (misleading information provided by accused about a murder suspect's whereabouts, voluntarily given to law enforcement agents, constitutes a false official statement).

(3) *United States v. Goldsmith*, 29 M.J. 979 (A.F.C.M.R. 1990) (untrue responses to a civilian cashier constituted a false official statement).

(4) *United States v. Ellis*, 31 M.J. 26 (C.M.A. 1990) (anonymous note can constitute a false official statement); *see generally* TJAGSA Practice Note, *An Anonymous Note Can Constitute a False Official Statement*, ARMY LAW., Mar. 1991, at 24 (discusses *Ellis*).

(5) *United States v. Hagee*, 37 M.J. 484 (C.M.A. 1993) (making and signing false official duty orders in order to deceive a private party who was entitled to rely on their integrity was a violation of Article 107).

(6) *United States v. Dorsey*, 38 M.J. 244 (C.M.A. 1993) (lying to investigator about reason for refusing a polygraph held to be an "official" statement).

(7) *United States v. Smith*, 44 M.J.369 (C.A.A.F. 1996) (falsifying an LES and ID card in order to obtain car loan was violation of Article 107; the official character of a false statement can be based upon its apparent issuing authority rather than the identity of the person receiving it or the purpose for which it is made).

(8) *United States v. Bailey*, 52 M.J. 786 (A.F. Ct. Crim. App 1999) (when AFOSI agents asked the accused, whom they suspected of threatening victims with guns and whose apartment they intended to search, whether his firearms were in his apartment, there was a clear governmental function underway), *aff'd,* 55 M.J. 38 (C.A.A.F. 2001).

(9) *United States v. Czeschin*, 56 M.J. 346 (C.A.A.F. 2002). Paragraph 31c(6)(a) of the Manual for Courts-Martial, which provides that a statement by an accused or suspect during an interrogation is not an official statement within the meaning of Article 107 if that person did not have an independent duty or obligation to speak, does not establish a right that may be asserted by an accused who is charged with violating Article 107. Statements to investigators can be prosecuted as false official statements.

(10) *United States v. Melbourne*, 58 M.J. 682 (N-M. Ct. Crim. App. 2003) (ruling that the language in the pre-2002 editions of the MCM, pt. IV, ¶ 31c(6)) is no longer an accurate statement of law, at least insofar as it would apply to statements made to law enforcement agents conducting official investigations).

(11) *United States v. McMahon*, 58 M.J. 362 (C.A.A.F. 2003) (accused convicted of false official statement for falsifying a certificate awarding himself a Bronze Star).

(12) *United States v. Day,* 66 M.J. 172 (C.A.A.F. 2008). False statements made to on-base emergency medical personnel were official for purposes of Art. 107, but false statements made to an off-base, civilian 911 operator were not.

3. Statement to Civilian Law Enforcement Authorities. Official statements include those made "in the line of duty". MCM, Part IV, ¶ 31c(1). An intentionally deceptive statement

made by a service member to civilian authorities may be nonetheless "official" and within the scope of Article 107.

 a) Analysis for Statements to Civilian Authorities.

  (1) Duty status at the time of the statement is not determinative. False official statements are not limited those made in the line of duty. Statements made outside of a servicemember's duties may still implicate official military functions. *United States v. Day,* 66 M.J. 172 (2008).

  (2) The critical distinction is whether the statements relate to the official duties of the speaker or hearer, and whether those official duties fall within the UCMJ's reach. *United States v. Day,* 66 M.J. 172 (2008).

  (3) The courts have used the following language to link the official duties and the reach of the UCMJ:

   (a) Statements are official for purposes of Article 107 where there is a "clear and direct relationship to the official duties" at issue and where the circumstances surrounding the statement "reflect a substantial military interest in the investigation." *United States v. Teffeau,* 58 M.J. 62 (C.A.A.F. 2003).

   (b) Statements may be official where there is "a predictable and necessary nexus to on-base persons performing official military functions on behalf of the command." *United States v. Day,* 66 M.J. 172 (C.A.A.F. 2008).

 b) Applications of Article 107 to False Statements to Civilian Authorities.

  (1) *United States v. Day,* 66 M.J. 172 (C.A.A.F. 2008). False statements made to on-base emergency medical personnel were official for purposes of Art. 107, but false statements made to an off-base, civilian 911 operator were not.

  (2) *United States v. Teffeau,* 58 M.J. 62 (C.A.A.F. 2003) (accused made false statements to local civilian police concerning an automobile accident in which a delayed-entry recruit was killed; the entire incident and investigation bore a direct relationship to the accused's duties and status as a recruiter; further, the subject matter of the police investigation was of interest to the military and within the jurisdiction of the courts-martial system).

  (3) *United States v. Morgan,* 65 M.J. 616 (N-M. Ct. Crim. App. 2007) (holding statements to civilian authorities were not "official" for Article 107 purposes).

  (4) *United States v. Holmes,* 65 M.J. 684 (N-M. Ct. Crim. App. 2007) (holding statements to civilian authorities were not "official" for Article 107 purposes).

  (5) *United States v. Caballero,* 65 M.J. 674 (C.G. Ct. Crim. App. 2007) (holding that false statements to civilian police detectives investigating a

shooting that had occurred off-post were not official for Article 107 purposes).

4. "Exculpatory No" Doctrine. A number of federal circuit courts apply this doctrine, which stands for the proposition that a person who merely gives a negative response to a law enforcement agent cannot be prosecuted for making a false statement. *See generally United States v. Solis*, 46 M.J. 31 (C.A.A.F. 1997).

    a) Statutory and constitutional concerns do not support continued application of the doctrine under the UCMJ. *United States v. Solis*, 46 M.J. 31 (1997); *United States v Black*, 47 M.J. 146 (1997); United *States v. Nelson*, 53 M.J. 319 (C.A.A.F. 2000).

    b) The doctrine was traditionally given limited scope under military law, but recent cases placed severe limits on its scope. *See United States v. Prater*, 32 M.J. 433 (C.M.A. 1991); *United States v. Frazier*, 34 M.J. 135 (C.M.A 1992); *United States v. Sanchez*, 39 M.J. 518 (A.C.M.R. 1993).

    c) The doctrine does not apply to false swearing offenses under Article 134, UCMJ. *United States v. Gay*, 24 M.J. 304 (C.M.A. 1987).

    d) The doctrine has no legitimate statutory or constitutional basis and is not a defense to 18 U.S.C. § 1001. *Brogan v. United States*, 118 S.Ct. 805 (1998).

5. Multiplicity. *See United States v. McCoy*, 32 M.J. 906 (A.F.C.M.R. 1991) (finding an accused guilty of violating Articles 107 and 131 when he lied to a trial counsel and the next day told the same lie in court is multiplicious for sentencing only).

6. Unreasonable Multiplication of Charges (UMC). *United States v. Esposito*, 57 M.J. 608 (C.G. Ct. Crim. App. 2002) (finding charging accused with false official statement and obstructing justice by making the same false statement was UMC. Also, charging accused with soliciting a false official statement and obstructing justice by that same solicitation was UMC).

7. Statute of Limitations. Prosecuting an accused for making a false official statement about instances of deviant sexual behavior that occurred outside the five-year statute of limitations for such offenses did not violate his due process rights. *United States v. Sills*, 56 M.J. 556 (A.F. Ct. Crim. App. 2001), *sentence set aside, rehearing granted by*, 58 M.J. 23 (C.A.A.F. 2002).

8. Statement. A physical act or nonverbal conduct intended by a soldier as an assertion is a "statement" that may form the basis for a charge of making "any other" false official statement under Article 107. *United States v. Newson*, 54 M.J. 823 (Army Ct. Crim App. 2001).

False Swearing. MCM, pt. IV, ¶ 79; UCMJ art. 134.

9. Elements. False swearing is the making, under a lawful oath, of any false statement which the declarant does not believe to be true. *United States v. Davenport*, 9 M.J. 364 (C.M.A. 1980). The offense of false swearing has seven elements: (1) that the accused took an oath or its equivalent; (2) that the oath or its equivalent was administered to the accused in a matter in which such oath or equivalent was required or authorized by law; (3) that the oath or equivalent was administered by a person having authority to do so, *United States v. Hill*, 31 M.J. 543 (N.M.C.M.R. 1990); (4) that upon this oath or equivalent the accused made or subscribed a certain statement; (5) that the statement was false; (6) that the accused did not then believe the statement to be true; and (7) that, under

the circumstances, the conduct of the accused was to the prejudice of good order and discipline in the armed forces or was of a nature to bring discredit upon the armed forces. MCM, pt. IV, ¶ 79b. It is service discrediting whether it occurs on or off post. *United States v. Greene*, 34 M.J. 713 (A.C.M.R. 1992).

10. Relation to Perjury. Although often used interchangeably, perjury and false swearing are different offenses. Perjury requires that the false statement be made in a judicial proceeding and be material to the issue. These requirements are not elements of false swearing, which is not a lesser included offense of perjury. *See United States v. Smith*, 26 C.M.R. 16 (C.M.A. 1958); *United States v. Byard*, 29 M.J. 803 (A.C.M.R. 1989); *United States v. Claypool*, 27 C.M.R. 533, 536 (A.B.R. 1958); *United States v. Kennedy*, 12 M.J. 620 (N.M.C.M.R. 1981); *United States v. Galchick*, 52 M.J. 815 (A.F. Ct. Crim. App. 2000)(Article 32 investigation is judicial); MCM, pt. IV, ¶ 79c(1); *but see* MCM, pt. IV, ¶ 57c(1). The drafters make no attempt to reconcile this provision with the authorities cited above. *See* MCM, pt. IV, ¶ 57 analysis at A23-16 (2002 Ed.). This provision, however, may be reconciled with those authorities if read in light of *United States v. Warble*, 30 C.M.R. 839, 841 n* (A.F.B.R. 1967) ("We are not called upon to decide whether the *Smith* case (dealing with *Article 131[1] perjury* and false swearing, as contrasted with *statutory perjury* and false swearing) would be held to be in any wise controlling in a statutory perjury charge")(emphasis in original), *aff'd*, 30 C.M.R. 386 (C.M.A. 1961); UCMJ art. 131(2). False swearing and perjury should thus be pled in alternative specifications when appropriate.

11. A civilian police officer authorized by state statute to administer an oath may satisfy the element of false swearing that requires that the "oath or equivalent was administered by a person having authority to do so." The element does not require that the person administering the oath be authorized to do so under Article 136, UCMJ. *United States v. Daniels*, 57 M.J. 560 (N-M. Ct. Crim. App. 2002).

12. Requirement for Falsity.

   a) The primary requirement for false swearing is that the statement actually be false. MCM, pt. IV, ¶ 79c(1). A statement need not be false in its entirety to constitute the offense of false swearing. *Id.*, Part IV, ¶ 79b. *See United States v. Fisher*, 58 M.J. 300 (C.A.A.F. 2003).

   b) A statement that is technically, literally, or legally true cannot form the basis of a conviction even if the statement succeeds in misleading the questioner. Literally true but unresponsive answers are properly to be remedied through precise questioning. *United States v. Arondel De Hayes*, 22 M.J. 54 (C.M.A. 1986) (accused lied when he said that the listed items were "missing" as he had an explanation for their absence); *United States v. McCarthy*, 29 C.M.R. 574 (C.M.A. 1960) (accused's friends stole some hubcaps which accused allegedly denied during a subsequent investigation).

   c) Doubts as to the meaning of an alleged false statement should be resolved in favor of truthfulness. *United States v. Kennedy*, 12 M.J. 620 (N.M.C.M.R. 1981) (only certain portions of accused's statements to a NIS agent were false).

   d) The truthfulness of the statement is to be judged from the facts at the time of the utterance. *United States v. Purgess*, 33 C.M.R. 97 (C.M.A. 1963) (evidence was insufficient in law to establish that accused made a false statement when accused stated that the seat covers in his car came from a German concern where the evidence showed that they did in fact come from a German concern, albeit by way of government purchase and theft from government stock); *see United States v. Arondel De Hayes*, 22 M.J. 54 (C.M.A. 1986).

13. Two Witness Rule. The rule is applicable to false swearing. *United States v. Yates*, 29 M.J. 888 (A.C.M.R. 1989), *aff'd*, 31 M.J. 380 (C.M.A. 1990); *see* TJAGSA Practice Note, *Judge's Incorrect Ruling Correctly Affirmed*, ARMY LAW., Apr. 1990, at 70 (discussing *Yates*). *See infra*, ¶ VII.D.5.a), this chapter.

14. Use of Circumstantial Evidence. *United States v. Veal*, 29 M.J. 600 (A.C.M.R. 1989); *see generally* TJAGSA Practice Note, *Using Circumstantial Evidence to Prove False Swearing*, ARMY LAW., Jan. 1990, at 36 (discusses *Veal*); *United States v. Hogue*, 42 M.J. 533 (A.F. Ct. Crim. App. 1995) (urinalysis result plus expert testimony satisfies direct evidence requirement), *aff'd*, 45 M.J. 300 (C.A.A.F. 1996).

15. "Exculpatory No" Doctrine. The doctrine is not applicable to false swearing, as the primary concern is the sanctity of the oath. *United States v. Gay*, 24 M.J. 304 (C.M.A. 1987); *see United States v. Tunstall*, 24 M.J. 235 (C.M.A. 1987); *United States v. Purgess*, 33 C.M.R. 97 (C.M.A. 1963); *United States v. Kennedy*, 12 M.J. 620 (N.M.C.M.R. 1981).

C. Perjury. MCM, pt. IV, ¶ 57; UCMJ art. 131.

1. Elements.

    a) Giving false testimony.

       (1) That the accused took an oath or affirmation in a certain judicial proceeding or course of justice;

       (2) That the oath or affirmation was administered to the accused in a matter in which an oath or affirmation was required or authorized by law;

       (3) That the oath or affirmation was administered by a person having authority to do so;

       (4) That upon the oath or affirmation that accused willfully gave certain testimony;

       (5) That the testimony was material;

       (6) That the testimony was false; and

       (7) That the accused did not then believe the testimony to be true.

    b) Subscribing false statement.

       (1) That the accused subscribed a certain statement in a judicial proceeding or course of justice;

       (2) That in the declaration, certification, verification, or statement under penalty of perjury, the accused declared, certified, verified, or stated the truth of that certain statement;

       (3) That the accused willfully subscribed the statement;

       (4) That the statement was material;

       (5) That the statement was false; and

       (6) That the accused did not then believe the statement to be true.

2. Distinguished From False Swearing and False Official Statement.

   a) Although often used interchangeably, perjury and false swearing are different offenses. The primary distinctions are that perjury requires that the false statement be made in a judicial proceeding and be material to the issue, whereas these matters are not part of the offense of false swearing. As such, false swearing is not a lesser included offense of perjury. *United States v. Smith*, 26 C.M.R. 16 (C.M.A. 1958).

   b) The offense of false official statement (UCMJ art. 107) differs from perjury in that such a statement can be made outside a judicial proceeding and materiality is not an essential element, but bears only on the issue of intent to deceive. It, too, is not a lesser included offense of perjury. *United States v. Warble*, 30 C.M.R. 839 (A.F.B.R. 1960).

3. "Judicial proceeding" includes a trial by court-martial and "course of justice" includes an investigation under Article 32, UCMJ. MCM, pt. IV, ¶ 57c(1).

4. Discussion of Elements.

   a) That the accused took an oath or its equivalent in a judicial proceeding or at an Article 32 investigation.

      (1) The oath must be one required or authorized by law. MCM, pt. IV, ¶ 57c(2)(d).

      (2) Article 42(b), UCMJ, requires that each witness before a court-martial be examined under oath. R.C.M. 405(h)(1)(A) provides that all witnesses who testify at an Article 32 investigation do so under oath.

      (3) R.C.M. 807 lists the various forms of oaths to be used at courts-martial and Article 32 investigations. A literal application of such formats is not essential. The oath is sufficient if it conforms in substance to the prescribed form. At the request of the party being sworn an affirmation may be substituted for an oath.

      (4) DA Pam 27-9, Military Judges' Benchbook, ¶ 3-149, defines an "oath" as a formal, external pledge, coupled with an appeal to the Supreme Being, that the truth will be stated. An "affirmation" is a solemn and formal, external pledge, binding upon one's conscience that the truth will be stated.

      (5) The oath must be duly administered by one authorized to administer it. MCM, pt. IV, ¶ 57c(2)(d).

      (6) Articles 41(c) and 136(a), UCMJ, along with R.C.M. 405 and R.C.M. 807, set out in detail those persons authorized to administer oaths at judicial proceedings and Article 32 investigations.

      (7) The president, military judge, trial counsel and assistant trial counsel for all general and special courts-martial, along with all investigating officers and judge advocates, are included in this group.

      (8) If the accused is charged with having committed perjury before a court-martial, the jurisdictional basis of the prior court-martial must be proved beyond a reasonable doubt.

(a) Ordinarily this may be shown by introducing in evidence pertinent parts of the record of trial of the case in which the perjury was allegedly committed or by the testimony of a person who was counsel, the military judge, or a member of the court in that case to the effect that the court was so detailed and constituted. *See United States v. Giles*, 58 M.J. 634 (N-M. Ct. Crim. App. 2003) *rev'd on other grounds and remanded by,* 59 M.J. 374 (C.A.A.F. 2004).

(b) Where (1) the evidence at trial on charges of perjury before another court-martial did not identify the convening authority of that court-martial; (2) no appointing order was either recited or introduced; and (3) no other evidence providing a factual basis for concluding the prior court was properly detailed and constituted is presented, the evidence was insufficient despite lack of objection by the defense at the trial level. *United States v. McQueen*, 49 C.M.R. 355 (N.C.M.R. 1974).

b)   That the accused willfully gave what he believed to be false testimony at the proceeding in question.

(1) A witness may commit perjury by testifying that he knows a thing to be true when in fact he either knows nothing about it at all or is not sure about it, and this is so whether the thing is true or false in fact. MCM, pt. IV, ¶ 57c(2)(a).

(2) A witness may also commit perjury in testifying falsely as to his belief, remembrance, or impression, or as to his judgment or opinion. Thus, if a witness swears that he does not remember certain matters when in fact he does or testifies that in his opinion a certain person was drunk when in fact he entertained the contrary opinion, he commits perjury if the other elements of the offense are present. MCM, pt. IV, ¶ 57c(2)(a).

(3) To undermine the willfulness and knowledge elements of this offense the following defenses are available:

(a) Voluntary intoxication. Intoxication may so impair the mental processes as to prevent a person from entertaining a particular intent or reaching a specific state of mind. To successfully argue this defense in a perjury prosecution, the evidence must show that the accused was intoxicated at the time he testified. Evidence that he was intoxicated at the time of the event about which he testified is immaterial insofar as raising this defense is concerned. *United States v. Chaney*, 30 C.M.R. 378 (C.M.A. 1961).

(b) Mistake of fact. Evidence that an accused charged with perjury was intoxicated at the time of the events about which he testified raises the defense of mistake since such evidence relates to his ability to see and recall what transpired. *United States v. Chaney*, 30 C.M.R. 378 (C.M.A. 1961).

(c) That the false testimony provided was in respect to a material matter.

(4) Determination of whether the false testimony was with respect to a material matter is a question of fact to be determined by the fact-finder. *United States v. Gaudin,* 515 U.S. 506 (1995); *see Johnson v. United States*, 520 U.S. 461, 463-66 (1997).

(5) To constitute a "material matter", the matter need not be the main issue in the case. The test is whether the false statement has a natural tendency to influence, or be capable of influencing, the decision of the tribunal in making a determination required to be made. *United States v. McLean*, 10 C.M.R. 183 (A.B.R. 1953). Materiality must be judged by the facts and circumstances in the particular case. The color of an accused's hair may be totally immaterial in one case, but decisively material in another. *Weinstock v. United States*, 231 F.2d 699 (D.C. Cir. 1956).

(a) False denial of prior convictions by a witness in response to cross-examination conducted to impeach him and attack his credibility constitutes perjury, as such false testimony relates to a material matter. *State v. Swisher*, 364 Mo. 157, 260 S.W.2d (1968).

(b) *United States v. Martin*, 23 C.M.R. 437 (A.B.R. 1956) (accused's testimony at a previous trial that he was authorized to wear certain decorations, which was not in fact the case, was a material matter for purposes of sustaining a charge of perjury).

(6) Even inadmissible evidence may be material and therefore the subject of a perjury charge. Where a court improperly admits evidence, such impropriety is not per se evidence of immateriality if the evidence goes to the jury. *See United States v. Whitlock*, 456 F.2d 1230 (10th Cir. 1972); *United States v. Parker*, 447 F.2d 826 (7th Cir. 1971).

5. Corroboration: Special Evidentiary Rules.

a) A unique characteristic of Article 131 is that it contains a quantitative norm as to what evidence must be presented to establish a crucial element of falsity. A mere showing of guilt beyond a reasonable doubt is not enough. Specifically:

(1) "Two witness rule." The falsity of accused's statement must be shown by the testimony of at least two witnesses or by the testimony of one witness which directly contradicts accused's statement plus other corroborating evidence. *See United States v. Olivero*, 39 M.J. 246 (C.M.A. 1994) (circumstantial evidence of marijuana use insufficient; must have at least one corroborated witness with direct proof of such use).

United States v. Tunstall, 24 M.J. 235 (C.M.A. 1987) (where alleged false oath relates to two or more facts that one witness contradicts accused as to the one fact and another witness as to another fact, the two witnesses corroborate each other in the fact that accused swore falsely, and their testimony will authorize conviction); *United States v. Lowman*, 50 C.M.R. 749 (A.C.M.R. 1975) (accused's testimony contradicted by two witnesses); *United States v. Jordan*, 20 M.J. 977 (A.C.M.R. 1985) (two witnesses rule not applicable where falsity of accused's oath is directly proved by documentary testimony).

(2) Direct proof required. No conviction may be had for perjury, regardless of how many witnesses testify as to falsity and no matter how compelling their testimony may be, if such testimony is wholly circumstantial. *See Olivero*, 39 M.J. 246 (C.M.A. 1994).

b) Documentary evidence directly disproving the truth of accused's statement need not be corroborated if the document is an official record shown to have been well known to the accused at the time he took the oath or if the documentary evidence appears to have sprung from the accused himself -or had in any manner been recognized by him as containing the truth - before the allegedly perjured statement was made. *See generally* Hall, *The Two-Witness Rule in Falsification Offenses*, ARMY LAW., May 1989, at 11.

c) With the passage of Title IV of the Organized Crime Control Act of 1970 (18 U.S.C. § 1623), Congress eliminated application of the two witnesses rule in federal court and grand jury proceedings. In its stead was adopted a beyond a reasonable doubt standard. This statute, however, has not been made applicable to the military. *See United States v. Lowman*, 50 C.M.R. 749 (A.C.M.R. 1975).

d) Inconsistent Sworn Statements. Because of the requirements of the "two witness rule," contradictory sworn statements made by a witness cannot by themselves be the basis of a perjury prosecution under Article 131. For example, X testifies under oath that on 15 March he was in a certain bar with accused from 1900-2100. At the same or subsequent trial he again testifies under oath, but this time states that although he was in the bar from 1900-2100, he never saw the accused. Under military law, insufficient evidence exists to prosecute X for perjury.

6. Application of evidentiary rules.

a) *United States v. Downing*, 6 C.M.R. 568 (A.F.B.R. 1952). Mere circumstantial evidence showing nonpresence at a hospital by nonexistence of entry in hospital records held to be insufficient.

b) *United States v. McLean*, 10 C.M.R. 183 (A.B.R. 1953). Weighty direct and circumstantial evidence of drinking which accused denied found sufficient.

c) *United States v. Taylor*, 19 C.M.R. 71 (C.M.A. 1955). Directly contradictory testimony of prosecution witness corroborated by strong circumstantial evidence held sufficient.

d) *United States v. Walker*, 19 C.M.R. 284 (C.M.A. 1955). Proof by circumstantial evidence alone of falsity of accused's negative assertion of what he saw - something by its nature not susceptible of direct proof - was held to be sufficient. This exception was subsequently embodied in MCM, 1969, ¶ 210 (currently in MCM, pt. IV, ¶ 57c(2)(c)).

e) *United States v. Guerra*, 32 C.M.R. 463 (C.M.A. 1963). Contradictory testimony held not directly so, therefore insufficient.

f) *United States v. Martin*, 23 C.M.R. 437 (A.B.R. 1956). Documentary evidence directly disproving accused's assertion of holding various decorations insufficient where uncorroborated.

g) *United States v. Anders*, 23 C.M.R. 448 (A.B.R. 1956). Facts similar to those in *United States v. Martin, supra*. Documentary evidence properly corroborated by testimony negating claim of awards.

h) *United States v. Giles,* 58 M.J. 634 (N-M. Ct. Crim. App. 2003)(accused's testimony that she "did not believe she was purchasing LSD" was sufficiently contradicted by her prior confession to CID that she knew she was buying LSD, her own handwritten note stating that she was got "acid" and from the observations of an informant; totality of the evidence supports conviction for perjury) *rev'd on improper joinder grounds, remanded by,* 59 M.J. 374 (C.A.A.F. 2004).

7. *Res Judicata* as a Defense.

a) The availability of *res judicata* as a defense to an accused charged with perjury is recognized in military law.

b) This doctrine is raised when accused testifies at his trial and is acquitted, but the Government wants to retry him for presenting false testimony at that trial. Under these circumstances *res judicata* will bar a conviction for perjury. *United States v. Martin*, 24 C.M.R. 156 (C.M.A. 1957); *United States v. Hooten*, 30 C.M.R. 339 (C.M.A. 1961); *see generally* Milhizer, *Effective Prosecution Following Appellate Reversal: Putting Teeth Into the Second Bite of the Apple*, II Trial Counsel Forum No. 4 (Apr. 1982).

c) When an accused is acquitted based on statements made at his trial and then makes similar statements at the trial of another person, *res judicata* is not available as a bar to a perjury prosecution for his subsequent statements because the principle of *res judicata* applies only to issues of fact or law put in issue and finally determined between the same parties. The accused was not a party to the second trial. *United States v. Guerra*, 32 C.M.R. 463 (C.M.A. 1963); *see generally* Hahn, *Previous Acquittals, Res Judicata, and Other Crimes Evidence Under Military Rule of Evidence 404(b)*, ARMY LAW., May 1983, at 1.

D. Obstructing Justice. MCM, pt. IV, ¶ 96; UCMJ art. 134.

1. Elements.

a) That the accused wrongfully did a certain act;

b) That the accused did so in the case of a certain person against whom the accused had reason to believe there were or would be criminal proceedings pending;

c) That the act was done with the intent to influence, impede, or otherwise obstruct the due administration of justice; and

d) That, under the circumstances, the conduct of the accused was to the prejudice of the good order and discipline in the armed forces or was of a nature to bring discredit upon the armed forces.

2. Scope. Obstructing justice under Article 134 is much broader than under the United States Code. *See United States v. Jones*, 20 M.J. 38 (C.M.A. 1985). It proscribes efforts to interfere with the administration of military justice throughout the investigation of a crime, not simply at pending judicial proceedings. The crime can be constituted where the accused had reason to believe that criminal proceedings were or would be pending. *United States v. Tedder*, 24 M.J. 176 (C.M.A. 1987); *United States v. Bailey*, 28 M.J. 1004 (A.C.M.R. 1989); *United States v. Chodkowski*, 11 M.J. 605 (A.F.C.M.R. 1981), *aff'd*, 14 M.J. 126 (C.M.A. 1982); *but cf. United States v. Kellough*, 19 M.J. 871 (A.F.C.M.R. 1985) (not obstruction to "plant" evidence where no proceeding pending; offense was a disorder under Article 134). Criminal proceedings are broadly defined to include nonjudicial punishment. MCM, pt. IV, ¶ 96c. An official act, inquiry, investigation, or other criminal proceeding with a view toward possible disposition in the military justice system is required. *United States v. Gray*, 28 M.J. 858 (A.C.M.R. 1989). MCM 1984, pt. IV 96F is amended by Change 5 by making wrongfulness a required element.

3. Applications.

a) Assault on witness who had testified at summary court-martial. *United States v. Long*, 6 C.M.R. 60 (C.M.A. 1952).

b) Intimidating witnesses who were to testify at a summary court-martial. *United States v. Rossi*, 13 C.M.R. 896 (A.F.B.R. 1953).

c) Intimidating a witness who was to appear before an Article 32 investigating officer. *United States v. Daminger*, 31 C.M.R. 521 (A.F.B.R. 1961). *But see United States v. Chodkowski*, 11 M.J. 605 (A.F.C.M.R. 1981) (arguing that *Daminger* no longer accurately represents controlling law on obstruction issue and that such a charge does not require that charges had been preferred in the underlying case or investigation).

d) Attempt to influence and intimidate a witness to retract a statement made during course of an Article 15 hearing. *United States v. Delaney*, 44 C.M.R. 367 (A.C.M.R. 1971).

e) MP tried to conceal money which came into his possession in the course of official duty when the money was possible evidence pertaining to an alleged criminal offense by another person. *United States v. Favors*, 48 C.M.R. 873 (A.C.M.R. 1974).

f) Communications among co-conspirators not embraced by the conspiracy. *United States v. Williams*, 29 M.J. 41 (C.M.A. 1989); *see United States v. Dowlat*, 28 M.J. 958 (A.F.C.M.R. 1989).

g) Endeavoring to impede trial by soliciting a murder. *United States v. Thurmond*, 29 M.J. 709 (A.C.M.R. 1989).

h) Accused's threat to airman, which airman understood as an inducement to testify falsely if he were called as a witness at the accused's trial, constituted offense even if accused was not on notice that airman would be a witness. *United States v. Caudill*, 10 M.J. 787 (A.F.C.M.R. 1981); *United States v. Rosario*, 19 M.J. 698 (A.C.M.R. 1984).

i) Attempt to have witness falsely provide an alibi. *United States v. Gomez*, 15 M.J. 954 (A.C.M.R. 1983).

j) Accused's act of simultaneously soliciting false testimony from two potential witnesses constituted a single obstruction of justice. *United States v. Guerro*, 28 M.J. 223 (C.M.A. 1989).

k) Asking witnesses to withdraw statements. *United States v. Latimer*, 30 M.J. 554 (A.C.M.R. 1990).

l) Accused's statement "don't report me" did not constitute obstruction of justice. *United States v. Asfeld*, 30 M.J. 917 (A.C.M.R. 1990).

m) Seeking to have minor daughter's boyfriend influence daughter to change her testimony at a state court proceeding, in exchange for consenting to daughter's marriage to boyfriend. *United States v. Smith*, 32 M.J. 567 (A.C.M.R. 1991) *rev'd on other grounds* 39 M.J. 448 (C.M.A. 1994) (merely requesting a soldier to contact a witness in a state proceeding, without evidence that accused also asked him to convince the witness to change her testimony, is not sufficient to sustain conviction for obstruction of justice).

n) No obstruction of justice where accused's conduct consisted only of calling friends and begging them not to press charges. *United States v. Kirks*, 34 M.J. 646 (A.C.M.R. 1992).

o) Making false and misleading statement to investigators may constitute obstruction of justice. *United States v. Arriaga*, 49 M.J. 9 (1998).

p) A senior drill instructor's attempt to get two trainees to change their story regarding a sexual assault against one of the trainees was legally sufficient to sustain convictions for two specifications of obstruction of justice. The accused's statement, "I'll do anything if you don't tell," and its converse implication of more severe treatment if the trainee did not accede was inconsistent with the duties of a senior drill sergeant. Additionally, the accused knew his offense against the trainee had been reported and that the trainee was pursuing the matter. *United States v. Barner*, 56 M.J. 131 (2001).

q) An interested party who advises, with a corrupt motive, a witness to exercise a constitutional right may obstruct the administration of justice. *United States v. Reeves*, 61 M.J. 108 (2005) (accused, a tech school instructor, told a trainee not to speak to investigators and to seek counsel once the accused came under suspicion for several offenses).

4. Applies to state court proceedings. *United States v. Smith*, 32 M.J. 567 (A.C.M.R. 1991), *rev'd on other grounds*, 39 M.J. 448 (C.M.A. 1994).

5. Requisite intent not found unless accused aware that there is or possibly could be an investigation. *United States v. Athey*, 34 M.J. 44 (C.M.A. 1992).

6. It is not necessary that the potential evidence be within the control of authorities or already seized when destroyed by the accused in order to be considered obstruction of justice. *United States v. Lennette*, 41 M.J. 488 (1995).

7. An accused can be convicted of obstruction of justice, even if the court-martial acquits him of the offense for which he was under investigation. *United States v. Bailey*, 52 M.J. 786 (A.F. Ct. Crim. App. 1999), *aff'd*, 55 M.J. 38 (C.A.A.F. 2001).

8. Using the U.S. Code.

   a) A more restrictive, and thus generally less desirable, way to charge this offense is under Article 134(3), UCMJ, as a violation of one of the below-listed sections of the U.S. Code:

   (1) 18 U.S.C. § 1503 (1982) - Obstruction of proceedings before any federal court, commissioner, magistrate, or grand jury. *United States v. Aguilar*, 115 S. Ct. 2357 (1995) (adopting the "nexus" requirement - that the conduct in question had the natural and probable effect of interfering with the due administration of justice).

   (2) 18 U.S.C. § 1505 (1982) - Obstruction of proceedings before departments, agencies and committees.

   (3) 18 U.S.C. § 1510 (1982) - Obstruction of criminal investigations. *See generally United States v. Casteen*, 17 M.J. 580 (A.F.C.M.R. 1983) (not intended to deal with communications between accomplices) *reconsidered on other grounds*, 17 MJ 800 (1983), *rev'd. in part*, 24 MJ 62 (C.M.A. 1987). *But see United States v. Williams*, 29 M.J. 41 (C.M.A. 1989) (disapproving of *Casteen* and stating that communications to an accomplice will be subject to obstruction charge under either Article 134(1) or 134(2)).

   (4) 18 U.S.C. § 1511 (1982) - Obstruction of state or local law enforcement.

   b) *See* Annot., 18 A.L.R. Fed. 875 (1974).

   c) If the offense is charged under the U.S. Code, the military judge must instruct on the elements set out in the statute and the Government must prove the same. *United States v. Canter*, 42 C.M.R. 753 (A.C.M.R. 1970); *see generally United States v. Ridgeway*, 13 M.J. 742 (A.C.M.R. 1982).

   d) The MCM obviates the need for proceeding under some of these statutes as Article 134 provides the offense of "Wrongful Interference With An Adverse Administrative Proceeding." *See* MCM, pt. IV, para 96a.

E. Destruction, Removal, or Disposal of Property to Prevent Seizure. MCM, pt. IV, ¶ 103; UCMJ art. 134.

   1. Elements.

      a) That one or more persons authorized to make searches and seizures were seizing, about to seize, or endeavoring to seize certain property;

      b) That the accused destroyed, removed, or otherwise disposed of that property with intent to prevent the seizure thereof;

      c) That the accused then knew that persons(s) authorized to make searches were seizing, about to seize, or endeavoring to seize certain property; and

      d) That, under the circumstances, the conduct of the accused was to the prejudice of the good order and discipline in the armed forces or was of a nature to bring discredit upon the armed forces.

   2. The offense has no requirement that criminal proceedings be pending or that the accused intended to impede the administration of justice. *Cf. United States v. Ridgeway*,

13 M.J. 742 (A.C.M.R. 1982). The crime is constituted where the accused intended to prevent the seizure of certain property that the accused knew persons authorized to make seizures were endeavoring to seize.

3. Not a defense that the search or seizure was technically defective. MCM, pt. IV, ¶ 103c.

F. Misprision of a Serious Offense. MCM, pt. IV, ¶ 95; UCMJ art. 134.

1. Elements.

   a) That a certain serious offense was committed by a certain person;

   b) That the accused knew that the said person had committed the serious offense;

   c) That, thereafter, the accused concealed the serious offense and failed to make it known to civilian or military authorities as soon as possible;

   d) That the concealing was wrongful; and

   e) That, under the circumstances, the conduct of the accused was to the prejudice of the good order and discipline in the armed forces or was of a nature to bring discredit upon the armed forces.

2. Taking affirmative steps to conceal the identity of the offender constitutes misprision; conviction of misprision of serious offense does not violate Fifth Amendment right against self-incrimination. *United States v. Sanchez*, 51 M.J. 165 (C.A.A.F. 1999) (accused took affirmative steps to conceal the identity of the offender).

3. *See supra*, ¶ II.D, ch. 1, for a discussion of differences between Misprision of a Serious Offense and Accessory After the Fact.

G. Lesser Included Offenses and Multiplicity. If properly pleaded, communicating a threat may be a lesser included offense of obstruction of justice. *United States v. Benavides*, 43 M.J. 723 (Army Ct. Crim. App. 1995) (relying on "pleading elements" analysis of *United States v. Weymouth*, 43 M.J. 329, 340 (1995)); *United States v. Craft*, 44 C.M.R. 664 (A.C.M.R. 1971). *But see United States v. Oatney*, 41 M.J. 619 (N-M. Ct. Crim. App. 1994) (relying on strict "statutory elements" analysis of *United States v. Teters*, 37 M.J. 370 (C.M.A. 1993), the Navy-Marine Court held that communication of a threat and obstruction of justice are not multiplicious, even in a particular case where the threat factually must be proved in order to prove the obstruction of justice), *aff'd*, 45 M.J. 185 (C.A.A.F. 1996).

VIII. "EVIL WORDS" OFFENSES.

A. Threat or Hoax Designed or Intended to Cause Panic or Public Fear. MCM, pt. IV, ¶ 109; UCMJ art. 134.

1. Expansion of Offense. In 2005, this offense was expanded from "bomb" threats or hoaxes to include threats and hoaxes of other types, including explosives, weapons of mass destruction, biological agents, chemical agents, and other hazardous material. See MCM, pt. IV, ¶ 109c; MCM, App. 23 ¶ 109.

2. Explanation. "Threat" and "hoax" offenses can be charged under either Article 134(1), UCMJ, as conduct prejudicial to good order and discipline or under Article 134(3), UCMJ, a non-capital federal crime violative of 18 U.S.C.

3. "Innocent Motive." Claim of joking motive is not a defense to "bomb hoax" charge, as the victim's concern, which satisfies the requirement for maliciousness, can be inferred. *United States v. Pugh*, 28 M.J. 71 (C.M.A. 1989); *see* TJAGSA Practice Note, *"I Was Only Joking" Not a Defense to "Bomb Hoax" Charge*, ARMY LAW., Jul. 1989, at 39 (discusses *Pugh*).

B. Communicating A Threat. MCM, pt. IV, ¶ 110; UCMJ art. 134.

1. Elements.

a) That the accused communicated certain language expressing a present determination or intent to wrongfully injure the person, property, or reputation of another person, presently or in the future;

b) That the communication was made known to that person or to a third person;

c) That the communication was wrongful; and

d) That, under the circumstances, the conduct of the accused was to the prejudice of good order and discipline in the armed forces or was of a nature to bring discredit upon the armed forces.

2. Explanation. This offense consists of wrongfully communicating an avowed present determination or intent to injure the person, property, or reputation of another presently or in the future. It relates to a potential violent disturbance of public peace and tranquility. *United States v. Grembowic*, 17 M.J. 720 (N.M.C.M.R. 1983).

3. Pleading. *United States v. Wartsbaugh*, 45 C.M.R. 309 (C.M.A. 1972) (pleading sufficient because evidence of surrounding circumstances may disclose the threatening nature of the words).

4. Applications.

a) Avowed present intent or determination to injure.

(1) Accused's statement that "I'd kill [my first sergeant] with no problem," made to health care professional while seeking help for drug addiction and suicidal urges, was not a present determination or intent to kill the putative victim. *United States v. Cotton*, 40 M.J. 93 (C.M.A. 1994); *United States v. Wright*, 65 M.J. 703 (N-M. Ct. Crim. App. 2007) (statements to health care professional not communicating a threat).

(2) Ineffective disclaimer. *United States v. Johnson*, 45 C.M.R. 53 (C.M.A. 1972) ("I am not threatening you . . . but in two days you are

going to be in a world of pain," constitutes a threat when considered within the totality of the circumstances).

(3) Conditional threat.

(a) The "impossible" variable. *United States v. Shropshire*, 43 C.M.R. 214 (C.M.A. 1971) (physical threat to guard by restrained prisoner not actionable as no reasonable possibility existed that threat would be carried out); *see also United States v. Gately*, 13 M.J. 757 (A.F.C.M.R. 1982) (upheld lesser included offense of provoking words).

(b) The "possible" variable. *United States v. Phillips*, 42 M.J. 127 (C.A.A.F. 1995) (accused's statement to airman to "keep her damn mouth shut and [she would] make it through basic training just fine" was not premised on an impossible condition, even if the victim was not inclined to report accused's misconduct); *United States v. Brown*, 65 M.J. 227 (2006) (accused could control the contingency, and the combination of words & circumstances could make a contingent threat immediate for purposes of Article 134); *United States v. Holiday*, 16 C.M.R. 28 (C.M.A. 1954) (unrestrained prisoner's threat to injure guard was actionable even though conditioned on guard's not pushing prisoner; the condition was one accused had no right to impose); *United States v. Bailey*, 52 M.J. 786 (A.F. Ct. Crim. App. 1999) (acts and words may express what accused can and will do in the future), *aff'd*, 55 M.J. 38 (C.A.A.F. 2001); *see United States v. Alford*, 32 M.J. 596 (A.C.M.R. 1991), *aff'd*, 34 M.J. 150 (C.M.A. 1992).

(4) Idle jest, banter, and hyperbole are not threatening words. *United States v. Gilluly*, 32 C.M.R. 458 (C.M.A. 1963). In appraising the legal sufficiency of the evidence to sustain a conviction of communicating a threat, the circumstances surrounding the uttering of the words and consideration of whether the words were stated in jest or seriousness are to be evaluated. *See United States v. Johnson*, 45 C.M.R. 53 (C.M.A. 1972) (Considered in the light of the circumstances of the situation the following was held to be an illegal threat, "I am not threatening you, but I am telling you that I am not personally going to do anything to you, but in two days you are going to be in a world of pain," adding a suggestion that the victim "damn well better sleep light").

(5) The words used by the accused are significant in that they may not evidence a technical threat but rather merely state an already completed act, *e.g.*, "I have just planted a bomb in the barracks." Such a statement may constitute a simple disorder under Article 134 or a false official statement under Article 107 if made to a person in an official capacity (*e.g.*, Charge of Quarters). To meet potential problems of proof, trial counsel should plead such offenses in the alternative. *See United States v. Gilluly*, 32 C.M.R. 458 (C.M.A. 1963).

(6) Lack of intent to actually carry out the threat is not a basis for rejecting a guilty plea. *United States v. Greig*, 44 M.J. 356 (C.A.A.F. 1996) (accused admitted making threats and wished that the individuals who heard the threats believed them).

(7) Consider language and surrounding circumstances to determine whether or not words express a present determination or intent to wrongfully injure. *United States v. Hall*, 52 M.J. 809 (N-M. Ct. Crim. App 1999).

b) Communication to the victim is unnecessary. *United States v. Gilluly*, 32 C.M.R. 458 (C.M.A. 1963).

c) No specific intent is required. The intent which establishes the offense is that expressed in the language of the declaration, not the intent locked in the mind of the declarant. This is not to say the declarant's actual intention has no significance as to his guilt or innocence. A statement may declare an intention to injure and thereby ostensibly establish this element of the offense, but the declarant's true intention, the understanding of the persons to whom the statement is communicated, and the surrounding circumstances may so belie or contradict the language of the declaration as to reveal it to be a mere jest or idle banter. *United States v. Humphrys*, 22 C.M.R. 96 (C.M.A. 1956).

d) A threat to reputation is sufficient. *United States v. Frayer*, 29 C.M.R. 416 (C.M.A. 1960); *see also United States v. Farkas*, 21 M.J. 458 (C.M.A. 1986) (threat to sell victim's diamond ring sufficient).

e) Threats not *directly* prejudicial to good order and discipline nor service discrediting do not constitute an offense. *United States v. Hill*, 48 C.M.R. 6, 7 (C.M.A. 1973) (lovers' quarrel).

f) Merger with an assault crime. *United States v. Metcalf*, 41 C.M.R. 574 (A.C.M.R. 1969) (threat after assault merges with assault for punishment purposes).

g) Threatening a potential witness is a separate offense from and may constitute obstruction of justice in violation of Article 134. *United States v. Oatney*, 41 M.J. 619 (N.M.C. Ct. Crim. App. 1994), *aff'd*, 45 M.J. 185 (C.A.A.F. 1996); *United States v. Rosario*, 19 M.J. 698 (A.C.M.R. 1984); *United States v. Baur*, 10 M.J. 789 (A.F.C.M.R. 1981).

C. Provoking Words or Gestures. UCMJ art. 117.

1. Elements.

a) That the accused wrongfully used words or gestures towards a certain person;

b) That the words or gestures used were provoking or reproachful; and

c) That the person toward whom the words or gestures were used was a person subject to the code.

2. Relationship to Communicating a Threat. This is a lesser included offense of communicating a threat.

3. *Mens Rea.* No specific intent is required. *United States v. Welsh*, 15 C.M.R. 573 (N.B.R. 1954).

4. Applications.

    a) The provoking words must be used in the presence of the victim and must be words which a reasonable person would expect to induce a breach of the peace under the circumstances. MCM, pt. IV, ¶ 42(c).

        (1) *United States v. Davis*, 37 M.J. 152 (C.M.A. 1993). Accused's statement to MP, "F___ you, Sergeant," and "F___ the MPs" was expected to induce a breach of the peace, even though the MP was not personally provoked and was trained to deal with such comments.

        (2) *United States v. Thompson*, 46 C.M.R. 88 (C.M.A. 1972). Because of the physical circumstances, the offensive words were unlikely to cause a fight.

        (3) *United States v. Shropshire*, 34 M.J. 757 (A.F.C.M.R. 1992). Insulting comments to policeman by handcuffed suspect under apprehension were insufficient to constitute provoking words as police are trained to overlook abuse.

        (4) *United States v. Meo*, 57 M.J. 744 (C.A.A.F. 2002). Guilty plea improvident when accused told ensign "[T]his is bullshit, I'm going to explode and I don't know when or on who." Although statement was disrespectful, it did not rise to the level of "fighting words."

        (5) *United States v. Ybarra*, 57 M.J. 807 (N-M. Ct. Crim. App. 2002) *pet. denied*, 58 M.J. 289 (C.A.A.F. 2003). Accused pled guilty to provoking speech for using racial slurs to an NCO who was trying to restrain him.

    b) Not necessary that the accused know that the person towards whom the words or gestures are directed is a person subject to the UCMJ.

    c) Merger with an assault crime. *United States v. Palms*, 47 C.M.R. 416 (A.C.M.R. 1973).

    d) Separate offense from disrespect. *United States v. McHerrin*, 42 M.J. 672 (Army Ct. Crim. App. 1995).

D. Extortion. UCMJ art. 127.

  1. Elements.

    a) That the accused communicated a certain threat to another; and

    b) That the acused intended to unlawfully obtain something of value, or any acquittance, advantage, or immunity.

  2. Applications. *United States v. Brown*, 67 M.J. 147 (C.A.A.F. 2009). Accused threatened to release videotape depicting the victim's sexual acts unless she engaged in sexual intercourse with him. The specification alleged that "with intent unlawfully to obtain an advantage, to wit: sexual relations, [the accused] communicate[d] to [PFC RA] a threat to expose to other members of the military their past sexual relationship and to use his rank, position, and connections to discredit her and ruin her military career." The CAAF held that the specification in this case was legally sufficient. The specification described the "advantage" that he accused sought to receive: sexual relations with the victim. By seeking to have her engage in sexual relations with him, the accused intended to "obtain an advantage." The specification also described the threat the accused

communicated in an effort to obtain the stated advantage: to expose their past sexual relationship in a manner that would harm the victim's military career.

E. Indecent Language. MCM, pt. IV, ¶ 89; UCMJ art. 134. *See supra* ¶ V.M., this chapter.

F. False Public Speech. Service member does not have unlimited freedom to make false official presentation to public forum, and giving false speech in public forum may constitute an offense under Article 134, Clause 2. *United States v. Stone*, 40 M.J. 420 (C.M.A. 1994).

G. Offensive Language.

1. *See supra* ¶ V.N., (obscenity), this chapter.

2. There is no generic "offensive language" offense under the UCMJ. *United States v. Herron*, 39 M.J. 860 (N.M.C.M.R. 1994) (uttering profanity in loud and angry manner in public setting was not "general disorder" and could not be prosecuted as such).

3. Any reasonable officer would have known that asking strangers of the opposite sex intimate questions about their sexual activities while using a false name, and a fictional publishing company as a cover was service discrediting conduct. *United States v. Sullivan*, 42 M.J. 360 (C.A.A.F. 1995).

IX. DRUG OFFENSES.

A. Drug offenses fall into several categories under the UCMJ.

1. UCMJ art. 112a. Covers certain drugs listed in the statutory language of Art. 112a, substances listed under Schedules I through V of the Controlled Substances Act (21 U.S.C. § 812), and any other drugs that the President may see fit to prohibit in the military.

2. AR 600-85, the Army Substance Abuse Program (2 February 2009), para. 4-2m. This is a punitive provision that expands the list of drugs that Soldiers are prohibited from using. Offenses are punished under UCMJ art. 92(1).

3. There are numerous hazardous substances that are not expressly contained in any of the two categories described above. Such substances may be prohibited by operation of other federal statutes, for example 21 U.S.C. § 813. In the absence of such a statute applicable to a particular hazardous substance, the use, possession, distribution, or manufacture or such substances may still be prohibited by other provisions of Title 21 of the U.S. Code. If this is the case, then such misconduct may be prosecuted under clause three of Article 134. *See, e.g., United States v. Reichenbach*, 29 M.J. 128 (C.M.A. 1989)

4. Finally, the abuse of substances not included in the categories described above may also violate clauses 1 and 2 of Article 134. *See generally United States v. Reichenbach*, 29 M.J. 128 (C.M.A. 1989); *see, e.g., United States v. Erickson*, 61 M.J. 230 (C.A.A.F. 2005) (wrongful inhalation of nitrous oxide that impaired thinking and could damage the brain); *United States v. Glover*, 50 M.J. 476 (C.A.A.F. 1999) (wrongful inhalation of aeresol "dust-off"). **NOTE:** After 2 Feb 09, the conduct in both *Erickson* and *Glover* of these cases would be covered under AR 600-85, para. 4-2m (4-2p after Rapid Action Revision on 2 Dec 09).

B. UCMJ art. 112a: The Statutory Framework.

1. Article 112a, UCMJ, provides in part: Any person subject to this chapter who wrongfully uses, possesses, manufactures, distributes, imports into the customs territory of the United States, exports from the United States, or introduces into an installation, vessel,

vehicle, or aircraft used by or under the control of the armed forces a substance described in subsection (b) shall be punished as a court-martial may direct.

2. Types of Controlled Substances Covered by Article 112a. Article 112a, UCMJ, is a statute of limited scope in that it only prescribes conduct relating to three specific categories of controlled substances; it does not purport to "ban every new drug mischief." *United States v. Tyhurst*, 28 M.J. 671, 675 (A.F.C.M.R.), *rev'd in part*, 29 M.J. 324 (C.M.A. 1989). Substances are "controlled" for purposes of this article (MCM, pt. IV, ¶ 37(a)(b)) if:

  a) Congress listed them in the text of Article 112a.

  b) The President listed them in the MCM for the purposes of Article 112a, UCMJ, or

  c) They are listed in schedules I through V of section 202 of the Controlled Substances Act (21 U.S.C. § 812).

3. Types of Conduct Prescribed by Article 112a, UCMJ. Article 112a prohibits an expansive array of conduct relating to controlled substances. The following types of conduct are expressly prohibited: Possession; Use; Manufacture; Distribution; Import/Export; Introduction; Possession, introduction, or manufacture with intent to distribute.

4. Time of war. When declared by Congress or in accordance with a factual determination by the President. R.C.M. 103(19); *United States v. Avarette*, 41 C.M.R. 363 (C.M.A. 1970); *United States v. Anderson*, 38 C.M.R. 386 (C.M.A. 1968).

5. Intent to distribute.

  a) Intent to distribute may be inferred from circumstantial evidence. Examples of evidence which may tend to support an inference of intent to distribute are: possession of a quantity of substance in excess of that which one would be likely to have for personal use; market value of the substance; the manner in which the substance is packaged; and that the accused is not a user of the substance. On the other hand, evidence that the accused is addicted to or is a heavy user of the substance may tend to negate an inference of intent to distribute. MCM, pt. IV, ¶ 37c(6).

  b) Possession with intent to distribute does not require ownership. *United States v. Davis*, 562 F.2d 681 (D.C. Cir. 1977).

  c) To convict for possession with intent to distribute, fact finder must be willing, where no evidence is presented of actual distribution, to find beyond a reasonable doubt that the accused would not have possessed so substantial a quantity of drugs if he merely intended to use them himself. *United States v. Morgan*, 581 F.2d 933 (D.C. Cir. 1978); see also *United States v. Turner*, 24 L.Ed.2d 610 (1970) (because accused's possession of 14.68 grams of a cocaine and sugar mixture of which 5% was cocaine might have been exclusively for his personal use, evidence was insufficient to support conviction for distribution).

  d) Evidence of resale value of drug may support inference of intent to distribute. *United States v. Raminez-Rodriguez*, 552 F.2d 883 (9th Cir. 1977).

  e) Circumstantial evidence of intent to distribute may require expert testimony as to dosage units, street value, and packaging. *See, e.g., United States v. Blake*,

484 F.2d 50 (7th Cir.), *cert. denied*, 422 U.S. 919 (1979) (expert testimony that 14.3 grams of 17.3% pure heroin would make 420 "dime bags" having a St. Louis street value of $4,200); *United States v. Wilkerson*, 478 F.2d 813, 815 n. 3 (8th Cir. 1973) (49 pounds of marijuana worth $58,000 when first broken up and $71,500 if broken into joints); *United States v. Echols*, 477 F.2d 37 (8th Cir.), *cert. denied*, 414 U.S. 825 (1973) (199.73 grams of cocaine worth $200,000); *United States v. Hollman*, 541 F.2d 196 (8th Cir. 1976) (127 foil packets of heroin worth $20 each). *See generally United States v. Gould*, 13 M.J. 734 (A.C.M.R. 1982) (35 individually wrapped pieces of hashish).

f) A finding of addiction may support an inference that a large quantity of drugs were kept for personal use. *See United States v. Raminez-Rodriguez*, 552 F.2d 883 (9th Cir. 1977); *United States v. Kelly*, 527 F.2d 961 (9th Cir. 1976).

C. Use.

1. Elements.

    a) Use of controlled substance.

    b) Knowledge that the substance was used.

    c) Knowledge of the contraband nature of the substance.

    d) Use was wrongful, i.e., without legal justification or authorization.

2. Defined.

    a) "[T]o inject, ingest, inhale, or otherwise introduce into the human body, any controlled substance." MCM, pt. IV, ¶ 37c(10).

    b) Administration or physical assimilation of a controlled substance into one's body or system. *United States v. Harper*, 22 M.J. 157 (C.M.A. 1986).

3. Pleadings.

    a) Because it is often impossible to prove the exact date and location of drug use and because time and location are not of the essence of this offense, courts allow some latitude in proving and pleading offenses of this sort. *United States v. Miller*, 34 M.J. 598 (A.C.M.R. 1992).

    b) However, where a specification alleges wrongful acts on "divers occasions," the members of a panel must be instructed that any findings by exceptions and substitutions that remove the "divers occasions" language must clearly reflect the specific instance of conduct upon which their modified findings are based by referring to a relevant date or other facts in evidence that will clearly put accused and reviewing courts on notice of what conduct served as basis for the findings. *United States v. Walters*, 58 M.J. 391 (C.A.A.F. 2003); *United States v. Seider*, 60 M.J. 36 (C.A.A.F. 2004); *United States v. Augspurger*, 61 M.J. 189 (2005) (citing the analysis in *Seider*).

    c) The prosecution must nonetheless prove beyond a reasonable doubt that the accused used controlled substance during the period of time alleged in the specification. *United States v. Williams*, 37 M.J. 972 (A.C.M.R. 1993); *United States v. Lopez*, 37 M.J. 702 (A.C.M.R. 1993).

4. Inferences and Proof of Use.

    a) Placebo effect. Expert testimony concerning herbal ecstasy and the effects described by the recipient in this case supported the factfinder's conclusion that this was MDMA rather than herbal ecstasy. In addition, a placebo effect was unlikely in this case because the recipient did not have any preconceived notion of what to expect. Finally, the government produced evidence that the participants used the term "ecstasy" rather than "herbal ecstasy" in referring to the drug. *United States v. Griggs,* 61 M.J. 402 (C.A.A.F. 2005).

    b) Permissive inference of wrongfulness drawn from the positive result on urinalysis test is sufficient to support a finding of wrongful use of marijuana. *United States v Pabon,* 42 M.J. 404 (1995); *United States v. Ford,* 23 M.J. 331 (C.M.A. 1987).

    c) Laboratory results of urinalysis, coupled with expert testimony explaining the results, constituted sufficient evidence to establish beyond a reasonable doubt that the accused knowingly and wrongfully used marijuana. *United States v Bond,* 46 M.J. 86 (1997); *United States v. Harper,* 22 M.J. 157 (C.M.A. 1986).

    d) When the sole evidence of drug use is a positive laboratory test result, knowledge of the presence of the controlled substance may be inferred if the prosecution presents expert testimony explaining the underlying scientific methodology and the significance of the test result, so as to provide a rational basis for inferring that the substance was knowingly and wrongfully used. *United States v. Campbell*, 52 M.J. 386 (C.A.A.F. 2000) (clarifying, on reconsideration, its earlier holding that evidence, in this case, insufficient to permit inference of wrongfulness from concentration of LSD reported through use of GC/MS/MS test); *but see United States v. Green*, 55 M.J. 76 (C.A.A.F. 2001) (positive urinalysis properly admitted under standards applicable to scientific evidence, when accompanied by interpretative expert testimony, provides legally sufficient basis to draw permissive inference of knowing, wrongful use of controlled substance); *but see United States v. Hunt*, 33 M.J. 345 (C.M.A. 1991) (result of urinalysis alone, with no expert testimony explaining the results, is insufficient to establish guilt).

    e) Results of urinalysis alone, with no expert testimony explaining the results, are insufficient to establish guilt. *United States v. Hunt*, 33 M.J. 345 (C.M.A. 1991); *United States v. Murphy*, 23 M.J. 310 (C.M.A. 1987); *United States v. Brewer*, 61 M.J. 425 (C.A.A.F. 2005) (testimony from witnesses (who knew the accused throughout the charged period) that they had never seen him use drugs or observed him under the influence of drugs goes to the issue of knowing and wrongful use, and could have bolstered an innocent ingestion defense).

    f) Manual provision that allows use of a permissive inference to prove wrongful use is constitutional. *United States v. Bassano*, 23 M.J. 661 (A.F.C.M.R. 1986).

    g) Conviction for drug use affirmed where government introduced lab report and stipulation explaining the report. *United States v. Spann*, 24 M.J. 508 (A.F.C.M.R. 1987).

    h) Hair analysis. Evidence was legally and factually sufficient to sustain conviction for unlawful use of cocaine; hair analysis revealed presence of cocaine in hair shafts, there was expert testimony that presence of cocaine in hair shafts was metabolically explained by ingestion, and that it did not occur as a natural phenomenon, accused's own witness conceded that there was cocaine in the hair sample tested, and chain of custody established that the sample was from the accused. *United States v. Bush*, 44 M.J. 646 (A.F. Ct. Crim. App. 1996), *aff'd,* 47 M.J. 305 (C.A.A.F. 1997).

5. Knowledge.

   a) There is no express mention of a mens rea requirement in the text of Article 112a for the use, possession, or distribution of controlled substances; the article merely prohibits the "wrongful" use, possession, or distribution of various controlled substances. *See* UCMJ art. 112a. Likewise the MCM does not identify a mens rea in its description of the elements of these offenses. *See* MCM, pt. IV, ¶ 37b(2). However, the Court of Military Appeals (COMA) has long held that the absence of knowledge as to the presence of the substance in question or its contraband nature may give rise to a mistake or ignorance of fact defense to charges of use or possession of controlled substance. *E.g., United States v. Greenwood*, 19 C.M.R. 335 (C.M.A. 1955). Later, COMA explicitly held that court-martial panels must be instructed that an accused must knowingly possess or use a controlled substance to be criminally liable for such an act. *United States v. Mance*, 26 M.J. 244 (C.M.A. 1988).

   b) There are two discrete types of knowledge that are relevant to the offenses in question: knowledge of the very presence of the substance, and knowledge of the physical composition of the substance. *United States v. Mance*, 26 M.J. 244 (C.M.A. 1988); *United States v. Williams*, 37 M.J. 972 (A.C.M.R. 1993); *United States v. Heitkamp*, 65 M.J. 861 (A. Ct. Crim. App. 2007).

   (1) If an accused is unaware of the presence of a controlled substance in another, lawful substance, then the accused may have a defense of ignorance of fact. Such a circumstance may arise when a controlled substance is placed in a drink or other foodstuffs without the knowledge of the accused. The accused would lack the knowledge required for "use" of a controlled substance. *Mance*, 26 M.J. at 253-54. However, the accused may not 'deliberately avoid" knowledge of the nature of the substance. *United States v. Brown*, 50 M.J. 262 (C.A.A.F. 1999) (defendant must be aware of the high probability that the substance was of a contraband nature and deliberately contrive to avoid knowledge of the substance's nature).

   (2) Alternatively, the accused may be aware of the presence of the substance but incorrectly believe that it is innocuous. This absence of knowledge as to the contraband nature of a substance may give rise to a mistake of fact defense. In this circumstance, the accused lacks the knowledge required to establish that the use was "wrongful." *Id.* at 254.

   (3) To be guilty of wrongful possession of a controlled substance, the accused need only know about the presence and the identity of the substance. *United States v. Heitkamp*, 65 M.J. 861 (A. Ct. Crim. App. 2007).

   c) Intersection with mistake of law. *United States v. Heitkamp*, 65 M.J. 861 (A. Ct. Crim. App. 2007). Accused possessed methandienone, a Schedule III controlled substance, but thought it was legal to possess the steroid. To be guilty of wrongful possession of a controlled substance, the accused need only know about the presence and the identity of the substance. His knowledge of the unlawfulness of the contraband item is not a defense. "[I]f an accused knows the identity of a substance that he is possessing or using but does not know that such possession or use is illegal, his ignorance is immaterial . . . because ignorance of the law is no defense."

d) The presence of the controlled substance gives rise to a permissive inference that an accused possessed both types of knowledge required to establish wrongful possession or use. *Mance*, 26 M.J. at 254.

6. Applications.

a) Use of leftover prescription drugs for a different ailment than that for which they were prescribed does not necessarily constitute wrongful use as a matter of law. *United States v. Lancaster*, 36 M.J. 1115 (A.F.C.M.R. 1993).

b) One who knowingly ingests a controlled substance that he believes to be only cocaine, but actually contains cocaine laced with methamphetamine, may be found guilty of wrongful use of *both* substances; an accused need not know the exact pharmacological identity of the substance, but merely that it is contraband. *United States v. Stringfellow*, 32 M.J. 335 (C.M.A. 1991); *see United States v. Miles*, 31 M.J. 7 (C.M.A. 1990). *United States v. Alexander*, 32 M.J. 664 (A.C.M.R. 1991), *aff'd,* 34 M.J. 121 (C.M.A. 1992). In *United States v. Dillon*, 61 M.J. 221 (2005) (ecstasy and methamphetamine).

c) Accused not guilty of wrongful use of marijuana if he is a law enforcement official conducting legitimate law enforcement activities. *United States v. Flannigan*, 31 M.J. 240 (C.M.A. 1990); *see generally* TJAGSA Practice Note, *Lawfully Using Marijuana to Protect One's Cover*, ARMY LAW., Mar. 1991, at 47 (discusses *Flannigan*). This rule does not apply, however, to possession or use of drugs caused by addiction, incurred as a result of earlier drug use necessitated when supplier forced accused, a drug informant who was not acting with approval of law enforcement authorities, to use drugs to prove that he was not an informer, occurring after accused was no longer an informant and his use was not necessary to protect his life or his cover. *United States v. Wilson*, 44 M.J. 223 (C.A.A.F. 1996).

d) Prosecution may not argue that the defense of innocent ingestion of marijuana should be rejected by court members to discourage other soldiers from raising it. *United States v. Causey*, 37 M.J. 308 (C.M.A. 1993).

D. Possession.

1. Elements.

a) Possession of controlled substance.

b) Knowledge of possession.

c) Knowledge of contraband nature of substance.

d) Possession is wrongful, *i.e.*, without legal justification or authorization.

2. Possession Defined.

a) Possession means the exercise of control over something, including the power to preclude control by others. *United States v. Zubko*, 18 M.J. 378 (C.M.A. 1984); MCM, pt. IV, ¶ 37c(2).

b) More than one person may possess an item simultaneously.

c) Possession may be direct or constructive.

3. Constructive Possession.

   a) An accused constructively possesses a contraband item when he is knowingly in a position or had the right to exercise dominion and control over an item, either directly or through others. *United States v. Traveler*, 20 M.J. 35 (C.M.A. 1985).

   b) Mere association with one who is known to possess illegal drugs is not sufficient to convict on a theory of constructive possession. *United States v. Seger*, 25 M.J. 420 (C.M.A. 1988).

   c) Mere presence on the premises where a controlled substance is found or proximity to a proscribed drug is insufficient to convict on a theory of constructive possession. *United States v. Wilson*, 7 M.J. 290 (C.M.A. 1979); *United States v. Corpening*, 38 M.J. 605 (A.C.M.R. 1993) (presence in automobile in which contraband found, without more, legally insufficient to sustain conviction).

4. Innocent Possession.

   a) Accused's possession of drugs cannot be innocent if the accused neither destroys the drug immediately nor delivers them to the police. *United States v. Kunkle*, 23 M.J. 213 (C.M.A. 1987).

   b) Innocent or "inadvertent" possession. The "inadvertent" possession defense requires that the drugs were planted or left in the accused's possession without his knowledge, coupled with certain subsequent actions taken with an intent to immediately destroy the contraband or deliver it to law enforcement agents. Returning contraband drugs to a prior possessor or owner will not entitle an accused to claim innocent possession unless the accused inadvertently comes into possession of contraband and reasonably believes that he would be exposing himself to immediate physical danger unless he returned it to the prior possessor. *United States v. Angone*, 57 M.J. 70 (C.A.A.F. 2002).

5. Deliberate Avoidance. MCM, pt. IV, ¶ 37c(11).

   a) Deliberate avoidance may also be called "deliberate ignorance," or "conscious avoidance." This doctrine allows the fact finder to infer knowledge by the defendant of a particular fact if the defendant intentionally decides to avoid knowledge of that fact. *See generally United States v. Rodriguez*, 983 F.2d 455, 457 (2d Cir. 1993).

   b) The rationale for the conscious avoidance doctrine is that a defendant's affirmative efforts to "'see no evil' and 'hear no evil' do not somehow magically invest him with the ability to 'do no evil.'" *United States v. Di Tommaso*, 817 F.2d 201, 218 n.26 (2d Cir. 1987).

   c) *United States v. Brown*, 50 M.J. 262 (1999) (military judge erroneously gave deliberate avoidance (a.k.a. "ostrich") instruction when evidence did not reach "high plateau" required for the instruction); *see also United States v. Newman*, 14 M.J. 474 (C.M.A. 1983).

6. Attempted Possession. One who possesses a legal drug believing it to be an illegal drug is guilty of attempted possession. *United States v. Newak*, 15 M.J. 541 (A.F.C.M.R. 1982), *rev'd in part on other grounds*, 24 M.J. 238 (C.M.A. 1987). If the evidence is insufficient to identify the substance beyond a reasonable doubt, the accused may be guilty of attempted possession. *United States v. LaFontant*, 16 M.J. 236 (C.M.A. 1983).

7. Awareness of the presence of a controlled substance may be inferred from circumstantial evidence. MCM, pt. IV, ¶ 37c(2). *United States v. Mahan*, 1 M.J. 303 (C.M.A. 1976); *see generally* DA Pam 27-9, ¶ 7-3; Hug, *Presumptions and Inferences in Criminal Law*, 56 Mil. L. Rev. 81 (1972).

8. Applications.

   a) Accused properly convicted of possession with intent to distribute when accused purchased 4.1 grams of marijuana, distributed 2.8 grams, but did not realize that 1.3 grams leaked out of the bag and remained in his pocket. *United States v. Gonzalez*, No. 20080111 (A. Ct. Crim. App. Jun. 26, 2009).

   b) Accused in stockade is in "possession" of package of drugs mailed by him and returned to the stockade for inability to deliver. *United States v. Ronholt*, 42 C.M.R. 933 (N.C.M.R. 1970).

   c) Possession is not present where accused tells another to hold marijuana while the accused decides whether to accept it in payment for a car. *United States v. Burns*, 4 M.J. 573 (A.C.M.R. 1978).

   d) Mere speculation as to the identity of a substance by one non-expert witness is not legally sufficient evidence to prove possession of marijuana. *United States v. Nicholson*, 49 M.J. 478 (C.A.A.F. 1998).

   e) Accused who comes into possession of drugs and who intended to return them to the original possessor is guilty of wrongful possession unless returning the drugs to the original possessor was motivated by fear for personal safety or to protect the identity/ safety of an undercover investigator. *United States v. Kunkle*, 23 M.J. 213 (C.M.A. 1987); MCM, pt. IV, ¶ 37 (analysis).

   f) Possessing drugs for the purpose of giving them over to authorities is no offense. *United States v. Grover*, 27 C.M.R. 165 (C.M.A. 1958).

   g) No "usable quantity" defense. *United States v. Birbeck*, 35 M.J. 519 (A.F.C.M.R. 1992) (small quantity of cocaine was found in bindle and entire amount consumed in testing; possession of a controlled substance is criminal without regard to amount possessed).

   h) An accused who involuntarily comes into possession and intends to give it to authorities, but forgets to do so, has a legitimate defense. *United States v. Bartee*, 50 C.M.R. 51 (N.C.M.R. 1974).

   i) An accused who acts on a commander's suggestion to buy drugs in order to further a drug investigation is in innocent possession. *United States v. Russell*, 2 M.J. 433 (A.C.M.R. 1955).

   j) Possession is not "wrongful" where an enlisted pharmacy specialist, pursuant to his understanding of local practice, maintains an average stock of narcotic drugs in order to supply sudden pharmacy needs or fill an inventory shortfall. This is so even though the stock was in his possession outside the pharmacy and its existence was prohibited by regulations. The latter fact might justify prosecution for violation of the regulation. *United States v. West*, 34 C.M.R. 449 (C.M.A. 1964).

k) Specification charging accused with possession of marijuana with intent to distribute was sufficient despite not alleging element of wrongfulness. *United States v. Berner*, 32 M.J. 570 (A.C.M.R. 1991).

l) Possession is a lesser included offense of possession with intent to distribute. *United States v. Gould*, 13 M.J. 734 (A.C.M.R. 1982); *United States v. Burno*, 624 F.2d 95 (10th Cir. 1980).

E. Distribution.

1. MCM, pt. IV, ¶ 37c(3) states: "Distribute" means to deliver to the possession of another. "Deliver" means the actual, constructive, or attempted transfer of an item, whether or not there is an agency relationship.

2. Mens Rea.

a) Distribution is a general intent crime. *United States v. Brown*, 19 M.J. 63 (C.M.A. 1984).

b) The only mens rea necessary for wrongful distribution of controlled substances is the intent to perform the act of distribution. Distribution can occur even if the recipient is unaware of the presence of drugs. *United States v. Sorrell*, 23 M.J. 122 (C.M.A. 1986).

c) Knowledge of the presence and the character of the controlled substance is an essential requirement of wrongful distribution. *United States v. Crumley*, 31 M.J. 21 (C.M.A. 1990).

d) Distribution may continue, for purposes of establishing aider and abettor liability, after the actual transfer if the "criminal venture" contemplates the exchange of drugs for cash. *United States v. Speer*, 40 M.J. 230 (C.M.A. 1994).

3. Pleading. Wrongfulness is an essential element of distribution. Failure to allege wrongfulness may not be fatal if the specifications as a whole can be reasonably construed to embrace an allegation of the element of wrongfulness required for conviction. *United States v. Brecheen*, 27 M.J. 67 (C.M.A. 1988).

4. Applications.

a) Distribution can consist of passing drugs from one co-conspirator to another. *United States v. Tuero*, 26 M.J. 106 (C.M.A. 1988); *see United States v. Figueroa*, 28 M.J. 570 (N.M.C.M.R. 1989).

b) Distribution can consist of passing drugs back to the original supplier. *United States v. Herring*, 31 M.J. 637 (N.M.C.M.R. 1990); *see generally* TJAGSA Practice Note, *Distributing Drugs to the Drug Distributor*, ARMY LAW., Mar. 1991, at 44 (discussing *Herring*).

c) Distribution includes the attempted transfer of drugs. *United States v. Omick*, 30 M.J. 1122 (N.M.C.M.R. 1989); *see generally* TJAGSA Practice Note, *Does*

Drug Distribution Require Physical Transfer? ARMY LAW., Nov. 1990, at 44 (discussing *Omick*).

   d)   The *Swiderski* exception.

   (1) Sharing drugs is distribution. *United States v. Branch*, 483 F.2d 955 (9th Cir. 1973); *United States v. Ramirez*, 608 F.2d 1261 (9th Cir. 1979). However, when two individuals simultaneously and jointly acquire possession of a drug for their own use, intending to share it together, their only crime is joint possession. *United States v. Swiderski*, 548 F.2d 445 (2d Cir. 1977).

   (2) The *Swiderski* exception probably does not apply to the military. *See United States v. Manley*, 52 M.J. 748 (N-M. Ct. Crim. App. 2000); *United States v. Ratleff*, 34 M.J. 80 (C.M.A. 1992) (PFC Ratleff went to mess hall with PFC Jaundoo who had hidden hashish in a can; PFC Jaundoo carried the can back to a barracks room and then gave the can to PFC Ratleff who opened the can and gave the hashish back to PFC Jaundoo; PFC Ratleff's distribution conviction affirmed). *But see United States v. Hill*, 25 M.J. 411 (C.M.A. 1988) (dicta).

   (3) Examples of cases where evidence did not raise the *Swiderski* exception. *United States v. Hill*, 25 M.J. 411 (C.M.A. 1988); *United States v. Viser*, 27 M.J. 562 (A.C.M.R. 1988); *United States v. Allen*, 22 M.J. 512 (A.C.M.R. 1986); *United States v. Tracey*, 33 M.J. 142 (C.M.A. 1991); *United States v. Lippoldt*, 34 M.J. 523 (A.F.C.M.R. 1991); *United States v. Espronceda*, 36 M.J. 535 (A.F.C.M.R. 1992).

e)   An accused cannot aid and abet a distribution between two government agents, where accused's former "agent" became a government agent and sold to a person known by the accused to be a government agent and the accused did not ratify the sale or accept the proceeds. *United States v. Bretz*, 19 M.J. 224 (C.M.A. 1985); *United States v. Elliott*, 30 M.J. 1064 (A.C.M.R. 1990). *But cf. United States v. Dayton*, 29 M.J. 6 (C.M.A. 1989) (accused guilty of distribution from source of one government agent to another government agent); *United States v. Lubitz*, 40 M.J. 165 (C.M.A. 1994) (accused not a "mere conduit" for drug distribution when he acted as buyer of cocaine with money supplie by government agent and subsequently transferred drugs to another covert government agent).

f)   Evidence that the distribution was a sale for profit will normally be admissible on the merits. If not, it may be admissible for aggravation in sentencing in a guilty plea or in a contested case. *United States v. Vickers*, 13 M.J. 403 (C.M.A. 1982); *see United States v. Stokes*, 12 M.J. 229 (C.M.A. 1982).

g)   Possession and Distribution. The elements of possession with intent to distribute are "necessarily included" within elements of distribution of a controlled substance, so accused cannot be found guilty of possession of marijuana with intent to distribute and distribution of the same marijuana on the same day. *United States v. Savage*, 50 M.J. 244 (C.A.A.F. 1999); see also *United States v. Scalarone*, 52 M.J. 539 (N-M. Ct. Crim. App. 1999).

5.   Use of Firearms. Carrying a firearm during a drug trafficking crime is a violation of 18 U.S.C. § 924(g) and may be separately punished.

6. Use of a communication facility (*e.g.*, telephone, fax, beeper) to facilitate a drug transaction is a violation of 21 U.S.C. § 843(b) and may be separately punished.

F. Manufacture.

1. MCM, pt. IV, ¶ 37c(4) states: "Manufacture" means the production, preparation, propagation, compounding, or processing of a drug or other substance, either directly or indirectly or by extraction from substances of natural origin, or independently by means of chemical synthesis or by a combination of extraction and chemical synthesis and includes any packaging or repackaging of such substance or labeling or relabeling of its container. The term "production" as used above includes the planting, cultivating, growing, or harvesting of a drug or other substance.

2. The definition is drawn from 21 U.S.C. § 802 (14) and (21).

3. Psilocybin mushrooms. Appellant planted spores from "magic mushroom" kit, but they failed to germinate. For the offense to be complete, the controlled substance must be present in the cultivated planting. Here, appellant is guilty only of an attempt to produce a controlled substance. Appellant ordered the "magic mushroom" kit, followed the instructions, and planted the spores with the specific intent of growing the contraband, acts that amounted to more than mere preparation. *United States v. Lee*, 61 M.J. 627 (C.G. Ct. Crim. App. 2005).

G. Introduction.

1. Introduction means to bring into or onto an installation, vessel, vehicle, or aircraft used by or under control of the Armed Forces. Installation is broadly defined and includes posts, camps, and stations. *See generally United States v. Jones*, 6 C.M.R. 80 (C.M.A. 1952) (Augsburg Autobahn Snack Bar a station).

2. An accused cannot be convicted of aiding and abetting introduction of marijuana by OSI agent where accused had already sold marijuana to agent off base and marijuana was agent's sole property when agent brought it onto base. *United States v. Mercer*, 18 M.J. 644 (A.F.C.M.R. 1984).

3. Accused must have actual knowledge that he is entering an installation to be guilty of introduction. *United States v. Thomas*, 65 M.J. 132 (C.A.A.F. 2007).

H. Drug Paraphernalia.

1. Because possession of "drug paraphernalia" constitutes only a remote and indirect threat to good order and discipline, it cannot be charged under Article 134(1) as an offense which is directly and palpably prejudicial to good order and discipline. This offense therefore must be charged under Article 92 as the violation of a general order/regulation or under Article 134(3), assimilating a local state statute under 18 U.S.C. §13. *United States v. Caballero*, 49 C.M.R. 594 (C.M.A. 1975)). The AFCCA has interpreted *Caballero* to mean that when a punitive lawful general order or regulation proscribing the possession of drug paraphernalia exists, the offense must be charged under Art. 92(1), UCMJ, and not Art. 134. *See also* 2008 MCM, pt IV, ¶ 60c.(2)(b); *United States v. Borunda*, 67 M.J. 607 (A.F. Ct. Crim. App. 2009). In the absence of a lawful general order or regulation, the Government is at liberty to charge the possession of drug paraphernalia under either Art. 92(3) or Art. 134. *Borunda*, 67 M.J. at 607.

2. Most installations have promulgated local punitive regulations dealing with drug paraphernalia.

3. The DEA model statute has come under attack for being unconstitutionally vague and overbroad. *Record Revolution No. 6, Inc. v. City of Parma*, 638 F.2d 916 (6th Cir. 1980), *vacated and remanded*, 451 U.S. 1013 (1981). *See generally Hoffman Estates v. Flipside, Hoffman Estates*, 455 U.S. 489 (1981) (ordinance requiring a business to obtain a license if it sells any items "designed or marketed for use with illegal cannabis or drugs" upheld; DEA code as adopted in Ohio struck down).

4. Military regulations have been challenged for vagueness and overbreadth. *United States v. Sweney*, 48 C.M.R. 476 (A.C.M.R. 1974) (regulation upheld as being neither vague nor overbroad); *see also United States v. Cannon*, 13 M.J. 777 (A.C.M.R. 1982) (upholding regulation prohibiting possession of instruments or devices that might be used to administer or dispense prohibited drugs). *See generally United States v. Clarke*, 13 M.J. 566 (A.C.M.R. 1982); *United States v. Bradley*, 15 M.J. 843 (A.F.C.M.R. 1983); *United States v. Hester*, 17 M.J. 1094 (A.F.C.M.R. 1984).

5. To show violation of a regulation by possessing drug paraphernalia, the government need only prove that the accused exercised dominion and control over the paraphernalia. *United States v. McKnight*, 30 M.J. 205 (C.M.A. 1990). Prosecutors must also establish a nexus between drug use and an article that is not intrinsically drug-related. *United States v. Camacho*, 58 M.J. 624 (N-M. Ct. Crim. App. 2003) (a butane torch).

6. Applications.

   a) Regulations will be closely scrutinized. Bindles, scales, zip-lock bags, and other materials associated with use or ingestion of drugs did not fall within regulatory prohibition of "drug abuse paraphernalia" of Navy Instruction. *United States v. Painter*, 39 M.J. 578 (N.M.C.M.R. 1993) (conviction set aside).

   b) Written instructions for producing controlled substances could constitute "drug paraphernalia" within meaning of Air Force Regulation. *United States v. McDavid*, 37 M.J. 861 (A.F.C.M.R. 1993).

I. Multiplicity.

1. Simultaneous possession of different drugs constitutes only one offense for sentencing. *United States v. Hughes*, 1 M.J. 346 (C.M.A. 1976); *United States v. Griffen*, 8 M.J. 66 (C.M.A. 1979). Simultaneous use of two substances is not necessarily multiplicious for findings but may be unreasonable multiplication of charges. *United States v. Ray*, 51 M.J. 511 (N-M. Ct. Crim. App. 1999) *overruled on other grounds by United States v. Quiroz*, 53 M.J. 600 (N-M.C.C.A. 2000). Not multiplicious to charge two separate specifications for the simultaneous use of ecstasy and methamphetamine. *United States v. Dillon*, 61 M.J. 221 (2005). Simultaneous distribution of two different substances is not multiplicious but may constitute unreasonable multiplication of charges. *See United States v. Inthavong*, 48 M.J. 628 (Army Ct. Crim. App. 1998).

2. No distinction between marijuana and hashish. *United States v. Kelly*, 527 F.2d 961 (9th Cir. 1976); *United States v. Lee*, 1 M.J. 15 (C.M.A. 1975); *United States v. Nelson*, 47 C.M.R. 395 (A.C.M.R. 1973).

3. Sales at the same place between same parties but fifteen minutes apart were separately punishable. *United States v. Hernandez*, 16 M.J. 674 (A.C.M.R. 1983).

4. Possession of drugs from one cache at another time and place constitutes a separate offense warranting separate punishment. *United States v. Marbury*, 4 M.J. 823 (A.C.M.R. 1978).

5. Solicitation to sell and transfer of drugs are separately punishable when respective acts occurred at separate times (four hours apart) and at separate locations. *United States v. Irving*, 3 M.J. 6 (C.M.A. 1977).

6. Use was separately punishable from possession and sale where quantity used was not same as quantity possessed. *United States v. Smith*, 14 M.J. 430 (C.M.A. 1983); *see United States v. Nixon*, 29 M.J. 505 (A.C.M.R. 1989). But if quantity used and possessed is the same, possession charge is multiplicious for findings. *United States v. Bullington*, 18 M.J. 164 (C.M.A. 1984); *see United States v. Hogan*, 20 M.J. 221 (C.M.A. 1985). *See generally United States v. Cumber*, 30 M.J. 736 (A.F.C.M.R. 1990) (use and distribution of same drug not multiplicious for sentencing).

7. Attempted sale of a proscribed drug and possession of the same substance were so integrated as to merge as a single event subject only to a single punishment. *United States v. Smith*, 1 M.J. 260 (C.M.A. 1976); *see also United States v. Clarke*, 13 M.J. 566 (A.C.M.R. 1982).

8. Where charges of possession and transfer of heroin were based on accused's retention of some heroin after transferring a quantity of the drug to two persons who were to sell it on the open market as accused's agents, the two offenses were treated as single for purposes of punishment. *United States v. Irving*, 3 M.J. 6 (C.M.A. 1977).

9. Possession of one packet of drugs and simultaneous distribution of a separate packet of drugs was separately punishable. *United States v. Wilson*, 20 M.J. 3 (C.M.A. 1985) (summary disposition). Possession with intent to distribute 35 hits of LSD was separately punishable from the simultaneous distribution of 15 hits of LSD. *United States v. Coast*, 20 M.J. 3 (C.M.A. 1985) (possession of LSD with intent to distribute was multiplicious with distribution of LSD); *see also United States v. Kitts*, 23 M.J. 105 (C.M.A. 1986); *United States v. Muller*, 21 M.J. 205 (C.M.A. 1986); *United States v. Jennings*, 20 M.J. 223 (C.M.A. 1985). Sale and possession of a separate, cross-town cache were separately punishable. *United States v. Isaacs*, 19 M.J. 220 (C.M.A. 1985). Where the accused bought a large amount of marijuana to be sold in smaller quantities at a profit, where he made a final sale of approximately one eighth of it to a friend, and where the remainder was retained for future sales or other disposition, different legal and societal norms were violated by the sale and possession, and separate punishments were proper. *United States v. Wessels*, 8 M.J. 747 (A.F.C.M.R. 1980); *accord United States v. Chisholm*, 10 M.J. 795 (A.F.C.M.R. 1981); *United States v. DeSoto*, 15 M.J. 645 (N.M.C.M.R. 1982); *United States v. Anglin*, 15 M.J. 1010 *United States v. Ansley*, 16 M.J. 584 (A.C.M.R. 1983); *United States v. Worden*, 17 M.J. 887 (A.F.C.M.R. 1984).

10. Possession and distribution of cocaine on divers occasions may be separate offenses under certain facts. *United States v. Bowers*, 20 M.J. 1003 (A.F.C.M.R. 1985) (considering guilty plea and facts before the court).

11. Distribution of a controlled substance necessarily includes possession with intent to distribute. *United States v. Savage*, 50 M.J. 244 (C.A.A.F. 1999); *United States v. Scalarone*, 52 M.J. 539 (N-M. Ct. Crim. App. 1999).

12. Introduction of drugs onto military installation and sale of portion on same day not multiplicious for sentencing. *United States v. Beardsley*, 13 M.J. 657 (N.M.C.M.R.

1982). Introduction and possession are, however, multiplicious. *United States v. Decker*, 19 M.J. 351 (C.M.A. 1985); *United States v. Roman-Luciano*, 13 M.J. 490 (C.M.A. 1982) (summary disposition); *United States v. Miles*, 15 M.J. 431 (C.M.A. 1983); *United States v. Hendrickson*, 16 M.J. 62 (C.M.A. 1983). But if the amount possessed is greater than the amount introduced, possession of the excess amount may not be multiplicious for any purpose if the excess amount is explained on the record. *United States v. Morrison*, 18 M.J. 108 (C.M.A. 1984) (summary disposition) (excess amount belonged to someone else); *cf. United States v. Hill*, 18 M.J. 459 (possession of excess amount dismissed where not explained on the record). Finally, introduction and possession with intent to distribute are not multiplicious. *United States v. Zupancic*, 18 M.J. 387 (C.M.A. 1984).

13. Introduction with intent to distribute and distribution are multiplicious for findings. *United States v. Wheatcraft*, 23 M.J. 687 (A.F.C.M.R. 1986); *contra United States v. Beesler*, 16 M.J. 988 (A.C.M.R. 1983).

14. Possession and distribution when time, place, and amount are the same are multiplicious for findings. *United States v. Zubko*, 18 M.J. 378 (C.M.A. 1984); *United States v. Brown*, 19 M.J. 63 (C.M.A. 1984).

15. Larceny of and possession of same drugs not multiplicious for sentencing. *United States v. Logan*, 13 M.J. 821 (A.C.M.R. 1982).

16. Possession and possession with intent to distribute are multiplicious for sentencing. The appropriate remedy is dismissal of the possession specification. *United States v. Forance*, 12 M.J. 312 (C.M.A. 1981) (summary disposition); *United States v. Conley*, 14 M.J. 229 (C.M.A. 1982) (summary disposition).

17. Possession of drugs and drug paraphernalia at the same time and place are multiplicious for sentencing. *United States v. Bell*, 16 M.J. 204 (C.M.A. 1983) (summary disposition).

18. Possession with intent to distribute and introduction are multiplicious. *United States v. Antonitis*, 29 M.J. 217 (C.M.A. 1989), *aff'd*, 32 M.J. 315 (C.M.A. 1991).

19. Distribution by injection and distribution of tablets of the same drug are multiplicious. *United States v. Gumbee*, 30 M.J. 736 (A.F.C.M.R. 1990).

20. Use and distribution based upon accused smoking a marijuana cigarette then passing it to a friend were not multiplicious for sentencing purposes. *United States v. Ticehurst*, 33 M.J. 965 (N.M.C.M.R. 1991).

21. For an example of prejudicial multiplicious pleading, see generally *United States v. Sturdivant*, 13 M.J. 323 (C.M.A. 1982) (charges dismissed where accused's phone conversation arguably setting up buy of his monthly marijuana ration led to 10 specifications being charged, a general court-martial conviction, and a sentence of dishonorable discharge, 3 years confinement and total forfeitures).

22. Simultaneous distribution not multiplicious. *United States v. Inthavong*, 48 M.J. 628 (C.A.A.F. 1998).

23. The offenses of introduction of a controlled substance, with the aggravating factor of intent to distribute, and distribution of the same controlled substance are not multiplicious. *United States v. Monday*, 52 M.J. 625 (Army Ct. Crim. App. 1999).

J. Special Rules of Evidence.

1. The laboratory report qualifies as a business record or public record exception to the hearsay rule and can be admitted into evidence once its authenticity is established. MRE 803(6) and (8); *United States v. Evans*, 45 C.M.R. 353 (C.M.A. 1972); *United States v. Miller*, 49 C.M.R. 380 (C.M.A. 1974); *United States v. Strangstalien*, 7 M.J. 225 (C.M.A. 1979); *United States v. Vietor*, 10 M.J. 69 (C.M.A. 1980).

2. The admission of a laboratory report into evidence as either a business or public record does not give accused an automatic right to the attendance of the person who performed the test. Rather, the accused must make a showing as to the necessity for producing the witness. *United States v. Vietor*, 10 M.J. 69 DA Form 4137 (the chain of custody form) is admissible as either a business record or public record exception to the hearsay rule. MRE 803(6) and (8). *Contra United States v. Nault*, 4 M.J. 318 (C.M.A. 1978); *United States v. Porter*, 7 M.J. 30 (C.M.A. 1979); *United States v. Neutze*, 7 M.J. 32 (C.M.A. 1979); *United States v. Oates*, 560 F.2d 45 (2nd Cir. 1977); *United States v. Helton*, 10 M.J. 820 *United States v. Scoles*, 33 C.M.R. 226 (C.M.A. 1963).

3. When dealing with fungible evidence such as drugs, military courts have traditionally required that an unbroken chain of custody be established to show that the drugs seized were in fact the drugs tested at the lab, and that they were not tampered with prior to testing. The Court of Military Appeals broadened this approach and declared that even fungible evidence may be introduced without showing an unbroken chain of custody so long as the government can establish that the substance was contained in a "readily identifiable" package and that the contents of that package were not altered in any significant way. *United States v. Parker*, 10 M.J. 415 (C.M.A. 1981); *United States v. Lewis*, 11 M.J. 188 (C.M.A. 1981); *United States v. Madela*, 12 M.J. 118 (C.M.A. 1981); *United States v. Ettelson*, 13 M.J. 348, 350-51 (C.M.A. 1982). *See generally United States v. Morsell*, 30 M.J. 808 *United States v. Hudson*, 20 M.J. 607 (A.C.M.R. 1985).

4. The chemical nature of a drug may be established without the aid of a laboratory report or expert witness but with the testimony of a lay witness familiar with the physical attributes of the drug. *United States v. Tyler*, 17 M.J. 381 (C.M.A. 1984) (lay witness qualified to testify what used was cocaine despite alcohol intoxication at time of use). Tests administered by investigators to determine lay witness' ability to identify drugs were relevant to ability to identify drugs at time of use. *Id.*; *United States v. Coen*, 46 C.M.R. 1201 (N.C.M.R. 1972) (accused's statement); *United States v. Torrence*, 3 M.J. 804 (C.G.C.M.R. 1977) (accomplice witness); *United States v. Watkins*, 5 M.J. 612 (A.C.M.R. 1978) (informer and CID agent); *United States v. Jenkins*, 5 M.J. 905 (A.C.M.R. 1978) (accused's admission is not enough to establish nature of drugs without corroborative evidence); *United States v. White*, 9 M.J. 168 (C.M.A. 1980) (accused's corroborated extrajudicial statement); *United States v. Morris*, 13 M.J. 666 (A.F.C.M.R. 1982) (transferee and witness); *United States v. Jessen*, 12 M.J. 122, 126 (C.M.A. 1981) ("simulated smoking" by undercover agent); *cf. United States v. Hickman*, 15 M.J. 674 (A.F.C.M.R. 1983) (witness merely calling the substance "marijuana" at trial insufficient); *but see United States v. LaFontant*, 16 M.J. 236 (C.M.A. 1983) (if evidence insufficient to identify substance beyond a reasonable doubt, accused may be guilty of an attempt).

5. The buyer in a drug sale case is an accomplice, and the defense is entitled to an accomplice instruction. *United States v. Hopewell*, 4 M.J. 806 (A.F.C.M.R. 1978); *United States v. Helton*, 10 M.J. 820 (A.F.C.M.R. 1981); *United States v. Scoles*, 33 C.M.R. 226 (C.M.A. 1963). No such instruction is required if buyer was Government informant. *United States v. Hand*, 8 M.J. 701 (A.F.C.M.R. 1980), *rev'd on other grounds*, 11 M.J. 321 (C.M.A. 1981); *United States v. Kelker*, 50 C.M.R. 410 (A.C.M.R. 1975).

K. Defenses.

1. The fact that the amount of controlled substance involved in any given offense is *de minimis* is no defense except as it may bear on the issues of the accused's knowledge. *United States v. Alvarez*, 27 C.M.R. 98 (C.M.A. 1958); *United States v. Nabors*, C.M.R. 101 (C.M.A. 1958); *see* MCM, pt. IV, ¶ 37c(7).

2. Knowledge, ignorance and mistake defenses.

   a) Ignorance of the law (not knowing that the substance was illegal) is no defense. *United States v. Mance*, 26 M.J. 244 (C.M.A. 1988); *United States v. Greenwood*, 19 C.M.R. 335 (C.M.A. 1955); *United States v. Heitkamp*, 65 M.J. 861 (A. Ct. Crim. App. 2007) (accused stated that he did not know it was illegal to possess methandienone, a Schedule III controlled substance).

   b) Ignorance of the physical presence of the substance is a legitimate defense ("I didn't know there was anything in the box . . . the locker . . . my pocket . . . the pipe."). *United States v. Mance*, 26 M.J. 244 (C.M.A. 1988).

   (1) Ignorance need not be reasonable, only honest. *United States v. Hansen*, 20 C.M.R. 298 (C.M.A. 1955).

   (2) Knowledge that a container was present, without knowledge of the presence of the substance within, will not defeat the defense. *United States v. Avant*, 42 C.M.R. 692 (A.C.M.R. 1970).

   (3) The accused's suspicion that a substance may be present is insufficient for guilt. *United States v. Whitehead*, 48 C.M.R. 344 (N.C.M.R. 1973); *United States v. Heicksen*, 40 C.M.R. 475 (A.B.R. 1969). *But see United States v. Valle-Valdez*, 554 F.2d 911 (9th Cir. 1977).

   (4) Under some circumstances deliberate ignorance of a fact can create the same criminal liability as actual knowledge. *United States v. Newman*, 14 M.J. 474 (C.M.A. 1983). *See supra* ¶ IX.C.5., this chapter.

   c) Ignorance or mistake as to "the physical composition or character" of the substance is a legitimate defense. ("I thought it was powdered sugar." "I didn't know what it was"). *United States v. Mance, supra*; *United States v. Greenwood*, 19 C.M.R. 335 (C.M.A. 1955); *United States v. Ashworth*, 47 C.M.R. 702 (A.F.C.M.R. 1973).

   (1) The ignorance or mistake need not be reasonable. *United States v. Fleener*, 43 C.M.R. 974 (A.F.C.M.R. 1971).

   (2) Knowledge of the name of the substance will not necessarily defeat the defense; to be guilty, the accused must know the "narcotic quality" of the substance. *United States v. Crawford*, 20 C.M.R. 233 (C.M.A. 1955); *United States v. Baylor*, 37 C.M.R. 122 (C.M.A. 1967) (Court approves instruction that accused "must know of the presence of the substance and its narcotic nature").

   (3) The mistake must be one which, if true, would exonerate the accused. *United States v. Jefferson*, 13 M.J. 779 (A.C.M.R. 1982) (mistake not exonerating where accused accepted heroin thinking he was getting hashish); *see also United States v. Morales*, 577 F.2d 769, 776 (2nd Cir.

1978); *United States v. Jewell*, 532 F.2d 697, 698 (9th Cir.) (en banc), *cert. denied*, 426 U.S. 951 (1978).

3. Defense of innocent ingestion does not require corroborative witnesses or direct evidence. *United States v. Lewis*, 51 M.J. 376 (C.A.A.F. 1999).

4. The defense of innocent possession does not apply in those cases where an accused exercises control over an item for the purpose of preventing its imminent seizure by law enforcement or other authorities, even if he intends to thereafter expeditiously destroy the item. *United States v. Angone*, 54 M.J. 945 (A. Ct. Crim. App. 2001), *aff'd,* 57 M.J. 70 (C.A.A.F. 2002); s*ee supra* ¶ IX.C.4, this chapter.

5. Regulatory immunity. Issue of whether accused was entitled to regulatory exemptions of Army Regulation 600-85 were waived if not raised at trial. *United States v. Gladdis*, 12 M.J. 1005 (A.C.M.R. 1982); *United States v. Mika*, 17 M.J. 812 (A.C.M.R. 1984).

6. Entrapment. *See infra* ch. 5, ¶ VII.

THIS PAGE INTENTIONALLY LEFT BLANK

CHAPTER 5: DEFENSES

I. "SPECIAL DEFENSES" VS. "OTHER DEFENSES."

Special defenses, the military's equivalent to affirmative defenses, are those which deny, wholly or partially, criminal responsibility for the objective acts committed, but do not deny that those acts were committed by the accused. Other defenses, such as alibi and mistaken identity, deny commission of the culpable act or other elements of the crime. R.C.M. 916(a).

II. PROCEDURE.

A. Raising a Defense.

1. The military judge must instruct upon all special defenses raised by the evidence. The test of whether a defense is raised is whether the record contains some evidence as to each element of the defense to which the trier of fact may attach credit if it so desires. *United States v. Ferguson*, 15 M.J. 12 (C.M.A. 1983); *United States v. Tan*, 43 C.M.R. 636 (A.C.M.R. 1971); *see also United States v. Jackson*, 12 M.J. 163 (C.M.A. 1982); *United States v. Jett*, 14 M.J. 941 (A.C.M.R. 1982). Generally, the reasonableness of the evidence is irrelevant to the military judge's determination to instruct. *United States v. Thomas*, 43 C.M.R. 89 (C.M.A. 1971); *United States v. Symister*, 19 M.J. 503 (A.F.C.M.R. 1984).

2. A defense may be raised by evidence presented by the defense, the Government, or the court-martial. R.C.M. 916(b) discussion; *United States v. Rose*, 28 M.J. 132 (C.M.A. 1989).

3. In deciding whether the defense is raised, the military judge is not to judge credibility or prejudge the evidence and preclude its introduction before the court members. *United States v. Tulin*, 14 M.J. 695 (N.M.C.M.R. 1982).

4. A defense is not raised, however, if it is wholly incredible or unworthy of belief. *United States v. Brown*, 19 C.M.R. 363 (C.M.A. 1955); *United States v. Franklin*, 4 M.J. 635 (A.F.C.M.R. 1977).

5. Appellate military courts are very generous in finding that a defense has been raised. *See, e.g., United States v. Goins*, 37 C.M.R. 396 (C.M.A. 1967) (self-defense raised against charge of assault with intent to commit rape). Any doubt whether the evidence is sufficient to require an instruction should be resolved in favor of the accused. *United States v. Steinruck*, 11 M.J. 322 (C.M.A. 1981); *United States v. Jenkins*, 59 M.J. 893 (A. Ct. Crim. App. 2004).

6. In a bench trial, the impact of the raised defense is resolved by the military judge, *sub silentio*, in reaching a determination on the merits.

7. Burden of Proof. Except for the defense of lack of mental responsibility and the defense of mistake of fact as to age as described in pt. IV, ¶ 45c(2) in a prosecution of carnal knowledge, the prosecution shall have the burden of proving beyond a reasonable doubt that the defense did not exist. The accused has the burden of proving the defense of lack of mental responsibility by clear and convincing evidence, and has the burden of proving mistake of fact as to age in a carnal knowledge prosecution by a preponderance of the evidence. R.C.M. 916(b).

B. Advising the Accused. If in the course of a guilty plea trial, the accused's comments or any other evidence raises a defense, the military judge must explain the elements of the defense to the accused. *See generally* UCMJ art. 45(a). The accused's comments raising the defense need not be credible. *United States v. Lee*, 16 M.J. 278 (C.M.A. 1983). Subsequently, if the accused does not negate the defense or other evidence belies the accused's negation of the defense, the military judge must withdraw the guilty plea, enter a plea of not guilty for the accused, and proceed to trial on the merits. *United States v. Jemmings*, 1 M.J. 414 (C.M.A. 1976).

C. Instructions.

1. In a members trial, the military judge must instruct the members, *sua sponte*, regarding all special defenses raised by the evidence. *United States v. Williams*, 21 M.J. 360 (C.M.A. 1986); *United States v. Sawyer*, 4 M.J. 64 (C.M.A. 1977); *United States v. Graves*, 1 M.J. 50 (C.M.A. 1975); R.C.M. 920(e)(3).

2. In instructing a military jury on a defense, the judge is under no obligation to summarize the evidence, but if he undertakes to do so, the summary must be fair and adequate. *United States v. Nickoson*, 35 C.M.R. 312 (C.M.A. 1965).

3. While the military judge must instruct upon every special defense in issue, there is no sua sponte duty to instruct upon every fact that may support a given defense. *United States v. Sanders*, 41 M.J. 485 (C.A.A.F. 1995) (holding no plain error to fail to mention victim's alleged invitation to assault).

D. Consistency of Defenses.

1. Generally, conflicting defenses may be raised and pursued at trial. R.C.M. 916(b) (discussion); *see also United States v. Viola*, 26 M.J. 822, 827-28 (A.C.M.R. 1988), *aff'd* 27 M.J. 456 (C.M.A. 1988); Nagle, *Inconsistent Defenses in Criminal Cases*, 92 Mil. L. Rev. 77 (1981). *See generally United States v. Garcia*, 1 M.J. 26 (C.M.A. 1975) (alibi and entrapment); *United States v. Walker*, 45 C.M.R. 150 (C.M.A. 1972) (lack of mental responsibility and self-defense); *United States v. Lincoln*, 38 C.M.R. 128 (C.M.A. 1967) (accident and self-defense); *United States v. Snyder*, 21 C.M.R. 14 (C.M.A. 1956) (heat of passion/voluntary manslaughter and self-defense); *United States v. Ravine*, 11 M.J. 325 (C.M.A. 1981) (entrapment and agency).

2. The defense of self-defense is eviscerated by the defendant's testimony that he did not inflict the injury, regardless of what other evidence might show. *United States v. Ducksworth*, 33 C.M.R. 47 (C.M.A. 1963); *United States v. Bellamy*, 47 C.M.R. 319 (A.C.M.R. 1973); *see also United States v. Crabtree*, 32 C.M.R. 652 (A.B.R. 1962) (both duress and denial may not be raised).

E. Burden of Proof.

1. Lack of mental responsibility. The accused has the burden of proving this defense by clear and convincing evidence. UCMJ Art. 50a(b); R.C.M. 916(b).

2. Mistake of fact as to age of victim of carnal knowledge. The accused has the burden of proving this defense by a preponderance of the evidence. The mistake must be both honest and reasonable. UCMJ Art. 120(d). *Cf. United States v. Strode*, 43 M.J. 29 (1995) (holding honest and reasonable mistake of fact as to age of victim of indecent acts with child may be a defense if acts would otherwise be lawful if victim was over age 16).

3. All other defenses. If a defense is raised, the prosecution then has the burden of proving beyond a reasonable doubt that the defense does not exist. R.C.M. 916(b); *United States v. Verdi*, 5 M.J. 330 (C.M.A. 1978).

III. ACCIDENT.

A. Defined. R.C.M. 916(f). To be excusable as an accident, the act resulting in death or injury must have been the result of doing a lawful act in a lawful manner, free of negligence and unaccompanied by any criminally careless or reckless conduct. *United States v. Rodriguez*, 31 M.J. 150 (C.M.A. 1990); *United States v. Moyler*, 47 C.M.R. 82, 85 (A.C.M.R. 1973). Accident is an unexpected act not due to negligence. It is not the unexpected consequence of a deliberate act. *United States v. Pemberton*, 36 C.M.R. 239 (C.M.A. 1966); R.C.M. 916(f). *See generally* TJAGSA Practice Note. *The Defense of Accident: More Limited Than You Might Think*, ARMY LAW., Jan. 1989, at 45.

> 1. The lawful act. The unlawful nature of an accused's actions are apparent when performed in the course of committing a malum in se offense, *e.g.*, robbery. Such is not the case, however, when a malum prohibitum offense is involved. In *United States v. Sandoval*, 15 C.M.R. 61 (C.M.A. 1954), the accused was charged with killing a fellow soldier. He claimed that the death resulted from an accidentally inflicted gunshot wound. The government argued that accident was not available as a defense because the accused's possession of the murder weapon was a violation of local regulations. The Court of Military Appeals' decision implied that violation of the regulation made the accused's act per se illegal and thus precluded access to the accident defense. Eighteen years later in *United States v. Small*, 45 C.M.R. 700 (A.C.M.R. 1972), the Army Court of Military Review stated that an accident instruction could be denied only if the act, illegal as violative of a general regulation, was the proximate cause of the injury inflicted. *See also United States v. Tucker*, 38 C.M.R. 349 (C.M.A. 1968); *United States v. Taliau*, 7 M.J. 845 (A.C.M.R. 1979).
>
> 2. The unexpected act. If an act is specifically intended and directed at another, the fact that the ultimate consequence of the act is unintended or unforeseen does not raise the accident defense.
>
>> a) *United States v. McMonagle*, 38 M.J. 53 (C.M.A. 1993) (the defense of accident is not raised where accused engages a target in a combat zone that turns out to be a noncombatant; the death of a human being is neither unexpected nor unforeseen under these circumstances).
>>
>> b) *United States v. Femmer*, 34 C.M.R. 138 (C.M.A. 1964) (no instruction on accident was required where the accused charged with aggravated assault admitted that the victim was injured by a razor blade in accused's hand which he used in a calculated effort to push the victim away from him. Because the injury resulted from an act intentionally directed at the victim, and the accused knew he held the razor blade when he carried out the act, accident of the kind that would absolve one of criminal liability was not involved).
>>
>> c) Accident is not synonymous with unintended injury. A particular act may be directed at another without any intention to inflict injury, but if the natural and direct consequence of the act results in injury, the wrong is not excusable because of accident. *United States v. Pemberton*, 36 C.M.R. 239 (C.M.A. 1968) (accused's act of struggling with victim over a broken beer bottle was not directed at the victim but rather at wresting the bottle from the victim. Accident defense was therefore available although the judge in this case instructed improperly).
>>
>> d) In military law, the defense of accident excuses a lawful act, in a lawful manner, which causes an unintentional and unexpected result. *United States v. Marbury*, 50 M.J. 526 (A. Ct. Crim. App. 1999), *aff'd* 56 M.J. 12 (C.A.A.F. 2001) (defense of accident did not apply where the accused intentionally engaged in an

offer type assault with a knife against a drunk and combative victim who was skilled in martial arts training).

3. Lawful manner. R.C.M. 916(f) discussion. The defense of accident is not available when the act which caused the death, injury, or event was a negligent act.

   a) *United States v. Sandoval*, 15 C.M.R. 61 (C.M.A. 1954) (pushing door open with a loaded weapon does not constitute due care to allow accused to interpose accident defense to homicide).

   b) *United States v. Redding*, 34 C.M.R. 22 (C.M.A. 1963) (in the course of playing "quick draw," accused shot a friend with a pistol. Even though the evidence established that the injury was unintentionally inflicted, no accident instruction was required because of the accused's culpable negligence).

   c) *United States v. Moyler*, 47 C.M.R. 82 (A.C.M.R. 1973) (carrying a weapon within the base camp with a magazine inserted, a round chambered, the safety off, and the selector on automatic, constitutes negligence as a matter of law). *See also United States v. Rodriguez*, 8 M.J. 648 (A.F.C.M.R. 1979).

   d) *United States v. Leach*, 22 M.J. 738 (N.M.C.M.R. 1986) (swinging a knife upwards in close quarters of victim was negligent, so the accident defense was not available).

   e) *United States v. Davis*, 53 M.J. 202 (C.A.A.F. 2000) (where the accused admitted that he was negligent by failing to properly secure his infant daughter in her car seat, the military judge did not err by failing to instruct *sua sponte* on the affirmative defense of accident).

   f) *United States v. Jenkins*, 59 M.J. 893 (A. Ct. Crim. App. 2004) (holding the military judge erred in refusing to give a requested accident instruction when there was evidence that the accused showed sufficient due care in firing a pistol).

   g) *United States v. Ferguson*, 15 M.J. 12 (C.M.A. 1983) (waving a loaded shotgun without placing the safety in operation was a negligent act).

4. Negligent self-defense. Acting in self-defense can be the lawful act in a lawful manner for purposes of the accident defense. Negligent self-defense would deprive an accused of the accident defense. *See United States v. Lett*, 9 M.J. 602 (A.F.C.M.R. 1980) (using switchblade knife as passive deterrent was negligent self-defense); *United States v. Taliau*, 7 M.J. 845 (A.C.M.R. 1979) (unintentional injury to innocent third party excused where accused was engaging in lawful self-defense); *see also United States v. Jenkins*, 59 M.J. 893 (Army Ct. Crim. App. 2004) (accident and defense of another). Instructions: MJ should instruct on both doctrines where death of a victim is unintended and deadly force is not authorized. *See* DA PAM 27-9, Military Judges' Benchbook ¶¶ 5-2, 5-4; *United States v. Jones*, 3 M.J. 279 (C.M.A. 1977); *United States v. Perry*, 36 C.M.R. 377 (C.M.A. 1966).

B. Assault by Culpable Negligence and the Defense of Accident.

1. Unavailability of the defense of accident because of the accused's failure to act with due care does not establish assault under the theory of a culpably negligent act. *See United States v. Tucker*, 38 C.M.R. 349 (C.M.A. 1968).

2. When raised by evidence, "defense" of accident applies to all allegations of assault; if accused is successful in raising reasonable doubt as to any requisite *mens rea* element, result is acquittal. *United States v. Curry*, 38 M.J. 77 (C.M.A. 1993).

IV. DEFECTIVE CAUSATION / INTERVENING CAUSE.

A. Defined. The accused is not criminally responsible for the loss/damage/injury if his or her act or omission was not a proximate cause.

1. Accused's act may be "proximate" even if it is not the sole or latest cause. *United States v. Moglia*, 3 M.J. 216 (C.M.A. 1977); *United States v. Taylor*, 44 M.J. 254 (C.A.A.F. 1996) (accused entitled to present evidence of negligent medical care given by paramedics to drowning victim even if eventual death did not result solely from such negligent medical care). *But see United States v. Reveles*, 41 M.J. 388 (C.A.A.F. 1995) (possibility that victim's death was caused by negligence of medical personnel subsequent to injury inflicted by accused was no defense because medical negligence did not loom so large that accused's act was not a substantial factor in victim's death).

2. The accused is not responsible unless his or her act plays a "major role" or "material role" in causing the loss/damage/injury. *United States v. Moglia*, 3 M.J. 216 (C.M.A. 1977) (manslaughter conviction affirmed where the accused's act of selling heroin played "major role" in overdose death of buyer); *United States v. Romero*, 1 M.J. 227 (C.M.A. 1975) (manslaughter conviction affirmed where the accused's act of assisting overdose victim in inserting syringe into vein played "material role" in victim's death).

3. In a crime of negligent omission, the accused is not criminally responsible unless his or her omission was a "substantial factor," among multiple causes, in producing the damage. *United States v. Day*, 23 C.M.R. 651 (N.B.R. 1957) (ship commander's failure to keep engines in readiness held proximate cause of ship grounding in gale).

4. *See generally* Benchbook ¶ 5-19.

B. Intervening Cause.

1. The accused is not criminally responsible for the crime if:

    a) The injury or death resulted from an independent, intervening cause;

    b) The accused did not participate in the intervening cause, and

    c) The intervening cause was not foreseeable.

2. Intervening cause test from 26 Am. Jur. *Homicide*, § 50, cited with approval in *United States v. Houghten*, 32 C.M.R. 3 (C.M.A. 1962), states that: "If it appears that the act of the accused was not the proximate cause of the death for which he is being prosecuted, but that another cause intervened, with which he was in no way connected and but for which death would not have occurred, such supervening cause is a good defense to the crime of homicide."

3. Intervening cause must be "new and wholly independent" of the original act of the defendant. *United States v. Eddy*, 26 C.M.R. 718 (A.B.R. 1958) (to constitute an intervening cause to the offense of murder, medical maltreatment must be so grossly erroneous as to constitute a new and independent cause of death); *see also United States v. Gomez*, 15 M.J. 954 (A.C.M.R. 1983).

4. The intervening cause must not be foreseeable. *United States v. Varraso*, 21 M.J. 129 (C.M.A. 1985) (defense not raised where accused helped victim hang herself by tying her

hands behind her back and putting her head in the noose; any later acts by the victim to complete the hanging were foreseeable).

5. Intervening cause must intrude between the original wrongful act or omission and the injury and produce a result which would not otherwise have followed. *United States v. King*, 4 M.J. 785 (N.C.M.R. 1977), *aff'd*, 7 M.J. 207 (C.M.A. 1979). Defense offered evidence that the accused drove onto the shoulder of the road to avoid the oncoming victim and that, in attempting to negotiate the sunken shoulder to regain the road, the accused crossed over the center line and struck the victim's vehicle. The court noted that intervening cause would have been present had a third vehicle been involved or had the accused offered evidence that one of the wheels of his vehicle dropped off or that an earthslide forced him into the oncoming lane.

6. *Henderson v. Kibbe*, 431 U.S. 145 (1977) (abandoning intoxicated robbery victim on an abandoned rural road in a snowstorm established culpability for death of victim resulting from his being struck by a speeding truck).

7. *United States v. Riley*, 58 M.J. 305 (C.A.A.F. 2003). Airman gave birth to a baby girl in the latrine of hospital. The baby died from blunt force trauma and left in the trashcan of the latrine. Appellant argued that the doctors' failure to discover her pregnancy on three prior medical visits was an intervening cause in the baby's death. CAAF disagreed, concluding that, at best, the negligence was a contributing cause. The doctors did not intervene between the birth of the baby and the ultimate death. *See also United States v. Cooke*, 18 M.J. 152 (C.M.A. 1984).

V. DURESS.

A. Defined. The defense of duress exists when the accused commits the offense because of a well-grounded apprehension of immediate death or serious bodily harm. R.C.M. 916(h); *see generally United States v. Rankins*, 34 M.J. 326 (C.M.A. 1992); *United States v. Montford*, 13 M.J. 829 (A.C.M.R. 1982).

1. Financial hardship, no matter how extreme, does not amount to duress under military law. *United States v. Alomarestrada*, 39 M.J. 1068 (A.C.M.R. 1994).

2. Duress is never a defense to homicide or to disobedience of valid military orders requiring performance of dangerous military duty. R.C.M. 916(h); *United States v. Talty*, 17 M.J. 1127 (N.M.C.M.R. 1984)(where sailor refused the order of his commander to enter the reactor chamber of a nuclear submarine to perform maintenance, based on his belief that radiation from the reactor could harm him); *United States v. Washington*, 57 M.J. 394 (C.A.A.F. 2002) (refusal to receive anthrax vaccination).

3. Reasonable opportunity to seek assistance negates a reasonable apprehension that another innocent person would immediately suffer death or serious bodily injury. *United States v. Vasquez*, 48 M.J. 426 (C.A.A.F. 1998).

4. What constitutes reasonable apprehension? Fear sufficient to cause a person of ordinary fortitude and courage to yield. *United States v. Logan*, 47 C.M.R. 1 (C.M.A. 1973) (reasonable fear did not exist where accused was in Korea and threats to harm his family in CONUS were made by local Korean nationals); *United States v. Olson*, 22 C.M.R. 250 (C.M.A. 1957) (prisoner-of-war who wrote anti-American articles while incarcerated was denied the duress instruction at his court-martial for aiding the enemy when the only evidence of coercion brought to bear on him consisted of veiled threats of future possible mistreatment); *United States v. Palus*, 13 M.J. 179 (C.M.A. 1982) (inadequate providency inquiry required reversal where accused in Germany stated he

feared for his family's safety when his wife was harassed in Las Vegas about his gambling debts). *See generally United States v. Ellerbee*, 30 M.J. 517 (A.F.C.M.R. 1990) (sufficient to raise duress); *United States v. Riofredo*, 30 M.J. 1251 (N.M.C.M.R. 1990) (evidence does not raise duress); TJAGSA Practice Note, *Duress and Absence Without Authority*, ARMY LAW., Dec. 1990, at 34 (discusses *Riofredo*).

5. The military apparently does not recognize the rule that one who recklessly or intentionally placed himself in a situation in which it was reasonably foreseeable that he or she would be subjected to coercion is not entitled to the defense of duress. *United States v. Jemmings*, 50 C.M.R. 247 (A.C.M.R. 1975), *rev'd*, 1 M.J. 414 (C.M.A. 1976); *see also United States v. Vandemark*, 14 M.J. 690 (N.M.C.M.R. 1982).

6. The defense requires fear of immediate death or great bodily harm and no reasonable opportunity to avoid committing the harm. *See generally United States v. Barnes*, 12 M.J. 779 (A.C.M.R. 1981).

   a) The accused must not only fear immediate death or great bodily harm but also have no reasonable opportunity to avoid committing the crime. R.C.M. 916(h). *See United States v. Banks*, 37 M.J. 700 (A.C.M.R. 1993) (defense of duress to charge of AWOL was not raised by accused's testimony that he failed to return from leave on time because of the serious illness of his mother); *United States v. Vasquez*, 48 M.J. 426 (C.A.A.F. 1998) (duress defense not raised in bigamy case where accused married Turkish woman three days after being caught with her and authorities threatened to put them in jail).

   b) The old rule. *United States v. Fleming*, 23 C.M.R. 7 (C.M.A. 1957) (even though accused was subjected to great deprivation as POW, actions of captors did not constitute defense against charge of collaboration with the enemy because accused's resistance had not brought him to the "last ditch.").

   c) The new rule. The immediacy element of the defense is designed to encourage individuals promptly to report threats rather than breaking the law themselves. *United States v. Jemmings*, 1 M.J. 414, 418 (C.M.A. 1976) (threat to inflict harm the next day held sufficient to activate defense where accused's company commander had previously refused to assist); *United States v. Campfield*, 17 M.J. 715 (N.M.C.M.R. 1983) *rev'd in part on other grounds (multiplicity)*, 20 M.J. 246 (C.M.A. 1985); *United States v. Biscoe*, 47 M.J. 398 (C.A.A.F. 1998) (sexual harassment did not constitute duress when victim conceded during providency that she did not fear for her life or the lives of her children when she went AWOL); *United States v. Vasquez*, 48 M.J. 426 (C.A.A.F. 1998) (in three days before threat to jail him and Turkish woman and his bigamous marriage, the accused could have sought legal assistance, sought assistance from the consulate, or sought help from his chain of command).

7. *United States v. Le*, 59 M.J. 859 (A. Ct. Crim. App. 2004). Appellant pled guilty to desertion. During his providence inquiry, appellant stated his primary reason for leaving was fear that his girlfriend's ex-boyfriend, a purported gang member, would kill or harm him. In response to the military judge's questions, appellant repeatedly said he did not fear "immediate" death or serious bodily injury, but he did not know when "they are going to come for me." The appeals court held that appellant's guilty plea was improvident because he raised the defense of duress, and the military judge failed to resolve the apparent inconsistency. Appellant's response that he did not fear immediate harm was merely a recitation of a conclusion of law. Duress has long been recognized as a defense

to absence offenses; however, it only applies so long as the accused surrenders at the earliest possible opportunity. Appellant's claim of duress could only apply while his reasonably grounded fear still existed. Once away from the source of the fear, the threat lost its coercive force.

8. *United States v. Barnes*, 60 M.J. 950 (N-M. Ct. Crim. App. 2005). Appellant pled guilty to a 52 month absence terminated by apprehension. Appellant claimed that he was beaten and threatened regularly and this contributed to his absence. HELD: The military judge erred when he granted a motion *in limine* to preclude the affirmative defense of duress, after ruling that the offense of desertion and the lesser included offense of unauthorized absence were not complete when appellant left the ship with the intent to remain away.

9. *See generally* Benchbook ¶ 5-5

B. Who Must Be Endangered. Any innocent person. R.C.M. 916(h); *see United States v. Barnes*, 12 M.J. 779 (A.C.M.R. 1981); *United States v. Pinkston*, 39 C.M.R. 261 (C.M.A. 1969) (threat against fiancée and illegitimate child can raise the defense of duress); *United States v. Jemmings*, 1 M.J. 414 (C.M.A. 1976) (threat against accused's children can raise the defense of duress).

C. Evidence. Accused's use of the duress defense creates an opportunity for the prosecution to introduce evidence of his other voluntary crimes in order to rebut the defense. *United States v. Hearst*, 563 F.2d 1331 (9th Cir. 1977); *see also* MRE 404(b).

D. The Nexus Requirement.

    1. A nexus between the threat and the crime committed must exist. *United States v. Barnes*, 12 M.J. 779 (A.C.M.R. 1981) (duress was not available to an accused who robbed a taxi driver where the threat was only to force payment of a debt; the coercion must be to commit a criminal act); *see also United States v. Banks*, 37 M.J. 700 (A.C.M.R. 1993) (defense of duress to charge of AWOL was not raised by accused's testimony that he failed to return from leave on time because of the serious illness of his mother); *United States v. Biscoe*, 47 M.J. 398 (C.A.A.F. 1998) (allegation of sexual harassment alone, absent threat of death or serious bodily injury, did not raise duress as a defense to AWOL).

    2. For requirements on instructions, see *United States v. Rankins*, 32 M.J. 971 (A.C.M.R. 1991), *aff'd,* 34 M.J. 326 (C.M.A. 1992).

E. The Military "Defense" of Necessity.

    1. Duress Distinguished. Necessity is a defense of justification; it exculpates a nominally unlawful act to avoid a greater evil. Duress is a defense of excuse; it excuses a threatened or coerced actor. *See generally* Milhizer, *Necessity and the Military Justice System: A Proposed Special Defense*, 121 Mil. L. Rev. 95 (1988).

    2. Duress and necessity are separate affirmative defenses, and the defense of necessity is not recognized in military law. *United States v. Banks*, 37 M.J. 700 (A.C.M.R. 1993). *But see United States v. Rockwood*, 52 M.J. 98 (C.A.A.F. 1999); *United States v. Olinger*, 50 M.J. 365 (1999) (common law defense of necessity, which may be broader than the defense of duress, may apply to the military).

    3. Necessity has arguably been recognized and applied de facto to the offenses of AWOL and escape from confinement, but always under the name of duress.

a) *United States v. Blair*, 36 C.M.R. 413 (C.M.A. 1966) (error not to instruct on defense raised by accused's flight from cell to avoid beating by a brig guard).

b) *United States v. Pierce*, 42 C.M.R. 390 (A.C.M.R. 1970) ("duress" to escape from confinement not raised by defense offer of proof regarding stockade conditions, but lacking a showing of imminent danger).

c) *United States v. Guzman*, 3 M.J. 740 (N.C.M.R. 1977) (accused with injury that would have been aggravated by duty assignment had no defense of "duress" to crime of AWOL because performing duty would not have caused *immediate* death or serious bodily injury), *rev'd on other grounds (court-martial improperly convened)*, 4 M.J. 115 (C.M.A. 1977).

d) In an early case in which a sailor went AWOL because of death threats by a shipmate, the Navy Board of Review held that the defense of duress was not raised. Noting that the accused was never in danger of imminent harm and that the threatener had never demanded that the accused leave his ship, the board concluded that the accused had no right to leave a duty station in order to find a place of greater safety. *United States v. Wilson*, 30 C.M.R. 630 (N.B.R. 1960).

e) Escapees are not entitled to duress or necessity instructions unless they offer evidence of bona fide efforts to surrender or return to custody once the coercive force of the alleged duress/necessity had dissipated. *United States v. Bailey*, 444 U.S. 394 (1979); *accord United States v. Clark*, NCM 79-1948 (N.C.M.R. 30 May 1980) (unpub.).

f) *United States v. Roberts*, 14 M.J. 671 (N.M.C.M.R. 1982), *rev'd*, 15 M.J. 106 (C.M.A. 1983) (summary disposition) (duress available to female sailor who went AWOL to avoid shipboard initiation when complaints about harassment went unheeded); *see also United States v. Tulin*, 14 M.J. 695 (N.M.C.M.R. 1982) (informant felt Navy could no longer protect him); *United States v. Hullum*, 15 M.J. 261 (C.M.A. 1983) (racial harassment).

g) Note, *Medical Necessity as a Defense to Criminal Liability*, 46 Geo. Wash. L. Rev. 273 (1978).

4. Controlled Substances. No implied medical necessity exception to prohibitions established by the Controlled Substances Act. The necessity defense is especially controversial under a constitutional system in which federal crimes are defined by statute rather than common law. The defense of necessity cannot succeed when the legislature itself has made a determination of values. *United States v. Oakland Cannabis Buyer's Cooperative*, 121 S.Ct. 1711 (2001).

5. Duress and Necessity. *United States v. Washington*, 54 M.J. 936 (A.F. Ct. Crim. App. 2001), *aff'd*, 58 M.J. 129 (C.A.A.F. 2003). The accused conceded that he was not under an unlawful threat; therefore, the defense of duress was not available to him. The court further held that the defense of necessity was not available because the accused's refusal to be inoculated was a direct flouting of military authority and detracted from the ability of his unit to perform its mission. A military accused cannot justify his disobedience of a lawful order by asserting that his health would be jeopardized.

VI. INABILITY / IMPOSSIBILITY—OBSTRUCTED COMPLIANCE.

A. Defined. Generally this defense pertains only to situations in which the accused has an affirmative duty to act and does not. The defense excuses a failure to act.

B. Physical (Health-Related) Obstructions to Compliance.

1. Physical impossibility. *See generally* Benchbook ¶ 5-9-1.

    a) The accused's conduct is excused if physical conditions made it impossible to obey or involuntarily caused the accused to disobey. *See United States v. Williams*, 21 M.J. 360 (C.M.A. 1986).

    b) When one's physical condition is such as actually to prevent compliance with orders or to cause the commission of an offense, the question is not one of reasonableness but whether the accused's illness was the proximate cause of the crime. The case is not one of balancing refusal and reason, but one of physical impossibility to maintain the strict standards required under military law. In such a situation, the accused is excused from the offense if its commission was directly caused by the physical condition and the question whether the accused acted reasonably does not enter into the matter. *United States v. Cooley*, 36 C.M.R. 180 (C.M.A. 1966). To apply a reasonableness standard in instructing the court is error. *United States v. Liggon*, 42 C.M.R. 614 (A.C.M.R. 1970).

    c) Physical impossibility may exist as a result of illness/injury of the accused. *United States v. Cooley*, 36 C.M.R. 180 (C.M.A. 1966) (the defense applied to a charge of sleeping on guard where the accused suffered from narcolepsy resulting in uncontrollable sleeping spells.) The defense also exists when requirements placed on the accused are physically impossible of performance. *United States v. Borell*, 46 C.M.R. 1108 (A.F.C.M.R. 1973) (discusses the impossibility of obeying an order to report to the orderly room within a very short period of time).

    d) *United States v. Roeseler*, 55 M.J. 286 (C.A.A.F. 2001) (because the impossibility of the fictitious victims being murdered was not a defense to either attempt or conspiracy, it was not a defense to the offense of attempted conspiracy).

    e) *United States v. Lee*, 16 M.J. 278 (C.M.A. 1983) (collects cases on impossibility and AWOL).

2. Physical Inability. *See generally* Benchbook ¶ 5-9-2.

    a) If the accused's noncompliance was reasonable under the circumstances, it is excused.

    b) Unlike physical impossibility, inability to act is a matter of degree. To determine whether a soldier's failure to act because of a physical shortcoming constitutes a defense, one must ask whether the non-performance was reasonable in light of the injury, the task imposed, and the pressing nature of circumstances. *United States v. Cooley*, 36 C.M.R. 180 (C.M.A. 1966).

    c) *United States v. Amie*, 22 C.M.R. 304 (C.M.A. 1957) (inability raised when accused testified that upon expiration of leave he was ill and, pursuant to medical advice, undertook to recuperate at home, thus resulting in late return to unit).

    d) *United States v. Heims*, 12 C.M.R. 174 (C.M.A. 1953) (law officer erred by failing to instruct on the physical inability defense where evidence established that accused was unable to comply with order to tie sandbags because he was suffering from a hand injury).

e) *United States v. King*, 17 C.M.R. 3 (C.M.A. 1954) (inability defense raised where accused refused order to return to his battle position allegedly because he was suffering from frostbitten feet).

f) *United States v. Barnes*, 39 M.J. 230 (C.M.A. 1994) (defense of physical inability to return to unit is available only when accused's failure to return was not the result of his own willful and deliberate conduct; defense was raised by testimony that accused's failure to return was due to his abduction by third parties, the subsequent theft of his car, and his forty mile walk back to his home).

g) If a physical inability occurred through the accused's own fault or design, it is not a defense. *United States v. New*, 50 M.J. 729 (Army Ct. Crim. App. 1999) (military judge did not err by failing to instruct on inability where the accused claimed that after he willfully reported to the company formation in the wrong uniform, he was removed from the formation and unable to comply with the order to be in the follow-on battalion formation in the Macedonia deployment uniform), *aff'd*, 55 M.J. 95 (C.A.A.F. 2001).

h) Relationship to mental responsibility defense. Military judge need not instruct on both lack of mental responsibility and physical inability when physical symptoms are insignificant compared to mental distress and are part and parcel of mental condition. *United States v. Meeks*, 41 M.J. 150 (C.M.A. 1994)

3. Financial and Other Inability.

   a) This defense is applicable if the accused can show the following:

      (1) An extrinsic factor caused noncompliance;

      (2) The accused had no control over the extrinsic factor;

      (3) Noncompliance was not due to the fault or design of the accused after he had an obligation to obey; and

      (4) The extrinsic factor could not be remedied by the accused's timely, legal efforts.

   b) *See generally* Benchbook ¶ 5-10.

   c) *United States v. Pinkston*, 21 C.M.R. 22 (C.M.A. 1966) (accused not guilty of disobeying order to procure new uniforms when, through no fault of his own, he was financially incapable of purchasing required uniforms).

   d) *United States v. Smith*, 16 M.J. 694 (A.F.C.M.R. 1983). Financial inability is a defense to dishonorable failure to pay a debt. *But cf. United States v. Hilton*, 39 M.J. 97 (C.M.A. 1994) (financial inability not a defense to dishonorable failure to pay just debt where accused's financial straits resulted from her own financial scheming, had debts of only $50 each month and was receiving monthly pay of $724.20).

   e) *United States v. Kuhn*, 28 C.M.R. 715 (C.G.C.M.R. 1959) (seaman who was granted leave to answer charges by civil authorities and who was detained in confinement after the expiration of his leave was not AWOL).

4. Physical Impossibility and Inability and Attempts. Generally physical impossibility and inability does not excuse an attempt. *United States v. Powell*, 24 M.J. 603 (A.F.C.M.R. 1987); *see supra*, chapter 1, section I.

VII. ENTRAPMENT: SUBJECTIVE AND DUE PROCESS.

A. Subjective Entrapment: The General Rule.

1. In *United States v. Vanzandt*, 14 M.J. 332 (C.M.A. 1982) the court set out the two elements of subjective entrapment.

   a) The suggestion to commit the crime originated in the government, *and*

   b) The accused had no predisposition to commit the offense.

2. A question of fact for the finder of fact. *United States v. Jursnick*, 24 M.J. 504 (A.F.C.M.R. 1987).

3. *See generally* TJAGSA Practice Note, *The Evolving Entrapment Defense*, ARMY LAW., Jan. 1989, at 40.

B. Predisposition to Commit the Crime.

1. The prosecution must prove beyond a reasonable doubt that the defendant was disposed to commit the criminal act prior to first being approached by government agents. *Jacobson v. United States*, 503 U.S. 540 (1992); *United States v. Vanzandt*, 14 M.J. 332 (C.M.A. 1982).

2. An accused who readily accepts the government's first invitation to commit the offense has no defense of entrapment. *United States v. Suter*, 45 C.M.R. 284 (C.M.A. 1972); *United States v. Garcia*, 1 M.J. 26 (C.M.A. 1975); *United States v. Collins*, 17 M.J. 901 (A.C.M.R. 1984); *see United States v. Rollins*, 28 M.J. 803 (A.C.M.R. 1989); *see also United States v. Clark*, 28 M.J. 401 (C.M.A. 1989) (accused's hesitancy did not raise entrapment, as it was a result of fearing apprehension rather than a lack of predisposition); *United States v. St. Mary*, 33 M.J. 836 (A.C.M.R. 1991) (evidence supported finding predisposition where accused procured hashish and sold it to undercover agent within 24 hours of first request.).

3. The government's reasonable suspicion of the accused's criminal activity is immaterial. *United States v. Vanzandt*, 14 M.J. 332 (C.M.A. 1982); *United States v. Gonzalez-Dominicci*, 14 M.J. 426 (C.M.A. 1983); *United States v. Eason*, 21 M.J. 79 (C.M.A. 1985) (holding error to instruct trier of fact that entrapment negated if gov't agents reasonably believed that accused involved in criminal activity).

4. To show predisposition the government may introduce evidence of relevant, uncharged misconduct to establish predisposition. *United States v. Hunter*, 21 M.J. 240 (C.M.A. 1986); *See* MRE 405(b).

5. Some authority suggests that reputation and hearsay evidence may be admissible to show predisposition. *See, e.g., United States v. Rocha*, 401 F.2d 529 (5th Cir. 1968); *United States v. Simon*, 488 F.2d 133 (5th Cir. 1973); *United States v. Woolfs*, 594 F.2d 77 (5th Cir. 1979). *But see United States v. Cunningham*, 529 F.2d 884 (6th Cir. 1976); *United States v. Whiting*, 295 F.2d 512 (1st Cir. 1961); *United States v. McClain*, 531 F.2d 431 (9th Cir. 1976). *See generally* Annot., 61 A.L.R. 3d 293, 314-18 (1975).

6. In a prosecution for possession of a large quantity of hashish for the purpose of trafficking, accused's prior possession and use of small quantities of hashish was held not to constitute "similar criminal conduct," and did not extinguish the defense of entrapment as to the large quantity. The accused would be found guilty, however, of possessing the lesser amount. *United States v. Fredrichs*, 49 C.M.R. 765 (A.C.M.R. 1974); *see also United States v. Jacobs*, 14 M.J. 999 (A.C.M.R. 1982). Prior possession or use of drugs

does not necessarily establish a predisposition to sell or distribute drugs. *United States v. Venus*, 15 M.J. 1095 (A.C.M.R. 1983); *United States v. Bailey*, 18 M.J. 749 (A.C.M.R. 1984), *aff'd*, 21 M.J. 244 (C.M.A. 1986).

7. Continuing Defense. A valid defense of entrapment to commit the first of a series of crimes is presumed to carry over into the later crimes. *United States v. Skrzek*, 47 C.M.R. 314 (A.C.M.R. 1973). Whether the presumption carries over to different kinds of drugs is a question of fact. *United States v. Jacobs*, 14 M.J. 999 (A.C.M.R. 1982). The taint can extend to a different type of crime as long as the acts come from the same inducement. *United States v. Bailey*, 18 M.J. 749 (A.C.M.R. 1984) (accused entrapped to distribute drugs could raise defense to larceny by trick arising from later distribution of counterfeit drugs), *aff'd*, 21 M.J. 244 (C.M.A. 1986).

8. Profit motive does not necessarily negate an entrapment defense. *United States v. Eckhoff*, 27 M.J. 142 (C.M.A. 1988); *United States v. Meyers*, 21 M.J. 1007 (A.C.M.R. 1986); *United States v. Cortes*, 29 M.J. 946 (A.C.M.R. 1990); *see* TJAGSA Practice Note, *Multiple Requests, Profit Motive, and Entrapment*, ARMY LAW., Jun. 1990, at 48 (discusses *Cortes*).

9. Predisposition is a question of fact. A military judge may not find predisposition as a matter of law and refuse to instruct on entrapment. *United States v. Johnson*, 17 M.J. 1056 (A.F.C.M.R. 1983).

C. Government Conduct.

1. *United States v. Williams*, 61 M.J. 584 (N-M. Ct. Crim. App. 2005) (wanting to get to know two attractive females (undercover government agents) is insufficient to raise entrapment and reject an otherwise provident plea).

2. Profit motive does not necessarily negate entrapment. *Eckhoff*, *Cortes* and *Meyers*, all *supra*.

3. Multiple requests by a government agent alone may not raise entrapment. *United States v. Sermons*, 14 M.J. 350 (C.M.A. 1982).

4. The latitude given the government in "inducing" the criminal act is considerably greater in drug cases than it would be in other kinds of crimes. *United States v. Vanzandt*, 14 M.J. 332, 344 (C.M.A. 1982); *United States v. Cortes*, 29 M.J. 946 (A.C.M.R. 1990). *But cf. United States v. Lemaster*, 40 M.J. 178 (C.M.A. 1994)

D. Not Confession and Avoidance. In order for the defense of entrapment to be raised and established, the accused need not admit the crime; indeed, he may deny it. *United States v. Garcia*, 1 M.J. 26 (C.M.A. 1975); *United States v. Williams*, 4 M.J. 507, 509 n. 1 (A.C.M.R. 1977).

E. Due Process Entrapment. *See generally* Benchbook ¶ 5-6, note 4.

1. The due process defense is recognized under military law. *United States v. Vanzandt*, 14 M.J. 332 (C.M.A. 1982) (but outrageous government conduct in drug cases will be especially difficult to prove given the greater latitude given government agents in drug cases); *United States v. Simmons*, 14 M.J. 624 (A.F.C.M.R. 1982); *United States v. Harms*, 14 M.J. 677 (A.F.C.M.R. 1982); *United States v. Lemaster*, 40 M.J. 178 (C.M.A. 1994) (targeting an emotionally unstable female suspect, sexually and emotionally exploiting her, and planting drugs upon her in a reverse sting operation violates the fundamental norms of military due process and is the functional equivalent of entrapment), *amended by*, 42 M.J. 91 (C.M.A. 1995).

2. The due process defense is a question of law for the military judge. *United States v. Vanzandt*, 14 M.J. 332, 343 n. 11 (C.M.A. 1982).

3. Reverse sting operation does not deprive accused of due process. *United States v. Frazier*, 30 M.J. 1231 (A.C.M.R. 1990).

4. Police did not violate due process in soliciting the accused's involvement in drug transactions where they had no knowledge of his enrollment in a drug rehabilitation program. *United States v. Harris*, 41 M.J. 433 (C.A.A.F. 1995); *United States v. Bell*, 38 M.J. 358 (C.M.A. 1993); *United States. v. Cooper*, 33 M.J. 356 (C.M.A. 1991), *cert. denied*, 507 U.S. 985 (1993).

5. *United States v. St. Mary*, 33 M.J. 836 (A.C.M.R. 1991) (government conduct did not violate due process where accused provided drugs to undercover female agent in hopes of having a future sexual relationship as the agent did not offer dating or sexual favors as an inducement); *accord United States v. Fegurgur*, 43 M.J. 871 (Army Ct. Crim. App. 1996) (undercover CID agent who repeatedly asked accused to obtain marijuana for her, knowing that he wished to date her, was not so outrageous as to bar prosecution of accused under either due process clause or fundamental norms of military due process).

6. *United States v. Bell*, 38 M.J. 358 (C.M.A. 1993) (sufficient evidence existed to show accused's predisposition to commit two separate offenses of distribution of cocaine; however, due process entrapment defense was available for drug use offenses where government improperly induced accused, a recovering cocaine addict enrolled in Army rehabilitation program, into using cocaine).

7. Court members should be instructed only on subjective entrapment, and not the due process defense. *United States v. Dayton*, 29 M.J. 6 (C.M.A. 1989).

F. Entrapment does not apply if carried out by foreign law enforcement activities. *See United States v. Perl*, 584 F.2d 1316, 1321 n. 3 (4th Cir. 1978).

VIII. **SELF-DEFENSE.**

A. "Preventive Self-Defense" in which no injury is inflicted. If no battery is committed, but the accused's acts constitute assault by offer, the accused may threaten the victim with any degree of force, provided only that the accused honestly and reasonably believes that the victim is about to commit a battery upon him. R.C.M. 916(e)(2). *United States v. Acosta-Vargas*, 32 C.M.R. 388 (C.M.A. 1962); *United States v. Johnson*, 25 C.M.R. 554 A.C.M.R. 1958); *United States v. Lett*, 9 M.J. 602 (A.F.C.M.R. 1980). *See generally* Benchbook ¶ 5-2-5.

B. Crimes in which an injury is inflicted upon the victim. Two separate standards of self-defense exist depending on the nature of the injury inflicted on the victim. *United States v. Thomas*, 11 M.J. 315 (C.M.A. 1981); *United States v. Sawyer*, 4 M.J. 64 (C.M.A. 1977); *United States v. Jackson*, 36 C.M.R. 101 (C.M.A. 1966).

1. R.C.M. 916(e)(1). Standard applied when homicide or aggravated assault is charged. The accused may justifiably inflict death or grievous bodily harm upon another if:

a) He apprehended, on reasonable grounds, that death or grievous bodily harm was about to be inflicted on him; and

b) He believed that the force he used was necessary to prevent death or grievous bodily harm.

c) *See United States v. Clayborne*, 7 M.J. 528 (A.C.M.R. 1979) (court set aside a conviction for unpremeditated murder because it "was not convinced beyond a reasonable doubt that the accused did not act in self-defense" in using a knife against a victim who attacked the accused with only his hands when the accused knew 1) the victim was an experienced boxer, 2) with a reputation for fighting anyone, 3) who had defeated three men in a street fight, and 4) had choked and beaten a sleeping soldier once before). *But see United States v. Ratliff,* 49 C.M.R. 775 (A.C.M.R. 1975) (reaching opposite result in a knife scenario).

2. R.C.M. 916(e)(3). Standard applied when simple assault or battery is charged. The accused may justifiably inflict injury short of death or grievous bodily harm if:

    a) He apprehended, upon reasonable grounds, that bodily harm was about to be inflicted on him, and

    b) He believed that the force he used was necessary to avoid that harm, but that the force actually used was not reasonably likely to result in death or grievous bodily harm.

    c) *See United States v. Jones*, 3 M.J. 279 (C.M.A. 1977) (one may respond to a simple fistic assault with similar force); *United States v. Perry*, 36 C.M.R. 377 (C.M.A. 1966).

3. Loss of Self-Defense by Aggressor / Mutual Combatant. A provoker, aggressor, or one who voluntarily engages in a mutual affray is not entitled to act in self defense unless he first withdraws in good faith and indicates his desire for peace. R.C.M. 916(e)(4). *United States v. Marbury*, 50 M.J. 526 (Army Ct. Crim. App. 1999) *aff'd* 56 M.J. 12 (C.A.A.F. 2001) (after the victim struck the accused in the face, the accused retreated from her room, unsuccessfully sought assistance from fellow NCOs, grabbed a knife, reentered her room, and then started a confrontation by threatening the victim with the knife). *United States v. Brown*, 33 C.M.R. 17 (C.M.A. 1963); *United States v. O'Neal*, 36 C.M.R. 189 (C.M.A. 1966); *United States v. Green*, 33 C.M.R. 77 (C.M.A. 1963).

4. Retreat / Withdrawal. The accused is not required to retreat when he is at a place where he has a right to be. The presence or absence of an opportunity to withdraw safely, however, may be a factor in deciding whether the accused had a reasonable belief that bodily harm was about to be inflicted upon him. R.C.M. 916(e)(4) (discussion); *United States v. Lincoln*, 38 C.M.R. 128 (C.M.A. 1967); *United States v. Smith*, 33 C.M.R. 3 (C.M.A. 1963); *United States v. Adams*, 18 C.M.R. 187 (C.M.A. 1955); *United States v. Jenkins*, 59 M.J. 893 (A. Ct. Crim. App. 2004) (holding when an aggressor, provoker, or mutual combatant who becomes unconscious and ceases resistance effectively withdraws, entitling another to exercise self-defense on his behalf).

5. Escalation. An accused who wrongfully engages in a simple assault and battery may have a right to use deadly force if the victim first uses deadly force upon the accused. *United States v. Cardwell*, 15 M.J. 124 (C.M.A. 1983); *United States v. Dearing*, 63 M.J. 478 (2006) (citing *Cardwell*); *United States v. Lewis*, 65 M.J. 85 (2007); *see United States v. Winston*, 27 M.J. 618 (A.C.M.R. 1988) (self-defense not raised where the accused aggressively participated in an escalating mutual affray);

6. Termination of Self-Defense. The right to self-defense ceases when the threat is removed. *United States v. Richey*, 20 M.J. 251 (C.M.A. 1985) (ejecting a tresspasser).

7. Voluntary Intoxication. The accused's voluntary intoxication cannot be considered in determining accused's perception of the potential threat which led him to believe that a battery was about to be inflicted, as this is measured objectively. *United States v. Judkins*, 34 C.M.R. 232 (C.M.A. 1964).

8. Requirement to Raise. Self-defense need not be raised by the accused's testimony, even if he testifies. *United States v. Rose*, 28 M.J. 132 (C.M.A. 1989); *see* TJAGSA Practice Note, *Self-Defense Need Not Be Raised by the Accused's Testimony*, ARMY LAW., Aug. 1989, at 40 (discusses *Rose*). *See United States v. Reid*, 32 M.J. 146 (C.M.A. 1991).

9. The "Egg-Shell" Victim. R.C.M. 916(e)(3) (discussion). If an accused is lawfully acting in self-defense and using less force than is likely to cause death or grievous bodily harm, the death of the victim does not deprive the accused of the defense, if:

   a) The accused's use of force was not disproportionate, and

   b) The death was unintended, and

   c) The death was not a reasonably foreseeable consequence. *United States v. Jones*, 3 M.J. 279 (C.M.A. 1977); *United States v. Perry*, 36 C.M.R. 377 (C.M.A. 1966).

   d) *See generally* Benchbook ¶ 5-2-4.

IX. DEFENSE OF ANOTHER.

A. Traditional View Adopted by Military. R.C.M. 916(e)(5). One who acts in defense of another has no greater right than the party defended. *United States v. Regalado*, 33 C.M.R. 12 (C.M.A. 1963); *United States v. Hernandez*, 19 C.M.R. 822 (A.F.B.R. 1955); *United States v. Cole*, 54 M.J. 572 (A. Ct. Crim. App. 2000) (where the victim did not attack or make an offer of violence to the accused's wife, he was not entitled to use deadly force in defense of his family), *aff'd*, 55 M.J. 466 (C.A.A.F. 2001). *See generally* Benchbook ¶ 5-3.

B. "Enlightened View" Rejected. Accused who honestly and reasonably believes he is justified in defending another does not escape criminal liability if the "defended party" is not entitled to the defense of self-defense. *United States v. Lanier*, 50 M.J. 772 (A. Ct. Crim. App. 1999), *aff'd* 53 M.J. 220 (C.A.A.F. 2000) (accused may not use more force than the person defended was lawfully entitled to use under the circumstances. This "alter ego" status imposes significant limitations on the availability and application of the defense of defense of another); *United States v. Tanksley*, 7 M.J. 573 (A.C.M.R. 1979), *aff'd*, 10 M.J. 180 (C.M.A. 1980); *United States v. Styron*, 21 C.M.R. 579 (C.G.B.R. 1956). *But see* LaFave & Scott, Criminal Law § 54 at 397-399 (1972). *See generally* Byler, *Defense of Another, Guilt Without Fault?*, ARMY LAW., June 1980.

C. Accident & Defense of Another. *United States v. Jenkins*, 59 M.J. 893 (A. Ct. Crim. App. 2004). Appellant and friends traveled to another unit's barracks area to solve a dispute with another group. Appellant carried with him a loaded handgun, which he gave to a friend to hold. A fight erupted between two members of the factions. A member of the opposing faction had beaten appellant's colleague unconscious and continued to beat him. Appellant retrieved his pistol and fired three shots; the third shot struck another soldier and caused the loss of his kidney. At trial, defense counsel requested instructions on accident, defense of another, and withdrawal as reviving the right to self-defense. The Military Judge (MJ) instructed the panel only on defense of another, and the panel convicted appellant of conspiracy to assault and intentional infliction of grievous bodily harm. The appellate court held that the MJ erred in refusing to give the requested instructions. When appellant's friend became unconscious during the fight, he effectively withdrew from the mutual affray, giving appellant the right to defend him. Further, there was evidence in the record that appellant showed due care in firing his pistol to prevent further injury to his friend. Finally, the panel's finding of guilt for intentional assault did not render the errors harmless.

X. INTOXICATION.

A. Voluntary Intoxication. R.C.M. 916(l)(2). *See generally* Milhizer, *Voluntary Intoxication as a Criminal Defense Under Military Law*, 127 Mil. L. Rev. 131 (1990).

1. Voluntary intoxication is a legitimate defense against an element of premeditation, specific intent, knowledge, or willfulness in any crime---except the element of specific intent in the crime of unpremeditated murder. R.C.M. 916(l)(2); MCM, pt. IV, ¶ 43c(2)(c); *United States v. Morgan*, 37 M.J. 407 (C.M.A. 1993) (voluntary intoxication no defense to unpremeditated murder; re-affirming the rule in face of lower courts calling the rule into question); *United States v. Ferguson*, 38 C.M.R. 239 (C.M.A. 1968). To constitute a valid defense, voluntary intoxication need not deprive the accused of his mental capacities nor substantially deprive him of his mental capacities. Rather, it need only be of such a degree as to create a reasonable doubt that he premeditated or entertained the required intent, knowledge, or willfulness. *See generally United States v. Gerston*, 15 M.J. 990 (N.M.C.M.R. 1983); *United States v. Ledbetter*, 32 M.J. 272 (C.M.A. 1991); *United States v. Cameron*, 37 M.J. 1042 (A.C.M.R. 1993) (defense to willful disobedience to a lawful order).

2. Voluntary intoxication is not a defense to crimes involving only a general intent. *United States v. Brosius*, 37 M.J. 652 (A.C.M.R. 1993) (voluntary intoxication no defense to general intent crime of communicating a threat), *aff'd,* 39 M.J. 378 (C.M.A. 1994); *United States v. Reitz*, 47 C.M.R. 608 (N.C.M.R. 1973) (voluntary intoxication no defense to drug sale, transfer, possession).

3. Where there is some evidence of excessive drinking and impairment of accused's faculties, military judge must *sua sponte* instruct on the defense of voluntary intoxication. *United States v. Yandle*, 34 M.J. 890 (N.M.C.M.R. 1992). If no evidence of excessive drinking or impairment, military judge is not required to instruct. *United States v. Watford*, 32 M.J. 176 (C.M.A. 1991).

4. Limitations on voluntary intoxication defense are constitutional. *Montana v. Egelhoff*, 116 S. Ct. 2013 (1996) (Montana's statutory ban on voluntary intoxication evidence in general intent crimes is consistent with state interests in deterring crime, holding one responsible for consequences of his actions, and excluding misleading evidence, and does not violate the due process clause).

5. *See generally* Benchbook ¶ 5-12 and 5-2-6, Note 4.

B. Involuntary Intoxication.

1. In issue when:

a) Intoxicant is introduced into accused's body either without her knowledge or by force; or

b) Accused is "pathologically intoxicated," i.e., grossly intoxicated in light of amount of intoxicant consumed and accused not aware of susceptibility; or

c) Long-term use of alcohol causes severe mental disease.

2. An accused is involuntarily intoxicated when he exercises no independent judgment in taking the intoxicant--as, for example, when he has been made drunk by fraudulent contrivances of others, by accident, or by error of his physician. If the accused's intoxication was involuntary and his capacity for control over his conduct was affected thereby and resulted in the criminal act charged, he should be acquitted. *United States v.*

Travels, 44 M.J. 654 (A.F. Ct. Crim. App. 1996) (involuntary intoxication exists when accused is intoxicated through force, fraud, or trickery or actual ignorance of intoxicating nature of the substance consumed); *but see United States v. Ward*, 14 M.J. 950 (A.C.M.R. 1982) (holding intoxication not "involuntary" where accused knew substance was marijuana but was unaware it was laced with PCP).

3. An accused who voluntarily takes the first drink, knowing from past experience that the natural and reasonably foreseeable consequences of that act will be a violent intoxicating reaction cannot claim that his condition was "involuntary" so as to interpose an affirmative defense. *United States v. Schumacher*, 11 M.J. 612 (A.C.M.R. 1981). *See generally* Kaczynski, *"I Did What?" The Defense of Involuntary Intoxication*, ARMY LAW., Apr. 1983, at 1.

Compulsion to drink that merely results from alcoholism that has not risen to the level of a severe mental disease or defect is considered "voluntary intoxication" and will not generally excuse crimes committed while intoxicated. Involuntary intoxication rises to level of affirmative defense only if it amounts to legal insanity, and is not available if accused is aware of his reduced tolerance for alcohol but chooses to consume it anyway. *United States v. Hensler*, 44 M.J. 184 (C.A.A.F. 1996).

XI. MISTAKEN BELIEF OR IGNORANCE.

A. Degrees of Mistake or Ignorance of Fact.

1. An honest (subjective) mistake of fact or ignorance is generally a defense to crimes requiring premeditation, specific intent, knowledge, or willfulness. For example, an accused's honest belief that he had permission to take certain property would excuse the crime of larceny or wrongful appropriation. R.C.M. 916(j). *United States v. McDonald* 57 M.J. 18 (2002) (accused entitled to mistake of fact instruction as to buying stolen retail merchandise); *United States v. Binegar*, 55 M.J. 1 (C.A.A.F. 2001) (honest mistake of fact a defense to larceny); *United States v. Turner*, 27 M.J. 217 (C.M.A. 1988) (honest mistake a defense to larceny); *see* TJAGSA Practice Note, *Recent Applications of the Mistake of Fact Defense*, ARMY LAW., Feb. 1989, at 66 (discusses *Turner*); *United States v. Hill*, 32 C.M.R. 158 (C.M.A. 1962) (honest belief owner gave permission to use car a good defense to wrongful appropriation); *see also United States v. Jett*, 14 M.J. 941 (A.C.M.R. 1982). Similarly, an honest mistake can be a defense to presenting a false claim, *United States v. Graves*, 23 M.J. 374 (C.M.A. 1987); *United States v. Ward*, 16 M.J. 341 (C.M.A. 1983), and false official statement. *United States v. Oglivie*, 29 M.J. 1069 (A.C.M.R. 1990). *See generally* Benchbook ¶ 5-11-1.

a) *United States v. Gillenwater*, 43 M.J. 10 (C.A.A.F. 1995) (mistake of fact defense raised in prosecution for wrongful appropriation of government tools where accused's former supervisor testified that he gave accused permission to take things home for government use & accused worked on several government projects at home); *United States v. Gunter*, 42 M.J. 292 (C.A.A.F. 1995) (discussing possible defenses of self-help and honest claim of right).

b) *United States v. McDivitt*, 41 M.J. 442 (C.A.A.F. 1995) (mistake of fact defense is not raised by evidence where accused signed official documents falsely asserting that he had supported dependents for prior two years in order to obtain higher allowances after being advised by finance clerk that he was entitled to allowances at higher rate until divorced).

2. An honest and reasonable (objective) mistake. A defense to general intent crimes—crimes lacking an element of premeditation, specific intent, knowledge or willfulness. R.C.M. 916(j). *United States v. Brown*, 22 M.J. 448 (C.M.A. 1986); *United States v. Carr*, 18 M.J. 297 (C.M.A. 1984) (rape); *United States v. Davis*, 27 M.J. 543 (A.C.M.R. 1988) (rape); *United States v. Graham*, 3 M.J. 962 (N.C.M.R. 1977) (accused's honest and reasonable mistaken belief he had permission to be gone held a legitimate defense to AWOL); *United States v. Jenkins*, 47 C.M.R. 120 (C.M.A. 1973) (accused's honest and reasonable belief he had a "permanent profile" held a legitimate defense to disobedience of a general regulation requiring shaving); *United States v. Oglivie*, 29 M.J. 1069 (A.C.M.R. 1990) (an honest and reasonable mistake is required for a defense to the general intent crime of bigamy); *United States v. Barnard*, 32 M.J. 530 (A.F.C.M.R. 1990) (an honest and reasonable mistake is required for a defense to general intent crime of dishonorable failure to maintain sufficient funds); *United States v. McMonagle*, 38 M.J. 53 (C.M.A. 1993) (mistake of fact can rebut state of mind required for depraved-heart murder and can negate element of unlawfulness and thus, killing was justified if accused honestly and reasonably thought that he was shooting at a combatant); *United States v. New*, 50 M.J. 729 (A. Ct. Crim. App. 1999), *aff'd* 55 M.J. 97 (C.A.A.F. 2001) (a mistake about the lawfulness of an order to wear UN accouterments must be both honest and reasonable); *See generally* Benchbook ¶ 5-11-2.

3. Honest mistake. Negates an element of premeditation, specific intent, willfulness, or actual knowledge. *United States v. Binegar*, 55 M.J. 1 (C.A.A.F. 2001) (larceny).

4. Certain offenses such as bad checks and dishonorable failure to pay debts require a special degree of prudence and the mistake and ignorance standards must be adjusted accordingly. For example, in UCMJ art. 134 check offenses the accused's ignorance or mistake to be exonerating must not have been the result of bad faith or gross indifference. *United States v. Barnard*, 32 M.J. 530 (A.F.C.M.R. 1990). *See generally* Benchbook ¶ 5-11-3.

5. Some offenses, like carnal knowledge, have strict liability elements. *See* Milhizer, *Mistake of Fact and Carnal Knowledge*, ARMY LAW., Oct. 1990, at 4. Deliberate ignorance can create criminal liability. *United States v. Dougal*, 32 M.J. 863 (N.M.C.M.R. 1991).

B. Result of Mistaken Belief. To be a successful defense, the mistaken belief must be one which would, if true, exonerate the accused. *United States v. Vega*, 29 M.J. 892 (A.F.C.M.R. 1989) (no defense where the accused believed he possessed marijuana rather than cocaine); *United States v. Fell*, 33 M.J. 628 (A.C.M.R. 1991) (against a charge of robbery, the accused's honest belief that the money was his is a legitimate defense to robbery of the money, though not a shield against conviction for assault on the victim); *United States v. Anderson*, 46 C.M.R. 1073 (A.F.C.M.R. 1973) (accused charged with LSD offense has no defense because he believed the substance to be mescaline); *United States v. Calley*, 46 C.M.R. 1131, 1179 (A.C.M.R. 1973) (no defense to homicide that accused believed victims were detained PWs rather than noncombatants); *United States v. Jefferson*, 13 M.J. 779 (A.C.M.R. 1982) (mistake not exonerating where accused accepted heroin thinking it was hashish); *United States v. Myles*, 31 M.J. 7 (C.M.A. 1990) (mistake as to type of controlled substance is not exculpatory); *see* TJAGSA Practice Note, *Mistake of Drug is Not Exculpatory*, ARMY LAW., Dec. 1990, at 36 (discusses *Myles*). *See generally United States v. Mance*, 26 M.J. 244 (C.M.A. 1988); *United States v. Heitkamp*, 65 M.J. 861 (A. Ct. Crim. App. 2007).

C. Mistake or Ignorance and Drug Offenses. *See supra* ¶ IX.K.2, ch. 4.

D. Mistake of Fact and Sex Offenses.

1. Consent and Mistake of Fact as to Consent (for offenses involving the new Article 120, effective 1 October 2007). Article 120 provides that consent and mistake of fact as to consent are affirmative defenses for Rape, Aggravated Sexual Assault, Aggravated Sexual Contact, and Abusive Sexual Contact. *See* UCMJ art. 120(r) & (t)(14). *See supra* Ch.4, ¶ V.B.8.

2. Mistake of Fact as to Consent (for offenses occurring prior to 1 October 2007). An honest and reasonable mistake of fact as to consent is a defense in rape cases. *United States v. Taylor*, 26 M.J. 127 (C.M.A. 1988) (mistake of fact not available in conspiracy to commit rape absent evidence that all co-conspirators had a mistaken belief that the victim consented); *United States v. Baran*, 22 M.J. 265 (C.M.A. 1986); *United States v. Carr*, 18 M.J. 297 (C.M.A. 1984); *United States v. Davis*, 27 M.J. 543 (A.C.M.R. 1988); *see* TJAGSA Practice Note, *Recent Applications of the Mistake of Fact Defense*, ARMY LAW., Feb. 1989, at 66 (discusses *Davis*); *see also United States v. Daniels*, 28 M.J. 743 (A.F.C.M.R. 1989) (discusses sufficiency of evidence to raise the defense).

a) Mistake of fact as to victim's consent to sexual intercourse cannot be predicated upon negligence of accused; mistake must be honest and reasonable to negate a general intent or knowledge. *United States v. True*, 41 M.J. 424 (1995).

b) Mistake of fact as to whether the victim consented to intercourse is a different defense than actual consent by the victim. When the evidence raises only an issue as to actual consent, the military judge has no sua sponte duty to instruct on mistake. *United States v. Willis*, 41 M.J. 435 (1995). *Cf. United States v. Brown*, 43 M.J. 187 (1995) (observing "[i]n every case where consent is a defense to a charge of rape, the military judge would be well advised to either give the mistake instruction or discuss on the record with counsel the applicability of the defense").

c) Applications.

(1) *United States v. Hibbard*, 58 M.J. 71 (C.A.A.F. 2003). Evidence cited by the defense in light of the totality of the circumstances, including the manner that the issue was litigated at trial, was insufficient to reasonably raise the issue of whether the accused had a reasonable belief that the victim consented to sexual intercourse.

(2) *United States v. Yarborough*, 39 M.J. 563 (A.C.M.R. 1994). Mistake of fact as to consent in a prosecution for rape is not reasonable where the 13-year-old victim is a virgin who was too intoxicated to consent or resist even if she was aware of the intercourse, notwithstanding her response of "yeah" when the accused asked her if she "wanted to do it."

(3) *United States v. Valentin-Nieves*, 57 M.J. 691 (N-M. Ct. Crim. App. 2002). Victim's alleged statement that she had told another witness she would not mind having sex with accused did not establish mistake of fact where, a few days later, accused had taken the very intoxicated victim into a bathroom and had sexual intercourse with victim, who at the time was "too weak to hold [her]self up let alone hold someone else away."

(4) *United States v. Barboza*, 39 M.J. 596 (A.C.M.R. 1994). There could be no honest or reasonable mistake of fact as to consent to intercourse and sodomy where the accused and victim had only slight acquaintance as classmates, no dating relationship, victim stated she did not want sex and asked accused to leave her room, accused forced her head to his penis to accomplish fellatio and threatened to kill her if she told anyone about the incident.

(5) *United States v. Campbell*, 55 M.J. 591 (C.G. Ct. Crim. App. 2001). The evidence established the affirmative defense of mistake of fact as to consent. The victim's failure to take action to stop the accused from touching her ribs and across her front after consenting to his giving her a back rub was sufficient to confirm in the mind of a reasonable person that she was consenting to his actions. His departure from the back rub to front side caress ultimately led to the touching of her breasts.

(6) *United States v. Parker*, 54 M.J. 700 (A. Ct. Crim. App. 2000), *rev'd on other grounds,* 59 M.J. 195 (C.A.A.F. 2003). The government did not disprove accused's defense that he mistakenly believed that the victim consented to the intercourse and sodomy. The victim admitted that she and the accused engaged in a consensual relationship for several months before the first alleged rape, and she sent mixed signals to the accused about their relationship. The relationship included consensual sexual acts, which were similar to the acts she claimed were nonconsensual.

(7) *United States v. Black*, 42 M.J. 505 (A. Ct. Crim. App. 1995) (evidence that victim of sex offenses may have engaged in oral sex with another individual prior to assault by accused was not relevant to show that accused was mistaken as to consent of victim to engage in such acts with accused). *Cf. United States v. Greaves*, 40 M.J. 432 (C.M.A. 1994)(excluding evidence of accused's projected beliefs of victim's sexual relations with others); *United States v. Traylor*, 40 M.J. 248 (C.M.A. 1994) (holding mistake of fact as to consent to intercourse not reasonable when based upon belief by accused that victim "would consent to intercourse with anyone").

(8) *United States v. Peterson*, 47 M.J. 231 (C.A.A.F. 1997) (holding consent element is a general intent element, even though indecent assault requires specific intent to gratify lust); *United States v. Johnson*, 25 M.J. 691 (A.C.M.R. 1987).

(9) Even though indecent assault is a specific intent crime, a mistake of fact as to the victim's consent must be both honest and reasonable as the defense goes to the *victim's* intent and not the accused's intent. *United States v. Johnson*, 25 M.J. 691 (A.C.M.R. 1987); *United States v. McFarlin*, 19 M.J. 790 (A.C.M.R. 1985). Compare this with assault with intent to commit rape, a specific intent crime, where a mistake of fact as to victim's consent need only be honest. *United States v. Langley*,

33 M.J. 278 (C.M.A. 1991); see also *United States v. Apilado*, 34 M.J. 773 (A.C.M.R. 1992).

(10) *United States v. Gaines*, 61 M.J. 689 (N-M. Ct. Crim. App. 2005). Appellant went into a dark room and touched the legs and pelvic area of the woman sleeping there, believing she was someone else. HELD: Mistake of fact was raised in this case, especially as to the issue of consent. Had the victim consented to the touching, there would be no assault. If appellant had an honest and reasonable belief that the victim consented to the touching, he would have a complete defense.

3. Mistake of Fact as to Age, Indecent Acts. *United States v. Zachary*, 63 M.J. 438 (C.A.A.F. 2006) (holding that it is a defense to indecent acts with a child that, at the time of the act, the accused held an honest and reasonable belief that the person with whom the accused committed the indecent act was at least sixteen years of age). *United States v. Strode*, 43 M.J. 29 (1995) (mistake of fact may be a defense if the accused had an honest and reasonable belief as to the age of the victim and the acts would otherwise be lawful were the victim 16 or older).

4. Mistake of Fact as to Age, Carnal Knowledge. The accused carries the burden to prove mistake of fact as to age by a preponderance of the evidence in a carnal knowledge case. R.C.M. 916(b).

5. Mistake of Fact as to Age, Sodomy. "There is no mistake of fact defense available with regard to the child's age in the Article 125, UCMJ, offense of sodomy with a child under the age of sixteen." *United States v. Wilson*, 66 M.J. 39 (C.A.A.F. 2008).

6. Accused not required to take stand to raise defense of mistake of fact. *United States v. Sellers*, 33 M.J. 364 (C.M.A. 1991).

E. Mistake of Law.

1. Ordinarily, mistake of law is not a defense. R.C.M. 916(l). *United States v. Bishop*, 2 M.J. 741 (A.F.C.M.R. 1977) (accused's belief that under state law he could carry a concealed weapon not a defense to carrying a concealed weapon on base in violation of Article 134, UCMJ); *United States v. Ivey*, 53 M.J. 685 (A. Ct. Crim. App. 2000) (accused argued that he did not know what was meant by "actual buyer" on ATF Form 4473 when purchasing firearms for friends), *aff'd,* 55 M.J. 251 (C.A.A.F. 2001); *United States v. Heitkamp*, 65 M.J. 861 (A. Ct. Crim. App. 2007) (accused believed it was lawful to possess methandienone; "[I]f an accused knows the identity of a substance that he is possessing or using but does not know that such possession or use is illegal, his ignorance is immaterial . . . because ignorance of the law is no defense.").

2. Under some circumstances, however, a mistake of law may negate a criminal intent or a state of mind necessary for an offense. R.C.M. 916(l)(1) discussion.

a) A mistake as to a separate, nonpenal law may exonerate. *See United States v. Sicley*, 20 C.M.R. 118 (C.M.A. 1955) (honest mistake of fact as to claim of right under property law negates criminal intent in larceny); *United States v. Ward*, 16 M.J. 341 (C.M.A. 1983) (honest mistake defense to presenting a false claim).

b) Reliance on decisions and pronouncements of authorized public officials and agencies may be a defense, although reliance on counsel's advice would not be. R.C.M. 916(l)(1) (discussion); R. Perkins and M. Boyce, Criminal Law 1041, 1043 (3rd ed. 1982). *Cf. United States v. Lawton*, 19 M.J. 886 (A.C.M.R. 1985) (behavior after obtaining lawyer's opinion that married at common law, *inter alia*, sufficient to raise mistake defense).

3. When an attorney advises an accused to act in manner that the accused knows is criminal, the accused should not escape responsibility on the basis of the attorney's bad advice. Thus, advice of counsel would not afford accused any protection for misconduct which is self-evidently criminal, such as injuring someone, violating a lawful regulation, or taking someone else's property without consent. *United States v. Sorbera*, 43 M.J. 818 (A.F. Ct. Crim. App. 1996).

F. Special Evidentiary Rule. MRE 404(b) allows the prosecution to present evidence of uncharged crimes, wrongs, or acts committed by the accused in order to show the absence of a mistake. This is particularly important because such extrinsic evidence may be admitted even though the accused does not testify on his own behalf. *See United States v. Beechum*, 582 F.2d 898 (5th cir. 1978) (en banc), *cert. denied*, 440 U.S. 920 (1979). Before such evidence will be admitted, however, it must be tested against the criteria of MRE 403. *See United States v. Reynolds*, 29 M.J. 105 (C.M.A. 1989).

XII. JUSTIFICATION.

A. Protection of Property.

1. Use of non-deadly force. Reasonable, non-deadly force may be used to protect personal property from trespass or theft. *United States v. Regalado*, 33 C.M.R. 12 (C.M.A. 1963) (one lawfully in charge of premises may use reasonable force to eject another, if the other has refused an oral request to leave and a reasonable time to depart has been allowed); *United States v. Hines*, 21 C.M.R. 201 (C.M.A. 1956) (with regard to on-post quarters, commander on military business is not a trespasser subject to accused's right to eject); *United States v. Gordon*, 33 C.M.R. 489 (A.B.R. 1963) (the necessity to use force in defense of personal property need not be real, but only reasonably apparent); *United States v. Wilson*, 7 M.J. 997 (A.C.M.R. 1979) (accused had no right to resist execution of a search warrant, even though warrant subsequently held to be invalid); *United States v. Adams*, 18 C.M.R. 187 (C.M.A. 1955) (generally a military person's place of abode is the place where he bunks and keeps his private possessions. His home is the particular place where the necessities of the service force him to live. This may be a barracks, a tent, or even a fox hole. Whatever the name of his place of abode, it is his sanctuary from unlawful intrusion and he is entitled to stand his ground against a trespasser, to the same extent that a civilian is entitled to stand fast in his civilian home); *see also United States v. Lincoln*, 38 C.M.R. 128 (C.M.A. 1967). *See generally* Peck, *The Use of Force to Protect Government Property*, 26 Mil. L. Rev. 81 (1964); Benchbook ¶ 5-7.

2. Use of deadly force. Deadly force may be employed to protect property only if (1) the crime is of a forceful, serious or aggravated nature, and (2) the accused honestly believes use of deadly force is necessary to prevent loss of the property. *United States v. Lee*, 13 C.M.R. 57 (C.M.A. 1953).

3. Reasonable force. While it is well established that a service member has a legal right to eject a trespasser from her military bedroom and a legal right to protect her personal property, the soldier has no legal right to do so unreasonably. *United States v. Marbury*, 56 M.J. 12 (C.A.A.F. 2001) (accused's immediate return to her bedroom brandishing a knife for the purpose of ejecting her assailant was excessive or unreasonable force and hence unlawful conduct).

B. Prevention of Crime.

    1. Under military law a private person may use force essential to prevent commission of a felony in his presence, although the degree of force should not exceed that demanded by the circumstances. *United States v. Hamilton*, 27 C.M.R. 204 (C.M.A. 1959). *See generally* Peck, *The Use of Force to Protect Government Property*, 26 Mil. L. Rev. 81 (1964). While felony is not defined in the 2008 Manual for Courts-Martial, 18 U.S.C. § 1 (1) (1982) defines it as any offense punishable by death or imprisonment for a term exceeding one year.

    2. Use of deadly force. *United States v. Person*, 7 C.M.R. 298 (A.B.R. 1953) (soldier on combat patrol justified in killing unknown attacker of another patrol member where (1) victim was committing a felony in the accused's presence, and (2) the accused attempted to inflict less than deadly force).

C. Performance of Duty.

    1. A death, injury, or other act caused or done in the proper performance of a legal duty is justified and not unlawful. R.C.M. 916(c).

    2. Justification is raised only if the accused was performing a legal duty at the time of the offense. *United States v. Rockwood*, 52 M.J. 98, 112 (1999) (holding that neither international law nor television speech by the President imposed on accused a duty to inspect Haitian penitentiary for possible human rights violations); *United States v. McMonagle*, 38 M.J. 53 (C.M.A. 1993) (killing civilian may be justified by a mistake of fact as to victim's identity, although not the facts of this case).

    3. *United States v. Little*, 43 M.J. 88 (C.A.A.F. 1995) (accused's statements in providence inquiry about his authorization for possession of a work knife were substantially inconsistent with guilty plea for unauthorized possession of a dangerous weapon on naval vessel).

    4. *United States v. Reap*, 43 M.J. 61 (C.A.A.F. 1995) (naval custom whereby goods are bartered or traded from department to department in order to avoid delays, red tape, and technicalities incident to acquisition through regular supply channels, is not a defense to wrongful disposition of government property unless it rises to the level of a claim of authority or honest and reasonable mistaken belief of authority).

    5. *United States v. Rockwood*, 52 M.J. 98 (C.A.A.F. 1999) (accused's interpretation of the President's command intent did not create a legal duty to inspect penitentiary in Haiti and accused could not base a special defense of justification on that ground. The commander, not the subordinate assesses competing concerns and develops command mission priorities).

D. Obedience to Orders.

    1. Orders of military superiors are inferred to be legal. MCM, pt. IV, ¶ 14c(2)(a); *United States v. Cherry*, 22 M.J. 284 (C.M.A. 1986).

    2. The accused is entitled to the defense where he committed the act pursuant to an order which (a) appeared legal and which (b) the accused did not know to be illegal. R.C.M. 916(d); *United States v. Calley*, 46 C.M.R. 1131, 1183 (A.C.M.R. 1973).

        a) Accused's actual knowledge of illegality required. *United States v. Whatley*, 20 C.M.R. 614 (A.F.B.R. 1955) (where superior ordered accused to violate a general regulation, the defense of obedience to orders will prevail unless the evidence shows not only that the accused had actual knowledge that the order was contrary to the regulation but, also, that he could not have reasonably believed that the superior's order may have been valid).

  b) Defense unavailable if man of ordinary sense and understanding would know the order to be unlawful. *United States v. Griffen*, 39 C.M.R. 586 (A.B.R. 1968) (no error to refuse request for instruction on defense where accused shot PW pursuant to a superior's order); *see United States v. Calley*, 46 C.M.R. 1131 (A.C.M.R. 1973) (instruction on obedience to orders given).

3. The processing of a conscientious objector application does not afford an accused a defense against his obligation to deploy, even if the orders to do so violate service regulations concerning conscientious objections. *United States v. Johnson*, 45 M.J. 88 (C.A.A.F. 1996).

4. *See generally* Benchbook ¶ 5-8.

E. The Right to Resist Restraint.

1. Illegal confinement. "Escape" is from lawful confinement only; if the confinement itself was illegal, then no escape. MCM, pt. IV, ¶ 19c(1)(e); *United States v. Gray*, 20 C.M.R. 331 (C.M.A. 1956) (no crime to escape from confinement where accused's incarceration was contrary to orders of a superior commander).

2. Illegal apprehension/arrest. An individual is not guilty of having resisted apprehension (UCMJ art. 95) if that apprehension was illegal. *United States v. Clark*, 37 C.M.R. 621 (A.B.R. 1967) (accused physically detained by private citizen for satisfaction of a debt may, under the standards of self-defense, forcefully resist and seek to escape); *United States v. Rozier*, 1 M.J. 469 (C.M.A. 1976) (by forcibly detaining accused immediately following his illegal apprehension, NCOs involved acted beyond scope of their offices); *United States v. Lewis*, 7 M.J. 348 (C.M.A. 1979) (accused cannot assert illegality of apprehension as defense to assault charge when apprehending official acted within the scope of his office); *United States v. Noble*, 2 M.J. 672 (A.F.C.M.R. 1976) (accused may resist apprehension if he has no "reason to believe" the person apprehending him is empowered to do so); *United States v. Braloski*, 50 C.M.R. 310 (A.C.M.R. 1975) (resisting apprehension by a German policeman is not an offense cognizable under UCMJ art. 95, but must be charged under UCMJ art. 134).

F. Parental Discipline.

1. The law has clearly recognized the right of a parent to discipline a minor child by means of moderate punishment. *United States v. Scofield*, 33 M.J. 857 (A.C.M.R. 1991). *See generally* Benchbook ¶ 5-16.

2. The use of force by parents or guardians is justifiable if:

  a) the force is used for the purpose of safeguarding or promoting the welfare of the minor, including the prevention or punishment of his misconduct; and

  b) the force is not designed to cause or known to create a substantial risk of causing death, serious bodily injury, disfigurement, extreme pain or mental distress or gross degradation. *United States v. Brown*, 26 M.J. 148 (C.M.A. 1988).

3. A parent who spanks a child with a leather belt using reasonable force and thereby unintentionally leaves welts or bruises nevertheless acts lawfully so long as the parent

acted with a bona fide parental purpose. *United States v. Scofield*, 33 M.J. 857 (A.C.M.R. 1991).

4. One acting in the capacity of parent is justified in spanking a child, but the disciplining must be done in good faith for correction of the child motivated by educational purpose and not for some malevolent motive. *United States v. Proctor*, 34 M.J. 549 (A.F.C.M.R. 1991), *aff'd*, 37 M.J. 330 (C.M.A. 1993); *United States v. Ward*, 39 M.J. 1085 (A.C.M.R. 1994) (not a license to abuse the child).

5. Applications.

a) Tying stepson's hands and legs and placing a plastic bag over his head went beyond use of reasonable or moderate force allowed in parental discipline. *United States v. Gowadia*, 34 M.J. 714 (A.C.M.R. 1992).

b) Accused who admitted striking his child out of frustration and as means of punishment and who made no claim that he honestly believed that force used was not such as would cause extreme pain, disfigurement, or serious bodily injury was not entitled to instruction on parental discipline defense. *United States v. Gooden*, 37 M.J. 1055 (N.M.C.M.R. 1993).

c) Evidence of one closed-fist punch, without evidence of actual physical harm, was legally sufficient to overcome the affirmative defense of parental discipline where the punch was hard enough to knock down the accused's 13-year old son. *United States v. Rivera*, 54 M.J. 489 (C.A.A.F 2001).

d) *See also United States v. Robertson*, 36 M.J. 190 (C.M.A. 1992); *United States v. Ziots*, 36 M.J. 1007 (A.C.M.R. 1993).

XIII. **ALIBI.**

A. Not an Affirmative Defense. R.C.M. 916(a) discussion.

B. Notice Required. R.C.M. 701(b)(2). Exclusion of alibi evidence because of lack of notice is a drastic remedy to be employed only after considering the disadvantage to opposing counsel and the reason for failing to provide notice. *United States v. Townsend*, 23 M.J. 848 (A.F.C.M.R. 1987). Military judge abused his discretion when he excluded defense testimony because R.C.M. 701(b)(1) notice requirements were not met. *United States v. Preuss*, 34 M.J. 688 (N.M.C.M.R. 1991).

C. Raised by Evidence. Alibi raised when some evidence shows that the accused was elsewhere at the time of the commission of a crime.

D. Instructions.

1. Military judge is under no *sua sponte* obligation to instruct on this theory of defense. R.C.M. 920(e)(3); *United States v. Boyd*, 17 M.J. 562 (A.F.C.M.R. 1983); *United States v. Bigger*, 8 C.M.R. 97 (C.M.A. 1953); *United States v. Wright*, 48 C.M.R. 295, 297 (A.F.C.M.R. 1974).

2. When defense is raised by the evidence and accused requests an instruction, failure to instruct is error. *United States v. Moore*, 35 C.M.R. 317 (C.M.A. 1965); *United States v. Jones*, 7 M.J. 441 (C.M.A. 1979).

E. Sufficiency.

1. If alibi raises a reasonable doubt as to guilt, the accused is entitled to an acquittal. *United States v. Stafford*, 22 M.J. 825 (N.M.C.M.R. 1986) (finding error to require defense to prove alibi beyond a reasonable doubt).

2. Rebuttal not required. *United States v. Rath*, 27 M.J. 600 (A.C.M.R. 1988) (holding alibi defense can be rejected by the trier of fact even absent rebuttal by government).

XIV. VOLUNTARY ABANDONMENT.

A. Special defense to a charge of attempted commission of a crime. M.C.M., pt. IV, ¶4c(4); *United States v. Byrd*, 24 M.J. 286 (C.M.A. 1987).

1. Not available as a defense to an attempt crime where the acts committed have caused substantial harm to the victim. *United States v. Smauley*, 42 M.J. 449 (C.A.A.F. 1995); *United States v. Thornsbury*, 59 M.J. 767 (A. Ct. Crim. App. 2004).

2. Available for a consummated attempt only when the accused has a genuine change of heart that causes her to renounce the criminal enterprise. *United States v. Schoof*, 37 M.J. 96 (C.M.A. 1993); *United States v. Walther*, 30 M.J. 829 (N.M.C.M.R. 1990).

B. Not raised when:

1. Not raised as a defense to attempted breaking restriction where the accused abandoned his efforts because of a fear of being detected or apprehended. *United States v. Miller*, 30 M.J. 999 (N.M.C.M.R. 1990).

2. Not raised as a defense where the accused merely postpones his criminal enterprise until a more advantageous time or transfers his criminal effort to another objective or victim, or where his criminal purpose is frustrated by external forces beyond his control. *United States v. Rios*, 33 M.J. 436 (C.M.A. 1991).

XV. MISCELLANEOUS DEFENSES.

A. Amnesia.

1. General. Inability to recall past events or the facts of one's identity is loosely described as amnesia. An accused who suffers from amnesia at the time of the trial is at a disadvantage. Failure to recall a past event may prevent the accused from disclaiming the possession of a particular intent, the existence of which is essential for conviction of the offenses charged. Similarly, inability to recall identity can prevent the accused from obtaining evidence of good character from friends and family. Amnesia, however, is, by itself, generally "a relatively neutral circumstance in its bearing on criminal responsibility." *United States v. Olvera*, 15 C.M.R. 134 (C.M.A. 1954). *See generally United States v. Boultinghouse*, 29 C.M.R. 537 (C.M.A. 1960); *United States v. Buran*, 23 M.J. 736 (A.F.C.M.R. 1986); *United States v. Barreto*, 57 M.J. 127 (C.A.A.F. 2002).

2. When Amnesia May be a Defense.

a) Military offenses requiring knowledge of accused's status as a service person.

(1) Inability to recall identity might include loss of awareness of being a member of the armed forces; in that situation, amnesia might be a defense to a charge of failing to obey an order given before the onset of the condition, as it would show the existence of a mental state which would serve to negate criminal responsibility. *United States v. Olvera, supra* ¶ XIV.A.

(2) An accused cannot be convicted of AWOL if he was temporarily without knowledge that he was in the military during the period of his alleged absence. *United States v. Wiseman*, 30 C.M.R. 724 (N.B.R. 1961).

b) Drug/alcohol induced amnesia.

(1) Lack of memory or amnesia resulting from drugs or alcohol has never constituted a complete defense. *United States v. Luebs*, 43 C.M.R. 315 (C.M.A. 1971); *United States v. Butler*, 43 C.M.R. 87 (C.M.A. 1971); *United States v. Day*, 33 C.M.R. 398 (C.M.A. 1963).

(2) Drug/alcohol induced amnesia in and of itself does not constitute a mental disease or defect which will excuse criminal conduct under the defense of lack of mental responsibility. *United States v. Olvera, supra* at ¶ XIV.A.; *United States v. Lopez-Malave*, 15 C.M.R. 341 (C.M.A. 1954).

(3) Under earlier law, in order to require an insanity instruction, the evidence must show that accused's alcoholism constitutes a mental disease or defect so as to impair substantially his capacity either to appreciate the criminality of his conduct or to conform his conduct to the requirements of law. *United States v. Brown*, 50 C.M.R. 374 (N.C.M.R. 1975); *United States v. Marriott*, 15 C.M.R. 390 (C.M.A. 1954).

(4) With the passage of UCMJ art. 50a, the standard for lack of mental responsibility is now complete impairment. For a complete discussion of Article 50a, see Chapter 6, *infra*.

3. Amnesia as Affecting Accused's Competency to Stand Trial.

a) The virtually unanimous weight of authority is that an accused is not incompetent to stand trial simply because he is suffering from amnesia. *Thomas v. State*, 301 S.W.2d 358 (Tenn. 1957); *Commonwealth v. Hubbard*, 371 Mass. 160 (1976).

b) The appropriate test when amnesia is found is whether an accused can receive, or has received, a fair trial. The test, as stated in *Dusky v. United States*, 362 U.S. 402 (1960), is "whether [the accused] has sufficient present ability to consult with his lawyer with a reasonable degree of rational understanding--and whether he has a rational as well as factual understanding of the proceedings against him."

c) The problem when the accused suffers from amnesia is not his ability to consult with his attorney but rather his inability to recall events during a crucial period.

d) Where the amnesia appears to be temporary, an appropriate solution might be to defer trial for a reasonable period to see if the accused's memory improves.

e) *Commonwealth v. Lombardi*, 393 N.E.2d 346 (Mass. 1979). Where the amnesia is apparently permanent, the fairness of proceeding to trial must be assessed on the basis of the particular circumstances of the case. A variety of factors may be significant in determining whether the trial shall proceed, to include:

(1) the nature of the crime,

(2) the extent to which the prosecution makes a full disclosure of its case and circumstances known to it,

(3) the degree to which the evidence establishes the accused's guilt,

(4) the likelihood that an alibi or some defense could be established but for the amnesia,

(5) the extent and effect of the accused's amnesia.

f) A pretrial determination of whether the accused's amnesia will deny him a fair trial is not always possible. In such a case, the trial judge may make a determination of fairness after trial with appropriate findings of fact and rulings concerning the relevant criteria.

4. Guilty Pleas. An accused who fails to recall the factual basis of the offenses but is satisfied from the evidence that he is guilty may plead guilty. *United States v. Luebs*, 43 C.M.R. 315 (C.M.A. 1971); *United States v. Butler*, 43 C.M.R. 87 (C.M.A. 1971).

B. Automatism / Unconsciousness.

1. Seizures attendant to epilepsy may render the accused unable to form the *mens rea* required for assault. *United States v. Rooks*, 29 M.J. 291 (C.M.A. 1989). *See generally* TJAGSA Practice Note, *Epileptic Seizures and Criminal Mens Rea*, ARMY LAW., Feb. 1990, at 65 (discusses *Rooks*).

2. Evidence was sufficient to convict accused of offenses of willfully disobeying and assaulting an NCO, notwithstanding accused's contention that he lacked required *mens rea* due to automatic and uncontrollable behavior brought on by claustrophobia. *United States v. Campos*, 37 M.J. 894 (A.C.M.R. 1993), *aff'd*, 42 M.J. 253 (C.A.A.F. 1995).

3. *United States v. Axelson*, 65 M.J. 501 (A. Ct. Crim. App. 2007). The ACCA concluded that the accused's plea to aggravated assault was knowing and no additional instructions on defenses were required because aggravated assault is a general intent crime to which partial mental responsibility is not a defense. Further, automatism is not a defense under R.C.M. 916 or other caselaw, and there was no evidence of automatism raised either in the providence inquiry or on the merits.

4. For an interesting survey of the law in this area, see Michael J. Davidson & Steve Walters, *United States v. Berri: The Automatism Defense Rears Its Ugly Little Head*, ARMY LAW., Oct. 1993, at 17.

C. Due Process Fair Warning. The touchstone of the fair warning requirement is whether the statute, either standing alone or as construed, made it reasonably clear at the relevant time that defendant's conduct was criminal. *United States v. Lanier*, 117 S.Ct. 1219 (1997).

D. Selective Prosecution. Accused was not subjected to selective or vindictive prosecution in regard to handling or adultery allegations, though charges were not preferred against two others alleged to have committed adultery, where charges were preferred against accused only after he violated a "no-contact" order. *United States v. Argo*, 46 M.J. 454 (C.A.A.F. 1997).

E. Jury Nullification. Because there is no right to jury nullification, military judge did not err either in declining to give a nullification instruction or in declining to otherwise instruct the members that they had the power to nullify his instructions on matters of law. *United States v. Hardy*, 46 M.J. 67 (C.A.A.F. 1997). *See generally* Lieutenant Colonel Donna M. Wright & Lieutenant Colonel (Ret.) Lawrence M. Cuculic, *Annual Review of Developments in Instructions – 1997*, ARMY LAW., Jul. 1998, at 39, 48 (discussing *Hardy*).

F. Religious Convictions. *United States v. Webster*, 65 M.J. 936 (A. Ct. Crim. App. 2008). The accused pled guilty to missing movement to Iraq by design and disobeying orders from two superior commissioned officers to deliver his bags for deployment. The accused had converted to Islam in 1994 and had doubts about whether he should participate in a war against Muslims. After consulting Islamic scholars on the Internet, the accused determined that the consensus was that Muslims are not permitted to participate in the war in Iraq. By participating as a combatant, the accused believed that he would be placed "in an unfavorable position on the Day of Judgment." The accused filed a conscientious objector packet prior to the deployment, but withdrew it. He filed another conscientious objector packet on the same day that he missed movement. During the guilty plea inquiry, the military judge ruled that his religious beliefs would not provide a defense to disobeying orders. The ACCA first held that the accused's guilty plea was knowing, voluntary, and provident. First, the accused confirmed that the defense of duress did not apply to him. Second, there is no authority for the proposition that conscientious objector status provides a defense for missing movement or violating lawful orders. Third, under AR 600-43, conscientious objector requests made after an individual has entered active duty will not be favorably considered when the objection is to a certain war, which was the case here. Finally, it is irrelevant that the offenses involving missing movement and failure to obey orders were based on religious motives where such motives and beliefs did not rise to the level of a duress defense and did not constitute any other defense. The court then held that the First Amendment does not require anything more to accommodate the accused's free exercise of religion than was offered here, and the accused's rights were not violated. The ACCA first identified the applicable standard for analyzing alleged government infringement on the free exercise of religion. Under the Religious Freedom Restoration Act of 1993, the state must have a "compelling state interest" before it can burden the free exercise of religion. Additionally, courts are enjoined to apply judicial deference when strictly scrutinizing the military's burden on the free exercise of religion. *See Goldman v. Weinberger*, 475 U.S. 503 (1986). Applying these two standards, the ACCA concluded that the government had a compelling interest in requiring soldiers to deploy with their units. The government furthered this compelling interest using the least restrictive means. The Army offers soldiers an opportunity to apply for conscientious objector status, and in this case, his command offered the accused the opportunity to deploy in a non-combat role. In applying the duly required judicial deference, the ACCA concluded that the Army furthered its compelling interest in the least restrictive manner possible. The accused "had no legal right or privilege under the First Amendment to refuse obedience to the orders, and the orders were not given for an illegal purpose." (citing *United States v. Barry*, 36 C.M.R. 829, 831 (C.G.B.R. 1966) (internal brackets omitted).

XVI. STATUTE OF LIMITATIONS

A. While not an affirmative or special defense, the statute of limitations operates like a defense in that it time-bars prosecutions. *See* UCMJ art. 43 (2008); R.C.M. 907(2)(B) and discussion.

B. The standard statute of limitations is five years. *See* UCMJ art. 43(a). Statute of limitations is tolled when the summary court-martial convening authority receives the sworn charges. *See* UCMJ art. 43(b)(1).

C. Offenses without a statute of limitations. UCMJ art. 43(a).

1. The following offenses may be tried at any time without limitation:

    a) Absence without leave.

    b) Missing movement in a time of war.

    c) Murder.

d) Rape and rape of a child.

e) Any offense punishable by death.

2. Applications.

a) *Willenbring v. Neurauter*, 48 M.J. 152 (C.A.A.F. 1998) (statute of limitations under Article 43 does not bar trial for rape, as any offense "punishable by death" may be tried at any time without limitation, even if it is referred as a noncapital case), *aff'd*, 57 M.J. 321 (C.A.A.F. 2002).

b) *United States v. Thompson*, 59 M.J. 432 (C.A.A.F. 2004). Appellant was charged with raping his stepdaughter on divers occasions within a specified four-year period. Evidence at trial showed a pattern of sexual abuse occurring over an eleven-year period at several duty stations. Over defense objection, the MJ instructed the members on carnal knowledge and indecent acts as LIOs. The members found appellant guilty of indecent acts or liberties. The MJ amended the charge sheet, deleting the time period during which the indecent acts would be barred by the statute of limitations, and asked the members whether the change did "violence" to their verdict. The president indicated that if the amended specification included a portion of the period at Fort Irwin, then that was satisfactory to the panel. The CAAF held that before instructing the members on any LIOs barred by the statute of limitations, the MJ failed to obtain a required waiver from the appellant. Because appellant did not waive the statute, the instructions erroneously included a time-barred period. The MJ was not authorized to modify the unambiguous findings of the panel, after announcement of the verdict, to reflect the non-time barred period.

D. Child Abuse Offenses. UCMJ art. 43(b)(2)(B) defines "child abuse offense."

1. Prior to 24 November 2003, the statute of limitations for child abuse offenses was 5 years.

2. Effective 24 November 2003, the statute of limitations for child abuse offenses was amended so that an accused could be tried as long as sworn charges were received by the SCMCA before the victim reached the age of 25.

3. Effective 6 January 2006, the the statute of limitations for child abuse offenses was amended once again, and an accused may now be tried for a child abuse offense as long as sworn charges are received by the SCMCA during the life of the child, or within 5 years of the offense, whichever is longer.

4. The applicable statute of limitations is the one effective at the time of the commission of the offense. *See United States v. Lopez de Victoria*, 66 M.J. 67 (C.A.A.F. 2008).

5. *United States v. McElhaney*, 54 M.J. 120 (C.A.A.F. 2000) (statute of limitations codified at 18 U.S.C. § 3283, which permits prosecution for offenses involving sexual or physical abuse of children under the age of 18 until the child reaches the age of 25, does not apply to courts-martial as UCMJ Article 43 provides the applicable statute of limitations for courts-martial).

E. Effect of Amendments to Art. 43.

1. An amendment to the statute of limitations may not revive and extend a statute of limitations that had run prior to the amendment. *Stogner v. California*, 539 U.S. 607 (2003) (holding that reviving time-barred offenses violated the Ex Post Facto Clause).

2. An amendment to the statute of limitations may extend a statute of limitations that had not run prior to the amendment ONLY when Congress evinces an intent to do so. *United States v. Lopez de Victoria*, 66 M.J. 67 (C.A.A.F. 2008) (holding an amendment to Article 43 that increased the statute of limitations for certain "child abuse" offenses did not extend existing limitations periods that had not run at the time of the amendment; the Article 43 amendment and its legislative history were silent as to retrospective application).

F. Extended Statute of Limitations for Certain Crimes in a Time of War. UCMJ art. 43.

1. Article 43(a). Covers AWOL and missing movement in a time of war. May be tried and punished at any time without limitation.

    a) Time of War for purposes of Art. 43(a) is a de facto determination. *See Broussard v. Patton* 466 F.2d 816 (9th Cir. 1972) ("time of war refers to *de facto* war and does not require a formal Congressional declaration").

    b) Korean Conflict. *United States v. Ayers* 15 C.M.R. 220 (C.M.R. 1954) (Korean Conflict is time of war for purposes of Article 43(a)); *United States v. Shell*, 23 C.M.R. 110 (C.M.R. 1957) (Armistice on July 27, 1953 terminated hostilities).

    c) Vietnam Conflict. *United States v. Anderson,* 38 C.M.R. 386 (C.M.R. 1968) (As of the Gulf of Tonkin Resolution on Aug. 10, 1964, the Vietnam Conflict is time of war for purposes of Article 43(a)); *United States v. Michaud*, 48 C.M.R. 379 (N.C.M.R. 1973) (Vietnam Conflict is time of war for purposes of Article 43(a)); *United States v. Reyes*, 48 C.M.R. 832 (A.C.M.R. 1974) (the Vietnam "time of war" terminated on 27 January 1973).

2. Article 43(f). Covers crimes against the United States or any agency thereof involving frauds, real or personal property, and contracting. Art. 43(f)(1–3).

    a) Statute of limitations is suspended during the time of war and for three years after the termination of hostilities. Art. 43(f).

    b) "Time of War."

        (1) *United States v. Swain,* 27 C.M.R. 111 (C.M.A. 1958) (Korean Conflict constituted a time of war for purposes of Article 43(f)).

        (2) There is no military caselaw addressing whether OIF or OEF constitute a "time of war" for purposes of Art. 43(f). For arguments that OIF and OEF should be considered a time of war for Art. 43, see Lieutenant Commander Joseph Romero, *Of War and Punishment: "Time of War" in Military Jurisprudence and a Call for Congress to Define its Meaning,* 51 NAVAL L. REV. 1 (2005).

        (3) One federal district court has concluded that both OIF and OEF were, at one point, a time of war, invoking the federal analogue to Article 43(f), 18 U.S.C. § 3287. *See United States v. Prosperi,* 2008 U.S. Dist. LEXIS 66470 (Dist. Mass. Aug. 29, 2008).

XVII. FORMER JEOPARDY (ART. 44, UCMJ)

A. No person may, without his consent, be tried a second time for the same offense. Article 44(a); U.S. CONST. AMEND V.

B. When Jeopardy Attaches.

1. A proceeding which, after introduction of evidence but before a finding, is dismissed or terminated by the convening authority or on motion of the prosecution for failure of available evidence or witnesses without any fault of the accused, is a trial. Article 44(c).

2. In the military, jeopardy does not attach until an accused is put to trial before the trier of the facts. *See United States v. Ragard*, 56 M.J. 852, 855 (A. Ct. Crim. App. 2003).

    a) In a military judge alone case, jeopardy attaches after an accused has been indicted and arraigned, has pleaded and the court has begun to hear evidence. *See United States v. McClain*, 65 M.J. 894 (A. Ct. Crim. App. 2008) (citing *McCarthy v. Zerbst*, 85 F.2d 640, 642 (10th Cir. 1936)).

    b) In a panel case, this occurs when the members are empaneled and sworn. *United States v. McClain*, 65 M.J. 894 (A. Ct. Crim. App. 2008) (citing *Serfass v. United States*, 420 U.S. 377, 390-91, 95 S. Ct. 1055, 43 L. Ed. 2d 265 (1975)).

3. Withdrawal of charges after arraignment but before presentation of evidence does not constitute former jeopardy, and denial of a motion to dismiss charges at a subsequent trial is proper. *United States v. Wells*, 26 C.M.R. 289 (C.M.A. 1958).

4. Double jeopardy does not attach when charges are dismissed for violating the statute of limitations. Thus, the government is not barred from prosecuting the accused on a charge sheet that had properly been received by the summary court-martial convening authority within the period of the statute, following dismissal of charges for the same offense (but on a different charge sheet) that was not received within the period of the statute. However, if evidence was introduced in the first proceeding, the first is considered a trial and jeopardy attaches. *United States v. Jackson*, 20 M.J. 83 (C.M.A. 1985).

C. When Former Jeopardy Bars a Second Trial.

1. A determination that jeopardy attaches does not end the analysis. Double jeopardy bars retrial only when the military judge or the panel has made a determination by regarding guilt or innocence. *See United States v. McClain*, 65 M.J. 894 (A. Ct. Crim. App. 2008); *United States v. Germono*, 16 M.J. 987, 988 (A.C.M.R. 1988).

2. An accused is "acquitted" only when a ruling of the judge actually resolves some or all of the factual elements of the offense charged in the accused's favor, even if some or all of that resolution may be incorrect. *See United States v. McClain*, 65 M.J. 894 (A. Ct. Crim. App. 2008) (citing *United States v. Hunt*, 24 M.J. 725, 728 (A.C.M.R. 1987) and *United States v. Martin Linen Supply Co.*, 430 U.S. 564, 572 (1977)).

3. Retrial for offenses was not barred when the military judge granted a defense motion to dismiss on speedy trial grounds after hearing evidence in the first trial, but before entering findings. *United States v. McClain*, 65 M.J. 894 (A. Ct. Crim. App. 2008).

D. Same Offense.

1. Once tried for a lesser offense, accused cannot be tried for a major offense that differs from the lesser offense in degree only. Trial for AWOL bars subsequent trial for desertion. *United States v. Hayes*, 14 C.M.R. 445 (N.B.R. 1953).

2. "The protection against double jeopardy does not rest upon a surface comparison of the allegations of the charges; it also involves consideration of whether there is a substantial relationship between the wrongdoing asserted in the one charge and the misconduct alleged in the other." *United States v. Lynch*, 47 C.M.R. 498, 500 (C.M.A.

1973) (doctrine of former jeopardy precluded another trial for unauthorized absence from different unit and shorter time period). *But see United States v. Robinson*, 21 C.M.R. 380 (A.B.R. 1956) (permitting, after conviction for an AWOL and after disapproval of findings and sentence by the convening authority, trial for AWOL for the same period but from a different unit than was previously charged); *United States v. Hutzler*, 5 C.M.R. 661, 664 n.3 (A.B.R. 1951).

3. Nonjudicial punishment previously imposed under Article 15 for a *minor* offense and punishment imposed under Article 15 for a *minor* disciplinary infraction may be interposed as a bar to trial for the same minor offense or infraction. R.C.M. 907(b)(2)(D)(iv).

    a) "Minor" normally does not include offenses for which the maximum punishment at a general court-martial could be dishonorable discharge or confinement for more than one year. MCM, pt. V, ¶ 1.e.

    b) If an accused has previously received punishment under Article 15 for other than a minor offense, the service member may be tried subsequently by court-martial; however, the prior punishment under Article 15 must be considered in determining the amount of punishment to be adjudged at trial if the accused is found guilty at the court-martial. *United States v. Jackson*, 20 M.J. 83 (C.M.A. 1985); *see* UCMJ art. 15(f); R.C.M. 1001(c)(1)(B); *United States v. Pierce*, 27 M.J. 367 (C.M.A. 1989) (accused must be given complete credit for any and all nonjudicial punishment suffered—day-for-day, dollar-for-dollar, and stripe-for-stripe).

THIS PAGE INTENTIONALLY LEFT BLANK

CHAPTER 6: MENTAL RESPONSIBILITY

I. **INTRODUCTION.**

    A. **Mental Responsibility.** Refers to the criminal culpability of the accused based on his mental state at the time of the offense and includes the complete defense commonly known as the "insanity defense" and the more limited defense of "partial mental responsibility."

    B. **Competency to Stand Trial.** Refers to the present ability of the accused to stand trial. An accused may not be tried unless mentally competent. *Godinez v. Moran*, 509 U.S 389, 396 (1993). To try a mentally incompetent accused is a violation of due process. *Medina v. California*, 505 U.S. 437, 453 (1992).

    C. **Sanity Boards.** Provision under Rule for Courts-Martial (RCM) 706 governing the process inquiring into the mental capacity or mental responsibility of an accused.

II. **REFERENCES.**

    A. Manual for Courts-Martial, United States (2008 ed.).

    B. TM 8-240, Military Mental Health Law (29 Sept. 1992).

    C. Major Timothy P. Hayes, Jr., *Post-Traumatic Stress Disorder on Trial*, 190-191 MIL L. REV. 67 (2007).

    D. Major Jeremy Ball, *Solving the Mystery of Insanity Law: Zealous Representation of Mentally Ill Servicemembers*, ARMY LAW., Dec. 2005, at 1.

    E. Captain Charles Trant, *The American Military Insanity Defense: A Moral, Philosophical, and Legal Dilemma*, 99 MIL. L. REV. 1 (1983).

    F. Major Rita Caroll, *Insanity Defense Reform*, 114 MIL. L. REV. 183 (1986).

    G. Lieutenant Colonel Donna M. Wright, *"Though this be madness, yet there is some method in it": A Practitioners Guide to Mental Responsibility and Competency to Stand Trial*, ARMY LAW., Sep. 1997, at 18.

    H. Major Jeff Bovarnick and Captain Jackie Thompson, *Trying to Remain Sane Trying an Insanity Case: United States v. Captain Thomas S. Payne*, ARMY LAW., June 2002 at 13.

III. **MENTAL RESPONSIBILITY.**

    A. **The Old Standard.** Court of Military Appeals adopted the ALI test for insanity in *United States v. Frederick*, 3 M.J. 230 (C.M.A. 1977). "A person is not responsible for criminal conduct if at the time of such conduct as a result of mental disease or defect he lacks substantial capacity either to appreciate the criminality of his conduct or to conform his conduct to the requirements of the law." *Frederick*, 3 M.J. at 234.

    B. **The Current Standard.** Codified in Article 50a, UCMJ.

        1. Definition. It is an **affirmative defense** in a trial by court-martial that, at the time of the commission of the acts constituting the offense, the accused, as a result of a severe mental disease or defect, was unable to appreciate the nature and quality or the wrongfulness of the acts. Mental disease or defect does not otherwise constitute a defense. RCM 916(k)(1). Article 50a was modeled on 18 U.S.C. § 17.

        2. Taken from Insanity Defense Reform Act, Pub. L. No. 98-473, § 402(a), 98 Stat. 2057 (1984).

    C. Significant aspects of the current standard.

1. Threshold Requirements.

   a) **Severe mental disease or defect**. The affirmative defense requires a "severe" mental disease or defect. *United States v. Martin*, 56 M.J. 97, 103 (C.A.A.F. 2001).

   (1) The MCM defines "severe mental disease or defect" negatively. A severe mental disease or defect "*does not* include an abnormality manifested only by repeated criminal or otherwise antisocial conduct, or minor disorders such as nonpsychotic behavior disorders and personality defects." RCM 706(c)(2)(A) (emphasis added).

   (2) However, case law indicates that a nonpsychotic disorder may constitute a severe mental disease or defect. *See United States v. Benedict*, 27 M.J. 253 (C.M.A. 1988) (discussing pedophilia).

   (3) Compare with Benchbook Instruction 6-4: "[A] severe mental disease or defect does not, in the legal sense, include an abnormality manifested only by repeated criminal or otherwise antisocial conduct or by nonpsychotic behavior disorders and personality disorders."

   (4) **Ultimate Opinion Testimony**. In 1986, the President rescinded adoption of Fed. R. Evid. 704(b), which prohibits expert testimony offering an opinion on the issue of a defendant's mental state or condition where such constituted an element or defense to a charged offense. Ultimate opinion testimony is admissible. *See, e.g., United States v. Combs*, 39 M.J. 288 (C.M.A. 1994). Testimony as to the ultimate opinion (diagnosis of severe mental disease or defect) does not, however, always equate to lack of mental responsibility. *United States. v. Jones*, 46 M.J. 535 (N-M. Ct. Crim. App. 1997), *rev'd on other grounds*, 50 M.J. 46 (C.A.A.F. 1998) (summary disposition), *on remand*, 1999 WL 356311 (N-M. Ct. Crim. App. May 7, 1999) (unpublished).

   b) As a result of severe mental disease or defect, accused unable to appreciate nature and quality *or* wrongfulness of the act. *Martin*, 56 M.J. at 103.

D. Procedure.

   1. The defense must give notice of the defense of lack of mental responsibility before the beginning of trial on the merits. RCM 701(b)(2). Reciprocal discovery may apply. RCM 701(b)(3) and (4).

   2. Burden and standard of proof.

   a) **Burden on the accused by clear and convincing evidence**. *Martin*, 56 M.J. at 103. A career Army Judge Advocate convicted, *inter alia*, of 29 specifications of larceny, alleged at trial and on appeal that he was not mentally responsible for his criminal misconduct because he suffered from bipolar disorder. Though the defense presented over 20 expert and lay witnesses (the accused did not testify), none of these witnesses described unusual or bizarre behavior on the dates of the alleged offenses.

   b) The constitutionality of shifting the burden. *See United States v. Martin*, 48 M.J. 820, 825 n.9 (A. Ct. Crim. App. 1998); *United States v. Freeman*, 804 F.2d 1574 (11th Cir. 1986), citing *Leland v. Oregon*, 343 U.S. 790 (1952).

3. **Instructions on mental responsibility**. The military judge has a *sua sponte* duty to instruct upon mental responsibility during final instructions if the defense is raised by the evidence. RCM 920(e)(3). Chapter 6, DA PAM 27-9. The defense can get a preliminary instruction (6-3) when some evidence has been adduced which tends to show insanity of accused. The MJ is not required to instruct the panel regarding the consequences to the accused of a not guilty only by reason of lack of mental responsibility verdict. *See Shannon v. United States*, 512 U.S. 573 (1994).

4. Bifurcated voting procedures. RCM 921(c)(4). *See also* DA PAM 27-9, 6-4 and 6-7 (procedural instructions on findings). Because of their complexity, the voting instructions should be given in writing.

    a) First vote on whether accused is guilty.

    b) If accused found guilty, the second vote is on mental responsibility.

5. RCM 1102A. Not guilty only by reason of lack of mental responsibility. <u>Within 40 days of verdict, court-martial must conduct a hearing</u>. UCMJ art. 76b. RCM 1102A sets out the procedural guidelines for the hearing.

    a) Before the hearing, the judge or convening authority shall order a psychiatric or psychological examination of the accused, with the resulting psychiatric or psychological report transmitted to the military judge for use in the post-trial hearing. RCM 1102A(b). *See also* 18 U.S.C. § 4243 (post-trial psychiatric examination).

    b) The convening authority *shall* commit the accused to a suitable facility until person is eligible for release IAW UCMJ, art. 76b(b). UCMJ, art. 76b(b)(1).

    c) Accused must prove that his release would not create a substantial risk of bodily injury or serious damage to property of another due to a mental disease or defect. If he fails to meet that burden, the GCMCA may commit the accused to the Attorney General, who turns the person over to a state or monitors the person until his release would not create a substantial risk of bodily injury or serious damage to another's property.

        (1) If the accused is found not guilty by reason of lack of mental responsibility for an offense involving bodily injury to another or serious damage to property of another, or substantial risk of such property or injury, the standard is <u>clear and convincing</u> evidence.

        (2) Any other offense, standard is <u>preponderance</u> of the evidence.

    d) **Right to Counsel**. RCM 1102A(c)(1) provides that an accused shall be represented by counsel.

6. Discovery of Evidence Post-Trial indicating Lack of Mental Responsibility. *See United States v. Harris*, 61 M.J. 391 (C.A.A.F. 2005). Good discussion of issues surrounding discovery, post-trial, of evidence of lack of mental responsibility.

IV. PARTIAL MENTAL RESPONSIBILITY.

A. **The Old (pre-2004 Amendment) Manual Standard**. A mental condition not amounting to a general lack of mental responsibility under subsection RCM 916(k)(1) is not a defense, *nor is evidence of such a mental condition admissible as to whether the accused entertained a state of mind necessary to be proven as an element of the offense.* RCM 916(k)(2). The old standard tried to prohibit a partial mental responsibility defense.

1. The CMA rejected the old RCM 916(k)(2) because it doubted the rule's constitutionality and found that the legislative history of the federal model lacked any Congressional intent to preclude defendants from attacking *mens rea* with contrary evidence.

2. Psychiatric testimony or evidence that serves to negate a specific intent is admissible. *Ellis v. Jacob*, 26 M.J. 90 (C.M.A. 1988); *see United States v. Berri*, 33 M.J. 337 (C.M.A. 1991); *United States v. Mansfield*, 38 M.J. 415, 419 n.5 (C.M.A. 1993); *see also United States v. Cameron*, 907 F.2d 1051 (11th Cir. 1990); *United States v. Pohlot*, 827 F.2d 889 (3d Cir. 1987); *United States v. Gold*, 661 F. Supp. 1127 (D.D.C. 1987); *United States v. Frisbee*, 623 F. Supp. 1217 (N.D. Cal. 1985).

B. **The Current (post-2004 Amendment) Manual Standard**. A mental condition not amounting to a lack of mental responsibility (i.e., a finding of not guilty only by reason of lack of mental responsibility) is not an affirmative defense, but may be admissible to determine whether the accused entertained the state of mind necessary to prove an element of the offense. In other words, partial mental responsibility is not an affirmative defense, but it is a deficiency of the government proof of a necessary element (e.g., specific intent).

1. Instruction on Partial Mental Responsibility. DA PAM 27-9, instruction 6-5. The affirmative defense of insanity and the defense of partial mental responsibility are separate defenses, but the panel members may consider the same evidence with respect to both defenses. With regard to partial mental responsibility, the burden never shifts from the government to prove, beyond a reasonable doubt, that the accused entertained the mental state necessary for the charged offense.

2. However, not all psychiatric evidence is now admissible. The evidence still must be relevant and permitted by UCMJ art. 50a.

   a) General intent crime. The psychiatric evidence must still rise to the level of a "severe mental disease or defect." The insanity defense cannot be resurrected under another guise. UCMJ art. 50a.

   b) Specific intent crime. The psychiatric evidence must be relevant to the *mens rea* element.

V. INTOXICATION.

A. **Voluntary Intoxication**. RCM 916(l)(2). Voluntary intoxication from alcohol or drugs may negate the elements of premeditation, specific intent, knowledge, or willfulness. Voluntary intoxication, by itself, will not reduce unpremeditated murder to a lesser offense. *United States v. Morgan*, 37 M.J. 407 (C.M.A. 1993). Voluntary intoxication not amounting to legal insanity is not a defense to general intent crimes.

B. **Involuntary Intoxication**. Generally, involuntary intoxication is a defense to a general or specific intent crime. *See United States v. Hensler*, 44 M.J. 184 (C.A.A.F. 1996). *But see United States v. Ward*, 14 M.J. 950 (A.C.M.R. 1982) (involuntary intoxication not available when accused knowingly used marijuana, but did not know it also contained PCP).

C. *See generally* Major Eugene Milhizer, *Weapons Systems Warranties: Voluntary Intoxication as a Defense Under Military Law*, 127 MIL. L. REV. 131 (1990).

VI. COMPETENCY TO STAND TRIAL.

A. **Current Standard**. "No person may be brought to trial by court-martial if that person is presently suffering from a mental disease or defect rendering him or her mentally incompetent to the extent that he or she is unable to understand the nature of the proceedings against them [sic] or to conduct or cooperate intelligently in the defense of the case." RCM 909(a). *See also* 18 U.S.C. § 4241(d). The accused is presumed to have capacity to stand trial. RCM 909(b).

B. **Old Standard**. "No person may be brought to trial by court-martial unless that person possesses **sufficient mental capacity** to understand the nature of the proceedings against that person and to conduct or cooperate intelligently in the defense of the case." MCM, RCM 909 (1984).

C. Differences between the standards.

    1. Mental disease or defect required (need not be "severe").

    2. "Unable to understand" vs. "sufficient mental capacity."

D. Cases.

    1. The real issue is whether the accused has sufficient present ability to consult with his lawyer with a reasonable degree of rational understanding and whether he has rational as well as factual understanding of the proceeding against him. It is not enough that he is oriented to time and place and has some recollection of events. *United States v. Proctor*, 37 M.J. 330, 336 (C.M.A. 1993) (quoting *Dusky v. United States*, 362 U.S. 402 (1960) (per curiam)).

    2. "The question is whether the accused is possessed of sufficient mental power, and has such understanding of his situation, such coherency of ideas, control of his mental facilities, and the requisite power of memory, as will enable him to testify in his own behalf, if he so desires, and otherwise to properly and intelligently aid his counsel in making a rational defense." *United States v. Lee*, 22 M.J. 767, 769 (A.F.C.M.R. 1986).

    3. *United States v. Schlarb*, 46 M.J. 708 (N-M. Ct. Crim. App. 1997). The accused did not establish a lack of mental capacity to stand trial where she testified clearly and at length on four occasions, showing a clear understanding of the proceedings.

    4. *Indiana v. Edwards*, 554 U.S. 164 (2008). The Constitution permits judges to take realistic account of the particular defendant's mental capacities by asking whether a defendant who seeks to conduct his own defense at trial is mentally competent to do so. Therefore, a defendant who is mentally competent to stand trial may still be denied the right to represent themselves, depending on the vagaries of the mental disease or illness.

E. **Compared to Amnesia**.

    1. Amnesia is not equivalent to a lack of capacity. "An inability to remember about the crime itself does not necessarily make a person incompetent to stand trial." *Lee*, 22 M.J. at 769; *see also United States v. Barreto*, 57 M.J. 127 (C.A.A.F. 2002). The ability of an accused to function is absolutely critical to the fairness of a criminal trial. In deciding whether an accused can function, a military judge can apply factors set out in *Wilson v. United States*, 391 F.2d 460 (D.C. Cir. 1968): (1) the extent to which the amnesia affects the accused's ability to consult and assist his lawyer; (2) the extent to which the amnesia affects the accused's ability to testify on his own behalf; (3) the extent to which the evidence could be extrinsically reconstructed, in view of the accused's amnesia; (4) the extent to which the Government assisted the accused and defense counsel in reconstruction; (5) the strength of the Government case; and, (6) any other facts and circumstances that would indicate whether the accused had a fair trial.

2. *United States v. Axelson*, 65 M.J. 501 (A. Ct. Crim. App. 2007). A failure to recall facts pertaining to an offense does not preclude an accused from pleading guilty so long as, after assessing the Government's evidence against him, he is convicted of his own guilt.

F. Procedure. UCMJ art. 76b and RCM 909.

    1. **Interlocutory question of fact.** After referral, military judge *may* conduct an incompetence determination hearing either *sua sponte* or on request of either party. RCM 909(d).

    2. Defense has the burden of proof by a preponderance of the evidence.

    3. Military judge *shall* conduct the hearing if sanity board completed IAW RCM 706 before or after referral concluded the accused is not competent.

    4. Military judge determines whether the accused is competent to stand trial. *United States v. Proctor*, 37 M.J. 330 (C.M.A. 1993); *Short v. Chambers*, 33 M.J. 49 (C.M.A. 1991).

    5. Once a sanity board is requested, the military judge must consider the sanity board report before ruling on the accused's capacity to stand trial. *United States v. Collins*, 41 M.J. 610 (A. Ct. Crim. App. 1994).

G. **Hospitalization of the accused.** An accused who is found incompetent to stand trial shall be hospitalized by the Attorney General for a reasonable period of time, not to exceed 4 months, to determine whether his condition will improve in foreseeable future, and for an additional reasonable period of time. The additional period of time ends when: the mental condition improves so that trial may proceed, or, charges are dismissed.

    1. Upon a finding of incompetence, if the convening authority agrees, there is no discretion regarding commitment. *United States. v. Salahuddin*, 54 M.J. 918 (A.F. Ct. Crim. App. 2001); *see also* RCM 909(e)(3) and 18 U.S.C. § 4241(d).

    2. The four-month time period may be extended. To justify extended commitment, the Government must prove by clear and convincing evidence that "a substantial probability exists that the continued administration of antipsychotic medication will result in a defendant attaining the capacity to permit the trial to proceed in the foreseeable future." *United States v. Weston*, 260 F. Supp. 2d 147, 154 (D.D.C. 2003) (approving a year-long extension from the case below in (3)(a)).

    3. Involuntary Medication.

        a) *United States v. Weston*, 255 F.3d 873 (D.C. Cir. 2001). Defendant indicted for the murders and attempted murder of federal law enforcement officers. A court-appointed forensic psychiatrist diagnosed defendant with paranoid schizophrenia, the severity of which rendered him incompetent to stand trial. Because he refused treatment with antipsychotic medication, he was simply placed in solitary confinement under constant supervision. The government sought a court order authorizing the involuntary administration of medication to render him competent to stand trial. The Circuit Court held that there was no basis to believe that defendant's worsening condition rendered him more dangerous, given his near-total incapacitation. However, the court affirmed the District Court's decision that the government's interest in administering antipsychotic drugs overrode his liberty interest and that restoring his competence in this way did not violate his right to a fair trial.

b) *Sell v. United States*, 539 U.S. 166 (2003). Defendant was charged with fraud. A federal magistrate found him incompetent to stand trial and ordered his hospitalization to determine whether he would attain capacity to allow his trial to proceed. Sell refused to take antipsychotic drugs. The magistrate found involuntary medication appropriate because Sell was a danger to himself and others, that medication was the only way to render him less dangerous, that any serious side effects could be ameliorated, that the benefits to him outweighed the risks, and that the drugs were substantially likely to return Sell to competence. The District Court, although determining that the Magistrate's conclusion regarding Sell's dangerousness was clearly erroneous, nonetheless affirmed the decision because it found that the medication was the only viable hope of rendering Sell competent and was necessary to serve the government's interest in adjudicating his guilt or innocence. The Circuit Court affirmed, finding that the government had an essential interest in bringing Sell to trial, that treatment was medically appropriate, and that the medical evidence indicated a reasonably probability that Sell would fairly be able to participate in his defense. The Supreme Court vacated and remanded the case. Determining that forced medication solely for trial competency purposes may be rare, the Court held that the Constitution permits involuntary medication to render a mentally ill defendant competent to stand trial on serious criminal charges if the treatment is medically appropriate, is substantially unlikely to have side effects that may undermine the trial's fairness, and, taking account of less intrusive alternatives, is necessary to significantly further important governmental trial-related interests.

c) *United States v. Bush*, 585 F.3d 806 (4th Cir. 2009). The court finds that the government must establish all of the *Sell* factors by clear and convincing evidence. The court also held that even where a defendant has been in an institution longer than the maximum punishment for the underlying offense, the government still has an important interest in bringing the defendant to trial. Certain consequences that convictions bring (such as firearms restrictions) are important governmental interests justifying continued prosecution and potential involuntary medication.

4. **Recovery.** If the accused has recovered and is competent to stand trial, the director of the facility notifies the GCMCA and sends a copy of the notice to accused's counsel. GCMCA must take prompt custody of the accused if the accused is still in a military status. The director of the facility may retain custody of the person for not more than 30 days after transmitting the required notifications.

a) **No Recovery**. If person does not improve (18 U.S.C. § 4246). If the director of the facility where the accused is confined certifies that the accused is presently suffering from a mental disease or defect and his release would create a substantial risk of bodily injury to another person or serious damage to property, the director notifies the GCMCA. The district court then conducts further hearings.

H. **Waiver**. *Moore v. Campbell*, 344 F.3d. 1313 (11th Cir. 2003). The Eleventh Circuit Court of Appeals looked at whether a defendant in a capital case can forfeit his right to competency – a case of first impression. Moore attempted suicide during his capital murder trial. After treatment at a hospital and subsequent examination by a psychiatrist, Moore appeared at trial, which resumed on 31 August. From 27 August until the evening of 1 September, Moore had refused anything to eat or drink, resulting in dehydration. The state court found Moore was competent to stand trial and that he took a "calculated and concerted effort to disrupt his murder trial." The state court also found Moore's asserted incompetence similar to a defendant whose behavior results in exclusion from a trial. Reviewing the state court proceedings during a federal *habeas* petition, the Court of Appeals determined that the "state court's determination that a capital defendant in Alabama can forfeit his right to be competent – that is mentally present – at trial" was not contrary to or an unreasonable application of clearly established Supreme Court precedent, if only because the issue has not been yet decided by the Supreme Court.

I. **Post-trial**. The convening authority may not approve a sentence while the accused lacks the mental capacity to cooperate and understand post-trial proceedings. RCM 1107(b)(5). Likewise, an appellate authority may not affirm the findings when the accused lacks the ability to understand and cooperate in appellate proceedings. RCM 1203(c)(5). *See Thompson v. United States*, 60 M.J. 880 (N-M. Ct. Crim. App. 2005) (holding that appellant demonstrated lack of mental capacity to assist in appeal; appeal stayed).

VII. **THE SANITY BOARD.**

   A. Sanity Board Request.

      1. Who can request? Any commander, investigating officer, trial counsel, defense counsel, military judge, or member. R.C.M. 706(a).

         a) Request goes to CA (before referral) and MJ (after referral).

         b) A sanity board should be granted if request is not frivolous and is made in good faith. *United States v. Nix*, 36 C.M.R. 76, 80-81 (C.M.A. 1965); *United States v. Kish*, 20 M.J. 652 (A.C.M.R. 1985).

         c) It may be prudent for trial counsel to join in the motion. *See United States v. James*, 47 M.J. 641 (A. Ct. Crim. App. 1997) (finding that a mental status evaluation was not an adequate substitute for a sanity board).

      2. Failure to direct a sanity inquiry.

         a) Though ultimate result may be "favorable" to the government, failure to timely direct a sanity board can result in lengthy appellate review. *United States v. Breese*, 47 M.J. 5 (C.A.A.F. 1997).

         b) **"A low threshold is nonetheless a threshold which the proponent must cross."** *United States v. Pattin*, 50 M.J. 637, 639 (A. Ct. Crim. App. 1999) (finding that the military judge's refusal to order a sanity board was not error where it appeared the motion for a sanity board was merely a frivolous attempt to get a trial delay).

      3. Sanity Board Order asks the following questions:

         a) At the time of the alleged criminal conduct, did the accused have a severe mental disease or defect?

         b) What is the clinical psychiatric diagnosis?

         c) Was the accused, at the time of the alleged criminal conduct and as a result of such severe mental disease or defect, unable to appreciate the nature and quality or wrongfulness of his conduct?

         d) Does the accused have sufficient mental capacity to understand the nature of the proceedings and to conduct or cooperate intelligently in the defense?

4. Composition of the sanity board.

   a) One or more persons.

   b) Physician or clinical psychologist.

   c) At least one psychiatrist or clinical psychologist.

   d) A provisional license may be enough to qualify a psychologist as a clinical psychologist. *United States v. Boasmond*, 48 M.J. 912 (N-M. Ct. Crim. App. 1998).

5. Conflict of interest. *United States v. Best*, 61 M.J. 376 (C.A.A.F. 2005). Two members of the accused's RCM 706 sanity board had a preexisting psychotherapist-patient relationship with the accused. In a case of first impression, the Army court stated that an actual conflict of interest would exist when prior participation that materially limits his or her ability to objectively participate in and evaluate the subject of an RCM 706 sanity board. The CAAF declined to adopt a presumptive rule that there would be an actual conflict of interest if a mental health provider, who has established a psychotherapist-patient relationship with an accused, also serves as a member in an RCM 706 sanity board. In this case, the CAAF held there was no evidence suggesting that the two members' participation would be materially limited by their prior relationship.

6. The accused's right to a speedy trial is not violated when the government delays the case for a time reasonably necessary to complete a thorough mental evaluation. *United States v. Colon-Angueira*, 16 M.J. 20 (C.M.A. 1983) (fifty-one days reasonable); *United States v. Carpenter*, 37 M.J. 291 (C.M.A. 1993) (the government's negligence or bad faith can be considered in determining whether the sanity board was completed within a reasonable time); *United States v. Pettaway*, 24 M.J. 589 (N.M.C.M.R. 1987) (thirty-six days was reasonable time for a second sanity board); *United States. v. Arab*, 55 M.J. 508 (A. Ct. Crim. App. 2001) (140 days was not unreasonable, where the record reflected due diligence by the government).

7. Results of board - limited distribution.

   a) Defense counsel gets full report.

   b) Trial counsel initially only gets answers to the above questions.

B. The Sanity Inquiry.

1. Compelled Examination. RCM 706.

   a) Article 31, UCMJ, not applicable.

   b) Failure to cooperate in an examination can result in the exclusion of defense expert evidence.

2. Privilege Concerning Mental Examination of an Accused. MRE 302.

   a) The general rule: Anything the accused says (and any derivative evidence) to the sanity board is privileged and cannot be used against him.

   b) This privilege may be claimed by the accused notwithstanding the fact that the accused may have been warned of the rights provided by MRE 305.

   c) Waiver. There is no privilege under this rule when the accused first introduces into evidence such statements or derivative evidence. Privilege applies only to examinations ordered under RCM 706. *See United States v. Toledo*, 25 M.J. 270 (C.M.A. 1987), *aff'd on reconsid.*, 26 M.J. 104 (C.M.A. 1988).

3. Derivative Evidence. In *United States v. Clark*, 62 M.J. 195 (C.A.A.F. 2005), the accused was charged, *inter alia*, with breaking restriction. Dr. Petersen treated the accused for almost a month after his command referred him to mental health. She concluded that the accused suffered a manic episode during the charged time period. Prior to trial, the defense requested a sanity board. Dr. Marrero was the lone member of the board, and he agreed with Dr. Petersen's diagnosis, but concluded that the accused was mentally responsible. At trial, Dr. Petersen, testifying for the defense, opined that there was a "high likelihood" that the accused suffered from a severe mental disease or defect during the relevant time period and that, as a result of that severe mental disease or defect, would have had a difficult time appreciating the nature and quality or wrongfulness of his conduct. During her testimony, Dr. Petersen acknowledged that she reviewed the sanity board report. The trial counsel renewed his motion to obtain a copy of the report (the MJ earlier denied the same request), which was granted. The CAAF held that it was error to release the statements of accused to Dr. Marrero as the derivative evidence provisions of MRE 302 had not been triggered. As a nonconstitutional error, the government would have to demonstrate that the error did not have a substantial influence on the findings. Given that the government relied heavily upon the testimony of Dr. Marrero, the court was left to conclude that the insanity defense may have succeeded had the military judge not erred in releasing the appellant's privileged statements to the government.

C. Are there substitutes for a sanity board?

1. Yes. "The point is that we do not believe that the drafters selected the sanity board format because they had determined that no other procedure was capable of detecting mental disorders or determining an accused person's mental capacity or responsibility. That being the case, *we believe we should look to the substance of the evaluation performed on the accused rather than on its form.*" *United States v. Jancarek*, 22 M.J. 600, 603 (A.C.M.R. 1986) (emphasis added).

2. *But see United States v. Mackie*, 65 M.J. 762 (A.F. Ct. Crim App. 2007), *aff'd*, 66 M.J. 198 (C.A.A.F. 2008) (finding that the mental health evaluation performed by a staff psychologist as a result of a pretrial suicide gesture was not an adequate substitute because of her inexperience in performing sanity boards); *United States v. James*, 47 M.J. 641 (A. Ct. Crim. App. 1997) (finding that mental status evaluation done by a mental health counselor was not an adequate substitute); *United States v. English*, 47 M.J. 215 (C.A.A.F. 1997) (finding that an examination by doctors for purposes of treatment of the accused was not an adequate substitute because the examination did not address the judicial standards for mental capacity or responsibility).

VIII. TRIAL CONSIDERATIONS.

A. In addition to a sanity board, an accused is entitled to access to a qualified psychiatrist or psychologist for the purpose of presenting an insanity defense if he establishes that his sanity will be a "significant factor" at the trial. *United States v. Mustafa*, 22 M.J. 165 (C.M.A. 1986); *see Ake v. Oklahoma*, 470 U.S. 68 (1985). Significant factor defined:

1. Mere assertion of insanity by accused or counsel is insufficient. *Volson v. Blackburn*, 794 F.2d 173 (5th Cir. 1986).

2. A "clear showing" by the accused that sanity is in issue and a "close" question that might be decided either way is required. *Cartwright v. Maynard*, 802 F.2d 1203 (10th Cir. 1986).

3. Expert must be made part of the "defense team" under MRE 502 to be covered by the attorney-client privilege. *United States v. Toledo*, 25 M.J. 270 (C.M.A. 1987), *aff'd on reconsid.*, 26 M.J. 104 (C.M.A. 1988). *United States v. Mansfield*, 38 M.J. 415 (C.M.A. 1993). A physician, psychotherapist who assists the defense in preparation of a defense may fall within the scope of the attorney-client privilege.

B. *United States v. Collins*, 60 M.J. 261 (C.A.A.F. 2004). The MJ must act when issues of mental responsibility and capacity arise during trial. In this case, the lone member of a sanity board testified in a manner apparently inconsistent with his conclusion in the report that the accused was mentally responsible for his actions. During trial, COL Richmond testified that the accused's actions were consistent with his delusional disorder and that the accused did *not* understand the nature and quality or wrongfulness of his conduct. The MJ did not order further inquiry under RCM 706 and the CAAF held that he should have.

C. **Defense use of statements of the accused to an RCM 706 Board.** *United States v. Schap*, 49 M.J. 317 (C.A.A.F. 1998). The judge did not err when he sustained trial counsel's objection and prevented former sanity board psychiatrist from testifying for defense at trial as to accused's statements and emotions at the time of the offense. The defense was attempting to smuggle the accused's statements in without subjecting him to cross-examination.

D. Once defense offers **expert** testimony of accused's mental condition, a prosecution expert may testify as to the reasons for the expert's conclusions concerning accused's mental state (may not extend to accused's statements unless the accused first introduces his own statement or derivative evidence). MRE 302.

E. **Disclosure of full sanity board report.** *United States v. Cole*, 54 M.J. 572 (A. Ct. Crim. App. 2000), *aff'd*, 55 M.J. 466 (C.A.A.F. 2001) (summary disposition). At trial, the Government moved to compel defense disclosure of entire report under MRE 302(c) because defense was requesting two experts to testify about accused's belief that his actions were necessary to protect his family (as opposed to lack of mental responsibility). The military judge's decision to defer ruling on the government motion, because it was unclear in advance of the testimony whether the experts would testify on the issue of mental responsibility and not just on the second prong of defense of another, was not an abuse of discretion.

1. *United States v. Savage*, 67 M.J. 656 (A. Ct. Crim. App. 2009). The appellant claimed that he was asleep when he stabbed his victim due to a disorder called parasomnia. An RCM 706 inquiry concluded that the appellant was competent to stand trial, that there was a reasonable possibility that the appellant suffered from "parasomnia, or somnambulism that produced an automatism or sleep-related behavior at the time of the assault," and that the appellant may not have been unable to appreciate the wrongfulness of his conduct. The defense provided the government with notice of intent to rely on the defense of lack of mental responsibility. Approximately six weeks later, the defense e-mailed the full RCM 706 report to the trial counsel without an order from the military judge. Six weeks after that, the appellant hired civilian counsel and excused the counsel who e-mailed the report. Eventually the civilian counsel notified the government that the defense would not pursue the defense of lack of mental responsibility, and instead would rely upon partial mental responsibility to negate *mens rea*. Some of those statements were eventually used in cross-examination of the appellant's expert. The ACCA held that MRE 302(c) was violated, but the error was harmless. The defense case-in-chief involved

statements from an expert that revealed specific statements made by the appellant captured in the RCM 706 inquiry. The defense could have avoided the government using any portion of the report by not calling experts who authored the report. *See United States v. Clark*, 62 M.J. 195 (C.A.A.F. 2005).

F. Although the rule seems to condition the use of expert testimony by the prosecution on prior use of **experts** by the defense, the Court of Military Appeals rejected such an interpretation, finding that lay testimony can permit the government to use its experts. *United States v. Bledsoe*, 26 M.J. 97 (C.M.A. 1988); *see also United States v. Matthews*, 14 M.J. 656 (A.C.M.R. 1982).

G. The sanity board report is not admissible under hearsay rules. *United States v. Benedict*, 27 M.J. 253 (C.M.A. 1988).

H. **Sentencing Considerations**. Extenuation and Mitigation. Evidence of the accused's mental condition can be used on sentencing but with caution. *See United States v. Bono*, 26 M.J. 240 (C.M.A. 1988).

I. Guilty Pleas and Sanity Issues.

    1. *United States v. Harris*, 61 M.J. 391 (C.A.A.F. 2005). After acceptance of the accused's pleas and announcement of sentence, but before the convening authority took action, the accused was diagnosed with bipolar disorder. At a post-trial Article 39(a) session, the military judge listened to expert testimony from mental health experts who disagreed as to whether the accused suffered from any mental illness. The accused did not testify at this hearing. In his findings of fact and conclusions of law, the military judge stated that the accused "suffered from a bipolar disorder that would equate to a severe mental disease or defect," but that he appreciated the wrongfulness of his actions and was subsequently competent to stand trial. The CAAF disagreed, the majority saying that they did not see how an accused can make an informed plea without knowledge that he suffers from a severe mental disease or defect at the time of the offense. The court also stated that it was not possible for a military judge to conduct the necessary *Care* inquiry without exploring with the accused the impact of any mental health issues on those pleas.

    2. *United States v. Shaw*, 64 M.J. 460 (C.A.A.F. 2007). The accused pled guilty to offenses during a guilty plea and findings were entered. During the accused's unsworn statement, he said that prior to the charged offenses he was assaulted by a man wielding a lead pipe and suffered severe injuries to his head and brain. The accused also said that he spent almost a month in the hospital and that he was diagnosed with bipolar syndrome. The CAAF determined that the military judge did not err when he failed to inquire into the accused mental condition because his statements were unsupported by other evidence entered into the record or his behavior during his providence inquiry or unsworn statement. <u>A military judge is only required to inquire into circumstances or statements that raise a possible defense, not circumstances or statements that raise the "mere possibility" of defense.</u> NOTE: the majority opinion recommend that a prudent military judge conduct an inquiry when a significant mental health condition is raised during the plea inquiry; s*ee also United States v. Falcon*, 65 M.J. 386 (C.A.A.F. 2008) (noting that "[the accused] has provided no authority that a diagnosis of pathological gambling can constitute a defense of lack of mental responsibility."); *United States v. Glenn*, 66 M.J. 64 (C.A.A.F. 2008) (stating that the accused's expert mitigation evidence that he suffered from a mood disorder and his unsworn and unsubstantiated statements that he suffered from bipolar disorder did not raise a substantial basis in law for questioning his guilty plea).

3. *United States v. Handy*, 48 M.J. 590, 593 (A.F. Ct. Crim. App. 1998). During a guilty plea, "[w]hen evidence of an accused's mental health rears its head, the judge should question defense counsel on whether he or she has explored the mental responsibility angle of the case, including whether evidence exists to negate an intent or knowledge element of the offense. The judge should ask the accused if defense counsel has discussed that issue and how it may apply to the particular case. The judge should accept the guilty plea only if the mental issues are resolved for the record and the accused disclaims any potential mental 'defense,' full or partial."

4. *United States v. Estes*, 62 M.J. 544 (A. Ct. Crim. App. 2005). Appellant argued that remarks made during his unsworn, indicating a hyper-religiosity, should have triggered further inquiry from the Military Judge regarding his lack of mental responsibility and competency. Appellant further argued that the inquiry, together with evidence of appellant's cannabis addiction, would have demonstrated significant issues of lack of mental responsibility. The Army court, in a carefully reasoned opinion, held appellant failed to show that a different verdict might reasonably have resulted if the trier of fact had evidence of a lack of mental responsibility that was not available for consideration at trial.

5. *United States v. McGuire*, 63 M.J. 678 (A. Ct. Crim. App. 2006). Appellant's providence inquiry referenced psychiatric treatment and he otherwise acting strangely during his colloquy with the military judge. A previous mental evaluation pursuant to RCM 706 determined that the accused possessed the requisite mental capacity to stand trial and that he did not lack the necessary mental responsibility at the time of the offense. The Army court determined that the military judge was not required sua sponte to order further evaluation of the appellant. With regard to the providence of the appellant's plea, the court, citing to *Estes*, reaffirmed that not every reference to psychiatric treatment or problems, no matter how vague or oblique, is sufficient to create a substantial basis for questioning a guilty plea.

6. *United States v. Riddle*, 67 M.J. 335 (C.A.A.F. 2009). In a stipulation of fact, the parties agreed that the appellant had a chronic alcohol and marijuana dependence, as well as a bipolar and borderline personality disorder. The military judge was aware of these conditions. The judge knew that before her absence, she was receiving mental health treatment at an "off-post installation that specializes in mental issues, mental and behavioral issues." The judge also knew that she arrived at the trial from the facility and would return there after trial. During the trial, the military judge asked the appellant if she was feeling OK when she referred to "getting the fishes high" by throwing a marijuana cigarette into a lake. The military judge also asked the appellant a series of questions regarding her mental health and competency at trial. A report of mental health status evaluation was admitted into evidence on sentencing, stating that appellant had attempted suicide twice, but was mentally responsible. Finally, the military judge noted before sentencing that he observed the appellant at trial, and that she was alert, articulate, and cognizant. The CAAF held that her guilty plea was not improvident. A military judge can presume, in the absence of contrary circumstances, that the accused is sane. *See United States v. Shaw*, 64 M.J. 460 (C.A.A.F. 2007). If the appellant's statement or facts in the record indicate a mental disease or defect, the military judge must determine if that information raises a conflict with the plea or merely a possibility of conflict with the plea. The former requires further inquiry, the latter does not. The CAAF finds that the facts of this case merely raised the possibility of conflict with the plea and the military judge was not required to inquire further. Moreover, the military judge appropriately inquired into her status, and captured his observations in the record.

7. Like other affirmative defenses, lack of mental responsibility is subject to the rule of waiver. *United States v. Boasmond*, 48 M.J. 912 (N-M. Ct. Crim. App. 1998).

CHAPTER 7: PLEADINGS

I. **THE CHARGING DECISION.**

    A.   One Method for Making the Charging Decision.

        1. Prosecutorial Discretion. Even in the absence of any formal limitations, it is important to remember that there is no ethical or legal obligation to plead *all* possible charges that the evidence might support. *Compare* ABA STANDARDS, Standard 3-3.9(b) (listing factors properly considered in exercise of prosecutorial discretion) *with* R.C.M. 306(b) discussion (listing factors to be considered by commanders in making an initial disposition of offenses).

        2. How To Make the Charging Decision: A Method.

            a) Review all the evidence.

            b) Develop a theory of the case.

            c) List possible charging options.

            d) Conduct elements/proof analysis of each charge.

            e) Consider ethical and legal limitations.

            f) Consider prudential/tactical factors.

                (1) Theory of the case.

                (2) Nature and degree of harm.

                (3) Panel's perception and sense of fairness.

                (4) Exigencies of proof and intentional multiplicity.

                (5) Use of "mega-specs".

                (6) Preservation of LIOs.

                (7) Maximum punishments.

                (8) Uncharged misconduct / MRE 404(b) issues.

                (9) Cooperation of accused.

                (10) Improper motives of witnesses or victims.

                (11) Reluctance of victim to testify.

            g) Draft the Charges. Consider these basic principles:

                (1) Charge the most serious offense consistent with the evidence. *See United States v. Foster,* 40 M.J. 140, 144 n. 4 (C.M.A. 1994) ("[T]here is prosecutorial discretion to charge the accused for the offense(s) which most accurately describe the misconduct and most appropriately punish the transgression(s).").

                (2) Err on the side of liberal charging and be prepared to withdraw as the case develops. *See* R.C.M. 401(c) and R.C.M. 604 concerning withdrawal of charges and specifications.

                (3) If charging conspiracy, ensure that it is important/necessary for your theory of the case.

    B. Ethical and Legal Limitations.

        1. Ethical Limitations.

a) Charges must be warranted by the evidence.

(1) ARMY REG. 27-26, Rule 3.8(a), provides that a trial counsel shall "recommend to the convening authority that any charge or specification not warranted by the evidence be withdrawn."

(2) ABA STANDARDS, Standard 3-3.9(a), provides that "a prosecutor should not . . . cause to be instituted, or permit the continued pendency of criminal charges" in two circumstances:

(a) When the prosecutor knows that the charges are not supported by probable cause, or

(b) In the absence of sufficient admissible evidence to support a conviction.

b) A supervising prosecutor cannot compel a subordinate to prosecute an offense about which the supervisor has a reasonable doubt as to the guilt of the accused. ABA STANDARDS, Standard 3-3.9(c). *Cf.* R.C.M. 307(a) discussion.

c) Charges should not be unreasonably multiplied.

(1) Nature of Charges. What is substantially one transaction should not be made the basis for an unreasonable multiplication of charges against one person. R.C.M. 307(c)(4). *Cf.* ABA STANDARDS, Standard 3-3.9(f) (A prosecutor should not "seek charges greater in number or degree . . . than are necessary to fairly reflect the gravity of the offense").

(2) Prosecutorial Motive. A prosecutor should not "pile on" charges to "unduly leverage an accused to forego his or her right to trial." ABA STANDARDS, Standard 3-3.9 commentary.

2. Constitutional Limitations.

a) A prosecutor cannot *selectively* prosecute an individual because of "race, religion, or other arbitrary classification." *Wayte v. United States*, 470 U.S. 598 (1985). Accused must show more than a mere possibility. *United States v. Hagen*, 25 M.J. 78 (C.M.A. 1987).

b) A prosecutor cannot *vindictively* prosecute to penalize an individual's exercise of constitutional or statutory rights. *Blackledge v. Perry*, 417 U.S. 21 (1974).

C. The Defense Response to the Charging Decision.

1. Motions to dismiss.

a) Failure to state an offense. R.C.M. 907(b)(1)(B).

b) Statute of limitations. R.C.M. 907(b)(2)(B).

c) Defective or misleading specifications. R.C.M. 907(b)(3)(A).

d) Unreasonable multiplication of charges. R.C.M. 907(b)(3)(B).

2. Motions for appropriate relief.

a) Determination of multiplicity. R.C.M. 906(b)(12).

b) Bill of particulars. R.C.M. 906(b)(6).

c) Sever duplicitous specifications. R.C.M. 906(b)(5).

d) Sever offenses. R.C.M. 906(b)(10).

e) Vindictive or Selective Prosecution. Fifth Amendment; *United States v. Hagen,* 25 M.J. 78 (C.M.A. 1987).

II. PLEADINGS GENERALLY.

A. Introduction.

1. Military pleadings follow the format of charge and specification. R.C.M. 307(c)(1).

2. Charge: The article of the UCMJ or law of war which the accused is alleged to have violated. R.C.M. 307(c)(2).

3. Specification: plain, concise, and definite statement of the essential facts constituting the offense charged. R.C.M. 307(c)(3).

B. Charges and Specifications.

1. Charges. Generally R.C.M. 307(c)(2).

a) A single charge is not numbered ("The Charge:").

b) If more than one charge, use Roman numerals ("Charge I:" "Charge II:").

c) Additional charges follow the same format and may be added until arraignment.

d) Error in, or omission of, the designation of the charge shall not be a ground for dismissal of a charge or reversal of a conviction unless the error prejudicially misleads the accused. R.C.M. 307(d); *see United States v. Bluitt,* 50 C.M.R. 675 (A.C.M.R. 1975).

2. Specifications. R.C.M. 307(c)(3) and discussion.

a) Numbering.

(1) A single specification is not numbered ("The Specification:").

(2) Multiple specifications use Arabic numbers ("Specification 1:" "Specification 2:").

b) Drafting the Language.

(1) Model specifications may be found in either:

(a) MCM, part IV; or,

(b) DEP'T OF ARMY, Pam. 27-9, *Military Judges' Benchbook,* Chapter 3 (15 Sep 2002). Note: Be sure to check for approved interim updates found on the Trial Judiciary page on JAGCNET.

(2) Legally Sufficient Specifications. *See infra* Chapter 7, Appendix A; *see also* R.C.M. 907(b)(1)(B), and R.C.M. 307(c)(3).

(3) Describe the accused.

(a) Name and rank.

(b) Armed force.

(c) Social security number of accused should not be stated in specification.

(4) Place of offense. "At or near . . ."

(5) Date and time of offense. "On or about . . ."

c) Novel Specifications.

(1) Counsel are unlikely to have novel specifications for most offenses. However, counsel may have to draft novel specifications for general disorders or service-discrediting conduct that are charged as violations of UCMJ art. 134, or for many forms of conduct unbecoming that are charged as violations of UCMJ art. 133.

(2) Designing a novel specification. *See United States v. Sell*, 11 C.M.R. 202 (C.M.A 1953).

(a) Identify and expressly plead the elements of the offense.

(i) Consult civilian case law or pattern jury instructions for the elements of crimes and offenses not capital integrated from federal law or assimilated from state law.

(ii) Conduct prejudicial to good order and discipline and service discrediting conduct not specifically listed as crimes by the President are more problematic.

(iii) The MCM provides that there are only two elements to such offenses: act or omission by accused, and a prejudicial or discrediting effect. MCM, pt. IV, para. 60.b.

(iv) Words of Criminality. If the act alleged is not *inherently* criminal, but is made an offense only by operation of custom, statute, or regulation, the specification must include words of criminality appropriate to the facts of the case, e.g., "without authority," "wrongfully," or "unlawfully." *See* R.C.M. 307(c)(3) discussion.

(b) Describe the offense with sufficient specificity to inform the accused of the conduct charged, to enable the accused to prepare a defense, and to protect the accused from subsequent reprosecution for the same offense. Notice pleading nevertheless remains the rule.

(c) Allege in the specification only those facts that make the accused's conduct a crime.

(d) Evidence supporting the allegation should ordinarily not be included in the specification.

C. General Rules of Pleading

1. Principals. All principals are charged as if they were the perpetrator. R.C.M. 307(c)(3) discussion at (H)(i). For a thorough discussion of principals, see UCMJ art. 77; MCM, pt. IV, ¶ 1; and Chapter 1 of the Crimes and Defenses Deskbook. The theory of liability does not need to be specified. *See United States v. Vidal*, 23 M.J. 319 (C.M.A. 1987)

2. Duplicity.

a) General. Duplicity is the practice of charging two or more offenses in one specification. Distinguish this from multiplicity, which is the practice of charging one offense in two or more separate charges or specifications.

b) Rule. Each specification shall state only one offense. R.C.M. 307(c)(4). If an accused is found guilty of a duplicitous specification, his maximum punishment is that for a single specification of the offense. Exception: "mega-specs;" see below.

c) Remedy. The sole remedy for duplicity is severance into separate specifications. R.C.M. 906(b)(5). *United States v. Hiatt*, 27 M.J. 818 (A.C.M.R. 1988) (conspiracy specification that alleged both conspiracy to commit larceny and to receive stolen property was duplicitous, but failure at trial to move to sever or strike constituted waiver). As a practical matter, severance is rarely requested, because it exposes the accused to multiple punishments.

d) Applications.

(1) "Mega-specs." The CAAF has held that the maximum punishment for some duplicitous specifications may be calculated as if each offense alleged in a duplicitous specification had been charged separately.

(a) Bad checks. *United States v. Mincey*, 42 M.J. 376 (C.A.A.F. 1995) (holding that maximum punishment in a bad-check case is calculated by the number and amount of checks as if they had been charged separately, regardless of whether Government joined multiple offenses in one specification).

(b) Check forgery. *United States v. Dawkins*, 51 M.J. 601 (A. Ct. Crim. App. 1999) (extending the *Mincey* rule to check forgery).

(2) Larceny.

(a) See pleading principles for value *infra* at Part II.C.4.

(b) *United States v. Rupert*, 25 M.J. 531 (A.C.M.R. 1987) (accused charged under one specification for larceny of different items "on divers occasions" over a 17-month period having a combined value of over $100). To be convicted of larceny over $100 either:

(i) One item must have that value, or

(ii) Several items taken at the same time and place must have that aggregate value.

Note: With the 2002 MCM Amendments, the threshold for increased punishment was raised to $500.

3. Matters in aggravation (*i.e.*, punishment enhancers).

a) Must be alleged and proven beyond a reasonable doubt. R.C.M. 307(c)(3).

b) Examples.

(1) Over 30 grams of marijuana. MCM, pt. IV, ¶ 37e(1).

(2) Value over $500; military property. MCM, pt. IV, ¶ 46e(1).

(3) Use of a firearm. MCM, pt. IV, ¶ 47e(1).

(4) Age of the victim. MCM, pt. IV, ¶ 54e(7).

4. Value.

a) Pleading value. ("of a value of about . . .," "of a value not less than . . .," "of some value").

b) Proving value. Value is a question of fact to be determined by all of the evidence admitted. MCM, pt. IV, ¶46c(1)(g).

(1) Government property. Listed in official publications.

(2) Other property. Legitimate market value.

(3) *United States v. Trisler*, 25 M.J. 611 (A.C.M.R. 1987) (hearsay testimony admissible to show value of stereo equalizer and two speakers <u>absent defense objection</u>).

c) Value in larceny cases.

(1) Multiple items taken at substantially the same time and place are a single larceny, even if the items belonged to more than one victim. In such cases, a single specification is used to allege theft of all items, and the values of the items are combined to determine the maximum punishment. *See* MCM, pt. IV, ¶47c(1)(h)(ii). The specification should state the value of each item followed by a statement of the aggregate value. R.C.M. 307(c)(3) discussion at (H)(iv).

(2) Cannot combine or aggregate values of items stolen from different places or on different dates.

(3) To be convicted of larceny over $500 either:

(a) One item must have that value (over $500.00), or

(b) Several items taken at the same time and place must have that aggregate value. *See* MCM, pt. IV, ¶47c(1)(h)(ii).

5. Joinder of offenses.

a) All offenses against an accused *may* be referred to the same court-martial for trial. R.C.M. 601(e)(2).

b) The military judge may sever offenses "only to prevent manifest injustice." R.C.M. 906(b)(10); *United States v. Duncan*, 53 M.J. 494 (C.A.A.F. 2000); *see also United States v. Simpson*, 56 M.J. 462 (C.A.A.F. 2002).

c) Joinder of perjury charges resulting from accused's testimony at previous trial. *United States v. Giles*, 59 M.J. 374 (C.A.A.F. 2004) (holding the military judge abused his discretion by failing to sever the perjury charge from the of attempted use and distribution charges at retrial; the instructions given were insufficient to prevent a manifest injustice).

d) After arraignment, charges cannot be added without the consent of the accused. R.C.M. 601(e)(2).

D. Amendments. R.C.M. 603.

1. Types of changes. R.C.M. 603(a).

a) Major change. Adds a party, offense, or substantial matter not fairly included in those previously preferred, or which is likely to mislead the accused.

b) Minor changes. All other changes.

2. Making minor changes.

a) Before arraignment. Any person forwarding, acting upon, or prosecuting the charges can make minor changes before arraignment. R.C.M. 603(b).

b) After arraignment. After arraignment, the military judge may, upon motion, permit minor changes any time before findings. R.C.M. 603(c).

3. Making Major Changes.

   a) Changes other than minor changes may **never** be made over the objection of the accused *unless* the charge or specification is preferred anew. R.C.M. 603(d).

   b) Applications.

   (1) Conspiracy. *United States v. Moreno,* 46 M.J. 216 (C.A.A.F. 1997) (holding that accused's ability to prepare a defense was not prejudiced by a change to conspiracy specification the day before trial).

   (2) Matters in aggravation. *United States v. Smith,* 49 M.J. 269 (C.A.A.F. 1998) (holding that amendment to larceny specification adding "military property" added a substantial matter within the meaning of the rule, but error was not prejudicial).

   (3) Lesser included offenses. *United States v. Brown,* 21 M.J. 995 (A.C.M.R. 1986); *United States v. Cowan,* 39 M.J. 950 (N.M.C.M.R. 1994).

   (4) Disobedience. *United States v. Longmire,* 39 M.J. 536 (A.C.M.R. 1994) (change to person issuing order and document used to issue order was major change).

   (5) General Article. *United States v. Sullivan,* 42 M.J. 360 (C.A.A.F. 1995) (change from clause three to clause two offense on day of trial was a minor change).

E. Variance. R.C.M. 918(a)(1)

   1. A variance between pleadings and proof exists when evidence at trial establishes the commission of a criminal offense by the accused, but the proof does not conform strictly with the offense alleged in the charge. *United States v. Allen,* 50 M.J. 84, 86 (C.A.A.F. 1999).

   2. Findings by exceptions and substitutions may not be used to substantially change the nature of the offense or to increase the seriousness of the offense or the maximum punishment for it. R.C.M. 918(a)(1).

   3. The specification and the findings may differ, provided the accused is not prejudiced. *United States v. Collier,* 14 M.J. 377 (C.M.A. 1983).

   4. Test for prejudice. *United States v. Lee,* 1 M.J. 15 (C.M.A. 1975); *United States v. Wray,* 17 M.J. 375 (C.M.A. 1984).

      a) The variance misled the accused to the extent that he was unable to adequately prepare for trial; or

      b) The variance puts accused at risk of another prosecution for the same offense; or

      c) The variance changes the nature or identity of the offense and the accused has been denied the opportunity to defend against the charge.

   5. Applications.

a) Substantially different offense. *United States v. Lovett*, 59 M.J. 230 (C.A.A.F. 2004) (holding variance was fatal when finding of guilt for solicitation to obstruct justice was substantially different from the charged solicitation to murder).

b) Different date. *United States v. Parker*, 59 M.J. 195 (C.A.A.F. 2003) (holding two-year variance in date of rape fatal); *United States v. Wray*, 17 M.J. 375 (C.M.A. 1984) (holding variance in date of larceny fatal). *But see United States v. Hunt*, 37 M.J. 344 (C.M.A. 1993) *cert. denied*, 114 S. Ct. 1052 (1993) (holding three-week variance in date of rape not fatal).

c) Different victim. *United States v. Marshall*, 67 M.J. 418 (C.A.A.F. 2009) (holding variance fatal in an Art. 95 prosecution when specification alleged that the accused escaped from the custody of "CPT Kreitman" and military judge entered findings by exceptions and substitutions convicting the accused of escaping the custody of "SSG Fleming").

d) Different injury. *United States v. Dailey*, 37 M.J. 1078 (N.M.C.M.R. 1993) (holding variance not fatal).

e) Different unit. *United States v. Atkinson*, 39 M.J. 462 (C.M.A. 1994) (holding variance in alleging unit of assignment rather than temporary place of duty not fatal).

f) Violation of different paragraph of general order. *United States v. Teffeau*, 58 M.J. 62 (C.A.A.F. 2003) (holding variance fatal where accused was charged with violating a lawful general order by providing alcohol to a recruit but convicted of violating of a different paragraph of the same order by engaging in a personal relationship with the recruit).

g) Statute of limitations—divers occasions. *United States v. Rollins*, 61 M.J. 338 (C.A.A.F. 2005). Appellant was charged with numerous offenses including attempted rape on divers occasions, and indecent acts on divers occasions. The panel found appellant not guilty of attempted rape, but guilty of indecent assault on divers occasions, and guilty of the divers occasions indecent act specification. Both of these specifications included periods which would later be time-barred by the holding in *United States v. McElhaney*, 54 M.J. 120 (C.A.A.F. 2000). The convening authority modified the findings to include only the dates not affected by the statute of limitations. HELD: The military judge erred by not providing the panel with instructions that focused their attention on the period not barred by the statute of limitations. The convening authority's action did not cure this prejudice and the affected findings were set aside. *See also United States v. Thompson*, 59 M.J. 432 (C.A.A.F. 2004).

6. Continuing course of conduct "on divers occasions."

a) On findings, when the phrase "on divers occasions" is removed from a specification, the effect is that the accused has been found guilty of misconduct on a single occasion and not guilty of the remaining occasions. *See United States v. Trew*, 68 M.J. 364 (C.A.A.F. 2010); *United States v. Augsberger*, 62 M.J. 189 (C.A.A.F. 2005).

b) Where the findings do not disclose the single occasion on which the conviction is based, appellate courts cannot conduct a factual sufficiency review or affirm findings because it cannot determine which occasion the servicemember was acquitted of. *See United States v. Trew*, 68 M.J. 364 (C.A.A.F. 2010); *United States v. Augsberger*, 62 M.J. 189 (C.A.A.F. 2005).

c) "Both trial practitioners and military judges need to be aware of the potential for ambiguous findings . . . and take appropriate steps through instruction and pre-announcement review of findings to ensure no ambiguity occurs." *United States v. Trew*, 68 M.J. 364 (C.A.A.F. 2010).

d) While a Court of Criminal Appeals may not review the record to determine which incident *most likely* formed the basis for the conviction, the court "may review the record to determine if there was *only a single possible incident* that met 'all the details of the specification' for which the [accused] was convicted. *United States v. Trew*, 68 M.J. 364 (C.A.A.F. 2010); *United States v. Ross*, 68 M.J. 415 (C.A.A.F. 2010). However, Government may prevail on appeal if legal sufficiency review reveals only one occasion that is legally sufficient. "Under those circumstances, . . . the verdinct would be unambiguous." *See United States v. Ross*, 68 M.J. 415 (C.A.A.F. 2010).

e) Applications. *United States v. Walters*, 58 M.J. 391 (C.A.A.F. 2003) (holding variance fatal where specification alleged wrongful drug use on "divers occasions" and findings by exceptions and substitutions removed the "divers occasions" language; the substituted language must clearly reflect the specific instance of conduct upon which the modified findings are based); *see also United States v. Trew*, 68 M.J. 364 (C.A.A.F. 2010) (accused charged with indecent acts upon a child on divers occasions, military judge convicted of assault consummated by battery on one occasion without clarification, ambiguous findings); *United States v. Ross*, 68 M.J. 415 (C.A.A.F. 2010)(charged with possession of child pornography on divers occasions, military judge excepts words "on divers occasions" without additional comment," ambiguous findings); *United States v. Wilson*, 67 M.J. 423 (C.A.A.F. 2009) (error for military judge to fail to identify the specific instance of conduct forming the basis for the conviction); *United States v. Seider*, 60 M.J. 36 (C.A.A.F. 2004) (fatal variance); *United States v. Augspurger*, 61 M.J. 189 (C.A.A.F. 2005) (fatal variance); and *United States v. Scheurer*, 62 M.J. 100 (C.A.A.F. 2005) (partially affirmed and partially set aside).

III. MULTIPLICITY.

A. Defined: "[T]he practice of charging the commission of a single offense in several counts." *Black's Law Dictionary* 1016 (6th ed. 1990).

B. The Constitutional Basis for the Doctrine.

1. "No person shall . . . be subject, for the same offense, to be twice put in jeopardy of life and limb." U.S. CONST. amend. V.

2. This prohibition extends to multiple punishments for the same offense at a single criminal trial. *Ohio v. Johnson*, 467 U.S. 493 (1984); Ball v. United States, 470 U.S. 856 (1985).

C. The Fundamental Rule. *United States v. Teters*, 37 M.J. 370 (C.M.A. 1993).

1. An accused may not be convicted of multiple offenses arising out of a single criminal transaction unless there is a clear expression of legislative intent to the contrary.

2. Legislative intent to allow multiple convictions for offenses arising out of a single criminal transaction may be inferred if each offense requires proof of a fact that the other does not. The determination that each offense requires proof of a unique fact is made by comparing the elements of the offenses. *See United States v. Dillon*, 61 M.J. 221 (C.A.A.F. 2005) (holding that separate specifications for different controlled substances used at the

same time not multiplicious; Congress clearly intended separate specifications for each controlled substance and this complies with the statutory elements test under *Teters*.).

3. "[T]hose elements required to be alleged in the specification, along with the statutory elements, constitute the elements of the offense for the purpose of the elements test." *United States v. Weymouth*, 43 M.J. 329, 340 (C.A.A.F. 1995).

4. The inference of legislative intent to allow separate convictions may be overcome if there are indications of contrary legislative intent. *See, e.g.*, UCMJ art. 120(b) (prior to 1 Oct. 2007) (2008 MCM, App. 27) (limiting carnal knowledge to "circumstances not amounting to rape").

5. Offenses found to be "separate" under this analysis may be considered separate for all purposes, including sentencing. *United States v. Morrison*, 41 M.J. 482 (1995).

6. Charges reflecting both an offense and a lesser included offense are impermissibly multiplicious. *United States v. Hudson*, 59 M.J. 357 (C.A.A.F. 2004); *United States v. Savage,* 50 M.J. 244 (C.A.A.F. 1999).

D. Multiplicity and Waiver.

1. Absent plain error, an unconditional guilty plea waives a multiplicity claim. *United States v. Lloyd*, 46 M.J. 19 (C.A.A.F. 1997). However, if two specifications are facially duplicative, i.e., "factually the same," then they are multiplicious, and it is plain error not to dismiss one of them. *United States v. Hudson*, 59 M.J. 357 (C.A.A.F. 2004) (holding, under the facts, that breaking restriction and AWOL are not factually the same, so the military judge did not commit plain error by not dismissing the AWOL charge as a lesser included offense).

2. Failing to object to charges as multiplicious waives the issue absent plain error. *See United States v. Britton*, 47 M.J. 195 (C.A.A.F. 1997); *United States v. Savage*, 50 M.J. 244 (C.A.A.F. 1999).

E. Suggested References for Multiplicity. Articles that may assist in understanding these principles include: Major Christopher S. Morgan, *Multiplicity: Reconciling the Manual for Courts-Martial*, 63 A. F. L. REV. 23 (2009); Lieutenant Colonel Michael Breslin & Lieutenant Colonel LeEllen Coacher, *Multiplicity and Unreasonable Multiplication of Charges: A Guide to the Perplexed*, 45 A. F. L. REV. 99 (1998); Major William T. Barto, *Alexander the Great, the Gordian Knot, and the Problem of Multiplicity in the Military Justice System*, 152 MIL. L. REV. 1 (1996).

IV. LESSER INCLUDED OFFENSES.

A. Fair Notice: A Fundamental Principle.

1. The Constitution requires that an accused be on notice as to the offense that must be defended against. *Jackson v. Virginia*, 443 U.S. 307 (1979); *Schmuck v. United States*, 489 U.S. 705 (1989).

2. This due process principle of fair notice mandates that an accused know for what offense and under what legal theory he may be convicted. This notice requirement is met when the lesser included offense is a subset of the greater offense alleged. *See United States v. Medina*, 66 M.J. 21 (C.A.A.F. 2008); *United States v. Miller*, 67 M.J. 385 (C.A.A.F. 2009); *United States v. Jones,* 68 M.J. 465 (C.A.A.F. 2010).

B. The Rule.

1. UCMJ art. 79. "An accused may be found guilty of an offense necessarily included in the offense charged or of an attempt to commit either the offense charged or an offense necessarily included therein."

2. An offense is "necessarily included" in another when its elements are a "subset" of the elements of the charged offense. *Schmuck v. United States*, 489 U.S. 705 (1989); *United States v. Teters,* 37 M.J. 270 (C.M.A. 1993) (adopting the elements test for military LIOs); *United States v. Foster*, 40 M.J. 140 (C.M.A. 1994); *United States v. Medina*, 66 M.J. 21 (C.A.A.F. 2008); *United States v. Miller*, 67 M.J. 385 (C.A.A.F. 2009); *United States v. Jones*, 68 M.J. 470 (C.A.A.F. 2010).

3. In order to determine if one offense is "necessarily included" in another, apply the elements test. "Under the elements test, one compares the elements of each offense. If all of the elements of offense X are also elements of offense Y, then X is an LIO of Y. Offense Y is called the greater offense because it contains all of the elements of offense X along with one or more additional elements." *United States v. Jones*, 68 M.J. 465, 470 (C.A.A.F. 2010).

4. Application to Article 134.

a) When comparing elements of offenses to determine whether an Article 134 offense stands as a lesser included offense to an offense under Articles 82 through 132, the CAAF has held that Articles 82 through 132 are not *per se* prejudicial to good order and discipline or service discreding. Clauses 1 and 2 of Article 134 are not *per se* included in every enumerated offense. *United States v. Miller,* 67 M.J. 325 (C.A.A.F. 2009), overruling in part, *United States v. Foster*, 40 M.J. 140 (C.M.A. 1994).

b) Offenses charged under clauses 1 and 2 of Article 134 are not *per se* lesser included offenses of offenses charged under Clause 3 of Article 134. *United States v. Medina,* 66 M.J. 21 (C.A.A.F. 2008).

5. Listings of LIOs in the MCM are not binding on the courts. Until Congress says otherwise, LIOs are determined by the elements defined by Congress for the greater offense. The President does not have the power to make one offense an LIO of another by listing it as such in the MCM. *United States v. Jones*, 68 M.J. 465, 471–72 (C.A.A.F. 2010). Practitioners should not rely on the LIOs listed under each punitive article in Part IV of the MCM, but should use the list as a guide and then apply the *Teters* elements test to be sure that the lesser offense is necessarily included.

C. Pleading Issues.

1. Lesser included offenses to the charged offense need not be separately pled. *See* R.C.M. 307(c)(4) discussion. However, if it is unclear whether an offense is a lesser included offense, it is prudent to allege both the greater and the purported lesser offenses.

2. If the MCM suggests that an enumerated article (Articles 82 through 132) has a lesser included offense in Art. 134, counsel should consider pleading both the enumerated offense and the Article 134 offense. *See United States v. Jones,* 68 M.J. 465 (C.A.A.F. 2010); *United States v. Miller*, 67 M.J. 385 (C.A.A.F. 2009); *United States v. Medina,* 66 M.J. 21 (C.A.A.F. 2008); *United States v. Foster*, 40 M.J. 140 (C.M.A. 1994).

3. If a lesser included offense is separately pled in addition to the greater offense, an accused may not be convicted of both the lesser and greater offense. *See United States v. Hudson*, 59 M.J. 357 (C.A.A.F. 2004).

4. The Three Clauses of Article 134. Clauses 1 and 2 are not necessarily included in Clause 3 of Article 134. In order to provide the requisite notice that the Government intends to pursue Clauses 1 and 2 in addition to Clause 3, the charge sheet should allege a violation of all three clauses. This is usually done by adding Clause 1 and/or Clause 2 language to a Clause 3 specicification. *See United States v. Medina*, 66 M.J. 21 (C.A.A.F. 2008).

D. Suggested references for multiplicity and lesser included offenses.

    1. A methodology for issues of multiplicity and lesser-included offenses may be found in Colonel James A. Young III, *Multiplicity and Lesser-Included Offenses*, 39 A.F.L. REV. 159 (1996).

    2. For an excellent discussion of the offense relation doctrines, see Major Howard H. Hoege, III, *Flying Without a Net:* United States v. Medina *and Its Implications for Article 134 Practice*, ARMY LAW., June 2008, at 37.

V. UNREASONABLE MULTIPLICATION OF CHARGES.

A. General. Even if offenses are <u>not</u> multiplicious, courts may apply the doctrine of unreasonable multiplication of charges (UMC).

    1. "What is substantially one transaction should not be made the basis for an unreasonable multiplication of charges against one person." R.C.M. 307(c)(4); *see also* R.C.M. 1003(c)(1)(C). *Cf.* R.C.M. 906(b)(12).

    2. Military judges must ensure that prosecutors do not needlessly "pile on" charges against a military accused. *United States v. Foster*, 40 M.J. 140, 144 n.4 (C.M.A. 1994).

B. The Doctrine. *United States v. Quiroz*, 55 M.J. 334 (C.A.A.F. 2001).

    1. Multiplicity and UMC are founded on distinct legal principles. The prohibition against multiplicity complies with the constitutional and statutory restrictions against double jeopardy. The prohibition against UMC addresses features of military law that increase the potential for overreaching in the exercise of prosecutorial discretion. After considering these factors, if the court finds the "piling on" of charges to be unreasonable, it will fashion an appropriate remedy on a case by case basis.

    2. In *Quiroz,* the CAAF endorsed the N-MCCA's non-exclusive list of factors to consider in weighing a claim of UMC: 1) Did accused object at trial? 2) Is each charge and specification aimed at a distinctly separate act? 3) Does the number of charges misrepresent or exaggerate accused's criminality? 4) Is there any evidence of prosecutorial overreaching in drafting? 5) Does number of charges and specifications unreasonably increase accused's punitive exposure?

C. Service courts may consider UMC claims waived or forfeited if not raised at trial. *United States v. Butcher*, 56 M.J. 87 (C.A.A.F. 2001).

D. Trial Judges may dismiss unreasonably multiplied charges on findings. *United States v. Roderick*, 62 M.J. 425 (C.A.A.F. 2006).

E. Unreasonable multiplication of charges can occur across multiple prosecutions. *See United States v. Raynor*, 66 M.J. 693 (A.F. Ct. Crim. App. 2008) (after the AFCCA ordered a rehearing on two charges, the government added charges for indecent liberties, sodomy, assault, and enticing minors to engage in sexually explicit conduct under 18 U.S.C. § 2251, which arose from the same conduct at issue at the first trial; not an unreasonable multiplication of charges).

F. Applications.

    1. *United States v. Campbell*, 66 M.J. 578 (N-M. Ct. Crim. App. 2008), aff'd ,68 M.J. 217 (C.A.A.F. 2009) (three specifications alleging possession of the same 38 images of child pornography on a government computer, 6 compact disks, and a personal hard drive did not constitute an unreasonable multiplication of charges, but the charges were multiplicious for sentencing).

    2. *United States v. Mazer*, 58 M.J. 691 (N-M. Ct. Crim. App. 2003). A commissioned officer exchanged sexually suggestive and explicit e-mail and "chat" messages with a 14-

year-old girl. Four specifications of an Article 133 charge was not UMC, because they did not reflect the same act or transaction. Each specification identified a discrete and unique communication.

3. *United States v. Esposito*, 57 M.J. 608 (C.G. Ct. Crim. App. 2002) Appellant made a false statement about the source of injuries sustained in a fight and asked a fellow crewmember to do the same. Charging appellant with false official statement and obstructing justice by making the same false statement was UMC. Also, charging appellant with soliciting a false official statement and obstructing justice by that same solicitation was UMC.

APPENDIX A
LEGALLY SUFFICIENT SPECIFICATIONS:
AN ANALYTICAL FRAMEWORK

A. The *Sell* Test. *United States v. Sell*, 11 C.M.R. 202 (C.M.A 1953). A legally sufficient specification must:

1. Allege all the *elements* of the offense,

2. Provide *notice* to the accused of the offense against which he must defend, &

3. Give *sufficient facts* to protect against re-prosecution.

B. Alleging the Elements.

1. Every element must be alleged either <u>directly</u> or by <u>fair implication</u>.

2. Applications.

   a) *United States v. Brown*, 42 C.M.R. 656 (A.C.M.R. 1970) ("club" alleges, by fair implication, a building or structure as required for housebreaking).

   b) *United States v. Knight*, 15 M.J. 202 (C.M.A. 1983) ("burglariously" enter does not allege, by fair implication, the element of breaking and entering required for burglary).

3. Omissions.

   a) Traditional, formal analysis. *United States v. Brice*, 38 C.M.R. 134 (C.M.A. 1967) (guilty plea; "wrongfully" omitted from attempted distribution spec; fatal defect).

   b) "Guilty plea" or "greater tolerance" test. *United States v. Watkins*, 21 M.J. 208 (C.M.A. 1986) ("without authority" omitted from AWOL specification; other AWOL specification had "without authority;" not fatal; flawed specifications first challenged on appeal are viewed with greater tolerance). *Watkins* "greater tolerance" test applies when:

      (1) The specification could reasonably be construed to charge a crime;

      (2) The specification is not challenged at trial;

      (3) The accused pleads guilty; and

      (4) No prejudice is shown.

   c) Applications.

      (1) Omitting "knowledge." *United States v. Brown*, 25 M.J. 793 (N.M.C.M.R. 1987) (having "knowledge of" a lawful order omitted; fatal omission, prejudicial).

      (2) Omitting "wrongful" - *Brice* revisited. *United States v. Brecheen*, 27 M.J. 67 (C.M.A. 1988) ("wrongful" omitted from both conspiracy to distribute specs in guilty plea case; not fatal); *see also United States v. Woods*, 28 M.J. 318 (C.M.A. 1989) (failure to allege traditional words of criminality in a UCMJ art. 134, clause 1 spec not fatal).

      (3) Omitting "wrongful." *United States v. Simpson*, 25 M.J. 865 (A.C.M.R. 1988) ("wrongful" omitted from one of four distribution specs; not fatal).

(a) Sufficiency of pleadings test: fair implication.

(b) Bootstrap "wrongful" from the charged article.

(4) Omitting "sexual intent." *United States v. LeProwse*, 26 M.J. 652 (A.C.M.R. 1988) ("with intent to arouse sexual desires . . ." omitted; alleged by fair implication).

(a) Contested case, challenged at trial.

(b) Relied on *Simpson* & bootstrapped MCM definition of "indecent."

(5) Omitting "wrongful" in a contested case. *United States v. Bryant*, 28 M.J. 504 (A.C.M.R. 1989) ("wrongful" omitted from conspiracy to distribute spec in a contested case; fairly implied from separate distribution spec); *see also United States v. Woods*, 28 M.J. 318 (C.M.A. 1989) (words of criminality omitted from art. 134 spec. alleging reckless endangerment for AIDS related misconduct; spec. adequate).

(a) The fact that *Watkins*, *Breechen*, and *Simpson* were guilty pleas "is a distinction without a difference".

(b) Accused failed to show that he was not on notice or that he would not be protected from further prosecution; accused must demonstrate prejudice.

C. Notice and Protection from Re-prosecution.

1. *United States v. Curtiss*, 42 C.M.R. 4 (C.M.A. 1970) (holding wrongful appropriation of "personal property" too vague).

2. *United States v. Alcantara*, 40 C.M.R. 84 (C.M.A. 1969) (holding larceny of "foodstuffs" sufficient).

3. *United States v. Weems*, 13 M.J. 609 (A.F.C.M.R. 1982) (holding larceny of "three unknown items" was vague but sufficient to protect the accused from re-prosecution for any three items on that date).

4. *United States v. Durham*, 21 M.J. 232 (C.M.A. 1986) (holding stolen property sufficiently identified in record to protect from a second prosecution; not fatally defective).

5. *United States v. Peszynski*, 40 M.J. 874 (N.M.C.M.R. 1994) (setting aside conviction on ground that conduct popularly styled sexual harassment did not state an offense).

6. *United States v. Harris*, 52 M.J. 665 (A. Ct. Crim. App. 2000) (holding specification alleging rape during 23-month period not too vague).

D. Bill of Particulars. R.C.M. 906(b)(6). Motion to compel the government to inform the accused of the precise misconduct alleged in the specification. *See, e.g., United States v. Mobley*, 31 M.J. 273 (C.M.A. 1990).

APPENDIX B
PLEADING NON-CAPITAL FEDERAL CRIMES
UNDER ARTICLE 134, CLAUSE 3

CHARGE: VIOLATION OF THE UNIFORM CODE OF MILITARY JUSTICE, ART. 134.

For Violation of U.S. Code:

Specification: In that SGT John Jones, U.S. Army, did, at Fort Bragg, North Carolina, a military installation within the special maritime and territorial jurisdiction of the United States, between on or about 1 October 2008 and 30 November 2008, unlawfully bring into the United States a firearm he obtained while deployed to Iraq during Operation Iraqi Freedom, to wit: a folding-stock AK-47 assault rifle with bayonet, in violation of 26 U.S.C. §5844, [such conduct being prejudicial to good order and discipline in the armed forces and being of a nature to bring discredit upon the armed forces]*.

[Assimilated State Law]

Specification: In that SPC Joseph Jones, U.S. Army, did, at Fort Hood, Texas, a military installation within the special maritime and territorial jurisdiction of the United States, on or about 4 February 2008, unlawfully enter a 2006 Honda Accord automobile, the property of SSG John M. Smith, with intent to commit a criminal offense therein, to wit: larceny of one car radio, in violation of §30.04 of the Texas Penal Code, and 18 U.S.C. §13, [such conduct being prejudicial to good order and discipline in the armed forces and being of a nature to bring discredit upon the armed forces]*.

* Language in brackets may be added to provide notice of Article 134, clauses 1 and 2, as lesser included offenses. *See United States v. Medina*, 66 M.J. 21 (C.A.A.F. 2008).

CHAPTER 8: IMPROPER SUPERIOR-SUBORDINATE RELATIONSHIPS & FRATERNIZATION

I. **REFERENCES.**

    A. Army References.

        1. Dep't of Army, Reg. 600-20, Personnel--General: Army Command Policy (18 Mar 2008). (Rapid Action Revision (RAR) Issue Date: 27 April 2010)

        2. Manual for Courts-Martial, United States [hereinafter MCM].

        3. Dep't of Army, Pam. 600-35, Personnel--General: Relationships Between Soldiers of Different Rank (21 Feb 2000). [This document is currently only available in draft format from the Army G-1.]

    B. Navy, Marine Corps, and Air Force References.

        1. OPNAVINST 5370.2C, Navy Fraternization Policy (26 Apr 2007).

        2. Marine Corps Manual 1100.4 (as amended by HQMC, ALMAR 185/96, 130800Z May 96, subject: Marine Corps Manual (MCM) Change 3) and MARCORMAN 1100.4 (13 May 96).

        3. Department of Air Force Instruction 36-2909, Personnel: Professional and Unprofessional Relationships (1 May 1999).

II. **INTRODUCTION.**

    A. Three Separate Concepts.

        1. Improper Superior – Subordinate Relationships.

        2. Fraternization.

        3. Sexual Harassment.

    B. A Spectrum of Misconduct.

III. **IMPROPER SUPERIOR - SUBORDINATE RELATIONSHIPS.**

    A. **History**:

        1. Task Force found disparate treatment between Services.

        2. New policy announced by Secretary Cohen on 29 Jul 98.

        3. Not effective immediately; gave Services 30 days to provide draft new policies to DoD. Essence of guidance now included within AR 600-20, paras 4-14 through 4-16.

        4. Does NOT cover all senior / subordinate relationships.

        5. Directs Service Secretaries to prohibit by policy:

            a. Personal relationships, such as dating, sharing living accommodations, engaging in intimate or sexual relations, business enterprises, commercial solicitations, gambling and borrowing between officer and enlisted regardless of their Service; and

            b. Personal relationships between recruiter and recruit, as well as between permanent party personnel and trainees.

    B. **The Old Army Policy**. Previous AR 600-20 (30 Mar 88), para 4-14. Two Part Analysis:

1. Part One: "Army policy does not hold dating or most other relationships between soldiers (sic) [of different ranks] as improper, barring the adverse effects listed in AR 600-20." Old DA Pam 600-35, Para. 1-5(e). Therefore, Army policy did <u>not</u> prohibit dating (even between officers and enlisted Soldiers), *per se*.

2. Part Two:

    a. "Relationships between soldiers (sic) of different rank that involve, or give the appearance of, partiality, preferential treatment, or the improper use of rank or position for personal gain, are prejudicial to good order, discipline, and high unit morale. It is Army policy that such relationships will be avoided." Old AR 600-20, paragraph 4-14.

    b. "Commanders and supervisors will counsel those involved or take other action, as appropriate, if relationships between soldiers (sic) of different rank

    (1) Cause actual or perceived partiality or unfairness.

    (2) Involve the improper use of rank or position for personal gain.

    (3) Create an actual or clearly predictable adverse impact on discipline, authority or morale." Old AR 600-20, para 4-14a.

    Key Note: <u>Old</u> AR 600-20 was not a punitive regulation. The revised paragraphs ARE PUNITIVE.

C. **The Current Army Policy**. Changes to AR 600-20, paras 4-14, 4-15 and 4-16.

   1. Now a **THREE** Part Analysis:

      a) Part 1: Is this a "strictly prohibited" category?

      b) Part 2: If not, are there any adverse effects?

      c) Part 3: If not "strictly prohibited" and there are no adverse effects, then the relationship is not prohibited.

   2. Para 4-14: Relationships between military members of different rank.

      a. "Officer" includes commissioned and warrant officers.

      b. Applies to relationships between Soldiers, and between Soldiers and members of other services.

      c. Is gender-neutral.

      d. (THIS IS PARA 4-14b.) The following relationships between Soldiers of **different ranks** are prohibited:

      (1) Relationships that compromise or appear to compromise the integrity of supervisory authority or the chain of command;

      (2) Relationships that cause actual or perceived partiality or unfairness;

      (3) Relationships that involve or appear to involve the improper use or rank or position for personal gain;

      (4) Relationships that are, or are perceived to be, exploitative or coercive in nature; and

(5) Relationships that cause an actual or clearly predictable adverse impact on discipline, authority, morale, or the ability of the command to accomplish its mission.

NOTE: Subparagraphs (1) and (4) are new additions to the three adverse effects looked for under the old policy's analysis.

e. (THIS IS PARA 4-14c.) Certain types of personal relationships between **officers and enlisted** personnel are prohibited. Prohibited relationships include:

(1) Ongoing business relationships (including borrowing or lending money, commercial solicitations and any other on-going financial or business relationships), **except**:

(a) Landlord / tenant; and

(b) One time transactions (such as car or home sales).

(c) All ongoing business relationships existing on the effective date of this prohibition, that were otherwise in compliance with the former policy, were not prohibited until 1 Mar 00 ("grace period").

(d) This prohibition does not apply to USAR / ARNG Soldiers when the ongoing business relationship is due to the Soldiers' civilian occupation or employment.

(2) Personal relationships, such as dating, shared living accommodations (other than as directed by operational requirements), and intimate or sexual relationships.

(a) This prohibition does not affect marriages (change as of 13 May 2002)

(b) Otherwise prohibited relationships (dating, shared living accommodations [other than directed by operational requirements] and intimate or sexual relationships), existing on the effective date of this prohibition, that were not prohibited under prior policy, were not prohibited until 1 Mar 00.

(c) Relationships otherwise in compliance with this policy are prohibited under this policy solely because of the change in status of one party to the relationship (such as commissioning). The couple does have one year to either terminate the relationship or marry within one year of the actual **start date** of the program or before the change in status occurs, whichever is later.

(d) Reserve Component (RC)/RC exclusion when the personal relationship is primarily due to civilian acquaintanceship, unless on active duty (AD) or full-time National Guard duty (FTNGD) other than annual training (AT).

(e) AD/RC exclusion when the personal relationship is primarily due to civilian association, unless on AD or FTNGD other than AT.

(3) Gambling. NO EXCEPTIONS.

(a) An NCAA basketball pool with a monetary buy-in is prohibited when there is a mix of officer and enlisted personnel participants. There is no prohibition against gambling between officers.

(b) An NCAA bracket competition with a certificate or trophy to the winner even with officer and enlisted personnel participants is permissible.

(c) Remember the Joint Ethics Regulation (JER), § 2-302 also addresses gambling. While it may not be prohibited under AR 600-20, it may violate the JER.

(4) These prohibitions are not intended to preclude normal team-building associations between Soldiers, which occur in the context of activities such as community organizations, religious activities, family gatherings, unit social functions or athletic teams or events.

(5) All Soldiers bear responsibility for maintaining appropriate relationships between military members. The senior military member is usually in the best position to terminate or limit relationships that may be in violation of this paragraph, but all Soldiers involved may be held accountable for relationships in violation of this paragraph.

3. Para 4-15: Other Prohibited Relationships.

   a. Trainee / Soldier. Any relationship between IET trainees and permanent party Soldiers (not defined) not required by the training mission is prohibited. This prohibition applies regardless of the unit of assignment of either the permanent party Soldier or the trainee.

   b. Recruit / Recruiter. Any relationship between a permanent party Soldier assigned or attached to USAREC, and potential prospects, applicants, members of the Delayed Entry Program or members of the Delayed Training Program, not required by the recruiting mission, is prohibited. The prohibition applies regardless of the unit of assignment or attachment of the parties involved.

4. Para 4-16: Paragraphs 4-14b. 4-14c and 4-15 are <u>punitive</u>. Violations can be punished as violations of Article 92, UCMJ.

D. **Commander's Analysis**: How does the commander determine what's improper?

   1. JAs must cultivate the idea that commanders should consult with OSJA.

   2. Use common sense. "The leader must be counted on to use good judgment, experience, and discretion...."

   3. Keep an open mind. Don't prejudge every male/female relationship. Relationships between males of different rank or between females of different rank can be as inappropriate as male/female relations. "[J]udge the results of the relationships and not the relationships themselves." DA Pam 600-35.

   4. Additional scrutiny should be given to relationships involving (1) direct command/supervisory authority, or (2) power to influence personnel or disciplinary actions. "[A]uthority or influence . . . is central to any discussion of

8 - 4

the propriety of a particular relationship." DA Pam 600-35. These relationships are most likely to generate adverse effects.

5. Be wary that **appearances of impropriety** can be as damaging to morale and discipline as actual wrongdoing.

E. **Command Response.**

1. The commander has a wide range of responses available to him and should use the one that will achieve a result that is "warranted, appropriate, and fair." Counseling the Soldiers concerned is usually the most appropriate initial action, particularly when only the potential for an appearance of actual preference or partiality, or an appearance without any adverse impact on morale, discipline or authority exists.

2. Adverse Administrative Actions: Order to terminate, relief, re-assign, bar to re-enlistment, reprimand, adverse OER/NCOER, administrative separation.

3. Criminal Sanctions: Fraternization, disobey lawful order, conduct unbecoming, adultery.

F. **Commander's Role.**

1. Commanders should seek to prevent inappropriate or unprofessional relationships through proper training and leadership by example. AR 600-20, para. 4-14(f).

2. Don't be gun-shy. Mentoring, coaching, and teaching of Soldiers by their seniors should not be inhibited by gender prejudices. Old AR 600-20, para. 4-14 (e)(1).

3. Training. DA Pam 600-35.

IV. **FRATERNIZATION AND RELATED OFFENSES**

A. General.

1. Fraternization is easier to describe than define.

2. There is no stereotypical case. Examples include sexual relations, drinking, and gambling buddies.

B. Fraternization. UCMJ art. 134.

1. The President has expressly forbidden officers from fraternizing on terms of military equality with enlisted personnel. MCM, pt. IV, ¶ 83b.

2. Elements: the accused

a) was a commissioned or warrant officer;

b) fraternized on terms of military equality with one or more certain enlisted member(s) in a certain manner;

c) knew the person(s) to be (an) enlisted member(s); and

d) such fraternization violated the custom of the accused's service that officers shall not fraternize with enlisted members on terms of military equality; and

e) under the circumstances, the conduct of the accused was to the prejudice of good order and discipline in the armed forces or was of a nature to bring discredit upon the armed forces.

3. "Hard to define it, but I know it when I see it."

4. Article 134 has also been successfully used to prosecute instances of officer-officer fraternization, *United States v. Callaway*, 21 M.J. 770 (A.C.M.R. 1986), and even enlisted-enlisted relationships. *United States v. Clarke*, 25 M.J. 631 (A.C.M.R. 1987), *aff'd*, 27 M.J. 361 (C.M.A. 1989).

5. Maximum punishment: dismissal/dishonorable discharge, total forfeitures and two years confinement. MCM, pt. IV, ¶ 83e.

6. Custom.

   a) The gist of this offense is a violation of the custom of the armed forces against fraternization; it does not prohibit all contact or association between officers and enlisted persons.

   b) Customs vary from service to service, and may change over time.

   c) Custom of the service must be proven through the testimony of a knowledgeable witness. *United States v. Wales*, 31 M.J. 301 (C.M.A. 1990).

7. Factors to Consider in Deciding How to Dispose of an Offense.

   a) Nature of the military relationship;

   b) Nature of the association;

   c) Number of witnesses;

   d) Likely effect on witnesses.

C. Failure to Obey Lawful General Order or Regulation. UCMJ art. 92.

1. Elements. MCM, pt. IV, ¶ 16b(1).

   a) There was in effect a certain lawful general order or regulation;

   b) the accused had a duty to obey it; and

   c) the accused violated or failed to obey the order or regulation.

2. Maximum punishment: dismissal/dishonorable discharge, total forfeitures and two years confinement. MCM, pt. IV, ¶ 16e(1).

3. Applications.

   a) Applicable to officers and enlisted.

   b) Most effective when used to charge violations of local punitive general regulations (for example, regulations prohibiting improper relationships between trainees and drill sergeants).

4. **Remember:** AR 600-20 re: improper relationships is NOW a punitive regulation.

D. Conduct Unbecoming an Officer. UCMJ art. 133.

1. Elements.

   a) Accused did or omitted to do certain acts; and

   b) That, under the circumstances, the acts or omissions constituted conduct unbecoming an officer and gentleman.

      2.   Only commissioned officers and commissioned warrant officers may be charged under article 133. Maximum punishment: dismissal, total forfeitures and confinement for a period not in excess of that authorized for the most analogous offense for which punishment is prescribed in the Manual, e.g., two years for fraternization.

    E.   Sexual Harassment.

      1.   Charged under Article 93 as Cruelty and Maltreatment.

      2.   Other offenses may be possible given the facts and circumstances of the case such as extortion, bribery, adultery, indecent acts or assault, communicating a threat, conduct unbecoming, and conduct prejudicial to good order/discipline.

V. CASE LAW

United States v. Pitre, 63 M.J. 163 (2006). The court held that simple disorder with a trainee is an LIO of Article 92, violation of a lawful general regulation, having a relationship not required by the training mission.

United States v. Fuller, 54 M.J. 107 (2000). Appellant was convicted of numerous offenses stemming from his sexual relations with subordinate female members of his unit. The CAAF granted review on the issue of whether the evidence was legally sufficient to sustain a conviction for cruelty and maltreatment of one of the victims. The evidence showed that while assigned to an inprocessing unit where the appellant was her platoon sergeant, the victim voluntarily went to the appellant's apartment with a friend, drank 10-12 oz. of liquor, kissed appellant, and got undressed and engaged in repeated sexual intercourse with appellant and another platoon sergeant. Additionally, the victim stated that in her decision to have sexual intercourse with the appellant, she never felt influenced by his rank and that he never threatened her or her career. Finally, the CAAF concluded that the evidence did not support a finding that the victim showed any visible signs of intoxication prior to the sexual intercourse with appellant. Although the CAAF found that the evidence was not legally sufficient to sustain a conviction for cruelty and maltreatment, they did find that it supported a conviction for the lesser-included offense of a simple disorder in violation of Article 134, UCMJ, since the appellant's conduct was prejudicial to good order and discipline or service discrediting. In mentioning that "appellant's actions clearly would support a conviction for violation the Army's prohibition against improper relationships between superiors and subordinates…", the CAAF cited to the current version of Army Regulation 600-20 (15 Aug[sic] 1999). The court, however, did not address the fact that the appellant's conduct occurred in 1996, when the regulation was not punitive and that therefore he could not have been found guilty for failure to obey a general regulation under Article 92, UCMJ.

United States v. Brown, 55 M.J. 375 (2001). ISSUES: The CAAF considered the issues, inter alia, of: 1) whether the trial court erred by admitting the Air Force's pamphlet on discrimination and sexual harassment for the members to consider on findings and sentencing; and 2) whether the charges of conduct unbecoming an officer were supported by legally sufficient evidence.
FACTS: The appellant, a captain and an Air Force nurse, was convicted of conduct unbecoming an officer for his comments to and physical contact with three co-workers over a ten month period. Appellant was married, had one child, and had served nearly ten years on active duty. All victims were female and, like the appellant, were company grade officers and Air Force nurses. All the victims worked in the operating room with the appellant at some point. The physical contact for which appellant was convicted included placing his hand on the other nurses' hair, thighs, knees, and buttock. The verbal conduct for which appellant was convicted included persistent complements on their hair, eyes, and physical appearance and questions about their weight,

whether they were happily married, whether they had a boyfriend, if they had ever had an affair, and in the case of one nurse, what type of bathing suit she wore and if women masturbated. Additionally, he asked them for their home phone numbers and asked them out for dates. Some of the victims showed their displeasure with appellant's physical contact with them by moving away from the appellant, and one told the appellant that she did not like the way he touched her. Contrarily, none of the complainants made their disapproval of the appellant's verbal comments known to him or to anyone in their chain-of-command.

HOLDING: The CAAF ruled that the military judge did not abuse his discretion when he admitted the nonpunitive Air Force Pamphlet (AFP) 36-2705, Discrimination and Sexual Harassment (28 February 1995) over defense objection. In so ruling, the CAAF agreed with the military judge that the AFP was relevant to establish notice of the prohibited conduct and the applicable standard of conduct in the Air Force community to the appellant. Additionally, the CAAF stated that in cases were evidence of the custom of the service is needed to prove an element of an offense, it is likely that the probative value will out weigh the prejudicial effect. With regard to the sufficiency of the evidence, the CAAF focused on the fact that government relied on the AFP to establish the applicable standard of conduct. When considering the standards in the AFP, combined with the facts of the case, the CAAF concluded that the government had to show that: "(1) appellant's conduct was 'unwelcomed'; (2) it consisted of verbal and physical conduct of a sexual nature and (3) it created an intimidating, hostile, or offensive work environment that was so severe or pervasive that a reasonable person would perceive that work environment as hostile or abusive, and the victim of the abuse perceived it as such." The CAAF went on to analyze the verbal comments and physical contact by the appellant separately. In finding the evidence legally insufficient to support appellant's convictions for the verbal comments, the CAAF noted that the record was clear that none of the victims ever informed the appellant that any of his remarks were unwelcome. While the AFP does not require a recipient of sexual remarks to tell the speaker that the remarks were unwelcome, the CAAF felt that a recipient's action or inaction in response to the remarks is relevant in determining whether the speech was unwelcome. The CAAF further noted from the record that the working atmosphere of the parties regularly accepted conversations involving physical appearance and sexual matters. This atmosphere cut against a finding that the appellant's comments created a work environment that was "hostile or abusive." However, the CAAF affirmed the convictions for the physical contact, concluding that it was not reasonable for the appellant "to assume that [the victims] would consent to physical contact of an intimate nature absent some communication of receptivity or consent."

United States v. Carson, 55 M.J. 656 (Army Ct.Crim.App. 2001). Appellant was convicted, contrary to his pleas, of maltreatment of subordinates (five specifications) and indecent exposure (three specifications). Appellant was the supervising desk sergeant in a military police station. While on duty appellant ordered a female MP to "physically search his crotch," and he repeatedly exposed his penis to three of his subordinate female MP Soldiers. The appellant challenged the maltreatment conviction stemming from his conduct with one of the victims, stating that his conduct did not result in "physical or mental pain or suffering" by this alleged victim. The victim of the challenged conviction testified that she never asked appellant to see his penis, that she was bothered and shocked when he exposed himself, and that she considered herself a victim. In holding that proof that the victim suffered "physical or mental pain" was not required in order to support a conviction for maltreatment of a subordinate, the ACCA relied on the fact that neither the UCMJ nor the Manual of Courts-Martial contained this requirement. In making this determination, ACCA expressly overruled its earlier contrary holding in *United States v. Rutko*, 36 M.J. 798 (A.C.M.R. 1993). *Affirmed by United States v. Carson*, 57 M.J. 410 (C.A.A.F. 2002)

United States v. Matthews, 55 M.J. 600 (C.G.Ct.Crim.App. 2001). Contrary to his pleas, appellant was convicted of attempted forcible sodomy, maltreatment by sexual harassment, indecent assault, and solicitation to commit sodomy. The charges arose from allegations of a subordinate female enlisted sailor who claimed that while she was on TDY with the appellant, he sexually assaulted her and attempted to force her to perform oral sodomy on him while they were in his hotel room. Contrarily, the appellant testified that it was the alleged victim who had initiated the sexual interaction, that the sexual foreplay was mutual, and that he never used force on her. Evidence presented at trial established that the appellant had sixteen years on active duty and had amassed an outstanding record and reputation for devotion to duty and honesty. In sharp contrast, several witnesses stated that they had little or no confidence in the alleged victim's truthfulness or integrity, and that she was a poor duty performer. The service court felt that this case boiled down to a swearing contest between the two parties, therefore, the issue of each of their credibility was paramount. In overturning the appellant's convictions for attempted forcible sodomy, maltreatment by sexual harassment, and indecent assault, the court relied heavily on the disparate opinion and reputation testimony concerning the two involved parties. The majority gave little weight to the testimony of medical and psychiatric experts who treated the alleged victim and found her credible and her reaction to the assault consistent with post-traumatic stress disorder. The court noted that these experts had assumed the accuracy of the facts related by the alleged victim and also pointed to the defense forensic psychiatrist who was skeptical of the alleged victim's account of events. The majority was quick to point out that under the facts of the case, the appellant was guilty of violating the service's general regulation against fraternization, but that he was never charged with that crime.

United States v Goddard, 54 M.J. 763 (N.M.Ct. Crim.App. 2000). Contrary to his pleas, the appellant was convicted of maltreatment and fraternization in violation of Articles 93 and 134, UCMJ. The charges resulted from a one time consensual sexual encounter with his female subordinate on the floor of the detachment's administrative office. In setting aside the maltreatment conviction, the service court cited the CAAF's decision in *U.S. v. Fuller*, 54 M.J. 107 (2000), in which it concluded that, "a consensual sexual relationship between a superior and a subordinate, without more, would not support a conviction for the offense of maltreatment." The court did, however, approve the lesser-included offense of a simple disorder in violation of Article 134, UCMJ. The fact that the sexual encounter took place in the detachment's administrative office, that after the sexual encounter was over the appellant instructed the victim leave the office in a manner that ensured that other personnel would not see her, and that the victim lost respect for and avoided the appellant because she had been briefed that such relationships were improper, all led the court to conclude that appellant's conduct was prejudicial to good order and discipline.

United States v. Sanchez, 50 M.J. 506 (A.F.Ct.Crim.App. 1998). Accused cannot be convicted of both conduct unbecoming (Art. 133) and fraternization (Art. 134) when the misconduct alleged in the specifications is identical; fraternization gets dismissed. Those fraternization allegations not alleged in conduct unbecoming specifications remain. Court cites *United States v. Harwood*, 46 M.J. 26, 28 (1997) in support.

United States v. Hawes, 51 M.J. 258 (1999). CAAF affirmed Air Force Court's decision to set aside fraternization conviction and to reassess the appellant's sentence without ordering a rehearing. CAAF agreed that the fraternization offense was "relatively trivial" when compared to other misconduct.

United States v. Mann, 50 M.J. 689 (A.F.Ct.Crim.App. 1999). Sexual relationship is not a prerequisite for fraternization. Evidence was legally and factually sufficient to support conviction for fraternization. No interference with accused's access to witnesses where order prohibiting accused from contact with his fraternization partner did not prohibit accused's counsel from such contact. A.F. court finds no unlawful command influence or unlawfulness with the order.

United States v. Rogers, 54 M.J. 244 (2000). Evidence legally sufficient to sustain Art. 133 conviction for the offense of conduct unbecoming an officer by engaging in an unprofessional relationship with a subordinate officer in appellant's chain of command. AF Court holds there is no need to prove breach of custom or violation of punitive regulation.

APPENDIX
AR 600-20 FRATERNIZATION (EXTRACT)

Rapid Action Revision (RAR) Issue Date: 27 April 2010

4-14. Relationships between Soldiers of different rank
a. The term "officer," as used in this paragraph, includes both commissioned and warrant officers unless otherwise stated. The provisions of this paragraph apply to both relationships between Army personnel (to include dual-status military technicians in the Army Reserve and the Army National Guard) and between Army personnel and personnel of other military services. This policy is effective immediately, except where noted below, and applies to different-gender relationships and same-gender relationships.

b. Relationships between Soldiers of different rank are prohibited if they—

(1) Compromise, or **appear** to compromise, the integrity of supervisory authority or the chain of command.

(2) Cause actual or **perceived** partiality or unfairness.

(3) Involve, or **appear** to involve, the improper use of rank or position for personal gain.

(4) Are, or are **perceived** to be, exploitative or coercive in nature.

(5) Create an actual or clearly predictable adverse impact on discipline, authority, morale, or the ability of the command to accomplish its mission.

c. Certain types of personal relationships between officers and enlisted personnel are prohibited. Prohibited relationships include—

(1) Ongoing business relationships between officers and enlisted personnel. This prohibition does not apply to landlord/tenant relationships or to one-time transactions such as the sale of an automobile or house, but does apply to borrowing or lending money, commercial solicitation, and any other type of on-going financial or business relationship. Business relationships which exist at the time this policy becomes effective, and that were authorized under previously existing rules and regulations, are exempt until March 1, 2000. In the case of Army National Guard or United States Army Reserve personnel, this prohibition does not apply to relationships that exist due to their civilian occupation or employment.

(2) Dating, shared living accommodations other than those directed by operational requirements, and intimate or sexual relationships between officers and enlisted personnel. This prohibition does not apply to—

(a) Marriages. When evidence of fraternization between an officer and enlisted member prior to their marriage exists, their marriage does not preclude appropriate command action based on the prior fraternization. Commanders have a wide range of responses available including counseling, reprimand, order to cease, reassignment, administrative action or adverse action. Commanders must carefully consider all of the facts and circumstances in reaching a disposition that is appropriate. Generally, the commander should take the minimum action necessary to ensure that the needs of good order and discipline are satisfied.

(b) Situations in which a relationship that complies with this policy would move into non-compliance due to a change in status of one of the members (for instance, a case where two enlisted members are dating and one is subsequently commissioned or selected as a warrant officer). In relationships where one of the enlisted members has entered into a program intended to result in a change in their status from enlisted to officer, the couple must terminate the relationship permanently or marry within either one year of the actual start date of the program, before the change in status occurs, or within one year of the publication date of this regulation, whichever occurs later.

(c) Personal relationships between members of the National Guard or Army Reserve, when the relationship primarily exists due to civilian acquaintanceships, unless the individuals are on active duty (other than annual training), on full-time National Guard duty (other than annual training), or serving as a dual status military technician.

(d) Personal relationships between members of the Regular Army and members of the National Guard or Army Reserve when the relationship primarily exists due to civilian association and the Reserve component member is not on active duty (other than annual training), on full-time National Guard duty (other than annual training), or serving as a dual status military technician.

(e) Prohibited relationships involving dual status military technicians, which were not prohibited under previously existing rules and regulations, are exempt until one year of publication date of this regulation.

(f) Soldiers and leaders share responsibility, however, for ensuring that these relationships do not interfere with good order and discipline. Commanders will ensure that personal relationships that exist between Soldiers of different ranks emanating from their civilian careers will not influence training, readiness, or personnel actions.

(3) Gambling between officers and enlisted personnel.

d. These prohibitions are not intended to preclude normal team building associations that occur in the context of activities such as community organizations, religious activities, Family gatherings, unit-based social functions, or athletic teams or events.

e. All military personnel share the responsibility for maintaining professional relationships. However, in any relationship between Soldiers of different grade or rank, the senior member is generally in the best position to terminate or limit the extent of the relationship. Nevertheless, all members may be held accountable for relationships that violate this policy.

f. Commanders should seek to prevent inappropriate or unprofessional relationships through proper training and leadership by example. Should inappropriate relationships occur, commanders have available a wide range of responses. These responses may include counseling, reprimand, order to cease, reassignment, or adverse action. Potential adverse action may include official reprimand, adverse evaluation report(s), nonjudicial punishment, separation, bar to reenlistment, promotion denial, demotion, and courts martial. Commanders must carefully consider all of the facts and circumstances in reaching a disposition that is warranted, appropriate, and fair.

4–15. Other prohibited relationships

a. Trainee and Soldier relationships. Any relationship between permanent party personnel and initial entry training (IET) trainees not required by the training mission is prohibited. This prohibition applies to permanent party personnel without regard to the installation of assignment of the permanent party member or the trainee.

b. Recruiter and recruit relationships. Any relationship between permanent party personnel assigned or attached to the United States Army Recruiting Command and potential prospects, applicants, members of the Delayed Entry Program (DEP), or members of the Delayed Training Program (DTP) not required by the recruiting mission is prohibited. This prohibition applies to United States Army Recruiting Command Personnel without regard to the unit of assignment of the permanent party member and the potential prospects, applicants, DEP members, or DTP members.

c. Training commands. Training commands (for example, TRADOC and AMEDDC) and the United States Army Recruiting Command are authorized to publish supplemental regulations to paragraph 4–15, which further detail proscribed conduct within their respective commands.

4–16. Fraternization

Violations of paragraphs 4–14*b*, 4–14*c*, and 4–15 may be punished under Article 92, UCMJ, as a violation of a lawful general regulation.

CRIMINAL LAW FACULTY
2010 – 2011

Chair and Professor:
  LTC Daniel G. Brookhart
  daniel.brookhart@us.army.mil
  434-971-3341 (DSN 521)
  Subjects: Unlawful Command Influence;
    Commander's Options & Duties;
    High Profile & Capital Litigation

Vice Chair and Professor:
  LTC Daniel M. Froehlich
  daniel.froehlich@us.army.mil
  434-971-3342 (DSN 521)
  Subjects: 6th Amendment – Confrontation
    Clause; Jurisdiction/MEJA

Professors:

LtCol Derek J. Brostek
derek.brostek@us.army.mil
434-971-3344 (DSN 521)
Subjects: Findings and Sentencing;
  Corrections; Search and Seizure;
  Protection of Military Installations
  (POMI)/SAUSA;
  Motions

LTC Eric R. Carpenter
eric.r.carpenter@us.army.mil
434-971-3346 (DSN 521)
Subjects: VWAP/SAPR/Lautenberg
  Amendment; Discovery;
  Instructions; Arguments; NJP;
  Trial Memo

MAJ Andrew D. Flor
andrew.flor@us.army.mil
434-971-3345 (DSN 521)
Subjects: Post-Trial Procedures;
  Self-Incrimination; Mental
  Responsibility; Urinalysis

MAJ Steven Charles Neill
steven.neill@us.army.mil
434-971-3343 (DSN 521)
Subjects: Voir Dire & Challenges;
  Court Personnel;
  Article 32/ Pre-trial Advice;
  Pleas & Pre-trial Agreements

MAJ Sean F. Mangan
sean.mangan@us.army.mil
434-971-3276 (DSN 521)
Subjects: Crimes; Defenses;
  Pleadings/Multiplicity;
  Role of Trial Counsel (OBC)

MAJ Tyesha L. Smith
tyesha.lowery@us.army.mil
434-971-3349 (DSN 521)
Subjects: Evidence; Classified Evidence;
  Writs & Government Appeals;
  Role of the Defense Counsel
  (OBC)

MAJ Jay Thoman
jay.thoman@us.army.mil
434-971-3348 (DSN 521)
Subjects: Professional Responsibility;
  Military Justice In a Deployed
  Environment; Speedy Trial & Pretrial
  Restraint; ISSFRT; 6th Amendment (IAC);
  Interviewing & Prep of Witnesses

PUBLICATION DATES FOR THE CRIMINAL LAW DESKBOOK ARE: JUNE – OCTOBER – FEBRUARY.

www.ingramcontent.com/pod-product-compliance
Lightning Source LLC
Chambersburg PA
CBHW080236180526
45167CB00006B/2292